Getting There With Faith

Adventures of a Travel Addict

Faith Bueltmann Stern

Faith Bueltmann Stern

Bielizna Press
Takoma Park, Maryland
2004

ISBN 0-9749675-0-5

Library of Congress Control Number: 2004102146

"We Couldn't Tiptoe Through the Tulips" was previously published in *The Cool Traveler*. "Floating the Buffalo" was previously published in *Canoe Cruisers*.

Other books by Faith Bueltmann Stern

Wise Guys: A Family History   1996
Lots of Loys: The Other Side   1995

Cover Photograph by Alan J. Stern

First Edition
Published by   Bielizna Press
               Takoma Park, MD
               Bieliznapress@aol.com

To my parents who got me started traveling

To Kurt, my favorite traveling companion, who shared the passion, encouraged the addiction, and made many trips possible

To Karen and Alan who enhanced the adventures

To Ruth, dear friend and all-seeing editor, whose enthusiasm kept me writing, correcting, and explaining, until I finished it.

Preface

It all began because my mother became tired of being pregnant. By the time I was three weeks overdue, Anna Marie Wise Bueltmann decided to take matters into her own hands. On Tuesday, June 26, she and my father, A. J. Bueltmann, took a long drive on a bumpy road in their model A Ford. I arrived early the next morning, and have been addicted to traveling ever since.

During my childhood, the longest time our family lived in one location was five years. Back and forth across the country we'd go, dragging our belongings with us, remembering friends we'd left behind, yet savoring new surroundings and adventures.

My husband's work kept him and us in one location. But we made up for this deprivation by giving vacation traveling a high priority. I enjoyed all our trips and invite you to sample the best of them in the pages that follow.

Faith Bueltmann Stern

PART I—THE GREAT OUTDOORS

PART II— A WORLD OF WONDERS

PART I — THE GREAT OUTDOORS

TRAILS TO GLORY

Mt. Washington

Alaska Basin and Lake Solitude

Sierra High

Revisiting the Pacific Northwest

Return to Mounts Washington and Katahdin

Arizona Canyons

Champions of the Chilkoot

Utah National Parks

Great Basin National Park

Two Months in the Alps

TRAILS TO GLORY

Hiking has been a constant in our lives. One of the places Kurt and I met was the Ozark Hiking Club (I was a graduate student and he was a very young faculty member at the University of Arkansas). We spent much of our honeymoon hiking. On weekends, Kurt found long walks in the woods and local stream valleys a rejuvenating tonic after long hours in the laboratory. For me, repeatedly trudging through deciduous forest in mid-Atlantic stifling heat and energy-draining humidity didn't do much. Getting to the top of some peak with a view, walking among aromatic evergreens or along a treeless ridge line, and scrambling over huge boulders were more to my liking. If a trail was new, I was interested. Born with a cat-like curiosity, I am fascinated by whatever is new, different, or seemingly exotic. I take the known for granted. So, why did I keep on hiking, almost every weekend when the weather permitted? A major incentive was that any day we hiked, I wouldn't have to cook dinner. Then, when we became interested in longer back-packing trips into wilderness areas, the one-day hikes were the only way to get in condition for those trips I really liked.

MT. WASHINGTON

Our weekend trips after we moved to Maryland were usually one-day hikes requiring a two-hour drive to reach Shenandoah National Park where many excellent trails were located. Vacations often involved hiking, though again, we'd make day trips from one particular campsite. Only small day packs were needed to hold our rain gear, water bottle, and a light lunch. And though many of these day trips were quite satisfying, others were frustrating. Often at the half-way point, when we had to turn back in order to reach camp before dark, I could see an intersecting trail inviting us to take it to either the left or the right. I was getting tired of always encountering these intriguing roads not taken. I knew that in order to follow these tantalizing trails, we would have to hike for several consecutive days and to carry heavier loads in larger packs, but it might be worth trying. Backpacking enabled us to hike into many incredibly beautiful wilderness areas and to experience and savor the quiet and solitude we found there.

In 1963, when our daughter was one year old, we tried to take a three-day hike in the Presidential Range in New Hampshire's White Mountains. Kurt carried Karen in a backpack, and I carried a pack loaded with baby-food jars and diapers. We planned to stay in the Appalachian Trail huts for two nights so we wouldn't have to carry sleeping bags or a tent. We began by taking the Tuckerman Ravine Trail to Mt. Washington. For the first two miles, the trail resembled a fire road. Though steep, it was broad and well-graded. Beyond a rest shelter, however, the trail became more difficult, staying close to the edge of a precipitous cliff and making us scramble up some ledges and carefully follow the piles of stones called cairns in Alpine Gardens, a tundra-like area with no trees. In good weather, the hike is strenuous but not impossible. The weather changes abruptly on Mt. Washington, so the careful hiker carries extra clothing, rain gear, and a flashlight, in addition to emergency food.

We were doing well, making slow but steady progress up the trail, until we reached the Alpine Gardens area. A light rain slowed us a bit, but all three of us had raingear, and we could still see the cairns that marked the trail above the tree line. Near the top, however, fog became mixed with the rain, so we decided to stay at the Mt. Washington Hotel, if they had a room. With poor visibility and bad weather, it would be difficult to find our way to the Lake of the Clouds Hut, our original destination, and we didn't want to endanger our young daughter.

Waking up to even heavier fog, we knew our three-day trip was over. Though disappointed, we decided the safest thing was simply to retrace our steps, if we could, rather than to follow an unknown trail to the next peak. As we started out, doing even this was questionable. In some places walking even slightly off the trail could be fatal. The dense fog increased the possibility of this happening. It also meant that the ledges we would have to scramble down would be wet and slick. We decided to aim for the longer but relatively safer carriage-road trail, as it had an easy grade and no drop-offs. Finding it was another problem. On treeless terrain, the trail is found by standing at one cairn, locating the next one, and moving in that direction. But when we stood at one cairn, we could see nothing but white fog in front of us. We devised a somewhat workable system. My red jacket was more visible than a pile of rocks, so I would begin walking in a direction that I thought was correct. When I reached the next cairn, I would stop and call to Kurt who was carrying Karen on his back. He then followed the direction my voice came from until he saw me, and finally the cairn. It was slow going, but safe. Fortunately, we had to use this method only in the Alpine Gardens area. Once we reached the carriage road, the way down was clear enough, and eventually we descended below the fog level and reached our car.

ALASKA BASIN AND LAKE SOLITUDE

Having spent some time in the Grand Teton area of Wyoming before we were married, Kurt and I had heard about Alaska Basin, but we also knew that seeing it would involve a two-night backpacking trip. If we planned carefully, we could do this trip within the context of a family vacation in the area, with special activities for each family member.

It was a logistically complex trip. In 1971, Karen, now eight, was already a seasoned hiker and experienced camper. At age six, she had hiked to the top of Hunter and Slide mountains in New York and had carried her own small pack on part of the Appalachian Trail in New Hampshire, while Kurt carried her one-year-old brother in a backpack But it was not good when Karen became bored or too tired on a hike. On our weekend day trips, rain and thunderstorms frequently curtailed any hike that Karen felt was too long or boring. Perhaps it was only a coincidence, but even as an adult, Karen seemed to have some control over the weather. At her outdoor engagement party, she managed to hold off threatening thunderstorms until the guests had left and everything had been put away. But that's another story. To forestall boredom on this trip, we invited our nine-year-old nephew, Greg, to keep Karen company. Alan presented a different challenge. Now three, he was too heavy to carry, but too young to walk long distances.

Because my mother couldn't join us, we found a substitute grandmother. Mrs. McKeever, a seventy-two-year-old farm wife and first-time camper, who had never been to the West, agreed to join us if we would provide a cot for her. She would care for all three children when Kurt and I did our three-day Alaska Basin hike and would also look after Alan while the rest of us did our planned overnight trip.

Karen, Alan, and I picked up Greg in Chicago and Mrs. McKeever in a small town in central Illinois before we headed for the Salt Lake City airport to pick up Kurt, who wanted to spend his limited vacation days in Wyoming, not in getting there and back. The first night we stayed in a motel, Greg asked me, "Are the robbers coming tonight?"

"I don't think so," I said. "I've stayed in motels many times and the robbers have never come. Why do you think they will?" Greg said he didn't know, so I never learned what caused his fear. Perhaps he was uneasy because this was the first time he had traveled anywhere without his parents. Greg and Karen usually entertained each other, and they competed to see who could eat the biggest breakfast, often ordering the Truck Driver's Special. I was amazed to see them eat everything that was served.

After meeting Kurt at the airport, we drove to Teton National Park, luckily found a campsite, and set up our family-sized tent, including the requested cot. While "Grandma" and little Alan stayed in camp, we took Karen and Greg on a twelve-mile warm-up hike without packs to Amphitheater Lake at 10,000 feet. The trail was steep and strenuous, with many switchbacks, but they made it with the help of numerous ghost stories and other tall tales I told to keep them moving. They had no problems with the altitude, so we felt they were ready for the overnight we'd planned for them. That trail was about nineteen miles long, but they would be doing it over two days, so we thought it would pose no problems.

But first we would check out Alaska Basin. Because Mrs. McKeever was not an experienced camper and we wanted her total focus to be on the children, we made arrangements for our temporary family to stay in a motel in town while we were gone. Jackson Hole would also provide more diversions for the children during our three-day adventure. Kurt and I waved goodbye, shouldered our backpacks, and started up the trail to Alaska Basin.

We began by hiking around the south side of Jenny Lake past Moose Pond to the Cascade Canyon trailhead at Hidden Falls. After gaining the top of Hidden Falls, the canyon trail straightened and flattened out for the next four and one-half miles. The trail was very popular, but most of the hikers took the north fork, which led to Solitude Lake. We took the south fork, which in the next five miles rose steeply to gain 2,600 feet. As we hiked, we passed many cascades and enjoyed great views of Table Mountain to the west. Gradually the Grand Teton came into view above the closer peaks. As the trail rose above the pines into the open, we were stunned by vast panoramas. Ahead we could see The Wall, a nearly vertical cliff along the park boundary. Just beyond the intersection for a trail to Avalanche Pass, the Grand Teton came into full view.

Carrying a pack requires a slow and steady pace, and before we reached the pass, we were happy to pitch our two-person tent in a beautiful alpine meadow filled with wildflowers. When the sun dipped below the horizon, we enjoyed a few minutes of alpenglow. The low-angle sunlight painted the highest peaks with a glowing golden-pink color just before twilight.

After breakfast, we re-shouldered our packs and hiked through stunted krumholz (twisted wood) trees to reach the terminal moraine, a cirque, and the beautiful aqua-colored lake created by run-off from Schoolhouse Glacier, a towering mass of ice rising above us. The Skyline Trail we were hiking bisected The Wall just as we reached Hurricane Pass. Now walking on tundra, we could see the three Tetons to the northeast. Directly north were Mt. Moran and a seeming endless sea of peaks. Ahead of us was Alaska Basin lying on the western flank of the Teton range–sublime!

A vast subalpine area with marvelous views on all sides, Alaska Basin also contained many beautiful tarns as well as snow patches still unmelted in July. We felt peaceful and content to walk slowly, absorbing the natural beauty surrounding us. A string of packhorses, part of a Sierra Club organized trip, passed by. Otherwise we saw very few hikers. It was a great feeling to have this wilderness to ourselves on a day of perfect weather. The temperature was very pleasant, the humidity low. Marmots (western woodchucks) and pikas (small alpine rodents) squeaked as they feverishly harvested grasses to store for winter fodder. What more could anyone want?

Our second campsite was near the intersection with Death Canyon, where we would descend in the morning. On our way out the next day, we entered this spectacular canyon, flanked on both north and south by remarkable rock walls. The trail, however, consisted of seemingly endless switchbacks. I was glad to be going down rather than up them. When we reached Phelps Lake at the end of the trail, Jenny Lake, where we'd parked our car, was still eleven miles away. We thought we could hitch a ride, since we were now on a paved road, but we had no luck with that. It was almost dark and we were very tired by the time we made it to Jenny Lake, but it had been a grand trip and well worth all the effort.

We rested the next day by taking a scenic float trip with our family on the Snake River where we looked for eagles, moose, and other wildlife from a raft on the quieter section of the river. That afternoon we filled the packs for our overnight hike with Karen and Greg. They each carried a small pack which contained rain gear and a sleeping bag. Kurt and I carried the tent, our bags, sleeping pads, the stove, food for all, a first aid kit, water bottles, and our own rain gear. This trip began the same way as our Alaska Basin hike, around Jenny Lake and up to Hidden Falls to the Cascade Canyon trailhead. For a while, on the level part of the trail, Karen and Greg were fine, but when the trail grew steeper, requests for rest stops became more frequent. A few ghost stories moved us on a bit farther. They loved seeing marmots and hearing their warning squeaks. Soon they developed a squeaking sound of their own to which the marmots actually responded.

Seeing a moose at the side of the trail was very exciting. But we were concerned because an adult hiker was chasing the moose and throwing rocks at it, in order to get a closer photograph. We tried to get past that scene as fast as we could. Moose are very unpredictable and can move very fast. I didn't want to find out what an irritated moose would do. But the kids couldn't move any faster with their packs, they claimed. So I tied their packs onto mine, and we moved away from danger.

We had hoped to camp that night at Holly Lake. That would have been more than half the total mileage. We would have seen the views, crossed over the pass, and would then have an easy way down Indian Paintbrush Canyon to Jenny Lake. But our pace was too slow. With constant urging we managed to reach Lake Solitude with just enough daylight left to set up the tent and cook dinner. The children were fascinated by the wonderful alpenglow on the high peaks and the pink and gold reflection in the lake below. Karen and Greg had a sense of accomplishment, and we all enjoyed the serenity at Lake Solitude, embracing this bit of nature's beauty that we had all to ourselves. We complimented the children for hiking so far in one day, not mentioning our earlier plan. But Greg didn't want to eat. We were worried that he might be having some altitude sickness. He said he just wasn't hungry. Finally, Kurt got him to eat an orange and drink some water. As darkness came, we crawled into our sleeping bags. We were almost asleep when we heard from Greg, "Uncle Kurt, help me. I can't get the sleeping bag closed." Kurt couldn't get the zipper to work either. By the flashlight's glow, we saw that the teeth of the zipper were clogged with Greg's chewing gum. Not much could be done till morning, so we told Greg not to worry. He probably wouldn't freeze overnight in an unzipped sleeping bag.

Clouds threatened in the morning, and Greg still didn't want to eat. If we stuck to our original plan, we would have to ascend to an un-named high pass at 10,650 feet where there still might be snow before we could head down. Although I wanted to see Indian Paintbrush Canyon, reputedly very beautiful, we began to realize that going that way was not the best choice for Greg and Karen. Greg had not eaten much and both of them would have to hike farther than they had the day before, even though most of it would be downhill. A park ranger who came by said we could probably make it okay, but he thought it best to retrace our steps. The biggest concern was possible exposure to bad weather in the pass where there were no sheltering trees. We couldn't spend too much time debating options as we needed most of the day for getting back to the car, even going the shorter way.

We made the trip back in good time. Karen and Greg moved right along since they were going downhill. Another motivation was a promise of a horseback ride the next day. Both of them were very proud of their overnight hike to Lake Solitude. We never told them of the trail not taken. But once we were back, we saw that Greg cleaned all the chewing gum out of the sleeping bag zipper before he was allowed to go horseback riding.

SIERRA HIGH

For about a year, we lived with the frustrating knowledge that we had failed in our 1976 attempt to hike to the top of Mt. Whitney, the highest peak in the contiguous United States. Then we decided to do something about it. In the summer of 1978, Kurt and I planned to approach Whitney from the west, preparing ourselves by a backpacking trip in the High Sierra region in California. We allowed ourselves twelve days for the actual hike. This meant that each day we would have to walk ten miles to reach our goal. Our average hiking speed in mountainous terrain was about two miles an hour. Even if our pace slowed to one mile an hour, we could do ten miles in a long day. It seemed like a reasonable plan.

As usual, there were some tricky logistics involved. Karen and Alan would be vacationing for two weeks with my mother. For one week, she took them to the summer camp in central Illinois where my brother was camp director. The four of us drove to my mother's home near Chicago, where we left our children and our car. Because we were beginning our hike on one side of a serious mountain range and ending it on the other, we had to find some way to use public transportation. It was possible but complicated and involved several connections.

Our flight from Chicago to San Francisco arrived at 3:00 a.m. From the downtown airport terminal where the airport bus dropped us, we had six blocks to walk carrying our packs to the Greyhound bus station. There didn't seem to be any way to avoid walking through a rather unsavory neighborhood, as we didn't have much time to waste. Most of the loungers and loiterers were sleeping off whatever they had enjoyed. No one moved to confront or even to panhandle us. But then we realized why. Groggy and jet-lagged, we looked fairly disreputable ourselves carrying beat-up backpacks and wearing hiking clothes. We weren't worth the effort. In the station we saw more people lying around half-asleep but watchful. None of the ticket windows were open. We weren't sure when we'd be able to get a ticket, but we knew that the bus to Fresno left at 5:00 a.m. The next bus to Fresno didn't leave until noon, too late for us to make our connection with the Sequoia Bus. Fortunately, one ticket window opened at 4:30 a.m., and there were seats available on the bus.

After arriving in Fresno at 9:30 a.m., we finally had breakfast. The Sequoia Bus didn't leave till the afternoon, so we tried to see what sights there were in Fresno besides the water tower and the murals in the library. The one historic building, Meux Mansion, that gave tours was closed for the summer. By eleven, the temperature was at least 102 degrees. We spent some time sitting in a park near a fountain and cooled off by eating frozen yogurt with fruit. Thirteen of us were waiting when the bus (actually a van) finally showed up at 2:45 p.m. It was a very full van with no air-conditioning. Even with the windows open, the ride was hot and uncomfortable until we reached higher elevations and Giant Forest Lodge in Sequoia National Park, the end of the line. We rented a housekeeping cabin to save ourselves the trouble of unpacking and putting up our tent. We'd also be able to make an early start the next day.

The cooler temperatures were delightful. After breakfast at the lodge's cafeteria, we took the King's Canyon tour bus, primarily for transportation to Cedar Grove, not far from the trailhead. But we enjoyed the sight-seeing stop at the General Sherman Tree, the largest known sequoia in the world. It is as tall as a twenty-six story building and very old. Although the age of the General Sherman, General Grant, and other large sequoias is unknown, it is estimated that these giants are between 1,800 and 2,700 years old. When the tour stopped for lunch at Grant Lodge, we had time to check out the other famous sequoia, the General Grant Tree. Reaching Cedar Grove, we set up our tent in Moraine campsite, next to the south fork of the King's River and about four miles from the road's end, where our hike would begin the next day. We'd brought plenty of freeze-dried food but realizing that the Cedar Grove Market offered what might be our last chance for a while to eat something fresh, we had supper there. That night a large church youth group serenaded us and anyone else within earshot.

By 7:00 the next morning we were on the way to the road's end. After we'd walked a little more than halfway, the driver of a National Park Service truck offered us a ride to where the Copper Creek Trail started. We signed the register, tied our backcountry permits onto our packs and started walking up the trail. It wasn't much fun. A hot, dusty, fly-ridden trail full of switchbacks took up most of the day. But at 3:00 p.m. we found a beautiful campsite, complete with a gorgeous view of distant peaks and tree-covered slopes. The site even had a fireplace. We hung our food bags high in the trees to discourage any bears and luckily had no such visitors. We did see three deer: one female, one male with four points, and one with eight points, and one hummingbird. Our campsite, somewhere above Lower Tent Meadow, was at 9,200 feet.

The following day, Friday, we didn't get started until after 8:00 a.m. Heading up into Granite Pass (10,673 feet), Kurt and I, who were hiking out of sight of each other, inadvertently took separate trails at a fork. Fortunately they were alternate routes which eventually rejoined. The trail led us to and across many streams which had to be crossed without the benefit of bridges. Sometimes large boulders could serve as stepping stones. Otherwise we had to wade, hoping we had sufficiently waterproofed our boots. We camped in sight of the Kennedy Trail crossing at about 9,500 feet beside a roaring brook. The mosquitoes were so ferocious that even our smoky campfire didn't discourage them. We'd had a fair day of hiking, sighting one very young deer and two fat marmots as we went. But we did have some problems. Kurt lost his rain jacket, leaving it behind when we packed up in the morning. And our pace wasn't what we had hoped, probably because our packs were too heavy. We realized we were carrying too much food– more than we could ever eat in ten days, since cookies seemed to be enough for lunch. But we couldn't just throw it away to lighten our loads. We tentatively decided that if our pace did not pick up, we would have to scratch Mt. Whitney. We'd be lucky to make Kearsarge Pass where we could hike down the eastern side of the mountain range.

On our third day of actual hiking, things went a little better. Our pace was faster because the trail was mostly downhill. Crossing swollen Dougherty Creek on a log bridge, I slipped, then recovered so that only one leg was soaking wet. I dried out quickly as the day was sunny with low humidity. We stopped for lunch at Simpson Meadow, where we soaked our aching feet in the stream, drank lemonade, and ate cookies and freeze-dried ice cream. We saw only one other hiker that day, early in the morning. It was pleasant to have all the gorgeous scenery to ourselves, but sobering to think that if we had an accident, help would be a long time coming.

With too little daylight left to make it to Cartridge Creek, we decided to camp at Windy Canyon Creek (6,200 feet). I was hesitant to stay when we saw evidence that bears had been in the area. But Kurt felt we should stop. I was becoming skilled at pitching a rope wrapped around a stone over high limbs from which we could suspend our precious food bags. We took extra time that night to select what we thought was a bear-proof tree. It had to be some distance from our tent and stand very tall with thin long branches a bear wouldn't try to reach. We also maintained a smoky fire as long as possible. Maybe I was just tired, but the desolate-looking area, the evidence of bears, and seeing only one hiker for two straight days, made me think about what would happen if we met with some disaster. We had identification, but no one would be at our home address to be notified. I thought a log or record of our trip should be made so anyone who might find our bodies would know what had happened. I would also tell the unknown reader to notify my mother. I had a pen, but no paper, until I remembered that the backs of our geological survey maps were totally blank. That night I jotted down an account of our first few days along with other pertinent information.

In the morning, we were still alive, the food bags were untouched, and we saw no evidence of unwanted visitors. We made good time to Cartridge Creek, where we saw a beautiful campsite complete with picnic table. I wished we had made it that far the previous night. Tempting as the site was, it was way too early in the day to stop, so we hiked on.

Soon we met a group of three hikers who warned us of a rocky trail ahead and a steep snowfield which blocked the trail. Face to face with the treacherous snowfield, we didn't dare to cross it at the level of the trail. Instead, we decided to climb up the steep hillside beside the snowfield, in order to cross above it on solid ground. Though it was tough and slow going with the packs, our plan worked. Then as we carefully picked our way down to the trail, we saw an unavoidable perilous creek crossing. Two wet logs were the so-called bridge. The water was fast, cold, and abundant. One slip and it would be difficult to recover. But if we were to continue on the trail, we had to cross that creek. I tied a rope around my waist, and Kurt belayed me as I carefully stepped along the logs. If I slipped he could keep me from being washed very far downstream. Once across, I held him secure as he crossed over. After a short rest to calm our nerves, we trudged on, ever upward beside the mighty Middle Fork of the Kings River with its constant roar and spectacular cascades, finally arriving at the intersection with the John Muir Trail. Here we found a lovely bridge crossing Palisade Creek and a pleasant campsite for lunch and rest. About a mile later in Aspen Flats at 8,000 feet, we found an irresistible campsite, so we stopped early. I even had time for laundry. A group of ten boy scouts with two leaders went by headed for Deer Meadow, not far away. Now at last we were getting some spectacular scenery, with the towering peaks of the Sierra range rising on all sides. After enjoying turkey tetrazzini for dinner, we found a perfect tree for hanging our food, noticing that we had consumed one of the three bags of food we'd brought–meaning our backpacks were getting lighter.

Waking up early, we soon caught up with the "boys" as we all worked our way up the Golden Staircase, a series of switchbacks to Palisades Lakes. They camped in this beautiful area surrounded by the rugged and alpine-like Palisade peaks with glacial basins lying beneath them.

We headed on to Mather pass, climbing up steep snowfields and scrambling up scree to 12,100 feet. Threatening weather made us hurry down the switchbacks on the trail until we saw an enormous snowfield with a track made by those who went before. Some hikers with ice axes glissaded down the snowfield, while we stayed in the prepared track, but it was a fast trip down anyway. Emerging from the snowfield and back again on the Muir Trail, we were pelted by a furious hailstorm. Because Kurt had lost his raingear, we sought shelter under some rocks where we waited out the worst of the storm. Kurt was already cold and wet, and the wind was howling. When the storm let up a bit, we hiked for about a mile and a half to find a reasonable camping spot at 11,000 feet, where we hurriedly prepared and ate dinner amid light rain. After cleaning up, we crawled into the tent, completing an eleven-mile day, up and over a high pass. The rain became serious, accompanied by howling wind and a flapping tent and rain cover. We contemplated having to spend the next day drying out.

Still tired from a restless night in the storm, we got a later start the next day. The guidebook described this area as containing a network of small tributary streams and lakes and interesting moraines. But the tributary streams were full and swollen. We spent most of the day building our own bridges. I felt that the trail had been designed by a madman who enjoyed crossing streams as frequently as possible. The streams were too swift, too deep, and too cold to ford. If there had been logs to use as bridges, they had been swept away by the raging torrents. Sometimes we could throw enough large boulders into the stream to create a way across. Other times we had to haul logs and parts of trees down to the water and wedge them in place. Several times we had to use a log to get halfway across a stream to a large boulder or a small island. Then we dragged our log onto the island and used it to get over the next half of the stream. In one spot, a log sloping downward was intended for a bridge. We sat on it and inched our way across, trying not to look at the wild current below us. We made very little mileage that day as bridge building was strenuous and time-consuming. That night we stopped early at a lovely lake above the Bench Lake Trail. When dark clouds dropped only a few raindrops and then blew over, we ate a leisurely dinner for a change. We even took an after-dinner walk without our packs amid clear skies, gorgeous scenery, twittering birds, and many fat marmots.

We'd now been walking for almost a week. Perhaps that enabled us to quickly ascend Pinchot Pass, 12,050 feet, the next morning. We met one hiker before walking down, down, down. There were beautiful lateral moraines and many lakes. Mt. Cedric Wright loomed above beautiful Twin Lakes. Our lunch by Woods Lake Trail was quick, though, as too many mosquitoes hovered, looking for a meal. Thunder rumbled above us, so we were surprised to see a low-flying airplane performing stunts or on a strange surveillance mission. Streams cascaded so wildly that in places where the water hit stones, the volume and impact sent high arcs of water flying up into the air. Finally we were down to Sixty Lake Basin and more level ground. Fairly early in the afternoon, we reached the campground at the intersection of Woods Creek with its south fork. There were many warning signs about bears and drownings. We were shocked at how filthy this campground was and spent a lot of time cleaning up candy, candy wrappers, and plastic. Not exactly what one goes to the wilderness to find.

That evening after dinner, Kurt said that his feet were really hurting and that he found every step painful. It was time to change our plan. We would not attempt Mt. Whitney and instead would take the first exit route we came to. Kurt wasn't sure how much longer he could hike, but there was no trail out until we reached Kearsarge Pass which lay at least one day's hike ahead. It had been a twelve-mile day, but though we went to bed early, we didn't sleep well. The shrimp creole we had for dinner was a bit too spicy for our digestions.

Compared to all the spectacular alpine scenery we'd experienced along the way, what we saw the next morning seemed a little dull. I felt we were just plodding along, not getting anywhere, when suddenly we were at Rae Lakes, where we stopped for early lunch. We read the guidebook description before starting on our afternoon hike. "From Rae Lakes the Muir Trail skirts the western shoreline to the upper end of Rae Lakes. It then climbs to the headwaters of a stream which feeds the lake, passing through a rough rocky basin strewn with lakelets and surrounded by forbidding cliffs. Above is Glen Pass. The trail zigzags up a rocky ridge to the base of the cliffs over steep sliding rock, then up the cliff to the summit of the spur ridge. The trail is difficult for stock when the snow has not been cleared."

We didn't consider ourselves stock, so we thought we'd be able to make it. I took the tent out of Kurt's pack, hoping that a lighter load might alleviate the pain in his feet. About 1:30 p.m. we started up to Glen Pass amidst sprinkles of rain and a very threatening sky. Many times we had to walk through thick snow patches on the trail, and a cold wind reminded us to put on mittens and wool caps. The trail did zigzag almost endlessly up, passing by barren, forbidding-looking black rocks. Beautiful frozen lakes below us were starting to thaw. After two hours we reached the top of the pass where we talked to a twenty-year-old hiker who told us he had only pancake mix to eat. Although we gave him some beef jerky, a package of beef stew, and a granola bar, he wasn't satisfied and asked Kurt to give him a roll of film. Kurt said he had no extra film, but the young man did not move on. He seemed rather strange and unstable, and he kept insisting that Kurt give him some film. Passing us would have been easy, but instead he stayed right behind us. I thought he either was having problems with altitude or was a druggie. Finally he must have realized he would not be getting any film from us and he left, much to our relief.

The way down from Glen Pass was also very steep and long, but a good dirt trail, clear of snow, with no sliding rocks, made it easier going. We had hoped to find a low trail to Bullfrog Lake and then Kearsarge Lakes, but somehow missed it. When we found a small lake high up on the beginning of the Kearsarge Pass Trail, we stopped, ate, and crawled into our tent for a surprisingly very restful evening surrounded by peaks with Kearsarge Lakes far below us. We'd completed another twelve- to thirteen-mile day.

In the morning we skirted Bullfrog Lake, closed to camping because it had been overused, and continued across the high meadow on the way to

Kearsarge Pass. We passed by the spur trail to Kearsarge Lakes, then started the zig-zag ascent into the pass at 11,823 feet. We knew we had four miles more to reach Onion Valley, but it was pleasant walking past four small lakes. No hamburger ever tasted as good as the one we had at Onion Valley. After ten days of eating freeze-dried trail food, the taste of fresh crunchy lettuce and juicy ripe tomato slices was refreshingly delicious.

If we had made it to Mt. Whitney and descended the Mt. Whitney Trail, we would have come out at Lone Pine, where we could take a bus back to San Francisco. Onion Valley, where we exited, was thirteen miles from Lone Pine. We'd already hiked about ninety miles, so when a friendly man offered us a free ride to town, we gladly accepted. Then we found out his truck wouldn't start. "It's downhill all the way," he said. "Hop in."

We weren't eager to coast down a very steep and windy road, but we didn't want to walk the miles either. Just outside town, the motor started, and we had about an hour before the bus left. Getting back to San Francisco wasn't so simple. We had to take one bus from Lone Pine to Mojave where we would transfer to another bus that would take us to Bakersfield. From there we could make a connection to San Francisco.

When the first bus was forty-five minutes late arriving in Lone Pine, I was certain we'd miss the connection in Mojave and have to spend the night and most of the day in the desert, since there was only one bus a day going to our destination. All the way to Mojave, I kept devising alternate plans. What a relief to see the Orange Line bus in the station! The driver had waited for our bus for over an hour.

Wretched as we looked after our nine-day hike and lengthy bus rides, the hotel in Bakersfield still gave us a room. We immediately went to a store and each bought a set of new clothes. Hot showers, clean clothes, and a good dinner restored us to respectability. Back in San Francisco, we did some sightseeing, visited Point Reyes National Seashore, its Morgan Horse Farm, and the San Andreas Fault. In our rental car we also drove the magnificent Big Sur coastline and visited Hearst Castle and Yosemite National Park. Despite the park's many outstanding natural sights and tempting hikes all located in one narrow ravine, we were content with a scenic drive through the area. We were giving our hiking boots a vacation for a while. Mt. Whitney remained unconquered. Eighteen years would pass before we tried again. See the chapter, "Getting High."

REVISITING THE PACIFIC NORTHWEST

In 1981, we decided to return to Washington State. We planned to spend two weeks exploring Olympic National Park on the coast and would then move farther inland to complete the second half of our 1973 back-packing trip in the North Cascades. (For the first half of that trip see the chapter, "Getting High.")

Kurt's hiking trip in the Olympic Mountains in 1957 with his brother had ended abruptly when Kurt twisted his ankle, so he was ready for a revisit. And though I had often see the Olympics during the five years I lived in Washington, I'd never gone hiking there.

Our son Alan, then fourteen, joined us. My aunt and uncle, the Spannauses, who lived in Seattle, agreed to serve as our base camp for rest and recovery between the two parts of our trip. They also wined and dined us on our Seattle sight-seeing days. The night four of us went to the Opera, Alan played ping-pong in the Spannaus basement. The three Sterns enjoyed visiting the Seattle Aquarium, watching the salmon in the fish ladders at the Ballard Locks, and exploring the Pacific Science Center and Seattle Underground. Concentrating on a five-block area around Pioneer Square in Seattle, the underground tour led through tunnels where we saw sidewalks and storefronts that had ended up underground when street levels were raised eight to thirty-five feet following a fire in 1869 that destroyed thirty blocks of downtown Seattle as well as ten piers on the wharf. We caught a bit of Alaska gold fever when we stopped at the National Park Service's Klondike headquarters. Photos of the famous Chilkoot Trail made a lasting impression on us, leading to an adventure there four years later (described below). One evening we rode the boat to Tillicum Island to eat smoked and alder-grilled salmon and to watch dances performed by the Native Americans who lived on the island.

Surprisingly good weather made our hikes in the Olympics a pleasure. Just inside the Olympic National Park boundary near Dosewallips, we took the trail to Lake Constance. We were late getting started but wanted at least to reach the lake before turning back, so we pushed a bit, moving faster than we usually did on a trail that steep. We did make it and were rewarded with awesome views of alpine quality surrounding the lake. On the way back, Alan and I saw a huge dark shape in a ravine at the side of the trail. As the shape moved nearer, we realized it was a Roosevelt elk, a species once nearly exterminated by hunting. Our knees and legs complained painfully after the hike, letting us know that we should have moved more slowly on the way down. All three of us walked rather stiffly the next day.

We drove next to the Hoh Rain Forest Visitor's Center. On the park's official Rain Forest Trail, lush vegetation made up of lichens, club mosses, and ferns covered everything, sometimes transforming old trees into grotesque shapes and making us feel we had better move fast before something started growing on us. Everywhere it was cool, green, and moist. Heavy and frequent rainfall and relatively mild winters had enabled Sitka spruce and Douglas fir trees to develop eight-foot trunks and to grow to heights of 275 feet. Western hemlock, western red cedar, Alaskan cedar, mountain hemlock, and subalpine fir mingled in vast protected stands of trees in this scenic wilderness. The main paved road skirted the outside of the park's area. The few roads that gave access to trails ended less than twenty miles into the park, and no roads passed through the park's interior.

Getting a good start on the Hoh River Trail, we stopped for the night in an attractive, tree-shaded trailside campground. The tent was up, sleeping bags unrolled, and a pot of water was starting to simmer on our trusty Optimus, a one-burner cooker ideal for backpacking. Dinner would soon be ready. Then we saw flames around the stove's fuel intake area. We had a leak! The stove was too hot and too dangerous to touch, so Kurt kicked it into the dirt to smother the flames. But it was too late. With a loud bang, the stove exploded. Fortunately no one was hurt by flames or flying pieces of the stove. Boiling water was needed to reconstitute our freeze-dried food. Hastily, we tried to get a wood fire going. Dinner would be a bit delayed.

With our Optimus stove, we could have camped in Glacier Meadows, giving us some views of the Blue Glacier and most of the next day for exploration. Now we would have to camp lower down the trail because wood fires were prohibited above a certain altitude. This would severely cut into the time we had for exploring the glacier on the flank of Mount Olympus, but we might still be able to take a look at it. The only wood we had for cooking that second night was very damp, and we had to wait even longer for our dinner.

We didn't bother with breakfast, but left our tent and hurried up the trail carrying our lunch of granola bars with us. The glacier was spectacular, huge, and full of crevasses. Rising above it were East and Middle Peak, two of the four that make up the complex summit of Mount Olympus. Though it rises only to 7,965 feet, the mountain receives a great deal of snow because of its latitude, elevation, and proximity to the Strait of Juan de Fuca. The route to the summit was fairly obvious. We had read that the average round-trip time from Glacier Meadows to the summit was ten hours, and that for the first mile, route-finding through the crevasse fields was the only problem. We took a trail down to the edge of the glacier, but without ice axes and rope, we didn't dare step out on the ice. Even under cloudy skies, the glacier had a bluish glow, the reason for its name. After eating our granola bars we turned back. Despite being somewhat disappointed at not having more time to explore, we enjoyed the splendid scenery–the snow-capped peaks all around and the dense conifer forests, lush ferns, and velvety moss at lower elevations.

Our amended plan had been to return to our campsite and spend another night where we could again cook on the wood fire. We'd then have about seven miles to hike out in the morning. But we did have another option. If we could walk a total of seventeen miles before dark, we could make it all the way back to the car. There was a quiet moment. Then at the same time we all said, "Let's go." It didn't take long to stow all our gear and shoulder our heavy packs. The trail seemed to go on and on, and our feet and legs began to let us know they had been working hard for us. It took two more days to get over what seemed like a resulting temporary paralysis from the waist down, but the pizza that night sure tasted good.

The next day, a fierce wind was assailing photogenic, glaciated Hurricane Ridge when we stopped there to take in the panorama of the park's jagged peaks, lowland lakes, and wildflower meadows. The area abounded with fearless deer, totally unaffected by the wind that almost blew me over.

Cape Flattery, the very northwestern tip of the Olympic Peninsula, provided a striking contrast with its caverns deeply undercut by the North Pacific's breaking waves. At Ruby Beach, another part of the park, we explored tidal-pool life. As we climbed over and around isolated weather-carved rocks along the coastline to reach the pools, the heavy morning fog that had given us an eerie sense of dislocation lifted for a gorgeous sunny day. Nearby we were fascinated by artifacts in the Makah Indian museum unearthed at an archeological site where a mud slide had preserved the ruins of an Indian civilization over two thousand years old.

After buying a replacement backpacking stove and doing laundry, we were ready to start on part two of our trip–a return to the unfinished 1973 North Cascades hike. The Spannauses drove the three of us to the trailhead at Ross Lake, where they planned to picnic after we left. We had just started up the trail when Alan said he didn't feel good, his legs were very painful, and he just couldn't do it. "Run back," we said, "maybe they haven't left yet." Of course, he couldn't run, but I could. Luckily the Spannauses had not left the parking lot and were happy to offer a week of tender, loving care to their grandnephew, who was suffering from aches and pains in his legs caused by a sudden rapid growth spurt.

For Kurt and me, it was satisfying to complete the trek we started in 1973 when we back-packed from Copper Canyon to Ross Dam, but had to scratch the second half of a planned trip. Now we began near Ross Dam, climbed twenty miles into Park Creek Pass, and were rewarded on the other side by an awe-inspiring view of range after range of snow-capped, glaciated peaks--and a campsite looking straight up into Mt. Buckner's double-glaciered crest. Finally we reached Lake Chelan, only then realizing that had we run the trip backwards we could have enjoyed the same view for only six miles of effort. Deer and marmots were absolutely fearless, circling our campfire and watching curiously while we ate. Once while getting water, Kurt slipped into neck-deep icy water, dousing his camera as well. Despite bright sunshine, his unexpected dip required an instant, on-trail, complete change of clothes, before the shivering stopped. He suffered no ill effects; but the camera, unfortunately, did not fare so well.

After we returned to Seattle to pick up Alan, we had three days left before our flight home. An unusual heat wave had hit Seattle, making it an ideal time for a revisit to Mt. Rainier. Lucky in getting a tent site, we were finally able to hike to the famed ice caves. They had been buried under heavy snow on all our previous visits. We enjoyed hikes on both sides of the massive and beautiful dormant volcano, remembering our 1971 summit climb, but not eager to repeat that adventure.

We couldn't leave Washington State and the Seattle area until we visited my father's uncle, Henry Joe Miller. At ninety-six, Great-uncle Henry had just started writing poetry. It didn't take much coaxing to get him to recite his latest clever and humorous creations. Then he regaled us with tales of the past and opinions on the present, showed us he could still touch his toes, and gave us the grand tour of the Masonic Home overlooking Puget Sound, where it was obvious his ever-cheerful and helpful personality had made him a favorite among the residents and staff.

RETURN TO MOUNTS WASHINGTON AND KATAHDIN

During the next two summers (1982 and 1983) we also took care of unfinished or aborted hikes. Off and on for twenty years we'd thought about hiking the Presidential Range in the White Mountains of New Hampshire. This range is the highest mountain group traversed by the Appalachian Trail north of Clingmans Dome on the North Carolina-Tennessee border. For most of the nearly twelve-mile distance between Mt. Madison and Mt. Pierce, the trail is above timberline. The elevation change, however, is mostly at the beginning and end of the ridge. Once Mt. Madison at 5,363 feet is reached, the trail continues on the ridge line, and the elevation varies at most by 900 feet. On clear days, the views are continuously spectacular.

Bud and Doris Aronson, who lived in Massachusetts, planned to join Kurt, Alan, and me. Bud and Kurt had both been very active in the University of Michigan Graduate School Outing Club in the 1950s and had maintained an intermittent correspondence. Although the Aronsons had not done much hiking, we knew they were in excellent condition. They were both marathon runners. With two cars available, we could hike for a week and not have to double back.

After meeting at a designated parking lot on the Kancagamus Highway in New Hampshire, we drove both cars to the Lafayette Place Campground, the planned endpoint of the trip. The five of us then drove to Pinkham Notch Headquarters to see what space was available in the mountain huts maintained by the American Mountaineering Club. For a fee, we could sleep on bunks in the huts and eat hot meals there. That way we would not have to carry packs and could make better time hiking.

Unfortunately, two huts on our planned route did not have room, so we had to take our sleeping bags in backpacks after all. A tent wasn't necessary, as three-sided shelters were available on a first-come, first-served basis. Because Alan had no backpack, we tried to patch together something to carry his sleeping bag, using a plastic garbage bag and some straps. It was an unwieldy burden. We avoided carrying any cooking equipment by planning to eat granola bars for two dinners and breakfasts.

Leaving the car at Pinkham Notch, we crossed U.S. Highway 16 to begin our long hike. We were very ambitious. First, we planned an easy ascent of

Wildcat Mountain by using the gondola. Then we'd have a short hike downward to the Carter Notch Hut, where we could spend the night. In the morning we'd take the Carter Trail over Carter Dome to the intersection with Imp Creek Trail, take that trail back down to the highway, cross over, and camp for a night in the Dolly Copp Campground. From Dolly Copp, we'd take the Daniel Webster Trail to the top of Mt. Madison and the Madison Springs Hut, where we had another hut reservation. The following day we'd hike along the Appalachian Trail on or near the ridge line to Mt. Adams, Mt. Jefferson, and Mt. Washington. Because the Lake of the Clouds Hut was already full, we'd have to make it to Mizpah Springs Hut. It would mean a long hiking day, but it was possible, if the weather were good and if we didn't dawdle. After more peaks, we'd spend two nights in shelters before we reached the car where we'd left it in the campground. It was a good plan on paper.

Our first hint of trouble began when we left Pinkham Notch and noticed dark clouds overhead. We thought the rain might hold off, though, until we reached Carter Notch Hut. We weren't that lucky. As soon as we got off the chairlift, the rain began. On went the ponchos and rainjackets. Mount Wildcat (4,397 feet), a popular ski resort in winter, is a long ridge comprising about ten more or less definite summits, the highest of which is that nearest Carter Notch. We would be crossing the five highest designated A, B, C, D, and E. Although we'd read the warning in the guide book that "this trail may be longer and harder than one would suppose," we thought we'd avoided most of the ascent and peak E by taking the gondola. Though the trail was well-marked, we wasted some time finding where it began from the gondola terminal. We also had avoided only the easiest peak. The rain made for slow going as rocks were slippery, and Doris kept stepping on her poncho when she had to scramble up a rock pile. It was also irritating that none of the grand views for which we'd taken this route were available because of the constant rain. Parts of the trail were quite steep and led to open ledges with no protection. Inside our raingear, we were sweaty from the exertion. Though the trail seemed endless, we did reach the hut in time for a hot dinner that was very comforting. We tried to wring out our drenched clothing and hung it over lines, but the continuing rain kept everything damp. At least we had a roof over our comfortable bunk beds.

Waking to rain in the morning, we immediately changed our plans. Imp Trail was scratched as was the Daniel Webster Trail. We didn't want to set up camp in the rain. If the rain continued, we might even have to forget the whole thing and lose the money we'd paid for the huts. We didn't bother hiking up Carter Dome, but took the first trail we came to, Nineteen-mile Brook Trail, down to the highway. Kurt and Bud hiked back to Pinkham Notch to pick up the car. After waiting patiently for some time, Doris, Alan, and I began to wonder why it was taking the men so long to return. When they finally pulled in to pick us up and left the motor running, we learned that the car's battery had died, and they'd had to wait to get a jump start. I was beginning to think this trip was not meant to be. We drove into the small town of Gorham, got motel rooms, dried our clothes, and prayed that the rain would stop. We had already devised an alternate plan.

Our clothes were dry, and the sun was shining as we drove the car around to the west side of the Presidential Range. Parking near the village of Randolph on U. S. Highway 2, at Appalachia parking space, we started up. A combination of intersecting trails would provide the shortest and quickest way to the Madison Hut.

We began with Air Line Trail, built in 1885. After about a mile, we intersected Short Line Trail, a graded path that led to the King Ravine Trail. About two miles later, the fun began. King Ravine Trail, built by Charles E. Lowe in 1876 as a branch of Lowe's Path, was fairly level for about another mile and a half. Then a short but very steep section took us to the upper floor of the ravine at 3,500 feet. The marvelous view was worth the tough go. Next the path wound over and under boulders ranging from the size of a small house down. A shortcut called the "Elevated" offered a way to avoid some of the boulder-caves. But we enjoyed the original trail called the "Subway"--550 feet long and lots of scrambling. In one of the boulder-caves, we saw ice that remains the year round. After another very steep section, the trail emerged between two crags and we could see our goal–the Madison Hut. Taking Gulfside Trail to the left we were soon inside, drinking lemonade and playing the piano until it was time to eat. Yes, a badly out-of-tune upright piano offered diversion for weary hikers. We never found out how it got there, perhaps delivered by helicopter. I can't imagine even a group of people carrying a piano up to the hut on any of the trails we'd taken.

Things were looking up as we strode along the ridge, trying to make sure that we stayed on the appropriate trail. Above timberline, it is easy to lose a sense of direction. Even the ridge trail had some ups and downs, so heading downhill wasn't a sure sign that you were going the wrong way. But every one of the other numerous trails led down either one side or the other of the ridge. Bud now took the lead striding on ahead, and Doris followed him. Kurt, Alan, and I always waited for a slower hiker at any trail intersection, just to make sure we were together. But we noticed that Bud didn't do this. "Oh, she'll be along," he said. We were on the summit of Mt. Washington (6,288 feet) by noon and stopped a bit to look around and to celebrate being there. Though we couldn't sleep at Lake of the Clouds Hut, we stopped for a bowl of soup, met Bud, and learned that Doris had taken a wrong turn and was back down on the highway at a ranch. She'd called Lake of the Clouds, thinking we might stop for lunch. Bud told her to stay there and he'd come to get her as soon as he could.

We had to move along to make it to Mizpah Spring Hut as we continued on the ridge past Mt. Monroe. We covered fourteen miles that day and barely made it in time for supper. Bud was about to leave when we arrived. He planned to take Crawford Path down to the highway in Crawford Notch, hitch a ride to

Appalachia where we'd left the car, pick up Doris, and head for home. He knew she was finished hiking for this trip. We said our goodbyes, but Alan wasn't paying much attention. He'd met a very attractive female hiker about his age-- fifteen. Krista was hiking part of the trail with her mother and younger brother. The three teenagers were getting acquainted while working on a jigsaw puzzle. Alan managed to sit opposite Krista both at dinner and at breakfast, and we noticed that our usually shy son was totally involved in animated conversation.

In the morning, as we headed towards Crawford Notch, I asked Alan about his new friend. "She's from Boston," he said. "She's lots of fun."

"Did you ask for her address?"

"I was too scared," he said. "But I got it anyway. I copied it out of the guest register book." It was good to know that his shyness did not prevent him from attaining his goals.

Alan was not moving very fast on the trail, so I added his sleeping bag in the plastic to the top of my pack. His knees were hurting, he said. Earlier in the summer he'd spent eleven days at the High Adventure Boy Scout Ranch in Philmont, New Mexico. He'd carried thirty-five pounds on his back and hiked fifty-five miles among other activities. By the time we reached Mizpah Spring Hut, we'd hiked about forty more miles. His knees deserved a rest.

After passing the summits of Mt. Jackson (4,052 feet) and Mt. Webster (3,910 feet) the trail descended steeply along Webster Cliffs for a winding 2,600 feet. When we finally reached the highway, Alan's knees were screaming. I had blisters on both my heels, so we made another change of plans. We'd all spend the night at the hostel in Crawford Notch, if there was room. If knees and heels recovered overnight, we'd all take the A-Z Trail, an alternate connecting trail to the Appalachian Trail. If not, in the morning Kurt would continue on, but without his heavy pack while Alan and I waited at the hostel for the shuttle bus to the Lafayette Place Campground.

We had a painful, long walk up the highway to the hostel, but Alan and I were offered a ride in a van. We must have looked rather pitiful. Kurt had gone on ahead, but we graciously picked him up too. When the heavy rains that had started as we walked continued, we were happy to be spending the night warm and dry inside.

In the morning, Alan and I decided to take the shuttle back to our car and the campground. I might have finished the hike, even with my blisters, but I didn't think Alan should be left on his own. At the campground, we set up our tent, cooked dinner, and enjoyed a campfire. Meanwhile Kurt, finishing the hike, made very good time without his pack and spent the night at Galehead Shelter. By early afternoon the next day, he joined us at the campground, and we headed home, happy to have finally hiked the Presidential Range in the White Mountains of New Hampshire. Although the distances between huts is not much, and though the summit elevations of 4,000 to 6,000 feet may seem minimal compared to the 14,000-foot peaks in Colorado, the terrain in the White

Mountains is rugged, and the trails are strenuous, minimally maintained, and challenging. Weather conditions change rapidly and can be quite severe, especially above timberline. We'd survived without a major mishap, had seen some gorgeous mountain scenery, and felt we'd had a good workout and satisfying vacation.

In August 1983, the following summer, we decided to try to reach the northern terminus of the Appalachian Trail, Mount Katahdin, in Maine. Kurt had hiked to the summit in 1953 and had been praising the knife-edge trail ever since. He and I had started up in 1961, but had to turn back when I became ill half-way up. In 1976, all four of us planned to do it following a conference Kurt had in New Hampshire, but as we drove towards Baxter State Park, we heard on the radio that extensive forest fires were creating a safety hazard, and the park was closed to all visitors until further notice. We enjoyed a few days in Acadia National Park on Maine's sea coast, but vowed to return to Katahdin.

When Kurt again had a conference in New Hampshire, it was time to go. Alan had kept up a correspondence with Krista and invited her to join us. We couldn't get a permit to camp at Chimney Pond which would have made our trip more leisurely, but we thought if we got an early start and kept moving we could make a round trip from Roaring Brook Campground. Alan and I picked up Krista in Boston and Kurt in New Hampshire and drove on to Maine.

One sunshiny day was all we needed. And it was all we got. On the way up we saw a moose casually munching grass at the side of the trail. I thought Alan was having altitude problems when he became pale and lost his breakfast part of the way up. It turned out that he had the flu. But he wouldn't give up. The picture of him at the summit looks as if he barely made it. From Chimney Pond, the aptly named Cathedral Trail led through huge, tall blocks of granite to the nerve-wracking and incredibly beautiful Knife Edge Trail. Made up of several peaks, Mount Katahdin at 5,287 feet is Maine's highest summit. The panoramic views of the surrounding lower peaks and hills covered with vegetation and of the uninhabited areas filled with trees, numerous lakes, and ponds were spectacular and impressive. The scramble to the summit was challenging and invigorating. Rain showers caught us on the way down, but we had been to the mountaintop and didn't care. After our two previously aborted attempts, success was sweet, satisfying, and worth the effort.

ARIZONA CANYONS

In October 1985, a Las Vegas conference for Kurt provided the excuse to fulfill another dream when I joined him at the conference's end to drive to the Grand Canyon's rim. We hoped that we could hike the Bright Angel Trail, but before we did, we planned an easier hike down a side canyon to the Havasupai Reservation. Access to Supai, a small farming village with one hotel, was only by foot, by horse, or by helicopter. Being cheap and wanting to condition ourselves, we hiked eight miles through the canyon surrounded by redstone walls, reviving memories of every Western movie ever seen. At any moment we expected to see cowboys or Geronimo and friends emerging from behind tall rocks or peering down at us from atop their Apaloosa or Pinto mounts. Instead we saw only a string of tourists riding on horses being led down the path. It was a pleasant hike mostly downhill. When we reached Havasu Creek, we also encountered grass, shrubs, and water-loving trees, all adding cool shade and beautiful contrasting tones of green to the otherwise arid scene.

The tiny village consisted of several streets of prefab houses, a small diner, the hotel, a ball field, a school, and peach orchards. Gathering piñon nuts is another source of income for the residents. Inside the diner, several people were trying fry bread, a favorite local treat. We'd made a reservation at the hotel and were glad we didn't have to walk four more miles to the campground. We'd hiked for eight miles and were ready to rest.

The next day, we hiked for several miles below the village to three incredibly beautiful aquamarine waterfalls. At the top of the falls, mineral deposits had created beautiful stone lacework. At the base of the falls, the same kind of mineral deposits had formed circular rimmed travertine pools large enough for swimmers. The pools resembled huge lily pads made of blue-green water. The path to the third and highest falls tunneled through the mountain itself at one point. When it traversed the rock surface, spikes with connecting cables had been installed to help hikers maneuver the steps cut into the stone. Exciting and awesome! Beyond this waterfall, we had a glimpse of the Colorado River into which the creek eventually flowed. But it was a long way down, and we still had several miles to hike back up to the village. We slept very well that night.

In the morning, we hiked the eight miles through the canyon to return to our car parked on the canyon's rim. Naturally the way up was more strenuous, but by then we were in pretty good shape and spent most of our time enjoying the beautiful scenery.

Successful in this training hike, we were ready for the Grand Canyon hike. Ideally, we wanted to hike down Kaibab Trail one day, camp overnight near the river, and return to the rim the next day on the Bright Angel Trail. The only question was whether any campsites were available. We knew staying at Phantom Ranch in the bottom of the canyon was impossible. Reservations there are made a year in advance. Campsites, too, are usually reserved in advance. Our fallback plan was to carry only water and hike down and back up in one day. I wasn't looking forward to that.

Luck was with us when we stopped at the Ranger Station. Someone had cancelled, and we not only got space at Cottonwood Creek at the bottom; we also got a spot for our second night at Indian Gardens, half-way up the Bright Angel Trail.

The night before we left, we camped in the National Park's Mather campground, awaking to a temperature of thirty-two degrees and a frosted windshield. In contrast we found a pleasant eighty degrees at Cottonwood campground beside the Colorado River when we arrived there after five hours on the steep South Kaibab Trail. On the way, we traversed geological time backward, noticing the changes in vegetation as we went. We did meet mule trains and tourists coming up, but the trail was wide enough (just barely) to accommodate everyone.

The day was perfect: the inner canyon with its dark, primordial, volcanic rock made us feel as if we had entered an ancient, mystical, enchanted dwelling place. That night the completely full moon illuminated not only the muddy Colorado River, but also sparkling Clear Creek and the other attractive campsites among the cottonwood trees, which we passed on our way to Phantom Ranch for the park ranger's evening talk. Learning more about the female architect who had designed many of the unique buildings on the canyon rim inspired us to take another look at these structures when we reached the top the next day.

The way up took longer, the packs were heavier, and the rest houses on Bright Angel Trail were welcome. But we reached Indian Gardens, our designated evening campsite, before noon. After a snack, we decided to try for the top. We didn't realize we'd only done the easy part and that the trail became increasingly demanding. As the switchbacks became seemingly interminable and progress slowed, we wondered why we had made such a stupid decision. We were dragging our way on the last bit to the rim, but we were on top before dark, and a hot bath in the motel room was a scrumptious reward.

On our way back to Las Vegas, we toured Hoover Dam, almost as impressive and unbelievable as the Vegas casinos, where grim-faced people supposedly enjoyed the "sport" of gambling. The surroundings, particularly MGM Palace and Caesar's Palace (site of Kurt's conference), were amazing and otherworldly. At Caesar's, huge muscled doormen were dressed as Roman guards in red and gold, complete with little skirts. We also took in an extravaganza girlie show, complete with orangutans, waterfalls, magic, a jungle sacrifice scene, and an ice-skating ballet—not too much continuity, but fun. We'd packed a variety of experiences into one short week and felt totally refreshed.

CHAMPIONS OF THE CHILKOOT

Five years after we'd seen photographs of the Chilkoot Trail in the National Park Service's Klondike Gold Rush Headquarters, we returned to Seattle to travel as deck passengers on the Alaska State Ferry to Skagway. My relatives, the Spannauses, met us at the airport the night we arrived and took us to the dock at 6:00 a.m. the next morning. Deck space was first-come, first served until the available spaces were full. The ferry trip, interesting in itself, is described in the chapter, "America the Beautiful."

Leaving the ferry when it docked in Skagway, the end of its route north, we checked in with the Park Service there, learning to our dismay that the train from Lake Bennett to Skagway had been discontinued. Instead, a bus from Whitehorse, headed for Skagway, came by twice a day, once in the morning and once in the evening. It stopped along the highway at a place called Log Cabin, ten miles from the end of the Chilkoot Trail. We had counted on the train to bring us back from Lake Bennett, the terminus of the Chilkoot trail, to Skagway. Now we would have to walk an extra ten miles from the end of the trail to Log Cabin and take the bus. We wrote down the posted bus schedule and boarded a van going to Dyea, a marshy area where the trail began.

The Chilkoot Trail became famous after gold was discovered in the Klondike River in 1896. Beginning in 1897 and continuing into the winter of 1897-98, between twenty and thirty thousand stampeders took this relatively fast and cheap route to the Yukon goldfields, unaware that most of the good claims had already been staked. It was only 33 miles from Skagway to Lake Bennett via the Chilkoot Trail, and from that point, all that remained was a 550-mile float trip on the Yukon River to reach Dawson City and the famous gold fields. But getting supplies over the pass was brutal. Because horses could not make it through the steep pass, all supplies had to be carried by the stampeders or by Indians they hired. The Canadian border lay in the pass, and it was there that the Mounted Police stopped each individual to see whether he or she had the requisite year's worth of supplies. No one was allowed to enter Canada without meeting this requirement. This rule probably saved many lives. A year's supply of goods amounted to about two thousand pounds, and since on average a single load was about seventy pounds, the stampeder had to make about thirty trips to the pass and back before moving on. He also had to find some way to distinguish his stack of stuff from everyone else's.

The famous Chilkoot Trail photograph showing a line of people from the base to the top of the "Golden Stairs" was taken in winter, when the steep, rocky trail was covered with snow and ice and 1,200 steps were cut into the ice so people could climb to the top of the ridge on these "stairs." If you stepped out of line to rest, you lost your place. Getting back down the hill was easier, as most people slid down on a shovel or a piece of metal. Indians offered to carry gear for twelve cents a pound from Dyea to the scales at the base of the pass, but they charged one dollar a pound over the pass. There were many stories of incredible feats. One man supposedly carried a piano over the pass. An Indian woman was said to have carried an iron stove. Eventually sleds and tramways were built to haul the goods up. But all these alternatives cost more than most people could afford, so they generally carried their own gear.

If the stampeders reached Lake Bennett before freezeup, they hurriedly built boats and rafts and left for Dawson City. Latecomers had to winter over, waiting for the spring thaw and breakup. Along the trail, entrepeneurs set up shop offering meals and bunks for the night. These people were the most likely to make a profit from the trip. Tent cities bloomed at Canyon City, the start of the tramway. Sheep Camp was the last stop before the pass where a bunk and a meal could be had. At The Scales, loads were weighed to ensure fairness when packers were employed. Hardships abounded. There were murders and suicides; disease and malnutrition; and death from hypothermia, avalanche, and perhaps heartbreak. In two years it was all over, and lively boomtowns became lonely ghost towns as the gold fever drew its victims to Nome and the latest find.

Today the Chilkoot Trail is part of the Klondike Gold Rush National Historical Park. The trail is unusual, being part wilderness and part history with explanatory photos of past glories posted at significant stops along the way and with many artifacts and ruins to be seen as one hikes by. Abandoned by the stampeders, worn-out boot soles, tin cans, tramway pilings, canvas boats, and iron cookstoves stir the imagination with thoughts of what happened here.

For the first fourteen miles, the trail is a series of steep ascents interspersed with level walking through the dense growth of wet ferns, moss-covered trees, dripping underbrush, mud, and slick exposed roots that constitute the coastal rainforest. Many streams are crossed, and sometimes boardwalks help the hiker traverse boggy, marsh areas. We walked under a green canopy, surrounded by green vegetation, often with green moss beneath our feet. As the trail rose from sea level to the pass at 3,739 feet, the coastal rain forest was replaced with tundra, and finally, near the pass, the walking surface was totally on rocks.

Heeding all bear warnings, wearing bear bells on our packs, and carrying only freeze-dried food (no gorp or peanut butter), we never encountered a bear, brown (grizzly) or black, though other hikers we met spotted one--with cubs. After a long day hiking through rain and mist, we welcomed the drying hut at Sheep Camp, despite the smelly, steamy wool clothing hanging everywhere. The hut was to be used only for getting warm, drying out, or cooking. No one was allowed to sleep inside, no matter how hard it rained. When our one-burner stove failed, other hikers shared fuel, boiling water for us.

In the morning, with better light, I spent considerable time trying unsuccessfully to get the stove working again. We were off to a late start, but made pretty good time along the fascinating trail up to the scales. Long Hill was a bit tiring, and the steep ascent to the pass, almost straight up over huge boulders and marked only by cairns, slowed us down even more. As a result, it was almost 5:00 p.m. when we reached Canada and the pass. We actually saw the enscribed bronze plaque that marked the highest point. Momentarily the clouds above the pass swirled in another direction–just for our benefit.

When the clouds swirled back, they were dark and threatening. We had at least two hours of hiking before we would reach the next campground, and our stove still wasn't working. About a mile on the far side of the pass near Stone

Crib, an emergency shelter, we were hailed by the Canadian Park Superintendent who graciously invited us to stay in the emergency shelter. The next campground, she said, was several hours and many snowfields ahead. Even if we reached it safely, it had only campsites, no shelters. She predicted the swirling dark clouds above meant heavy rain or snow. Even as we spoke, the torrent began, and we scuttled inside the tiny shelter for the night. Other hikers had told her of our stove problems. From a cabin she shared with her seventy-two-year-old mother, she brought a walking stick, hot chocolate, a space heater, hot water, and plastic bags to wear inside our boots for traversing the snowfields and swollen streams she said we would encounter the next day.

Ignoring the foggy, foggy dew the next morning, we headed down through what were probably gorgeous high alpine areas with green glacial tarns and many snowfields--a wild barren beauty. By early afternoon we had entered the boreal forest, the sun was shining, and we were drying out at Lake Lindeman hut in front of a roaring pot-bellied stove tended by a six-foot- four-inch retired Methodist minister in walking shorts who carried a ninety-pound pack. He had hiked in forty-nine states, he said, and found this trail the most demanding one he had tried. After finishing this hike, he planned to fly to Hawaii to complete his three-year, fifty-state trek. Near beautiful Lake Lindeman, adjacent to the warming hut, the Canadians provided an emergency food cache and a fascinating outdoor museum on the history of the trail, the railroad, and the town of Bennett.

Because camping was not allowed at Lake Lindeman, we pressed on and camped at Bare Loon Lake instead. We rose early and shared one granola bar, saving the last remaining one for an emergency. Then we hiked fast, passing other hikers still in their tents. Once we reached the railroad tracks, we still had to cover nine miles along them before we reached Log Cabin, the designated pickup point for the bus. Delighted to see that we were twenty minutes ahead of time, we devoured our emergency granola bar and drank our last water. But the bus didn't come. Instead a cold wind started up, which cut through all our warm clothing. As time went on, I thought about setting up the tent or starting a fire, but I was afraid the bus would come at any minute. Though the day was sunny, the persistent wind made the ditch by the side of the road rather inviting.

With unlimited time to think, we came to the realization that we had neglected to factor in the time difference. British Columbia is not on Alaskan time. Instead of being twenty minutes early, we had missed the morning bus by fifteen minutes. The next one would not arrive until late in the evening. It would be a long, long, cold day with no food or water.

We tried hitchhiking, sometimes together, sometimes separately, but nothing worked. Recreational vehicles whizzed by us. Drivers of sedans never looked our way. There was nothing else around–for miles. It was twenty-seven miles back to Skagway, but we'd already hiked thirteen that morning and the idea of twenty-seven more had no appeal. We preferred to wait in the ditch all day if we had to. As it turned out, we waited there for four hours.

Finally some Canadian hikers we'd met earlier came out the same way. Part of a larger group, they had stashed one of their cars at the trailhead and saved us from eight hours of waterless and foodless waiting by driving us back to Skagway.

As we drove into Skagway, we saw the ferry was in the dock. Thanking our saviors for the ride, we ran on board. We knew there was a cafeteria on the ferry, and we were eager to be on our way to Juneau. We quit talking about the wonders of the Chilkoot Trail only long enough to listen to two Australians who told us if we liked the Chilkoot, we should really try the Milford Trek in New Zealand. From that conversation, a new goal emerged. Amazingly, three years later, we were in New Zealand, tramping the Milford. You can read about that in the chapter, "Island Survivors."

HIMALAYAN DREAM

Almost from the time we met, Kurt and I talked about places we'd like to go, hikes we'd like to take, and mountains we'd like to climb. On our honeymoon trip to the Crestone Mountains in Colorado, we told each other, "One day we'll go trekking in the Himalayas." It was more of a fantasy than anything we thought we'd actually do, given our financial resources at that time.

Thirty years later, when Kurt retired in 1990, he asked me for ideas to mark the occasion. "What would you really like to do?" he asked.

"Do you remember our fantasy from thirty years ago?"

He did remember and started gathering information almost immediately. We read books and brochures, attended lectures and slide shows, and carefully examined our savings. We planned to visit India on the same trip. One potential problem was whether I would be allowed to take leave without pay from my job. I didn't have two months of vacation time. Luckily the Copyright Office needed to save money and readily granted my request.

Because this was the longest of our hikes and unexpectedly included attendance at an important Buddhist yearly celebration, my descriptions and impressions can be found in a separate chapter, "Himalayan Happening."

UTAH CANYONS

During the summer of 1996, when we drove to Arizona for a two-week raft trip on the Colorado River through the Grand Canyon, we agreed that if we survived we'd also visit the famed national parks in Southern Utah. Now, having successfully completed the raft trip, we headed for Utah. It was early June when we reached Canyonlands National Park, an area filled with fantastically shaped rock pillars and monoliths of sandstone. On our first hike, we made a wrong turn, but since the temperature was about ninety-five degrees, we relished the cool, shaded rock canyon we found. While we ate lunch and rested, we planned a second try very early in the morning. The night sky away from anywhere showed us brilliant stars and a vivid Milky Way.

On the trail at 7:00 a.m., we made the correct turn and hiked down to Elephant Canyon through long passages with high-sided walls. The trail then led up one side of the canyon over red rocks, making interesting twists and turns. Chesler Park itself was beautiful, a high, grassy plateau encircled by grotesquely shaped needles--spindly monoliths carved from cedar mesa sandstone. Many had arches or holes caused by erosion. We had the trail all to ourselves. Only after we started back at 9:00 a.m. did we meet any hikers, and they were starting up the trail.

It was only 10:15 a.m. when we left for Arches National Park, but when we arrived fifteen minutes later, the campground was already filled. After finding a cheap motel room in Moab, we spent the day visiting the Windows area of the park, where the wind and weather had carved hollows in the sandstone. In one spot, the rocks looked like giant spectacles. Arches National Park, famous for its fins and towers, balanced rocks, petrified sand dunes, and over 1,500 natural arches and windows formed by the action of ice, water, and wind on Entrada sandstone, sits on a plateau high above the canyon of the Colorado River, a slickrock land of fantasy. Climbing or scrambling over the rocks is fairly easy in dry weather, but we learned the reason for the name *slickrock* when we were caught in an afternoon rain.

The next morning we hiked through Park Avenue, an area full of tall slabs of rocks which resembled skyscrapers. The trail followed narrow pathways between the slabs. First in line for campsites, we felt lucky to find one that had some shade. After setting up camp, we tried to hike to Broken Arch, but gave it up when we felt we were getting overheated. Later we learned the temperature had been 103 degrees. Instead we drove to Dead Horse Canyon Point, a plateau from which we had phenomenal views of the twists and turns of the river below. The huge neon-blue pools we spotted in one area were part of the process for drying potash, not the result of some evil enchantment. We also visited Island in the Sky, but had only enough energy to get out at the viewpoints and wonder how people managed to hike through the hot and arid territory.

When we woke the next morning at 5:30, four mule deer were visiting our campsite. Only a few hikers were at the trailhead when we arrived at 7:00 a.m. For a while the trail was level and the formations such as Pine and Tunnel arches were just at the side of it. More effort was required to see Wall, Partition, Navajo, and Landscape arches. To reach Double O and a view of Dark Angel, a formation of black stone resembling an angel, we had to scramble along rocky ridges and ledges. The way was not always clearly marked, but the views were wonderful. By the time we returned, busloads of European tourists and many other visitors were coming up the trail, making us doubly glad we'd started early.

After stopping to photograph more red sandstone arches and bluffs, we drove to Colorado National Monument, where we camped and marveled at the shapes inside the steep-walled canyons. On a short hike, we encountered a beautifully-colored lizard that seemed to enjoy posing for us.

On our way to Capitol Reef National Park, I insisted we stop at Goblin Valley State Park. Here we hiked the Curtis Bench Trail through canyons of dried mud. This area had very whimsical formations carved out of cocoa brown Entrada sandstone and capped by the greenish Curtis formation. While some shapes resembled space aliens, others looked like giant toadstools. As we hiked, the view towards Wild Horse Butte became dramatic as dark clouds and lightning arrived. The threatening weather followed us to the campground in Capitol Reef, but we still had time for a short hike in the area, after setting up camp in wonderfully cool weather. The scenery now, though totally different from the red sandstone, was also very beautiful. Massive stone areas culminated in spires, pinnacles, and domes with descriptive names such as Golden Throne, Egyptian Temple, and Capitol Dome.

At breakfast, sixteen deer ambled through the campground in two herds. Then on the way to our five-hour hike, we saw a chukar with four chicks. This bird, new to us, appeared to be a fat cousin of the grouse. The hike was superb. We walked to Grand Wash, took the Cassidy Arch Trail, then Frying Pan Trail and finally Cohab. The trails were well marked and well graded with new and different vistas at every turn and shady spots when it got warm. We saw two marmots and a black-headed grosbeak. In Cohab, a narrow chasm, some of the rock was pitted with holes, giving it a Swiss cheese appearance. The canyon got its name because it was once a refuge for some Mormon polygamists or cohabitationists who were trying to evade a federal posse. Grand Wash, a 500-foot-deep canyon, impressed us by its twists and turns and by the high, impregnable smooth canyon walls that offered no route to climb out. In one section of the canyon called "the narrows," the wash is only twenty feet wide. Pioneers who drove horses and wagons through the wash were careful to do so only on dry days. In a flash flood, there would be no way out as there are very few alternate exit routes.

Our destination the next day was Lower Muley Twist Canyon. Supposedly given its name by early Mormon pioneers who declared the canyon sinuous enough to "twist a mule," the canyon passed through a portion of the 100-mile-long eroded uplift called the Waterpocket Fold. We drove for about two hours south on Highway 12, then took the Burr Trail Road through a landscape of beautiful dark red hills overlooking land dotted with pale gray-green sagebrush. After parking at the trailhead, we walked for a little more than three miles before we took a side trail to the Strike Valley Overlook. The vista was enormous and magnificent. Back on the trail, we continued up the wash to magnificent Saddle Arch and beyond. I wanted to try the rim trail and continue for about thirty minutes, but a very dark cloud was sitting just over the trail. We definitely didn't dare to follow the rim trail. When we heard thunder, we headed back toward the car. For a while we kept up with or were slightly ahead of the front edge of the darker clouds, but as the two arms of clouds swirled to a meeting, the raindrops started. Out came our raingear and we trudged on.

We noticed the rain was increasing just about the time we came upon a large overhang, inviting us to pause and shelter underneath it. Shortly thereafter a downpour including hail descended. Torrents poured off the rocks above creating brown mini waterfalls and mini showers where streams of water clung to the rocks' underside until the last possible moment before forced to drop into a quickly forming pool below. Where the torrent hit the trail, a small creek developed that hurried down the wash. After thirty minutes the rain slackened a bit and we moved on, keeping other overhangs in mind should there be another downpour. Lightning and thunder continued, hurrying us on our way. Just as we reached the car, we had to walk on a red clay road. The red clay stuck to our boots creating a massive cleanup job. The wet slickrock glistened in the late afternoon sun, looking like cake with icing. It was an excellent day. We'd hiked more than ten miles.

Arriving the next day at Bryce National Park, we noticed how comfortable the temperature was–ideal for hiking. But after our exertions the previous day in Muley Twist Canyon, we opted for the scenic drive and stops at the viewpoints. The view of the amphitheater was fabulous–a wonderland of red, white, and cream-colored castles, spires, and pinnacles.

The following day we didn't even start our hike until 10:00 a.m., since we didn't have to worry about high temperature. The eight-mile Fairyland Trail was magical despite its many ups and downs and we enjoyed the spires, pinnacles, windows, towers, and bridges. Exotic formations such as the Palace of the Fairy Queen and the Ruins of Athens were enchanting. The Chinese Wall resembled the original for which it was named. Though there were masses of people and many tour buses at the viewpoints, the trail was not too crowded.

We couldn't leave without hiking the short three-mile Queen's Garden Trail with its hoodoos: Gulliver's Castle and Queens Castle along with a formation resembling the profile of Queen Victoria. Navajo Loop, a connecting trail, showed us formations such as Two Bridges, The Pope, and Thor's Hammer, a slender orange pinnacle capped by a mallet-shaped stone. The white stone tops of spires backlit by the rising sun were almost translucent, a gorgeous reward for being on the trail at 7:00 a.m.

Cedar Breaks National Monument, our next stop, was at 10,000 feet elevation. Our campsite nestled under tall evergreen trees and was visited by Clark's nutcracker, the usual camp robber. Here in mid-June on the Alpine Pond Trail, we found mountain bluebells, lupine, Engleman spruce, and sub-alpine firs. We were intrigued by the elkweed plant, a member of the gentian family. Every two years it grows a fat green stalk with star-like flowers that have a lavender center, surrounded by pale yellow and white petals. Hikes here were short. Bristlecone Pine Trail was only two miles; the Wasatch Rampart Hike was four, but the views were great--into deep, pine-covered canyons. At night a ranger program on astronomy helped us locate many constellations. Stars were brilliant as only a thin sliver of the new moon competed. Despite wearing long underwear, we grew cold when the wind started, so we left at about 10:15 p.m. for our warm sleeping bags in the tent.

Even the drive to Zion National Park is spectacular, passing through several tunnels. Deer were everywhere in the park. Arriving fairly early, we had time to hike to the Emerald Pools, after setting up camp and visiting the museum. The lower pool was spectacular, and part of the trail led under an overhang dripping with water. But it was hot here, and we got tired of tramping. We also hiked the Weeping Rock Trail to a spring and took the Riverside Trail until the point where continuing meant walking in the Virgin River.

It was a good introduction to the park, but the real treat was the hike to Angel's Landing. What fun! Although the trail is only one mile round-trip, it is very strenuous. The trail climbs steeply to the top of a tall fin that juts out into the middle of the canyon at 5,785 feet, nearly 1,400 feet above the river. The entire canyon is visible at a glance, but not everyone feels comfortable looking down. From the Grotto parking area we followed the trail up through cool, shady Refrigerator Canyon. Walter's Wiggles, a series of twenty-one switchbacks named for the park's first superintendent, were strenuous and tiring, but they did take us to a fairly broad top with a good view. As we drank water and rested a bit we saw that to reach Angel's Landing a narrow saddle had to be crossed. We watched other hikers making their way carefully across and saw that it was actually wide enough for two people to pass, unless they worried too much about the very steep dropoffs on either side. The trail on the other side of the saddle looked totally impossible. Not only did the trail to the summit look very steep, but I could see that spikes and chains had been placed in some probably horrific spots. But I had come too far not to try it. The exposure in the saddle wouldn't bother me, and once across, I could always come back if it was too difficult. Actually, it looked worse than it was, and we both enjoyed a great scramble in good weather. Though many of the hikers relaxed and slept in the sun, we didn't linger long. The views were great, and we enjoyed them, but I was taking no chances on being around when the usual afternoon thunder shower came by. No way would I want to do that trail when the rock was wet.

That afternoon the heat was so bad that we spent several hours inside the elegant air-conditioned lodge, pretending to be guests. Around 4:30 p.m. we went back to Riverside Trail and this time continued for a while in the Virgin River. By then there was some shade, and the water up to our knees was wonderfully cooling. The heat was so intense that candles we'd left at the campground melted.

The unique beauty of the southwest canyons of Utah remains a vivid memory. I had feared the heat of the desert, but learned that it could be tamed by taking on the habits of the animals that lived there. Get up early and hike before noon. Take a long noon-time siesta in the shade. Come out again only in the late afternoon. Carry and drink lots of water and enjoy the magnificent colors and shapes nature displays in this part of the world.

GREAT BASIN NATIONAL PARK

We hadn't planned to do any hiking in Nevada, but then we heard about Mt. Wheeler and Great Basin National Park. The park was fairly new, established in 1986. A fellow camper at the Cedar Breaks astronomy program was so enthusiastic about it that we decided to check it out.

At 10,000 feet, the campground would probably have comfortable temperatures, and we would sleep well. Bristlecone Pines Trail offered a chance to see trees that are among the oldest living things on our planet–4,000-year-old bristlecone pines. They were stunted and twisted by the extreme winter weather, but they were still alive. Glacier hike was also very pleasant, leading through fields of wildflowers to the base of a glacier. On the way back we took an alternate route that passed two small but beautiful alpine lakes. When we were almost back to the campground, a tree fell, crashing into another, which also fell– both fairly near the trail. It was very windy and we were glad to get back to our tent.

The next morning about 8:00, we started up Wheeler Peak (13,063), Nevada's second highest mountain. For a while the trail was a graded path and we made good time. But all too soon it became mostly rock and scree. The trail was fairly well marked or it was obvious, except where it was covered by snow. Some clouds looked somewhat threatening, but the wind kept pushing them beyond the summit, so we kept moving forward. We reached the summit about 11:30 a.m. and ate lunch, such as it was, with no bread. All we had was cookies, rotting oranges, and water. While Kurt rested, I went along the ridge to the pyramids built of rock. Here I found the register and signed it. When we started down, we followed two hikers who had reached the summit earlier, thinking they knew the way. I'm not sure what they were doing, but we ended up having to make a long traverse over chunky rocks to find the original trail. This was very slow going and because so much of the trail was snow-covered, we were never quite certain where the original trail was until we were actually on it.

Once there we made good time. We were surprised when a low cloud we thought was merely fog turned out to be snow flurries. Almost back in camp, Kurt slipped on a pebble, falling to his knees and gouging a finger. Repairs were made back in camp when we got there around 4:00 p.m. It had been a long day.

Before we left the park we visited Lehman Cave. Though fairly small, the cave was crammed full of stalactites, stalagmites, and the other beautiful formations. New to us were shields or palettes, perfectly round variations of

41

draperies. Our stop in Nevada had been a good warm-up for what would come next, our climb up Mt. Whitney in California, described in the chapter, "Getting High."

TWO MONTHS IN THE ALPS

While making plans in 1972 to climb the Grossglockner with the Innsbruck Climbing School, we had noticed that walking tours in other parts of the Austrian Alps were offered. "We can do that on our own when we're older," we said. Twenty-five years later, in the summer of 1997, that's just what we did, combining our walks with visits to museums, castles, and churches.

The snowline was still low in June, and cloudy skies obscured some of the views in the Zugspitze area near Garmisch-Partenkirchen, Germany, where impressive trails had been cut into the gorges created by waterfalls. It was incredible to walk on a slanting narrow rock trail blasted out of the side of a cliff next to the edge of a raging torrent of water. Guardrails helped calm any anxieties. Emerging from a narrow opening between the cliffs, we were greeted by spectacular views of huge glaciers--an exciting beginning to two months of hiking in the Alps, riding trains and buses in Austria carrying only backpacks like overage college students, and visiting the usual tourist sites on rainy days. Staying in youth hostels, alpine huts, and bed and breakfasts was more interesting as well as cheaper than staying in hotels. Though we had no reservations, we always found a room or bed.

The charming bed-and-breakfast in Garmisch had red geraniums in the windows and shiny copper pots and pans decorating the kitchen walls. From that location we took several hikes up nearby lower mountains. Restaurants and small cafes along the way offered tasty refreshments. We enjoyed hiking in the cool temperatures even when we lost the trail once and took the long way back, but the cloud cover was too thick to make a cable-car ride to the high summit of the Zugspitze itself worth the expense. Sometimes we caught a breathtaking view of that peak from the place we stayed.

At the first train station in Austria, we purchased senior passes that entitled us to half-price fares on all forms of transportation. Our ride to Vienna, Kurt's birthplace, was so long that the pass paid for itself. In just three days we were able to visit the old inner city, Stefansdom, the church with the beautiful tiled roof and spire, and the Prater, a park at the edge of the city where a famous Ferris wheel still takes tourists up for a splendid panoramic view. These were all nostalgic visits for Kurt. But he had never visited Belevedere, former estate and palace of Prince Eugen, now magnificent art galleries situated in beautifully landscaped gardens from which one can see another view of Vienna. One night we went to a concert given by the touring Quincy Symphony Chorus in the Votivkirche, primarily because my brother was one of their soloists. We spent some time photographing Stern homesites and looking for information about Kurt's great-uncle and great-aunt who had been well known in the Hofburg Theater from 1890 to 1910. It was really exciting to find Aunt Ferdinande's will and a book Uncle Heinrich had written about his training and life in the Viennese theater.

From Vienna we traveled to Graz, second largest city in Austria, located in the southeast part of the country. Home to the emperor in the late middle ages, Graz retains its medieval city center, even though it is also a modern university town and cultural center. Out of the midst of old buildings nestled side by side, faced by twisting roads, rises the Schlossberg, an impressive castle, built in the fifteenth century. As we walked up the steep path through extensive park and forest lands to reach the castle, we paused to inspect the clock tower with its wood balconies, where many Graz residents enjoy their first kiss. The clock, built in 1382, is one of the oldest clocks in Europe that is still working.

Austria's oldest and largest provincial museum, the Styrian Landesmuseum Joanneum offered so much to be seen we had to select favorites. The Old Gallery held wonderful paintings by Cranach and the Breughels. In the New Gallery, we preferred the colorful mosaic-like paintings of Gustav Klimt to the mostly grim work of Egon Schiele, both from the period 1890 to 1925.

Outside town at Schloss Eggenberg, we toured the incredible castle with its richly decorated state rooms and 365 windows. Peacocks perching on the sills of second-story windows were a surprising sight. We were fascinated by the collection of artifacts depicting the history of civilization in Styria from the paleolithic age to the early middle ages. The most remarkable, mysterious, and beautifully crafted item was the ritual chariot of Strettweg, a bronze cart (600 B.C.) carrying a large decorative bowl supported by a primitive Atlas-like figure who was surrounded by horned animals and human figures.

Though the hunting museum did not appeal to us, we did enjoy the park outside the castle where sheep, deer, pheasants, and peacocks roamed freely. Back in Graz, a restaurant featuring food from Cyprus was a delicious way to end the day.

The train from Graz to Bad Gastein traveled through several tunnels, remained high on the mountainside and gave us postcard views of small alpine villages below. It was still winter in Bad Gastein, a famous resort where a huge waterfall flows between two eight-story hotels perched on the hillside and connected by a bridge over the plunging water. Many people were wearing coats, and there was lots of snow at the visible higher elevations. Luckily we arrived just in time for an delightful unexpected noon concert by a visiting choir from Bellingham, Washington. At least they were accustomed to rainy, dreary weather.

At the hostel we had a very nice room to ourselves and good food for a reasonable price. A large youth group ate in a separate area from the walk-ins or people who had previously made reservations. We found all the information we needed about hiking and huts in the National Park. From Bad Gastein we planned two trips. We first hiked from the hostel to Bockstein for great views of mountains and waterfalls. Beautiful caramel-colored horses with white manes stood under shade trees near a quaint 1743 church painted yellow. This was a good warm-up for the longer trip we attempted the next day.

Despite the clouds overhead, we started up the trail to Stubnerkogel past a meadow filled with tall spikes of lupine in differing shades of pink and blue interspersed with Queen Anne's lace. We tried to ignore a few sprinkles of rain, but by the time we reached the top of the chair lift, we were drenched by a serious downpour. When it finally stopped, we shook out our rain gear and continued on a trail to the Angertal valley, enjoying views of farms, grazing lands, and cattle in lush green valleys below barren peaks. When the bus was late and the clouds became darker, we worried about walking a long way back in a storm. But our patience was rewarded when a bus finally showed up--thirty minutes late.

In Zell am See, our next stop, we found a room in a charming white stucco house with shuttered windows and window boxes filled with colorful flowers. The room was spacious and comfortable, but we had to ascend three long flights of stairs with our heavy packs on our backs. In the afternoon, we hiked around the huge lake admiring the far-off peaks on all sides and a swan and her fuzzy cygnets at the lakeside. In the town itself, a visiting band from Norway entertained visitors having lunch or a snack at outdoor tables near the impressive stone Romanesque church built in 940.

We'd already discovered that our big packs were too heavy for making a continuous hut-to-hut trek, but we thought a stuffed day pack would see us through a two-hut trip, along a spectacular ridge, and down to a village in a new valley. We wanted to try the Pinzgauer Spaziergang, a splendid alpine trail with constant views of even higher Alps. In the morning we stored our heavy packs at the railroad station, then hiked to the cable car we took to the ridge, saving our energy for getting to the first hut. The hut had room for us, dinner was a hearty goulash stew and chocolate cake, and the view from the window of the full moon on snow-drenched peaks across a deep valley below us was magical.

Leaving the hut early in the morning, we followed the red-and-white painted trail markers above treeline to alpine meadows. A large herd of sheep meandered about the hillside seemingly without a shepherd. When I stopped to look back for Kurt, the sheep ran towards me. One nipped at my bootstrings; another nuzzled my hand. When I moved, they moved–all fifty of them. If I stopped, they initiated body contact. There was no escape. For reasons of their own, never disclosed, they had decided I was their shepherd. Perhaps the stick I carried was convincing evidence or the broad-brimmed hat and the knickers I wore. When a second "shepherd" showed up, they knew I was an imposter. As Kurt caught up with me, the sheep went back to grazing.

Once past the sheep, we made good progress until we saw three trail choices, none appearing on the schematic map we had. The trail we chose seemed to have more exposure than we had expected, but it posed no real problems except for somewhat slowing our pace. Just as we reached a barren rocky ridge above both tree and grassline, the clouds rolled in, accompanied by a wind so strong we could barely move forward against it. By then we were too far along the trail to go back, but we also did not know how far away the next hut was. Ahead were black thunderclouds, and the severe cold wind never stopped. Below us on the opposite side of the ridge from our destination, we could see the sun shining on gorgeous green pastures and farmhouses, but if we went that way, we were not sure if we could get back to our starting point.

At the trail intersection, as we stopped to consider our options, a family coming up the trail shared their better map. We saw that the trail we had chosen was an alternate and more difficult trail. From where we were, we probably could not reach the second hut until after dark. It was a long way down to that sunny valley we'd seen, but an exposed ridge in the dark in a storm is no joke. The family said they had come up from Hinterglemm. I vaguely remembered seeing a bus giving its destination as Hinterglemm as we walked out of town in the morning. If my memory was correct, we could get back "home" easily. If not, it would take a while. In the valley as we entered the town of Hinterglemm, we went to the first bed-and-breakfast we saw; fluffy featherbeds, a private bath, and an enormous breakfast buffet were most welcome.

Fortunately, my memory had been correct, and in the morning, a local bus took us back to Zell am See. Walking to the train station to retrieve our big packs, we encountered a parade of village bands and groups of young and old dressed in their village's traditional folk dress. The incredibly long parade included a decorated wagon pulled by a team of five horses. A group of six men in costume hauled a large cannon by ropes, firing it occasionally. Some groups danced schuhplattler and ring dances. Others carried farm implements as if they were weapons. The costumes were varied and beautiful: lots of dirndls, loden, lederhosen, red knee socks, top hats, gold crowns and woven caps. Onlookers lined the streets; many sat eating and drinking at tables along the way, applauding as their friends or a particularly appealing group went by. Our train left at noon, so when the parade stalled for a while, we hurried down the narrow cobblestone street at the side of the marchers and walkers. As we passed some tables, I heard applause, but nothing was moving except us. We did look strange, dressed in our hiking gear (knickers, long wool socks, boots, daypacks, and walking sticks). Kurt wore a white golfing hat; I wore a collapsible broad-brimmed white sun hat. We were obviously neither tourists nor natives. We acknowledged the applause by bowing, waving, smiling, and moving quickly out of the range of the video camera I saw focused on us.

The train took us next to St. Johan in Tirol, a picturesque village. The buildings surrounding the square had beautifully painted stucco walls. While the band gave a concert on a raised platform in the middle of the square, a costumed woman carrying a small keg and a silver cup made her way through the crowd offering a sip of schnapps in return for a donation to be used for the band. From St. Johan, our first hike was to Griesenau, past sharp craggy peaks and waterfalls to the end of the valley, where an inn was perched offering food and drink to travelers.

Kitzbühel, the famous ski resort we visited the next day, was a short bus ride from St. Johan. Though busy with tourists and their tour buses, the town built on a hillside was very attractive, having many arcaded walks and a church built in 1140 that contained sculptures which looked even older. We enjoyed a short hike past beautiful larch trees to the skiing area below Kitsbüheler Horn. The varying green patches of trees and fields in the valley below resembled a patchwork quilt. In the distance we could see the dazzling peaks of Austria's two highest mountains, the Grossglockner and Gross Venediger.

The forbidding peaks and jagged walls of the Wilder Kaiser were also accessible by bus from St. Johan. From the bus stop below the peaks, the trail began amidst meadows and fields, but it was not long before we encountered a barren glacial area and a very long, steep snow field. Most hikers that day ate lunch below the snowfield where crows came to snatch up scraps. Despite some sunshine, we wore caps and gloves. Carefully we climbed up the snow field to reach the gloomy pass. The trail markings leading into a rocky abyss and further adventures were inviting, but when dark clouds gathered, we decided to retrace our steps. On the way back, Kurt's walking stick caught in a crevice and hurled him forward towards a sharp rock. He scraped his nose and tore his pants, but he wouldn't stop to rest. He was afraid we'd miss the last bus back to St. Johan. We reached the bus stop just in time to board before a wild thunderstorm let loose, frightening the two dogs who were also riding the bus. A reduced fare is charged for the dogs, but they are allowed to ride, as long as they are muzzled and accompanied by a friend.

We next traveled to Vorarlberg, Austria's most western province, stopping in Feldkirch, a town on the border of Liechtenstein and Switzerland. The Feldkirch youth hostel was a large half-timbered building constructed in 1350, used as an infirmary during the black plague, and renovated in 1985. Thoroughly modern inside, this most picturesque hostel had a medieval aura about it. So did the town itself. Narrow cobble-stoned passages led through arches to the square where the town hall displayed painted coats of arms and historic figures on its stucco exterior. Red geraniums filled windowboxes everywhere. In the shadow of an arcade, a cozy restaurant served a delicious goulash on a dreary cold day. A striking orange building was topped with black onion-shaped domes. Stone watch towers marked the earlier city boundaries.

Near Feldkirch a trail led to the Three Sisters, a dramatic rocky summit with three peaks side by side. For quite a while we hiked along the actual border between Austria and Liechtenstein, marked by barbed wire. At the top of one of the foothills, we stopped for lunch. As soon as we did, we were surrounded by a group of very large cows showing a great deal of interest in our food. All of them wore huge cowbells and had horns. They seemed to be much larger than cows we were used to. When we tried to shoo them away, they ignored us. But an Austrian hiking couple had more success. Waving their arms wildly about, they loudly shouted at the animals. Somewhat intimidated, the animals strolled off to greener and quieter pastures on another hillside. Perhaps they understood only German.

On another hike we'd encountered more obliging cows. Although these enormous, placid beasts were comfortably resting their huge bodies in the middle of the trail, they politely vacated the area when a legitimate hiker came by. At first we were hesitant to walk through these herds of cows, fearing we might antagonize a bull, but since we never saw any males, we gradually became used to sharing the hillsides with them.

Vaduz, the capital of Leichtenstein was only a half-hour bus ride from Feldkirch. The castle fortress high on a hill was an impressive building, but casual visitors were not welcomed, since the castle was actually occupied by the ruler, the Prince of Liechtenstein. Near old half-timbered homes stood quite modern stucco designs painted pastel colors as if they were in California or Florida. The town was filled with tourists and tourist buses, despite threatening dark clouds overhead and very high prices for everything. An ice-cream cone cost about five dollars, so we went without and solaced ourselves by visiting the covered bridge over the Rhine river. In the middle of the bridge, signs marked the boundary between Liechtenstein and Switzerland. It was difficult to believe that this small river was actually the Rhine of legend and song.

Finally we found the sun in Italy, where we enjoyed a time-share week in Cervinia, at the foot of the Matterhorn (Monte Cervino). To get there, we took a train across Switzerland from Feldkirch, changing trains twice. To reach St. Bernard pass, we had to take a special train to Orsieres, a ski resort. At the resort, a bus waited to take us to the pass. Then we waited for two hours in the pass for an Italian bus to arrive from below in order to carry the waiting passengers into sunny Italy. The pass was momentarily clear and the views of surrounding jagged, snowy, glaciated peaks was awesome. The larger-than-life statue of St. Bernard placed on a pillar amidst the barren rock and high mountains attracted photographers. Many tourists arrived in cars to visit the Benedictine hospice on the lake, known for its trained Alpine rescue dogs, the huge St. Bernard dogs that carry small kegs of alcohol.

After spending the night in Aosta, we still had to take another train and a bus in order to reach Breuil-Cervinia. With so many changes and switching from train to bus and back again, we were glad our only luggage was our backpacks. Primarily a ski resort, the town sits just below the Matterhorn. From the time-share condo we could see the magnificent peak every day. The condo itself was quite comfortable and complete with cooking facilities and access to the exercise facility. One piece of equipment we tried at the urging of the manager was an electronic Shiatsu massage couch. Kurt said his back felt worse after the massage. It was strange to feel the couch rippling and sometimes almost punching at various body parts. Once was enough. The condo had been designed for residents with cars to drive up the long, gently graded winding approach. The shortcut we found to walk to town for groceries was quite steep, but much more direct. On the other hand, one of the trails we wanted to take conveniently left directly from our building.

Our first hike took us through meadows filled with wildflowers: anemones, clumps of almost fuchsia-colored rhododendrons, blue gentians, yellow buttercups and tri-colored violas in shades of pink, white, and lavender. After about three miles we reached the reservoir, Lago Goillet, in which we could see a stunning reflection of the Matterhorn and the walls of mountains that adjoined it. Continuing on the trail above the lake, we met skiers enjoying the snow still remaining on the Monte Rosa Plateau.

The next day we hiked on the other side of the valley to the Cherillon Glacier, impressive in its size and in its location near the Grandes Murailles marking the boundary with Switzerland. On the way back, we got a glimpse of Furggen pass and a high-altitude ski area not in use. Successful in this trip, we thought we could handle the trail to the Rifugio Rionde, also named for the Duke of Ambruzzi, who was known for his climbs in the alps.

That trail was very popular and the Rifugio Rionde was crammed with young people buying snacks and drinks. A good day allowed everyone to enjoy lunch outdoors while soaking in very close-up views of the Matterhorn. Some people with binoculars claimed they saw climbers on the peak, but we weren't convinced their vision was that good.

Another day we hiked a more difficult trail to Rifugio Jumeaux. On the way we passed an abandoned stone shelter used in World War II, but now inhabited only by marmots. Though most of the way was on a well-marked trail on barren rock and scree, the refuge was accessible only to those who could scramble up narrow ledges. Views from the top were worth the effort, but when clouds gathered, we turned back, waiting out a torrential downpour in a building near a skiing area.

A rocky climb to the formation known as the Beak of the Pious Blackbird, but which looked more like a prairie dog, was very enjoyable as was our visit to the waterfall inside the cave at Gouffre de Busserailles, on our last day before we took the train to Courmayeur, hoping to hike on the Italian side of Mont Blanc.

Courmayeur was a very up-scale resort with many elegant private homes and luxury condominiums. Ritzy jewelry and clothing stores lined the well-kept avenues, but we were still able to find a reasonably priced room, though it was somewhat shabby and had a slightly moldy smell. The next morning we were off early to take the Val Veni bus for about six miles to the end of the pavement. The trail began just beyond a stone bridge at an elevation of near six thousand feet. From the first, we had marvelous sweeping views of Mont Blanc or Monte

Bianco. These only improved as we continued towards Rifugio Elisabetta where we had early lunch. To continue, we had to wade across a glacial stream and then make our way up a long trail with many switchbacks. To our amazement, we saw mountain bikers riding down this trail. Thinking we had plenty of time, we took the side trip up Mont Fortin, only to find the way down was a seldom used trail which had considerable exposure and uneven footing on unbalanced rocky slabs and chunks. We began to worry that we might miss the last bus back and have to walk an additional six miles. But we still took a few moments to enjoy the marvelous views in both directions. Once we reached the shoulder of Mont Favre we could take in the majestic Mont Blanc across the valley with at least five huge glaciers spilling off its massive cone. Finally reaching the Col Checrouit, we took the short way through the woods to the bus stop. We'd been hiking for ten hours. The bus arrived ten minutes later.

The following day we took the bus in the other direction to Arnuva to hike to the Grand Col du Ferret, a shorter trip of about seven miles round-trip. From the parking lot, the trail switch-backed up into steep meadows. The scenery here was dominated by Les Grandes Jorasses, the Teeth of the Giant, and the Needles, all jagged, awe-inspiring, glaciated peaks. Views of them changed constantly as the trail gained elevation until it reached the cairn marking the Italian-Swiss border at about 8,000 feet. Some hikers with backpacks continued over the pass into Switzerland, but we were satisfied to return the way we came. Although neither distance nor altitude were extreme, the trail itself was very steep and tiring. Because it was close to the time the bus would leave, when the trail flattened, I ran, catching the bus just as it was about to leave. "Wait, my husband comes," I said in Italian, hoping the driver understood. It was no problem. He remembered driving the two of us out in the morning and knew someone was missing.

For the next three weeks of hiking, we returned to Austria, where living was cheaper. By now our packs were overloaded with detailed maps we'd collected along the way. To lighten our loads, we mailed a large package back to the states from Feldkirch where we stayed overnight before taking the train to Bludenz, home of the Suchard chocolate factory. The only room we could find was very expensive, so we skipped the factory tour and free samples and took the bus to Bieler Höhe, back up into the Austrian Alps. The bus dropped us off at Silvretta Stausee, a huge reservoir. Within the first mile we could see two huge glaciers: Ochsentaler and Vermunt. One had many crevasses and very long snowfields; the other was shorter but covered a broad expanse. As we neared the Wiesbadener Hütte (about 7,000 feet high) we could see two more smaller glaciers, but we could also feel raindrops. We walked the last mile and a half in pouring rain. After taking a few photos and drying out in the hut where we had some warm soup and coffee, there was no question about our next move. Vetoing the rest of the round-trip, we returned the way we came to spend the night in Madlener Hütte near the Silvretta Stausee.

Landeck, where parallel city streets were connected by steep stairways, offered a folk museum featuring beautiful carved wooden furniture and doors inside a former Schloss with a stucco tower that could be climbed. Across the river on a crag jutting out from the mountain stood the ruin Schrofenstein, a square-towered castle with a second story entrance approachable only on a high bridge–a perfect setting for a gothic novel. We couldn't resist an afternoon hike to this romantic site, passing through plum orchards on our way back through a neighboring suburb spread out on the hillside.

Then it was back to serious hiking as we explored the Ötztaler Alps, southeast of Landeck. From Sölden, a ski town where we stayed for four days, we had access by bus to yet another group of beautiful peaks and glaciers. By now we acted like most natives, taking the available chair lifts as far as possible, saving our energy for the exciting trails that began where the chair lifts ended. This helped us reach the top of Schwarzkogel, where a huge iron cross topping a pile of stones marked the summit. On the way to the summit, as we hiked through snowfields beside the glacial lake, Scharzkogel See, a helicopter landed near the shoreline. No one beckoned for our help, so we moved on, never learning why it was there. From the top, we had stunning views of the huge Rettenbach Glacier, where some skiers still found something to ski on.

The next day we took a bus to Vent, a very small village that gave us access to trails up Wildspitze. Reaching the 11,000-foot summit required crossing glaciers, so we never considered it. There were plenty of fascinating routes farther down. We enjoyed a long but beautiful day hiking a loop trail along the side of a ravine below Wildes Mannle and traversing the flank of Wildspitze to reach Breslauer Hütte before we returned using a different route. When a helicopter landed just below Breslauer Hütte, some hikers ran down to see what was going on. A few of us started up the trail towards an even higher hut, but we couldn't go very far, since we had to get back first to Rofen, another tiny village where farmers were cutting hay with scythes on steep hillsides, and then to Vent in time to catch the bus to Sölden.

Across from Wildspitze stood Kreuzspitze and another range of peaks. If we could reach the Martin Busch Hut, we'd get a view of the incredibly large Marzell Glacier and several others. Because the day was sunny, many hikers were out on the long trail leading to Martin Busch Hut. Beyond the hut, the trail became more of a scramble up rocky ledges. We went as far as a small hut, now abandoned, before turning back. We were close to the Italian border and near the place where Ötzi, the pre-historic iceman had been found a few years earlier.

Because the weather seemed to be more stable with fewer clouds, we decided to return to Innsbruck for a few days. During our earlier stop there, we'd taken a tour of the Royal Palace admiring the ornate furnishings and decor, visited the folk museum to see detailed displays of the costumes and ways of life in the varied and somewhat isolated villages of Tirol, and spent a day at the Schloss Ambras, a former medieval castle transformed into a beautiful

Renaissance castle by Duke Ferdinand of Tirol. Besides a huge collection of armor and artwork, the Duke's Cabinet--an amazing collection of all kinds of curiosities from all over the world--kept us spellbound. Continuous rain had kept us off the mountain trails.

On this second visit to Innsbruck, better weather let us visit mountain areas on both sides of the Inn valley in which Innsbruck is situated. Our luck wasn't the best though. After we took the cable car to the top, fog made it difficult to find the trail leading to a formation called Frau Hitt. But when the sun burned through, we enjoyed a lovely afternoon and great views of the city far below us. The next day on the other side of the valley, we took a cable car from Igls to Patscherkogel at 6,600 feet, then hiked along a beautiful but challenging trail to Glungezer Hut at 7,800 feet. Here we found not only snow, but also a cold wind and some rain. The split-pea soup at the hut was delicious. On the way down, after getting past a stony treacherous area, we encountered a functioning chair lift and saved our knees by riding it down to the valley. We were far from where we had started, but we knew a bus to Innsbruck would come by sometime. What a joy it was to sit in the choir stalls in the Hofkirche that night for a marvelous free concert played on the church's sixteenth-century organ.

We still had one more alpine area to explore before leaving Austria. Traveling east of Innsbruck to Mittersill, we then took a bus through a long tunnel to gain access to the Venediger group of peaks from the town of Matrei in East Tirol. Three of the four hikes we took in this area required early departure as only one morning bus left for the trailhead. We expected to pick up some rolls and coffee on the way, but the woman from whom we rented our room would not hear of it. She rose before dawn in order to fetch our fresh rolls from the bakery and had our coffee ready by 5:30 a.m.

For our first hike we rode the bus from Matrei west through the villages of Bichl and Hinterbichl to the end of the line at Ströden. Here we took Trail 911 to Clarahütte, a charming alpine hut with food and drink. Situated at more than 6,000 feet, Clarahütte was built in 1872, but had been renovated in 1974. The primary attraction, however, was the very popular waterfall trail which passed three magnificent waterfalls each falling about three hundred feet. From the gently rising trail, we also enjoyed views of high snow-clad peaks farther on. On this pleasant, sunny day, many fellow travelers had stopped at Clarahütte to enjoy a leisurely beer at the tables outside.

The next day we headed north for about forty-five minutes, then changed buses to go west to the end of the road at Innergeschloss. As many hikers milled around the large inn, Venediger Haus, where the trail began, a horse-drawn wagon arrived, offering transportation over the next two miles to where the trail led up over rocky foothills and outcroppings to the huge Schrofen Glacier. Thinking this would save us some time, we squeezed into the two remaining spaces. But the seats were hard, and the horses did not move very fast. Still, the ride gave us the chance to admire the beauty of Austria's second-highest peak, the Gross Venediger, instead of watching our feet to make sure we didn't stumble.

The hike was strenuous, and it was a long way to the Alte Prager Hütte, perched just at the edge of the enormous glacier. The weather held, though, and it was thrilling to be so close to the heavily crevassed glacier and the classic-shaped triangular peaks above it. The area was a wonderland in varying shades of white and gray. It felt as if we'd been transported to another world. Some hikers played in the snow and examined the crevasses close up, but we drank hot chocolate and planned for our descent. Connecting trails offered shortcuts across the glacier or continued to the summit. Some led to other glaciers, but we had only the afternoon left and a bus to catch back to Matrei. We had just enough time for pastry and coffee with the jovial returning hikers crowding the cozy Venediger Haus before our bus arrived.

Encouraged by our success in completing the Venediger hike, we planned a longer circuit hike the next day. Once more we took the bus to Ströden, but this time the trail to Essener-Rostocker hut went north along the Mauerbach, a stream formed by the runoff from the Mauer Glacier. We quickly rose out of the forest and lush meadowlands into fragile subarctic vegetation. Below towering snow-capped peaks, some over 10,000 feet high, we traversed open, boulder-strewn slopes. The trail was not always easy to find, causing some anxiety at times and some backtracking. The vast panoramic sights and the many glaciers were awesome. From the hut, we intended to take the Schweriner Weg, a rough but well-marked route to Johannis Hütte, according to the guidebook. Finding where this route began gave us some problems, as it wasn't quite as well-marked as we'd expected. It was challenging, but eventually we did reach Turmljoch, a high pass at 9,067 feet where the weathered rock stood in grotesque but beautiful shapes, somewhat like abstract sculptures. Snow and sleet made us bring out our raingear and convinced us to move on quickly after taking a photograph with their camera of another hiking couple we met in the pass. Then it was a long winding way down a slippery path through wet rocks and grass until we reached Johannis Hütte, where the sun finally shone again. Warm soup strengthened us for the rest of the hike, a somewhat tedious walk along the Dorferbach back to Hinterbichl where we caught the bus.

Tired of long bus rides, we walked in the morning across the main highway to take the cable car to the top of the ridge where the Europa Panoramaweg began near the Goldried Bergrestaurant. On this beautiful day, many hikers were out, greeting each other with the usual Austrian alpine greeting: "Grüss Gott." Wherever we hiked in Austria, every Austrian or Bavarian we met greeted us with this phrase which sounds like "grease god," but means something close to our "Go with God" or "God be with you." A few people simply said "Tag" or "Guten Tag," but very few hikers passed without saying something.

The trail ran along the top of a ridge at almost 7,000 feet. From this vantage point, more than seventy of East Tirol's highest peaks, most near or over 9,000 feet high, could be seen. We recognized the Grossglockner and the Venediger Gruppe even without binoculars. We'd intended to go only part of the way, but we did so well that we continued to where the trail descended to reach the top of the Glocknerblick chair lift bringing up hikers from the valley on the other side of the ridge. Many groups ate lunch in the sun, some people napped, while others, including me, hiked to the top of a steep mound called Blauspitze. The trail continued farther to distant huts and other inspiring mountain scenery, but our train for Munich left early in the morning, so we reluctantly made our way back. This lovely day had unexpectedly served as a summary of our adventure, showing us from a distance a vast panorama of some of the many alpine areas in which we'd hiked.

After two months of walking, we decided to spend our last week driving and sightseeing in Bavaria and Baden-Württemberg. From Augsburg with its magnificently restored city hall, we drove to Ulm to see its awesome cathedral. After one short hike in the Black Forest, we stopped at the medieval town of Freiburg, home of Erasmus. On the way to Heidelberg, we took photographs of the older buildings in the two villages where my father's maternal grandparents had been born. Heidelberg, where Kurt had been stationed in 1945, had changed; but the castle ruins and the bridge over the Neckar River were still the same. Returning to Bavaria, we spent a day in picturesque Rothenburg on the Tauber; and Dinkelsbühl. And when we arrived in Bayreuth the one day tours were not being given, we just moved on to Nürnberg and enjoyed watching a colorful joust in Nürnberg Castle's dry moat before flying home from Munich.

Maroon Bells and Kurt

North Cascades - Faith and George

Matterhorn as seen from Italy

Cervinia, Italy

**Canyonlands
Utah**

Arches National Park

Kurt descending Angel s Landing

Chilkoot Pass

Bryce National Park

GETTING HIGH

Colorado Peaks - Technical Matters

The Grand Teton

Mount Rainier

Austria's Grossglockner

The Lyells in Canada

Mount Whitney

GETTING HIGH

Maybe it's the lack of oxygen, maybe the feeling of being on top of everything, maybe it's the vast, panoramic views one takes in. Whatever the reason, we developed a great interest in reaching the summits of high peaks, standing on their geological markers, and signing the register books usually contained in a nearby weatherproof canister. On many of Colorado's fourteen-thousand-foot peaks, a trail leads to the top. Reaching the top, however, is often arduous and takes a long time. Sometimes it requires an overnight stay in wilderness areas. But getting there is possible for anyone with stamina, good legs, healthy lungs, and the desire to do it. Oh, and good weather is also a necessary component.

COLORADO PEAKS

One of the first peaks we reached together was Hallett Peak in Rocky Mountain National Park, near Estes Park, Colorado. It was a tough go to reach 12,713 feet, and the usual summer- afternoon showers pelted us when we made our way, off trail, through Chaos Canyon, a jumble of boulders, on our way back to our tent.

That hike was good training for the second week of our honeymoon spent in the Crestone Peaks of the Sangre de Cristo range in Southern Colorado. We were only a few hundred yards from the summit of Humboldt Peak (14,064 feet) when a sudden thunderstorm, with lightning strikes so close we couldn't even count to one, chased us downhill into a sheltering cave. From there we could see snow falling on Crestone Peak and Crestone Needles across a valley facing us, as we shivered, sharing the one candy bar we'd brought along for lunch. Because we were afraid to go back up towards the top, we couldn't catch the trail back and had to bushwhack our way down the mountain in the general direction of our tent. It was way past suppertime and getting dark when we finally reached our campsite on the edge of lower South Colony Lake.

Our fascination with Colorado's "fourteeners" as the state's fifty-four peaks with summits above fourteen thousand feet are affectionately called, has been a constant in our lives. Although other adventures intervened, including technical rock, snow, and ice climbs on lower peaks, we often returned to this or that peak in Colorado for various reasons. But we were not always successful in reaching the summits of mountains we ascended.

In the summer of 1977 we hoped to get used to the high altitude by hiking a week in Rocky Mountain National Park before taking on Mount of the Holy Cross and the beautiful Maroon Bells. The contrast between Takoma Park, Maryland's humid ninety-three degrees at sea-level and Glacier Basin Campground's forty degrees at eight thousand feet took some getting used to. Our fifteen-year-old daughter fell in love with the Rockies, especially after her twelve-hour horseback trip across the continental divide, which gave her memorable views of Hallett and Longs peaks. Ten-year-old Alan was able to manage the short hikes we took to glacial lakes without any altitude problems.

After we picked up my mother, who had been vacationing in Cheyenne, Wyoming, Kurt and I hiked to Spearhead, a somewhat isolated peak in a back valley of Longs Peak, its face used mostly by super rock-climbers. We found an alternate route to the top to enjoy spectacular glacial scenery, even though I had some migraine problems despite wearing dark glacier goggles.

When we headed south to Georgetown and Leadville, Colorado, the sky became overcast. Camping lost some of its allure, and we checked into a motel. The next day looked a little better, but we weren't ready to embark on a two-day wilderness trip. Instead, Kurt, Karen, and I hiked to the top of Mt. Elbert, Colorado's highest peak at 14,431 feet. No technical climbing techniques were needed. The trail was good and well-marked, but it was a seemingly endless slog to the top. Almost there, Karen said she was cold and wanted to stop and wait for us. We agreed, assuming that she was having some altitude difficulty. We were close enough to keep her in sight and didn't want to push her beyond where she felt comfortable. But just as we reached the summit, we saw her close behind us. She'd changed her mind and made it to the top. On our return, I developed a cramp in my leg. I could still walk, but only very slowly, and it was a long way down.

As the rains continued, we investigated Colorado Springs, visiting museums on woodcarving and mining. We drove to Aspen, just to say we'd been there, and used the laundromat. We visited every historic site and museum in Leadville, hoping the rain would stop. Finally we gave up and took a raincheck on Holy Cross Mountain and Maroon Bells, eating in the World's Highest Pizza Hut (ten thousand feet) in Leadville before we left for home.

In 1993, when the Nepal trekkers decided to have a reunion hike in Colorado Springs seven months after we met, we saw this as an opportunity to revisit the Sangre de Cristo range and the Crestone Mountains. By then we'd been married for thirty-three years, so our honeymoon camping spot was somewhat overgrown. The mountain peaks didn't seem quite as high as we remembered, though they were still spectacular. The road leading to South Colony Lakes was just as rutted and wretched as it had been before, but now all-terrain-vehicles drove the long road we'd wearily hiked. It was good preparation and acclimation for the hike up Pikes Peak.

Shirley Hurtado had invited all of our trekking group to join her annual family hike up the Barr Recreational trail to the top of Pikes Peak, (14,110 feet), and all nine of us showed up. Kurt and I had driven to the top of Pikes Peak twice in the past, but had not known there was a trail. I remembered the road as winding its way up to the summit on a dry hillside. There were excellent views, of course, but the thought of hiking a dry, dusty trail all day long did not appeal I also knew the trail was thirteen miles long one-way and almost eight thousand feet up. Shirley said her family did this every year I was totally impressed by a family, young and old, that could in one day hike twenty-six miles with that elevation change.

The night before the hike, a spaghetti and pasta feast at Shirley's enabled us to load up on carbohydrates. She said the hike would start in Manitou Springs at 5:30 a.m., before sunrise. This might give me a chance to make it before it got really dark again, though I wasn't looking forward to fourteen hours of hiking. But if they could do it, so could I--somehow. Imagine my great relief when Shirley explained that those who arrived at the summit first should take time for a hot drink, but should not hang around too long, as the trucks and vans would need to make another trip for those who arrived later. She was also concerned about everyone being off the mountain top before the afternoon thunder and lightning storms arrived. Cars? Vans? We only had to make it to the top? I was overjoyed. I didn't have to worry about "losing face." I now had all the time in the world--or at least all day--to do only thirteen miles and the elevation gain.

The weather that day was perfect, and the trail a wonderful surprise. It had been laid out on the wet or green side of Pikes Peak and wound its way through lush evergreen forests. About five miles up at ten thousand feet, the Barr Camp shelter had tables and benches, providing a most pleasant resting spot. Views of distant peaks got better and better the higher we went. We thought we were doing quite well, but runners, training for a marathon to be held the following week, passed us, wearing shorts and carrying only bottles of water. Near the top we met mountain bikers descending the trail. They had biked up the road and were now trying to ride the steep trail down.

As the trail approached the top of the mountain, the last two miles or so were called the "golden steps." Above timberline at this point, the trail had no trees or shrubs and resembled a huge rock pile over which switchbacks took the hiker to the broad summit. The trail itself was made up of boulders which were not always stable. Smart bikers walked or carried their bikes until they reached the dirt trail below, still challenging enough. Others lost control and tumbled onto the rocks, cursing, with their bikes falling on top of them. No one was seriously hurt, and perhaps they learned something.

It was breathtaking to reach the top--literally. But it was also a thrill to be there before noon, in the first group to arrive. As we caught our breath and had something hot to drink, the sky clouded up and some serious snowflakes encouraged us to put on our jackets. Photos of the jubilant conquerors were taken and the shuttle began. That night at dinner, the day's adventures were shared before the nine of us who did not live in Colorado headed home. Because one couple lived in California and several us had wanted to hike up Mt. Whitney, the highest peak in the lower forty-eight states, we thought we'd have our next reunion hike there.

When the Mt. Whitney reunion hike didn't materialize the following year, we decided to revisit Colorado and to attempt some of the other fourteeners. In preparation, we hiked daily at home, trying to increase our speed and stamina. Flying to Denver, we acclimated by hiking to Ypsilon Lake and Mt. Chiquita (13,069 feet) in the Mummy Range of Rocky Mountain National Park. We didn't move as fast as we usually did, but we weren't left breathless either.
Just to keep in practice, after setting up our tent in Longs Peak Campground, we spent the afternoon hiking up nearby Estes Cone (11,008 feet). Since this hike went very well, we thought we were ready for a big one.

Apparently we weren't. Our try for the summit of Longs Peak (14,255 feet) was unsuccessful. We didn't start early enough, and Kurt was moving more slowly than usual. As we passed the boulder field, we could see roped rock climbers making their way up some of the many technical climbing routes on the sheer north face of the mountain. We were taking the keyhole route, a longer, but non-technical route with some exposure, but basically a hiking and scrambling rugged trail to the broad top. Threatening weather turned us back about an hour from the summit, but not before we'd seen the impressive panorama on the backside of the keyhole, above the boulder field. Some people start from the Longs Peak campground before dawn and others carry tents and sleeping bags up to the boulder field where they spend the night before making the final scramble to the top. We learned about these strategies too late, and we didn't want to spend more days on Longs. There were many other mountains to try, and Kurt had successfully completed a technical climb of Longs with a guide thirty-four years earlier in 1960.

On this trip, the morning skies were always a beautiful blue, though clouds gathered in the late afternoon. But we didn't have the steady rain we'd encountered in 1977 when we gave up on Maroon Bells. Perhaps it was time to cash in our raincheck. Heading south, we stopped for the night in Frisco, staying at a motel to save time in the morning. It was only a short drive down state highway 24 to the trailhead (10,400 feet) for Mount of the Holy Cross, and we wouldn't have to break camp. June is the best time to see the famous cross for which the mountain is named. Melting winter snows have left the face of the mountain then and linger only in several deep ravines. The huge cross is created by this remaining snow.

The image of this mountain was imbedded in my psyche. I had grown up admiring and wanting to visit this mountain because a painting of it had formed the cover of a family photo album. Unfortunately we were there in August, so all the snow had melted. But from the highway, we could still see the ravines that formed the pattern of the cross.

Up at five, we got a good start on the trail and were doing well up to Half Moon Pass (11,600 feet). Wildflowers like Indian paintbrush, mountain columbine, and shooting star adorned the hillsides. Marmots seemed to pose for pictures. Pikas squeaked warnings to each other as they gathered grass for their pantries. The air was cool and fresh and the mountain views magnificent. We were gaining altitude, but from the top of the pass we'd worked so hard to reach, the trail descended a steep 900 feet to 10,700 in order to cross a creek. After all that work we were only three hundred feet higher than our starting point. We'd have to work our way up all over again. Still, we made good progress until we reached timberline.

Here a sign warned hikers that from the top it was easy to mistakenly follow a trail downwards that led too far west and into a wilderness area far from any roads or habitation. Though the correct route back was tougher and more tedious, it was important to stay on the rocks and keep to the right of a high rocky ridge in order to return to one's starting point.

Tilting boulders and scree piles above timberline made for slower going. Though marked by cairns (distinctive piles of rocks), the trail was not always so easy to find. Sometimes the cairns had fallen down and several alternative pathways seemed to offer a better route. As we hiked, we reminded ourselves of two important mountain facts. One, it's very easy to twist an ankle or lose balance if a hiker is hesitant to move ahead or slow to react to the unexpected. And two, the summit is always just a bit farther away than it looks.

Along the trail I saw a large back pack that seemed to have been abandoned. Shortly after that I noticed a pair of green binoculars in a small hole over which I stepped. Overhead a helicopter kept circling. Now past noon, the sky began to cloud up and a few raindrops fell, but we were nearing the ridgeline. We could see three hikers on top who were waving to the helicopter. Once we reached the ridge, it would be an easy go to the summit.

Stopping only briefly to pull on our rain jackets and rain pants, we kept moving higher. When the helicopter left, we welcomed the silence. Suddenly the low rumble of thunder echoed around us. Lightning leaped from one cloud to another. It was no time to be on the ridgeline. The only wise thing to do was to go down. Rain and hail pelted us as we carefully picked our way over the now wet and potentially slick rocks above timberline. It was a long, tiresome, wet way back to our starting point, but we had remembered the warning and had resisted the easy trail into wilderness. The next day's paper told of a twenty-two-year-old hiker and his dog who had been lost in the Holy Cross Wilderness for several days after making the summit and then taking the wrong trail down. They had been the object of the helicopter's fruitless search, but had finally, in an emaciated state, found their way out to a highway and help.

When we learned that between mid-June and Labor Day the Maroon Creek road was closed every day from 8:30 a.m. to 5:00 p.m., with bus service provided to reduce congestion in the very scenic and extremely popular area near Aspen, we made sure we arrived early before the gates closed. Even so, we weren't the first cars in the parking lot. Because the day we visited was a Sunday, the spectacular shapes and dark reddish rocks of the aptly named Maroon Bells (Maroon and North Maroon Peaks) drew hundreds of people, though numbers thinned as the trail neared the pass. Many people had come to picnic at Maroon Lake and enjoy the remarkable views of three steep peaks clustered together: Maroon Peak, North Maroon Peak, and Pyramid Peak. We saw a few serious rock climbers wearing helmets and carrying ropes and other climbing equipment. The rock, though beautiful, is weak and crumbles easily, making climbing very hazardous even for the skilled.

Our goal was just to reach Buckskin pass, a high ridge that promised awesome views of Snowmass and Capitol peaks, two more fourteeners. The trail switchbacked up the sides of hills covered with meadows and wildflowers on a beautiful day. The dramatic reddish peaks were always in view, though the maroon color often changed, revealing darker purple shades, depending on the angle of the light striking it. Despite our early start, darkening skies and thunder arrived when we were just fifteen minutes from Buckskin Pass. I hurried for the top, determined to grab that view, hoping lightning wouldn't strike me. The taller hikers already strolling on the ridge would be more vulnerable, I thought. I made it, looked, and hurried back down in pelting rain, meeting Kurt on the way. Though some people stayed on the ridge, most of the others, like us, headed back to the lake. By the time we arrived, the storm was over, and we enjoyed a gorgeous sunset when we reached our new campground.

La Plata Peak and Handies Peak also defeated us. But we were at last successful in reaching the summits of Mt. Princeton (14,197 feet) and Uncompaghre Peak (14,309 feet). Mt. Princeton is one of the five collegiate peaks, named after important colleges of the late 1800s. The others are Columbia, Harvard, Oxford, and Yale. The trail up Mt. Princeton was fairly easy and also a bit dull. The sun, reflecting off the rocky slabs, bathed us in heat, and the trail kept moving upward. We did see some mountain goats, and the summit was visible the entire time. Views from the top of vast valleys and other high peaks were excellent, and it was good to know that we'd finally reached the summit of one of the fourteeners and could write our names in the official register book.

Uncompahgre Peak was more beautiful. Viewing the precipitous east face of this mountain from timberline, we thought reaching the summit was impossible. But the trail led us below this frightening side of the mountain and around to the southeast ridge, which is long but doable. At 13,400 feet we had a great view of Wetterhorn Peak, a snow-covered beauty. We could also see Mount Sneffels. A short section of the trail gave Kurt some problems as it entered a craggy cliff area with some exposure and continued up a short, steep gully. Feeling tired, he considered turning back. But when I told him that from the top of the gully, an easy trail led to the summit, he forged ahead and was happy to reach the top. Though we saw a few dark clouds above us, they soon blew over, perhaps in answer to our prayers.

Along with several other hikes, we tried a total of six fourteeners, but made only two summits. Later we learned that many of the fourteeners we didn't try were much easier to climb. Somehow it didn't make that much difference. We had enjoyed the beauty we'd experienced on our climbing days, and the physical workout had been good for us whether we reached the top or not.

On a day off when we didn't climb, we rafted, paddling and screaming our way through Brown's Canyon on the Arkansas River where a majestic isolated mountain goat stood sentinel on an inaccessible rock outcropping above us. Later we camped at the impressively steep, narrow Black Canyon of the Gunnison, marveled at the amazingly vast Sand Dunes National Monument on the western side of the Sangre de Cristo mountain range, and walked around former silver-mining towns such as Ouray, Silverton, and Cripple Creek which now mine tourists. Though we didn't gamble in Cripple Creek, we couldn't pass up the cheap but delicious food offered by the casinos.

TECHNICAL MATTERS

Hiking trails and general mountaineering skills can take you only so far. Was it the frustration of having to turn back when going higher demanded more than scrambling over rocks? Or had we simply fallen in love with certain peaks, or at least in love with the idea of standing on top of them? Early in the 1960s we realized that if we wanted to fulfill some of our ambitions, we would have to acquire additional skills.

For several years we learned and practiced rock-climbing skills with a specialized offshoot of the Potomac Appalachian Trail Club at an area along the Potomac River called Carderock Cliffs. Coaches and teachers in the group were climbers like Arnold Wexler and Don Hubbard, famous for first ascents. Don, a physicist, wrote a pamphlet on the science of the dynamic belay. We practiced our knots, learned to Prussik up a rope, before mechanical jumar clamps were invented, and tested belaying skills on "Oscar." The group had rigged a huge blob of cement into a high tree. The belayer's job was to stop the cement blob, named Oscar, from hitting the ground when it fell from the tree. I can't remember what started its descent, but it took quick reactions and practice in holding the rope in just the correct way, while putting all one's weight on it, to prevent the awful and embarrassing sound of a heavy thud as Oscar hit the dirt. Beginner's Crack was a favorite practice place where climbers could easily be belayed by a trusted friend standing at the bottom of the climb who was thus able to offer suggestions for the next handhold or foothold available. If a step or hold was missed, this friend would hold the climber secure, as he or she swung out or down to start up again from the bottom.

THE GRAND TETON

Finally we thought we might be able to tackle the Grand Teton, a magnificent 13,766-foot peak in Wyoming, near Yellowstone National Park. Kurt had attended the Exum Climbing School on an earlier trip to the Tetons before we were married, and he had climbed Ice Peak with a guide. But he had his heart set on the Grand, and I was eager to see what I could do. Camping at Gros Ventre campground for a couple of weeks in the summer of 1968, we took the two-day climbing school to review and to prepare ourselves for the 120-foot free rappel which we knew was part of the easiest route of many on this famous climbing mountain. Practice climbs helped us review skills and execute harder moves than we had ever done before. For safety, a climber should always have three points of contact while moving the fourth. One of the practice routes had a 5.8 move, just out of reach for a shortie like me. The guide, relaxing safety requirements, told me to jump for it; so I did, and made it.

Rappeling involves wrapping a rope around your body and stepping off a ledge backwards in order to gradually slide down the rope, which has been secured around a tree above you. It is a fast way down the mountain, avoiding some spots which might be very dangerous to climb down. It is mostly a matter of trust and remembering never to let go of the rope with your right hand, or was it the left hand? Done correctly, rappeling is great fun. It also allows you to move across the face of the mountain from left to right and back again, if you are close enough for your feet to touch a rocky face. A free rappel simply means that the face of the cliff is probably undercut, so there is no place against which to brace your feet, and you just slide down the rope, like an elevator sliding down its cable. You control your own speed by slowly sliding your hand down the rope or grabbing it to stop. If you don't mind dangling on a rope and swaying back and forth, you can take all the time you want going down, as long as you don't let go of the rope. We were given leather patches to wear on our shoulders so the moving rope wouldn't give us rope burns, but Kurt's rope slid off the patch, tore into his neck, and left scars that remain to this day.

We passed the climbing school, but before we were allowed to sign up for a guided trip up the Grand Teton, we had to pass one more test. "Hike up to Amphitheater Lake as fast as you can," the head guide said. "Come back and tell us how long you took." The time we reported convinced him that we would be fast enough and that we didn't have problems with altitude.

The guide, Bill Griggs, and a couple from San Francisco completed our group of five. Having gathered all the items on a required gear list, we left Teton Valley around noon to hike up Garnet Canyon to the Lower Saddle, at 11,644 feet, a flat area between the Grand and Middle Teton mountains. Here, in the saddle, we would spend the night, sleeping in a Quonset hut and arising at 3:00

a.m. to start for the summit. Once we reached the summit and had lunch, we would have to make it all the way back to Teton Valley where we started. If we wanted a chance for a long, leisurely lunch stop on the mountain top, an early start was mandatory.

Clear skies and a pleasant temperature made the afternoon hike up the ravine a pleasure. Great views of distant craggy mountains heightened our anticipation, although the Grand Teton disappeared from our view as we ascended its flanks. Dinner was a mixture of cans of soup and stew, but it tasted good. We talked for a little while before crawling into our sleeping bags eager for our adventure the next day.

Everyone overslept. Bill's alarm didn't ring, and we woke only when climbers heading for a different route passed by. We didn't bother with breakfast, left our things in a corner of the hut, and took off at an accelerated speed, at least until the serious climbing began. One chimney climb, where you inch your way up between two walls, with your feet on one wall and your behind on the other, still harbored some ice, increasing its difficulty. We passed through "the eye of the needle," a tunnel which leads under an enormous boulder to a look-out ledge. The route was certainly challenging. The "Crawl," a ledge about eighteen inches wide, directly under a severe overhang, requires most climbers to crawl on their stomachs, as the overhang prevents standing or even going on hands and knees. Another spot was not difficult, but it was frightening because its short descending traverse was extremely exposed. To avoid looking down, a climber momentarily is tempted to close his or her eyes, but that is definitely not advisable. After ascending several more chimneys, we scrambled to the summit. Our lunch stop on top was abbreviated, but we did have time for a good look around in continuing glorious weather. From the top of the continental divide we marveled at the fantastic panorama of seemingly endless mountain ranges that lay around and below us.

On the way down, the 120-foot free-fall rappel allowed us to avoid the hazardous aspects of the crawl and the exposed ledge. Bill asked for a volunteer to be first on the rope down. Only that first backward step made me hesitate a bit, but once I started down, it was a trip! After packing up all the gear left at the Quonset hut, we started down the barren ravine. Then we heard the wind. Farther down the mountain, when we reached the tree line, we saw the wind toppling tall pines. Some fell across the trail just in front of us. We picked up the pace until we were practically running, tired as we were. Getting back to our tent, pitched on a treeless plain, became our highest priority. The Grand Teton was the only summit we made together which required being roped and using technical rock-climbing skills to reach the top. For the next several years, our interests switched to snow and ice climbing.

MOUNT RAINIER

Kurt and his brother had climbed Mt. Popocatepetl, a snow-covered volcano in Mexico, although they stopped short of the summit. They later tried to climb Mt. Rainier in Washington State, but were turned back by foul weather. For me, Mt. Rainier had been our favorite family excursion during the four years I lived in Tacoma, Washington, with my family, while commuting to college. On clear days, this massive, gorgeous dormant and snow-covered volcano could be seen from the campus, an inspiring sight for every book-laden, exam-weary student. Mt. Rainier stood alone, resplendent over the meadows surrounding it, an inviting challenge.

In 1971 we combined this climb with a family vacation. Kurt flew to Seattle, saving valuable annual leave. Driving from the east coast to the west, the rest of us, including my widowed mother, broke up the trip with several stops along the way. In South Dakota, the Corn Palace's decorative designs amazed us. The constantly repeated Wall Drug signs were effective in luring us in, and the complex itself offered an unusual conglomeration of souvenirs, antiques, and other amusements. The Badlands and Mt. Rushmore were on our "must see" list. Reptile Gardens, Bedrock City, and Dinosaur Park delighted our two children, then under ten, and were successful bribes for reducing bickering and boredom on the long ride.

After picking up Kurt at the airport, we headed for Lake Chelan, on the eastern side of Washington State's Cascade Mountain range. We hoped to get in some conditioning hikes there. Grandma and the children camped, while Kurt and I backpacked to the base of Bonanza Peak at the southeast edge of the Glacier Peak Wilderness area. There a fearless deer invaded our glacier-surrounded solitude to inspect our reconstituted dehydrated dinner. The hiking conditions were excellent.

A week later we moved to a campground near Mt. Rainier. The weather was fantastically good. We saw Rainier from top to bottom every day, and often could also see Mt. Adams and Mt. St. Helens. Karen and Alan thoroughly enjoyed the special children's campfire programs the rangers gave each night. During the day they hiked with their grandmother and looked for wildflowers and marmots, while Kurt and I successfully passed the summit school, required before anyone is allowed to sign up for an ascent. It's quite exciting to attempt a self-arrest with an ice axe while careening down a steep snow-covered hill, head first on your back. A strong death wish helps.

We also practiced ascending steep slopes wearing crampons on our boots and tied to other class members by nylon rope. Although walking in crampons felt awkward at first, and we had to be careful not to trip ourselves, the bite of the metal spikes gave us a great feeling of security on the melting snow. A sickening accident taught us the value of paying attention to the teacher. We'd been told that we should never walk directly below another class member. If

66

someone slipped, a person directly below might not be able to move out of the way quickly enough. We were horrified when just such an accident occurred. One class member was taken to the hospital to have a doctor sew up the bleeding gashes, inflicted by crampons, just above his eye.

The climb up Mt. Rainier began with a hike from Paradise (about 7,000 feet) to Muir Cabin at 10,000 feet. Since there are no high peaks around on which to practice, this hike was a good test of the climber's conditioning and sensitivity to high altitude. One father and son pair were late getting to the cabin, and the father's face had lost healthy color. The guides tried to persuade him not to go with the group the next morning, but he wouldn't agree. Bunk beds filled the cabin and were assigned to whoever got there first. Some independent climbers camped in their tents outside. With no electricity available, it was dark at sunset, and most people tried to sleep. Either adrenaline or the altitude made good sound sleep an impossibility. Nightmares of falling into crevasses or encountering sudden snowstorms made me uneasy.

Leaving at 2:00 a.m. by an almost full moon, the roped teams started for the 14,410-foot summit. The line of climbers, each carrying a flashlight, ascending the diagonal trail across dark rocks before reaching the glaciers, created an unforgettable vision. Unable to persuade the father who had experienced altitude problems to wait in the cabin, one guide carried along an extra sleeping bag. About an hour after we started climbing, the stricken man begged to stop. He could go no farther. The guide tucked him into the sleeping bag, placed him for safety in a depression under a huge boulder, and the rest of the group moved on. We crossed three snow-covered glaciers, hoping to avoid falling into the beautiful but treacherous crevasses. Deep inside them, greenish and blue colors glowed eerily among grotesquely-shaped slabs and towers of ice. Before dawn, the moon-glow was hauntingly lovely. Instead of walking out to the narrow point of a crevasse and then back on the opposite side, our guide told us all to jump the yawning chasm. I gave a mighty leap; the front edges of my crampons touched the opposite edge of the crevasse but then slid backwards, dropping me safely to a ledge just below the lip from which I could scramble up. I wasn't hurt at all, just embarrassed.

Usually guides are sensitive to the needs of their paying clients. We had learned the rest step, often needed as the air becomes less oxygen-rich. We had plenty of time to reach the top and return before the warming sun created avalanches. But a few of the guides, who regularly make several such trips a week, decided to race each other to the top. Perhaps they were trying to impress the lead guide. This meant everyone roped to a particular guide had to move at his pace. Fortunately, we didn't have a problem with that, but there were several climbers in another group who began having breathing problems and called out to their guide for mercy.

On top by 9:00 a.m., we had about an hour in which we could either rest or run across the crater to the summit register. The sky was totally clear, and we could see Mt. St. Helens and other volcanoes to the south. The temperature seemed almost balmy at thirty-four degrees. Usually it's around zero on the top of Mt. Rainier, but Seattle was having a heat wave that year.

Altitude affects everyone differently. Some people did not feel like eating at all. I was ravenous and euphoric. Unlike my wiser husband who chose to rest, I crossed the crater, though I didn't run, and signed our names in the register. Our descent to Paradise from upper earth took the rest of the day. I developed a nasty migraine headache, probably because I didn't rest on top. By 5:00 p.m. we reached our camp, exhausted and hungry, but soul-satisfied.

After rejoining the family, we all headed for the North Cascades, savoring a beautiful sunset with fog at Deception Pass and Mt. Erie. Cascade Pass, Mt. Baker, and Mt. Shuksan were informally surveyed and noted for future trips. We stopped for a day in Vancouver, British Columbia, to get new shock absorbers for the car, to see the city and the killer whales, and to investigate the curiously named "Chinese smorgasbord."

With not enough time for a major assault or expedition, we took several strenuous hikes in the Lake Louise area. One all-day fourteen-miler included two passes, with a final ascent which seemed interminable. On another day Karen had a horseback trail ride, and we all dipped into one of the Banff hot spring pools, entered the buffalo paddocks, and saw much wildlife. There were bears at Rainier and Lake Louise, but they were mainly interested in garbage cans. Kurt got some excellent photos of marmots. Wildlife in Canada seemed completely undisturbed by human visitors. Grandma, Karen, and Alan rode the snowcat on the Columbia icefields, and Kurt was amazed at how much the glacier had receded since he last saw it in 1954. The entire drive from Lake Louise to Jasper was spectacular, 189 miles of continuous, glaciated mountains interspersed with lovely differently-hued glacial lakes. When Kurt flew home from Calgary, he left his raincoat in the airport coffee shop. Surprisingly, one letter to the airport resulted in a prompt reply and a bit later the raincoat itself.

AUSTRIA'S GROSSGLOCKNER

A scientific conference in Italy gave us the opportunity to add some vacation time and try some snow and ice climbing with a mountain-climbing school from Innsbruck, Austria. From their catalog, we chose a week in the Grossglockner area. This gave us the possibility, though not the guarantee, of having a chance to climb Austria's highest peak, the Grossglockner. An extremely beautiful mountain, it is named "Great Bell" for its bell-like shape.

Just getting to the school's meeting place meant driving through snow, fog, and ice, in and about desolate mountain stretches on an often frightening, but well-engineered road. When we arrived at the end of the road, where the stone-walled Franz Josef Hutte offered food, drink, beds, and marvelous views down to the huge Pasterze glacier and up at the surrounding Austrian Alps, we couldn't find any trail leading to the meeting place, Hoffman's Hutte. Finding the trail after it grew dark would be impossible, even with flashlights, and the sun was sinking fast. Finally we asked someone in the so-called hut, which was more like a hotel, and were told, "Take the elevator to the basement and go through a tunnel to the trailhead." We would never have found this trail without asking. Once on the trail, we obeyed the request to each hiker to carry up some firewood from a huge pile, to keep the higher cabin warm. Beyond the trailhead there were no roads: only trails, snow, ice, rock, and perilously perched huts serving the hikers.

To our delight, only four people had signed up for the climbing week. For a very reasonable price, we essentially had a private guide. One man was from Munich, Germany, and Gustav, a very tall man, was from Denmark. Our guide, Walter, was from Tyrol. I did have two concerns. One was whether I'd be able to keep up with the others. I also worried that if an emergency occurred, I might not understand the German commands correctly. No English was spoken. Kurt could always translate for me, but he might be too far away to help.

The snow began the night we arrived. It continued for two days without stopping, forcing us to remain in the cabin. The man from Munich left after the first day, preferring to climb in better weather. The remaining three of us talked, read climbing magazines, all in German, and kept checking on the weather. Our chances of climbing the Grossglockner were dwindling. But my German was improving, as no one else, except Kurt, spoke English and the only reading material available was in German.

When the sun came out, so did we. In glorious sunshine that first climbing day, we had to work very hard to prove ourselves. Walter would not take us up the Grossglockner until he saw how we coped with the altitude and how we managed on other, easier climbs. This seemed a reasonable approach, but it also heightened my anxiety about the difficulty of the climb we really wanted to do. All the new and deep snow made climbing very strenuous, but what beauty! In many places, ours were the first steps. After sitting in the hut for two days, we found the pace a bit fast, but we were rewarded by successful attempts on Hohe Riffel and Johannisberg peaks. Walter was satisfied that we were reasonably capable, and, weather permitting, we would be allowed to try the Grossglockner on our final climbing day.

As we talked over our plans the night before the attempt, an eavesdropper asked our guide if he could join us. He said he had a heart condition and didn't want to climb alone. Walter was too polite to turn him down, but I was shocked that someone in that condition had the nerve to invite himself. Walter agreed to let him come, but told the man that if he changed his mind, he could easily return to the hut on his own.

Leaving before dawn, we almost ran down the trail to the immense glacier named Pasterze. I couldn't believe the fast pace, but kept up with it. Soon after we had traversed the glacier's width of about a mile, we took off our crampons and then started to climb steeply. At that point the self-invited guest decided he couldn't go any farther and turned back. Walter, our guide, thanked us for keeping up the very fast pace he had set in order to discourage the man from going. He had wanted the man to make that decision himself.

The climb over large boulders and rocks to Hoffman's Glacier went well. Walter was uncanny. He always stopped for a few minutes just before we had to ask for a break. We reached Adler's Ruhe (Eagle's Rest), a hut unbelievably nestled in a saddle below the summit, in time for breakfast. The extensive menu was possible only because supplies were sent from the valley on the other side in boxes conveyed by a rope-and-pulley system. A small kitten played inside. One of the workers, who stay in the hut for six weeks at a time, had carried the pet along when she crossed the glacier earlier in the year.

Leaving Adler's at 9:00 a.m., we had to scale a steep glazed-ice wall, belayed through iron stanchions and praying that our crampons really would hold. Most of the steps carved into the ice were okay, but one or two were made for people with much longer legs than mine. These required quite a stretch, on ice made wet by the warming sun. When I first saw that ice wall, I couldn't believe that was where the trail led.

We then faced two summits, and between them a snow- and ice-covered narrow ledge. Belayed and clinging to a cable, we crossed the hazardous ledge singly and tentatively only to face a perpendicular rock wall on which another climbing party was plastered--petrified with fear. The first clear day for some time had called out climbers of every skill, so that the next greatest challenge, after the ice wall, was avoiding entanglements with other bodies and ropes. Walter led the way as we scrambled up the rock face, successfully reaching the summit. Here a gigantic, rime-crusted iron cross, anchored firmly into the mountain top by several cables, was ideal for taking impressive photos and shouting the Austrian greeting to those who make the top–Berg Heil!

We'd had perfect weather all day, but as we enjoyed the incredible views of the surrounding Alpine peaks, we noticed a cloud bank beginning to form in the distance. On our way down, we could see snowflakes falling on an adjacent peak. We must have descended the ice-covered wall, but I don't remember doing so. We jumped crevasses instead of going the long way around and probed snow bridges with our ice axes to make sure they were sturdy enough to hold us. At the end of a very long day, we welcomed our bunk beds in the hut. Early the next morning, well-satisfied and savoring thrilling memories and awesome scenery, we hiked back to our car and drove to Innsbruck.

THE LYELLS IN CANADA

Having had the experience of traveling over snow, glaciers, and crevasses, Kurt and I thought we were ready to try the Picket Traverse of the North Cascades. Yes, there was a lower trail we could have followed. But the traverse which skirted the mighty Challenger Glacier, giving the hiker incredible views of surrounding peaks, intrigued us. With our newly-minted training and successful climbs of Mt. Rainier and the Grossglockner, we thought we could do the traverse with the help of the guide book. For safe glacier crossing, we needed a third person. If one person fell into a crevasse, rescue was more likely with two others pulling on the rope. Kurt's friend, George, was interested in going with us. He also recommended a week of climbing in the Lyell Mountain range of the Canadian Rockies, which was offered by the Canadian Alpine Club. George had previously taken one of the club's trips and had enjoyed it. We did some trial climbs and hikes locally and were all satisfied with each other's skills, so we decided to add the Canadian week to our plans, using the two-week back-packing trip of the Picket Traverse to get in shape for it.

While the two Stern children visited their grandmother, Kurt, George, and I flew to Seattle where friends from my college days met us at the airport and provided food and beds for the night. Evie and Wayne had also located a student willing to drive us to the trailhead about forty miles east of Bellingham in the North Cascades National Park.

We'd seen the snowy North Cascades from the plane and were eager to meet them, but the first day was tough. Were we really out of condition, or just suffering from jet lag? The second day was better, until we lost time bridge building--hauling rocks and fallen trees to create a safe passage over swollen streams. Still, we reached the ridge before dark, set up camp quickly and relished our reconstituted freeze-dried meal. The blueberry cheesecake was memorable.

In the morning fog closed in, but we pressed on hoping for burn-off. We thought we were following the ridge trail, but it was hard to see anything, and we weren't sure how steeply the other side of the ridge fell off. When we found a trail just below the ridge, we were happy with it until it deteriorated and fog thickened, just as we reached sickeningly steep snow patches. Our thirty-five- to fifty-pound packs made balance precarious, so we roped up and started out, even though we couldn't see where or in what the snowfield ended until we were halfway across. Momentarily the fog lifted, revealing a sharp rock buttress blocking us, forcing us to traverse the lower end of the rocky wall, where we found another snowfield, another rocky wall, and so forth. We had survey maps, but no altimeter. Thus we knew what mountain we were on, but not where we were on it.

Because there was no level spot, human-size, on the hillside, we spent the waning light lugging boulders and digging away at the slope to build a platform large enough for three-fourths of the tent. I felt bad about disturbing the ecosystem and causing erosion, but this was survival. It was cozy for the three of us, but we kept warm. When there was no improvement in the weather the next morning, we gave up on the Picket traverse. If our orientation of the map to what we saw on the ground was correct, we would be able to escape the wilderness by going downwards to the creek valley. Then, if we followed the creek downstream we should at some point intersect a marked trail. We would then know where we were.

At times, the steepness of the slope forced us to let our packs down separately on the rope, then to lower ourselves, clutching to branches and/or anything. George lost his pack twice, once because he used a slip knot to attach the rope. We gasped in dismay when we saw the pack slip off the rope and tumble to the edge of a waterfall. Then we had to find a way to reach that spot ourselves, without tumbling, in order to retrieve it. Another time, he took the pack off, forgot to secure it, and his own movements knocked it off a broad ledge to a narrow crevice far below us. We tied George into a rope to make sure he wouldn't fall, then gradually gave him slack as he worked his way down to the crevice. Getting the pack out this time was his responsibility we felt. Each one of these mishaps consumed a lot of precious time and energy. I resented both the mishaps and George because I was afraid we would not reach the trail before dark or before we became too tired to continue. Then we would have to camp somewhere on the valley floor.

The valley floor had its own problems: thick undergrowth constantly clutched at our by now monster packs or the slide alder pushed us into the icy-cold creek bed itself. Next, an endless succession of deep ravines which we had to descend and ascend in order to maintain our direction, huge fallen tree-giants, and pernicious "devil's club" so harried and slowed us that only mosquitoes and the fear of not finding the trail before dark kept us moving. Finally, we intersected the trail and found our well-built bridge intact. We ate in the dark; but it was a real campsite after fourteen hours of unrelenting struggle.

We were now committed to a much longer, though technically easier route. Magnificent forests, ancient mammoth cedars, and splendid vistas of the mighty Challenger glacier and snow- and ice-covered Challenger Peak from Whatcom Pass somewhat compensated for our suffering. When we later learned that our projected route was not being done that year because of hazardous conditions that made it horrendously difficult, our wounded egos were somewhat salved as we endured biting flies (twenty-five on each leg all day long), dust, dried-up streams, and a discontinued boat service that added unexpected mileage to our trip.

Although nothing was ever said, we quickly learned that the three of us were not as compatible as we thought. It was mostly a matter of style, with a bit of macho embarrassment thrown in. Kurt and I had adapted to each other from the many trips we'd taken together. We had our routine. It's no fun to set up camp or eat in darkness, so our first priority on reaching a camping site was to set up the tent, then cook and eat the meal. If any daylight was left, we could then wander around exploring the area, sticking our hot and tired feet in cooling streams, examining wildflowers or birds. George's first order of business was to head for a stream, take his shoes off, relax, and birdwatch. This meant that each night Kurt and I were doing all the work and calling George to come eat his dinner. To his credit, George did his fair share the night we had to construct the sleeping platform. George also liked to take many long rests along the way. Perhaps this kept him from tiring, but it also made it feel as if we weren't making much progress. Short rests are fine, but I lose momentum and incentive if I sit too long. It wouldn't matter if time weren't critical, but on this trip time had become an issue.

For an experienced hiker, George also made an incredible mistake. He bought new boots for the trip and did not break them in. In a very short time, blisters developed. He changed to his sneakers, but this didn't help much and made it difficult for him to carry a full load. At six feet, and weighing about 180 pounds, he was capable of carrying a heavier load than either of us. Our plan had been to empty something from each pack as we went along, giving everyone a break. George was carrying fifty-five pounds; Kurt, who was five-feet-seven, carried forty-five pounds. My load of thirty-five pounds was close to one-third of my body weight, and I was looking forward to some relief. In order to help George as much as we could, we now shifted things around, so that only his load was lighter each day. A feeling of tension settled in after a while. To some extent George probably felt like a fifth wheel. Though not demonstrative in public, Kurt and I were obviously a closely attached couple, used to each other's ways. George's wife did not like hiking. I also think George finally became embarrassed because the smallest person and a female at that was having to fill in for him, and could still cover the miles at a better pace.

Despite having his load lightened, George moved more and more slowly. We didn't want to get too far ahead of him, but on the last day I was worried that his slow pace and long rest stops would make us miss the last ferry for the day on Lake Diablo. Sure, there would be another ferry in the morning, but we'd been hiking for over a week, and I was more than ready for a hot shower and a real bed. I was determined not to miss that ferry, even though we would have to keep up a hurried pace for sixteen miles in order to reach the dock before 3:15 p.m.

We packed up camp quickly and were on the trail early; we agreed to meet at a shelter at lunch time. By then there was already a problem. We ate our lunch and waited for George to appear. Thirty minutes later he arrived, needing to eat lunch and rest. Given the time of day and the miles we had yet to go, Kurt and I decided to move on. Actually, I just left as soon as George arrived. Kurt stayed to talk with him for a few minutes. The two of us reached the boat landing with about ten minutes to spare. But when the boat arrived, George was nowhere in sight. We had no idea where he was, except that he was farther behind us somewhere, probably resting. The boat had to keep to its schedule, although it waited, at our request, for five more minutes. Kurt was concerned about leaving, because we were carrying all the food and the tent as well. "Whose fault is that?" I countered as I happily boarded the boat. "George won't die if he goes without food one night."

Diablo Lake Resort had an available cabin, and the hot shower was heavenly. We bought real food at the camp store and enjoyed eating dinner while sitting in a chair at a table. We slept very well. Early in the morning, George came knocking on our door. He told us he had been an hour too late for the ferry, had eaten berries he found along the way, had crawled part of the way on his hands and knees to rest his feet, and had slept under the stars. I was relieved to see him, though I still did not regret leaving him behind.

After sharing breakfast, we all agreed there was no sense in trying to complete the hike. We were about half-way to Lake Chelan, our original destination. In one more week, we three were scheduled to climb with the Canadian Alpine Club. George's feet, which now had two sets of blisters on them, needed rest and recovery. He headed out immediately for Lake Louise in Canada, hitching a ride. We stayed for two more days, eating the huge wild raspberries that grew everywhere. We tried unsuccessfully to climb some nearby peaks, but the vegetation, thick with vines and thorny bushes, was too much for us. Gladly accepting a ride from the owner of the Diablo Lake Resort who was making his weekly marketing trip to Bellingham, Washington, we then took a bus from there to Vancouver and Victoria, British Columbia, to enjoy some city life for a few days before going to Lake Louise.

At Lake Louise, we picked up the clothes and gear we'd mailed to ourselves and met George, whose feet had recovered, prior to the twelve-mile trek in the afternoon to the Lyell Glacier campsite of the Canadian Alpine Club. There were packhorses available, for an additional fee, but toughened by our previous week's adventures, we carried our own things. Tea and cake ready on our arrival had great restorative powers.

In a large meadow at the foot of the glacier a small group of tents had been set up. The larger tent was the dining area. Fellow campers had varied interests. Some had come to climb, some had come to paint the scenery; some preferred bird watching. In addition to three delicious and bountiful meals with fresh fruits and vegetables, tea was served every afternoon, for those in camp.

The guides were all volunteers, experienced members of the club who felt capable of leading climbs. A proposed schedule was listed for each day, and those who wanted to participate in a particular climb signed up. Refresher courses in tying knots and belaying were offered. Climbing days were strenuous with 4:00 a.m. breakfast and 7:00 p.m. dinner. It was a long slog up some very steep snow-packed couloirs on the day we reached the ten-thousand-foot summits of the Lyell Mountains. Although the mountains are not as high as some we had summited, they were glaciated and had huge snowfields because they were so far north. The Lyells had two summits, but some people stopped after climbing one. The rest of us kept going to claim two victories. On the way back to camp, my group decided to run down the slope. Because we were roped together we had to go at the same pace. Some members were very tall and had very long legs, so sometimes for a few moments I was lifted completely into the air.

Some hikes offered were primarily rock; others were ice and snow. The volunteer guide on one climb decided to take a shortcut, leading us up a very steep snow-covered slope. Five of us were roped together. As the leader climbed, he dug handholds and footholds into the snow wall. Going up was more like climbing a ladder than going up a mountain. Below us yawned a wide and probably bottomless crevasse. The wall was so high that before long we were all stretched out, hands and feet in the steps, with no one in a safety position either on the top or the bottom. Although we all had ice-axes, if someone had slipped, we would probably all have been lost in the chasm below. It was a very frightening thought. But there was no way out. We tried not to look down while moving forward swiftly and carefully to the broad summit where we all breathed a sigh of relief. After that, we were careful to avoid the trips that particular volunteer led.

Fellow campers were gracious and friendly even to Yanks. We learned a lot and re-experienced that supremely unique and soul-stirring sunrise beauty of glaciated and snow-covered mountains, renewing my joy in this special world of wonder. Kurt, George, and I celebrated this marvelous alpine week with a twenty-ounce steak in Calgary before flying home.

MT. WHITNEY

Because Mt. Whitney at 14,494 feet is the highest peak in the contiguous United States, I had assumed that it would be difficult to climb it. Once I learned that there was a trail to the top, I was eager to go. Kurt said it was just a pile of rock and not a very interesting mountain, but I still wanted to get to the top. On the east side, Death Valley and the desert are nearby. As if to make up for the extreme height of Mt. Whitney, the altitude at Death Valley is below sea level. Even the valley next to Whitney is only about four thousand feet high.

Our first attempt to hike up Mt. Whitney was part of our family's long bi-centennial coast-to-coast trip. On our way home from California, we planned to spend a week backpacking on part of the John Muir Trail leading to the Whitney Trail. This would have us in good shape and used to the high altitude before the four of us attempted to reach the summit. We drove our car to the Onion Valley campground at 9,000 feet, and spent the night there, hoping that would help us. Having a week's time for the hike, we could move slowly enough for our nine-year-old to feel comfortable. We started up the sloping trail to the pass at 12,000 feet. Kurt and Karen, our fourteen-year-old daughter, were moving along very well. Alan, our nine year old, did well at first. But near the pass he asked me to carry his pack, and just as he reached the junction, he said his head hurt. We decided we'd camp at the first reasonable campsite we could find by a glacial lake. I woke with a terribly painful migraine headache. Alan had lost his lunch and supper and still didn't feel well. If we went on, hoping the two of us would get better, we would be farther and farther from help, if instead we got worse. We decided to save Whitney for another year.

Two years later in 1978, Kurt suggested that we try to reach Whitney from the West. Karen and Alan would vacation with their grandmother while the two of us took a ten-day backpacking trip in the High Sierras ending with a hike up Whitney. We'd be in great condition from the hike, and we would be used to the higher elevation before we went to the top. This time our hopes were crushed by the numerous swollen, flooded streams with dangerous crossings created by exceptionally heavy spring rains and by the very painful callouses that developed on Kurt's feet after ninety miles of hiking. We quit and descended at Onion Valley again, promising to return. A daily account of this Sierra hiking trip can be found in the chapter, "Trails to Glory."

Our next chance did not occur until eighteen years later. We'd thought the Nepal trekking group would hold a reunion hike of Mt. Whitney in 1994, but that didn't even get off the ground.

In the summer of 1996 we planned a two-week group raft trip in the Grand Canyon followed by our own exploration of the National Parks in southwestern Utah. Once we were that far West, I thought, Mt. Whitney was almost next door. But regulations had changed. Now permits were required for entering the Whitney area, and those interested in getting one were advised to fax or call beginning April 1. Only a limited number of people were allowed to be in the area each day. We knew that at Kurt's pace, we could not possibly do the whole trip in one day, as some people did. After our fourteener experiences, we planned to carry our packs, camp out on the way, take our time, enjoy the scenery, and maybe, if we were lucky, get to the top. I asked for a four-day permit and got it.

We hadn't planned to stop in Nevada, but at a campground in Utah, we heard about Nevada's Great Basin Park. It was practically on our way and deliciously cool at 10,000 feet. Lehman Cave, an attraction within the park, was remarkably rich in formations for a small area. We stretched our hiking legs on the Glacier and Bristlecone walks, admiring the oldest pine trees in the world. Wheeler Peak at 13,000 feet took us all day and was good practice for Mt. Whitney. (See "Trails to Glory.")

After a look at nearby Mammoth Lake and the Devil's Postpile, a remarkable outcropping of basalt, we camped for one night at Whitney Portal. From the campsite at 8,500 feet, we could get a good start. We'd seen the Whitney pinnacles from below and were quite excited about finally doing the hike. Starting early, we had carefully crossed a waterfall and reached an area where many shooting stars were clustered together, creating pink splotches of color. As we got higher, the dark clouds we had tried to ignore insisted that we notice them by pouring out both snow and sleet. If the weather was this bad here, what would it be like higher up? Disappointed, we turned back as the precipitation became serious. On our way down, we met a hiker and his dog going up the trail. The dog, a handsome malamute, wore leather booties on each foot, but we never learned the reason why. Both dog and owner were moving fast, and they didn't turn back as we did.

While having a second breakfast at a diner in the valley, we grumbled about the storm. A waitress said it was just one of those things that blows in and blows out. The next few days, she claimed, would be perfect. We would now have only three days in which to do the trip, but it was still possible, if we got good weather. We took a motel for the night. If we woke to rain, we could get an early start home.

A beautiful clear morning the next day sent us up to Trail Camp, at twelve thousand feet. On the way, Kurt tripped crossing a creek, but dried out while we ate lunch. We hadn't carried full packs for quite a while but were okay. As the trail rose above timberline, small birds and chipmunks begged for food. We had constant views of the pinnacles and other peaks.

Trail camp was simply gorgeous, surrounded by high peaks and next to a lake which froze over each night. Although one or two tent sites were already taken, we found a secluded spot, sheltered from the wind. Illuminated by a full moon, the lake and the haunting landscape were magical.

We awoke in the morning to frost, but the rising sun in a beautifully clear sky quickly took care of that. While having our breakfast, we noticed some groups already starting up the trail. We didn't leave until 9:00 a.m. From this point we had to carry only a day pack with lunch and water, and we had all day to hike. Soon we caught up with a troop of boy scouts who were doing the trip. They hiked at a fast pace for a while, but then took frequent rests on the switchbacks.

One of the boys told me there were ninety-nine switchbacks to reach the saddle. He intended to count every one, but found this impossible. Even though it was late June, many of the trail switchbacks were partially or entirely covered with snow. Twice we had to traverse long, steep snowfields. Deep steps left by previous hikers and the comfort of rented ice axes helped. Most exciting were two treacherous icy steps around a frozen waterfall at the edge of a cliff. A protective chain had been installed, but most hikers still traversed this bit very cautiously.

Beyond the saddle, the trail was clear of snow as it gradually ascended the gentler backside of the mountain. Kurt and I had agreed at the beginning of the day that wherever we were at 1:00 p.m. we would turn back, to make sure we made it back to camp before dark. Keeping that in mind, I stepped up my pace. I was determined to make the top by that time. Most of the trail was not a problem, though it was longer than it looked. An optional snowfield offered a quicker way to the summit, so I took it. I signed the official register book on Mt. Whitney at 12:30 p.m., and used my extra half hour to drink in the vast panorama on all sides. It was a thrill to know I was standing on the highest point in California and in the contiguous United States.

I waited until 1:10 p.m. to start back, thinking Kurt would be arriving at any time. Ten minutes after I left the summit, I saw him coming up, so I stopped and returned to the top with him. What a grand trip it was, a quite satisfying high point after our two aborted attempts. Views were spectacular, and the weather held. It was great to know that we could still do it. We made the 14,494-foot summit the day after my sixty-second birthday; a truly fitting way to start my new year. I was totally energized by the experience.

We were back in camp in time to cook dinner before dark. But what a change! Instead of our lovely spot with only one neighbor at a distance, Trail Camp became Tent City for the many people planning to leave for the summit on Saturday morning.

As we hiked down the mountain that morning, the trail became a superhighway full of ascending hikers in all kinds of attire, with all sorts of preconceptions and misconceptions. Some people wore shorts and flip-flops and carried no jacket and no water. Some women even wore high heels. Obviously they hadn't reached the rocks yet and had no idea of what was to come. Others carried huge backpacks with all kinds of gear, as if they were climbing Mt. Everest. Small children asked their parents if they were there yet. Perhaps some groups were simply making day trips, intending to picnic near the lower waterfalls and small lakes along the way. We didn't stay to find out. We had finally achieved our goal and were ready to head home.

HIMALAYAN   HAPPENING

HIMALAYAN   HAPPENING

"We've climbed Mt. Rainier and the Grossglockner in Austria," Kurt insisted.

"But that was twenty years ago, and what have we done since?" I countered. "My highest altitude is around 14,000 feet, and this trek goes to about 18,000. Remember how you had to turn back in Mexico at 17,000, and then you were only twenty-nine?"

"Don't you want to go?"

"No question, but are we really capable? Our high altitude stuff was years ago; our longest hike was ten days, not thirty. And what about malaria, with my sensitivity to mosquitoes?"

"Kathmandu is already above the mosquito range, so that shouldn't be a problem," Kurt responded, ignoring my other concerns. It was time to try to fulfill a thirty-two-year-old dream. When we married, we had grandiosely and half-jokingly claimed that one day we'd trek in Nepal. It was more of a fantasy than anything we thought we'd actually do, given our financial resources at the time. After many years, an opportunity arose that made us think seriously about making the fantasy happen.

Looking for a way to celebrate his retirement in 1990, Kurt eagerly jumped at my suggestion that we go for the dream. Now I was having second thoughts or what I called practical considerations. It didn't help that only a few months earlier, a Thai plane had crashed in Kathmandu, but we bolsteed our courage by saying that going now would be the safest time to travel since everyone would be more safety conscious as a result.

Our children were grown, and we had a little nest egg. Kurt did the research, and I obtained a leave of absence from work. Although we had lots of experience hiking and backpacking in the United States, we did not trust ourselves to attempt this trip on our own. If we developed high altitude sickness or some other medical problems, the resources of a reliable trekking company would be a great benefit.

As usual, we wanted to get the best value for our money, and we did not have unlimited funds. This ruled out all the up-scale companies such as Mountain Travels Sobek and Abercrombie and Fitch. Eventually we narrowed the field to four companies that offered treks to the area we were interested in–the Solo Khumbu. In particular we wanted a trip that went to Kala Pattar, a famous 18,000-foot knob from which the view of Mt. Everest and the Khumbu icefall would be spectacular–in good weather.

The lecture-slide shows presented by Above the Clouds; Men, Mountains, and Myths; and R.E.I. strengthened our resolve, increased our desire to make the trek, and also gave us a better idea of what company might be the most comfortable fit for us. Comparing the length of the trips offered and the destinations was an important part of our planning. In addition to the treks to various Nepalese destinations, all the companies included sight-seeing in the three major cities in the Kathmandu valley: Bhaktapur, Patan, and Kathmandu.

Cost considerations and itineraries led us to focus finally on R.E.I. (a Seattle-based recreational equipment firm) and Journeys (a company based in Michigan). In the same amount of trekking time, both these companies went to Kala Pattar, but R.E.I. included an optional climb of 20,000-foot Island Peak. In order to do this, I figured, the R.E.I. trek would have to move faster each day, and this was an issue to be considered. A faster pace would mean a more rapid elevation gain, which could lead to altitude sickness. If we got altitude sickness we wouldn't be able to even attempt the 20,000-foot peak. Those who couldn't or didn't want to do the climb would spend two days resting in the campsite, a waste of time it seemed to me. Besides, our primary goal was to see as much of the area as we could, not to climb Island Peak.

The better choice seemed to be Journeys. Though the company founder lived in Ann Arbor, Michigan, his partner and co-founder, Pemba Sherpa, lived in Kathmandu. Journeys offered two versions of their Everest Sherpa Country Trek. A two-week trip to Kala Pattar began and ended with a flight from Kathmandu to Lukla. The brochure, however, recommended the longer twenty-three-day trip for cultural interest and for altitude acclimation. This trip began with a bus ride to the village of Jiri and a week of walking through villages to reach Lukla. On the way back, trekkers would fly from Lukla to Kathmandu. Journeys also offered a five-day extension trekking from Lobuche to Gokyo Ri, another 18,000-foot peak with an awesome view of Mt. Everest amidst a circle of majestic peaks, before returning to Lukla on an alternate trail.

We chose the longer version of the trek, thinking it would help us avoid altitude sickness and that we would also be able to see and experience more of the Nepalese culture as we walked through various tribal villages. We also signed up for the Gokyo extension. This part of the trek was somewhat dependent on weather conditions, but it also depended on the fitness and capability of those who signed up for it. We would be allowed to continue on it only if we did well on the regular trip. When we saw that the reservation form asked for a list of our previous hiking and climbing experience and for other likes and dislikes, we hoped this information would be used by the company to put together compatible groupings of trekkers.

After getting the required immunizations, we read and reread the trip preparation materials and purchased what we didn't have as well as travel insurance in case we needed costly medical evacuation. For weeks I wore my new hiking boots in the house and even to work. The week before we left, I finally decided we actually were going, bought a Nepali language tape, and practiced every night. Besides *Namaste* (I greet the God within you), I knew two phrases very well, *Charpi kahaa cha?* (Where is the toilet?) and *Kukhurako maasu* (chicken meat). The last phrase stuck in my mind only because of its musical rooster-like sound.

We were on our way October 17, 1992, encouraged by a conversation with the eighty-year-old man sitting beside me on the flight from Los Angeles to Bangkok via Tokyo. From Binghamton, New York, he was heading for his eleventh trek–couldn't get enough of it, he said.

Sleeping for several hours in Bangkok helped, but we were still slow in realizing the security folks at the airport wanted us to remove the batteries from the flashlights in our duffel bags. Trekkers of all ages wearing various tour company tee-shirts filled the entire waiting room, raising concerns about how crowded the trails might be. When we introduced ourselves to three people in line for tickets who wore Journeys tee-shirts, we learned that Sherri from Washington, D.C., Jeff from Boston, and Roger from Seattle were taking the same trek we were.

As our flight approached Kathmandu, a glimpse of Everest above the clouds thrilled us as did the narrow pass where a plane could definitely have a problem if visibility were limited and it came in too low, too soon. Ignoring the pawing hordes trying to carry our bags, we finally found the Journeys' guides and were whisked away on a wild ride through the city with many near encounters with animals and other maniac drivers before being deposited at a substitute hotel; we had been displaced by an entourage of the Indian Prime Minister, who was visiting. Turned loose on our own, we were advised not to drink the water, while being handed mango juice, in which ice cubes were clearly floating. Had I missed something?

Kurt, Sherri, and I inadvertently passed by the main road downtown and instead walked a winding back road past numerous tiny shops. Some sold fabrics, others modern light fixtures, hair ornaments, wood carvings, and drums. Fly-encrusted carcasses announced the meat market which also sold rotting legs of unknown animals and unidentifiable bloody entrails. Next door was the cassette tape and video store.

Passing by Hindu shrines, large bells, fascinating carvings, and *sadhus* (professional holy men) carrying tridents, their matted uncut hair brushing against chests daubed red, we reached Durbar Square, busy, but much tamer than I expected, remembering its reputation as a drug-saturated hippie hangout in the 1960s. Everyone asked for money, almost it seemed out of habit. All too soon we were able to ignore the constant appeals, just as the middle-class natives did.

The next morning, an incredible traffic jam made up of buses, motorcycles, people walking, and cows taking their ease delayed our visit to Bhaktapur, the sixteenth-century city where the pillar bearing the statue of one of the Malla Kings faced the Golden Gate, entrance to the fifty-five-window palace. Adjoining the palace was the King's private bath, an open-air empty pool encircled by a protective carved-stone cobra. The natural spring feeding the pool had ceased to flow after an earthquake in 1934, and it had not been used since. Bhaktapur also showed us the Palace of the Five Roofs, the largest and oldest pagoda in Nepal. Statues in ascending power adorned the stepped approach. Two warriors on the first step were overpowered by elephants, ten times stronger, on step two. The lions on step three, ten times stronger than the elephants, were dominated by the griffins of step four. At the top of this power pyramid stood two goddesses–a heartwarming line-up for any feminist.

Pashupatinath, most sacred temple of the Hindus, was off-limits to non-Hindus, but many miniatures of the stylized *lingam* (phallus) of Shiva and the *yoni* (vulva) of his consort were placed on a hill opposite to accommodate tourists. Next to the temple was a "sick house" where Hindus feeling they were about to die came to spend their final days to ensure that their ashes would be put into the Bagmati River, a tributary of the sacred Ganges. Having one's ashes put into the Bagmati assures one of coming back at a higher level. One pyre was almost finished burning, but another was fairly new. When the father dies, it is the duty and honor of the son to put the fire first to the mouth of his father and then to the rest of the pyre. The royal *ghat* (boat landing on the river where corpses are cremated) was also located here. Although Shiva represents both rebirth and destruction, the place had only a somber feeling to it. Several *sadhus* lounged around waiting for donations.

At Bhodinath in the Buddhist part of Kathmandu, beggars and peddlers were less aggressive. The *stupa* (dome-shaped Buddhist shrine) with its all-seeing eyes on all sides was the largest in Nepal. We learned that the figure resembling a nose beneath the eyes was really the numeral one, intended to symbolize the absoluteness of Buddha. This area of the city was noticeably cleaner than anywhere else we had been in Kathmandu.

That night after dinner at the Amber Restaurant, where we sampled Vistari Beer in oversized bottles along with delicious Nepali food, we met Pemba Sherpa, Journey's Nepalese partner and head of the Kathmandu office. We also met some of our guides and the other three trekkers in our group: Patti and Bill Bright and Patti's sister Shirley Hurtado from Colorado. We were at least ten to fifteen years older than any of the other trekkers in our group.

When Pemba distributed itineraries, we noticed that only Jeff had also signed up for the Gokyo extension. We worried whether they would do the trip for just three trekkers.

Our trek began in the morning with a seven-hour bus trip from Kathmandu past the end of the paved road to the trailhead at the village of Jiri. Beyond Jiri there were no vehicular roads and no vehicles. Everyone walked. Our goal for this part of the trip was to reach Phakding in six days. Near Phakding, two people who had signed up for a shorter trek would join us.

Another group of ten who were taking the shorter trip would also begin their trip to Kala Pattar at that point. Our itinerary beyond Jiri showed the following nightly stops: Kasrobash, Kenja, Thak Tok, Trakshindu, Bupsa, Surkhe, and Phakding. But we were told everything was subject to change.

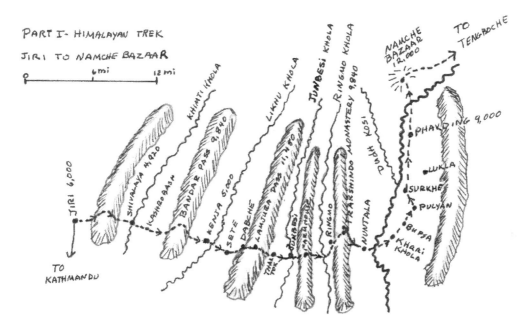

PART I- HIMALAYAN TREK
JIRI TO NAMCHE BAZAAR

The second part of the trip began with a day's walk from Phakding to Namche Bazaar. After we reached Namche, one rest day was scheduled before we would move on to Tengboche, then Dingboche for two nights, and Lobuche for three nights. Kala Pattar would be a full-day trip from Lobuche and back again. After sleeping at Lobuche, the regular trekkers would then hike back to Lukla, and Kurt, Jeff, and I would cross the pass (Cho La), weather permitting, to reach Gokyo Ri before returning to the airport at Lukla.

After posing for a group photo against our aging yellow bus, we eagerly climbed aboard. At lunchtime, we received another culture shock. We already had a box lunch, but we stopped to buy drinks at a roadside teahouse. When Sherri used the toilet there, she reported that anything deposited therein dropped directly into the river below. No wonder water purification was extremely important.

Despite stopping for tire repair, running out of gas, and nearly colliding with wild drivers and buses along the highway which climbed steeply towards the border with China, we arrived in Jiri before nightfall. Camp, including a *charpi* (toilet) tent, was already set up in a field at the edge of town. Surrounded almost instantly by many children, we practiced our Nepali phrases on them, asking how old they were, their names, and if they knew English. Forewarned, I had brought photos of my children, of our house, and of Washington, D.C., since we live in the Maryland suburbs. The children, their mothers, and their grandmothers were intensely interested in seeing these, quickly giving me additional vocabulary words as they pointed out various items in the photos and asked me questions.

Our first day of hiking began at 6:00 a.m. with the greeting, *"Namaste Aama"* (good morning, mother) and the welcome *"Chai, tato-rato"* (tea, red hot). Delivered to each tent, the delicious and warming wake-up tea was followed by a basin of warm water for washing. Before breakfast at 6:30 a.m., we were expected to have rolled up our sleeping bags and packed our duffel bags to expedite our departure. We ate breakfast seated at a long table, then started up the trail from Jiri to Kasrobash while tents were dismantled and packed, supplies were purchased, and our *sirdar* (chief guide) Baburam tried to hire porters.

We'd already had some changes of altitude. From sea level, where we live, we'd spent two days at Kathmandu's 3,000 feet and overnight at Jiri, about 6,000. Between Jiri and Kasrobash, we would descend to Shivalaya at 4,920 feet, then climb to about 8,000.

After passing some simple stone houses at the edge of town, we climbed towards the top of the ridge, where we hiked through deep forests, then more open fields, passing some tiny settlements. By about 10:30 a.m. we reached what looked like high pastureland, and there were the cooks and their packs. I remembered our chief guide Baburam's advice, "Go at your own pace, but don't pass the cooks–unless you don't mind missing a meal." I assumed this was a tea break, as I saw the kerosene stoves set up, and we were waved in to take a rest. Hot lemonade was refreshing, but no one made a move to hike on. Were we just waiting for the porters to catch up with us? We were, but it was also the usual time that our two-hour lunch stop began. Each day we would hike for about three hours, rest for two, and then hike for three more before stopping for the night. We always had a hot meal, and the guides and porters ate after we finished. Local greens were purchased for the porters, whose meal consisted of rice and greens and *chai* (tea). Offered a taste of non-tourist food, I tried it, but it had been laced with chili peppers so hot that tears came to my eyes. After washing our hands, we had yak cheese and tomato sandwiches and cabbage and carrot salad beautifully arranged and previously soaked in iodine water to kill harmful bacteria.

Crossing the ridge we walked farther, admiring the steep, terraced hillsides. In Nepal so little land is flat that the hills are farmed, using terraced plots to slow down erosion. The terracing created beautiful visual patterns. Gradually we descended beside a stream, finally crossing it on a small wooden bridge, emerging into the main valley of the Khimti Khola River. This large river was spanned by a high suspension bridge that led to Shivalaya, a small town, where cold drinks were available. Our afternoon break at about 3:00 p.m. lengthened into an overnight stay because the porters carrying our tents, sleeping bags, and clothing had not yet arrived at 5:00 p.m., and the next part of the trail was very steep.

Baburam warned us to sleep with our duffel bags in the center of the tents. He also set up a a twenty-four-hour guard tent, because there had been a recent robbery incident near Shivalaya. "Once we're farther away from the larger towns," he said, "we won't have this problem." Dinner was late and was followed by medical consultation. Kurt's gray beard and my wrinkles qualified us as wise elders, I suppose. Why else would the porters be brought to us seeking medical assistance? It was a good thing we had both been scouts. I wrapped a sprained ankle in an ace bandage and supplied antibiotic and a band-aid for a scraped leg, shocked to learn that there were no communal first aid supplies. We'd been told to bring a personal kit, but we didn't expect to be called on to assist the staff.

From Shivalya, the trail ascended steeply–almost like scrambling rather than hiking–to Kasrobash. Up higher through a slightly wooded area, rhododendron bushes covered a hillside. Lunch was waiting on a high platform overlooking the trail. A large blue tarp had been spread to provide a clean eating and sleeping surface. Many in our group napped or sun dried laundry after eating. The afternoon hike took us through a covered bridge, then up another steep hill, beside quince and cotoneaster forests. At the top of Bhandar pass (9,840 feet) stood a large hotel made primarily of stone with beautiful painted blue window frames. Here we had a small rest stop, enjoying the fabulous view of the Likhu Khola Valley and inspecting the several rows of long *mani* walls there. Now entering an area dominated by Tibetan culture, we were careful to pass the *mani* (memorial stones with carved inscriptions) on the left side of the wall, saying the *mantra* (prayer) *"Om Mani Padme Hum,"* as the Buddhists do, not only to show respect, but also to ensure a safe trip. This most widely used of all Buddhist mantras is open to anyone who feels inspired to repeat it. The phrase is most often interpreted in English as "Hail to the Jewel in the Lotus," but its significance and power are not readily understood from this phrase. At the most simple level, the jewel in the lotus refers to Buddha, but the person reciting the mantra is not simply greeting Buddha. Rather in reciting the mantra, we are to contemplate or imagine ourselves becoming one with the Buddha of Compassion, thus replacing our self-focus with Buddha's focus on the needs of others. In another explanation of the phrase, each of the six syllables helps in the perfection of a different aspect of life: generosity, ethics, tolerance and patience, perseverance, concentration, wisdom. Reciting the mantra is a way of asking to be blessed or helped in purifying oneself of obstacles preventing the perfection of these qualities within oneself.

On the even steeper way down, walking cornstalks made me rub my eyes until I realized there would be no tractors here, and everything–absolutely everything–that had to be moved anywhere traveled either on an animal or a human back.

Because we were allowed to go at our own pace, the group of hikers often spread out. One guide led the way with Jeff, Sherri, Shirley, Kurt and I usually close behind, though not necessarily within sight of each other. Bill, Patti, and Roger took their time, chatting as they walked together. The cooks began after we did, but always passed everyone along the way. Assistant guides tried to accompany unnoticeably anyone they thought might require help. Last came the porters, but they were carrying all the duffel bags. Behind them was our sirdar, Baburam, making sure everything had been taken care of and that no one was left behind. At times, though, he would suddenly appear at the middle or the front of the group checking on our well-being. But there was nothing rigid about the order in which we walked, and it often changed depending on how energetic each hiker felt. The feeling of freedom with security was exhilarating.

Kurt and I missed the main trail when it took a sharp turn through a small town. Reaching the top of a terrace, I saw Roger's jacket disappear around a corner on a trail farther down the mountain. Yelling and motioning for us to follow him, a small child ran toward us. I kept repeating Kenja, the name of our day-three destination, and he answered yes. But I also knew by then that in their desire to please, many Nepalese answer yes, no matter what. It's safer to ask which trail to Kenja, thereby forcing a decision to be made, rather than receiving an amenable but perhaps unreliable answer. When the boy saw we were finally going the right way, he wanted a rupee for helping, a very reasonable price.

I hiked in a cotton shirt and an ankle-length red skirt. We'd been advised that Nepalese women did not wear trousers. I'd always hiked in long pants, but I knew that many long-skirted Victorian women had scaled serious peaks in the early days of mountaineering, so I decided to give it a try, bringing safety pins in case I needed to make adjustments. Actually, the skirt gave me a great range of motion, could be tucked up when scrambling, and provided better privacy than jeans when nature called between villages. Red was also the favorite color in Nepal, and my long red skirt often brought favorable comments from women I met. Some women asked to touch it. They approved the fabric, sturdier than the beautifully patterned, but thin cotton sarongs they wore.

Everyone we met greeted us with "Namaste," and we responded as we admired the amazing strength and agility of these people. While we wore hiking boots and carried day packs, many of the men carried sixty-pound bags and wore only flip-flops or zorries. Sometimes they wore holey tennis shoes. The women wore blouses and sarongs and many bracelets. They either wore flip-flops or went bare-footed. Not only did they have long, beautiful dangling earrings, but they also wore intricate nose-rings. I suppose they removed them if they had a cold or a runny nose. Men sometimes wore embroidered hats and frequently wore earrings in both ears. Their earrings, however, were usually simple gold loops. Children imitated their parents, and from an early age, many of them practiced carrying the typical large woven pack baskets. The beautiful smiles which we saw on every face made us feel very welcome.

Descending a long trail, we finally neared a farmhouse on a terrace, where I asked again about Kenja. The farmer pointed, and we made yet another zigzag, walking in water for a bit and still wondering when we would see someone from our group. We passed a gorgeous waterfall amidst lush greenery, and then around the corner we saw Ekraj and Damaiching, two of the cooks, setting up the kitchen near a beautiful two-story farmhouse. We knew we would not reach Kenja that night, but there didn't seem to be any flat space nearby large enough for our tents. We wondered where we would be sleeping.

While we waited for the rest of our group and the porters, an older Nepalese man, accompanied by several small children, came up and asked Kurt how old he was. I could tell that he was also curious about my age but felt it would be impolite to ask a woman, so I volunteered the information in Nepali. He then told us that he was eighty-four, that the children were his grandchildren, and that his son was building the two-story farmhouse, or at least that's what we thought he said. We were amazed. We knew life expectancy in Nepal was fifty-seven.

The farm had quite a variety of trees and plants. Citrus trees, a banana tree, cabbages, turnips, and potatoes grew along with taro in this fertile soil. Negotiations took place between the farmer and our head guide, and soon our tents were being set up in what had been a taro field. Two chickens were also purchased and kept secure in small overturned bamboo baskets which served as chicken coops. Dinner was alfresco by lantern with the farmer and his extended family watching how the foreigners ate.

In the morning before we left on the fourth day of our trek, the family gave us permission to take photos of them. They proudly gathered on the porch and included the family goat which the grandfather drew towards him and kissed on the mouth–just another member of the family. Breakup of camp was quick, and we were on the trail by 7:00 a.m. traveling across a high suspension bridge with beautiful views, then along another streamside trail, and finally arriving in Kenja, a lovely little city where the usual dirt walkway had been paved with flat stones. From now on we would trek completely in Sherpa country. While we waited for our *sirdar* to bring the required permits for traveling beyond Kenja, the community *charpi* was located and was judged acceptable.

Leaving Kenja, we began the ascent towards the high Lamjura ridge. The guidebook had described the first part of the ascent as very steep, then becoming less severe as elevation is gained. Damaiching, one of the cooks, started up the fairly steep way, and I followed. He moved faster than the comfortable pace Lakpa, an assistant guide, usually set, but I assumed that he was to be the leader that day and tried to keep up, though I wasn't sure how long I could. Damaiching asked if I were going to Gokyo, and when I replied that I hoped so, he said I was very strong and asked how old I was. Behind me, Kurt had also tried to keep pace, but he slipped, scraping his arm and banging his elbow against a large rock. At the first rest stop we bandaged it.

My given name was difficult for the Sherpas to pronounce, so I received two nicknames: *bolshoe* (grandmother) and *aama* (mother). The Nepalese prefer to address other individuals with some term indicating a relationship to the person speaking. This is also why they are so interested in knowing your age. If you are about the same age as the person addressing you, you will be either *didi* or *daai* (older sister or older brother) or you might be *bahini* or *bhaai* (younger sister or younger brother). Lakpa asked which name I liked best. I was old enough to be a *bolshoe* for some of the Sherpas, cooks, and porters, but since I really had only a grandkitty at home, I said *aama* would do fine. Everyone laughed when I refused to let Ekraj, an older cook, call me *aama*. For Ekraj, I would only answer to *didi,* not *aama.* Kurt wasn't given a choice. When they saw his gray beard, he was grandfather.

Our lunchtime stop was near a small house where a woman was beating soybeans with a stick to break open the pods. We bought sodas that had traveled there on someone's back. They served as an additional source of income for the woman, though the cost was no higher than in the states. The harvested soybeans, roasted in a pan on the fire, tasted somewhat like popcorn–a good snack. Although it was only 10:30 a.m., the sandwiches, salad, orange juice, tea with lime, and freshly made potato chips were eagerly devoured.

Fortified, we continued up and up until we reached Sete, about 8,500 feet. We'd been at 5,000 feet in Kenja. Views were spectacular all around, but the trail continued up. More frequent rest stops were needed, and when we met several mule trains, we had to step aside. Still the porters were far behind. At one rest stop, Damaiching met a group of porters who were on their way home. A long conversation took place, and we thought perhaps new porters had been hired.

Our goal was to reach Goyem, a small village that had already been substituted for Thak Tok, our original destination. But we had only reached Dabche when twilight came on. At this elevation, when darkness came, so did cold temperatures. A mist began settling in as we huddled together in the yard surrounding a small hut. We had only sweaters and rain jackets in the day packs we were carrying. After a while, we were invited in and given tea prepared by the kitchen crew. This was a far cry from the description in the brochure we'd all read. It had stated that we would arrive at each site in the afternoon in time for tea and rest in our tents that would be waiting for us. All eight of us lay down side by side on the floor trying to keep warm in the unheated, low-roofed hut. Concerned about us, the kitchen crew shared their food: noodle soup, rice, and some vegetables. When the porters arrived long after dark, we eagerly crawled inside the tents and warm sleeping bags. Some trekkers were beginning to wish they'd never come.

Before we left Dabche the next morning, another problem arose. Our food was cooked on stoves using kerosene. This meant porters carried the kerosene we needed in huge tins. One kerosene container lacking a proper lid had been sealed with only a rag and a cork. The steepness and unevenness of the trail caused the kerosene to slosh out of the container and onto the back of the porter carrying it. A layer of skin on his back hung like a sack, filled with the kerosene that had burned him. We drained the fluid, then applied burn ointment and whatever large bandages we could find in our own supplies. One trekker donated a tee-shirt, as the porter wanted to continue despite his ghastly chemical burn. I had never seen anything like it. How he could continue to carry a load in what must have been excruciating pain was incredible. His twelve-year-old son, Schumann, was also carrying things for us. Because carrying was a good-paying job, they wanted to continue.

Leaving Dabche, we continued to climb through a fine, moist mountain forest, with huge, gnarled, moss-covered rhododendrons and magnolia, maple, and birch trees. There were few villages on the way. The trail climbed steeply to the rather barren ridge, before it contoured toward Lamjura Pass, at 11,480 feet, the highest point on the trek between Jiri and Namche Bazaar, marked by a tangle of stones, twigs, and prayer flags erected by devout travelers. We paused there, taking photos of the stark, dramatic scenery. Patti put on her knee brace for the long descent, and we scurried on to Thak Tok, waiting for the rest of our group at a tea house where I gave my small Thai airline orchid I'd carried on my hat for several days to a little girl who watched but didn't beg.

We lunched in a beautiful pine and maple forest, then three of us hurried on to squeeze in a short side trip to see Serlo Monastery with its stained-glass windows and its monks who produced books for other monasteries. Our fast pace allowed us to catch up with the rest of our group at the amazing Junbesi Monastery. Painted yellow, it was a landmark for us, visible for a long distance. Outside the main building, gargoyles protected the front arch; inside a Buddha and a female guardian could be seen. Our stop was short, since we still had not made up lost time, and we had to be in Lukla on our seventh day. Two more trekkers, flying in from Los Angeles, expected to join our group there.

Trudging up yet another hill, we came to a lovely whitewashed two-story farmhouse where we were invited into a newly-built sleeping or guest room. Again our tents and duffel bags had not arrived. Tea was served in the guest room while Jeff played with a scrawny kitten, and a young boy read English sentences to us. We also had dinner in this room, as the cooking crew had rented space below. Our tents finally arrived and were set up in the farmer's yard, but when all the porters had arrived, two duffel bags were missing, so two people had no sleeping bags or extra clothes. One of them was Kurt, so I gave him my long underwear to put on, and we opened my sleeping bag to blanket size. Finally about 9:30 p.m. Kurt's sleeping bag arrived, but only because Baburam had run back down to Junbesi for it. Ekraj, the cook, also made a second trip to bring things up that had been left behind.

When Jeff's bag still hadn't arrived by 10:30 p.m. Damaiching, who had taken over for Baburam, borrowed blankets and a sleeping pad for Jeff from the farm family. There was some talk of hiring animals, as each night of the trip there had been some problem or inconvenience caused by the porters. Strange as it seemed, hiring animals cost more than hiring people. Some porters who had started in Jiri had tried to carry double loads in order to get double pay, but they made it only as far as Dabche on the night they were so late. Following some disagreement and a long discussion, several porters left the next morning, including the one who was wearing our good ace bandage. Two new porters now joined us. More potential porters had seemed glad for the job offer a few days ago when we met them on the trail, but they never showed up at the designated meeting place.

In the morning of our sixth day, we gave our hostess pens for her children: four boys and one girl. Only three boys were home, for the girl and her older brother were attending school in Kathmandu. The trail now made a long traverse high up on a hillside. We could see various trails heading into other valleys, but our way to the Khumbu was the trail on the left that went uphill through Ringmo and its apple orchards to Trakshindu Pass at 9,840 feet and the monastery located there. On the way we were treated to glimpses of Everest, called *Sagamartha* in Nepali, Chamlang, and Makalu.

About lunch time Jeff, Sherri, and I had reached the pass and were enjoying the view as the others joined us. Suddenly the temperature dropped, and a strong wind blew in sleet and hail. We had lunch and some of the local apples inside a small store, where a fire in the corner added warmth to the room. When the store owner mentioned his nagging headache, someone offered him Tylenol. Medications of any kind were scarce, and headaches frequently developed whenever Westerners appeared.

As we descended on the other side of the pass, the hail changed to a heavy mist surrounding us until we reached Trakshindu Monastery. For a small donation, we could see a large Buddha, hand-painted decorative pillars supporting the roof, and many sacred scrolls. A small protective dragon face on the building warded off evil spirits. To help support the monastery, a small gift shop sold wood blocks carved with a mantra. The calligraphy was attractive, and the blocks did not add too much weight to our daypacks.

In the middle of a lovely green woods below the monastery, just as we had to cross a creek on logs, we met a group of friendly Buddhist nuns. Dressed in burgundy robes, they were on their way to visit the monastery for the festival of *Dasain* or *Durga Puja*. This ten-day celebration of Durga's triumph over evil, the biggest festival in Nepal, was similar to our Thanksgiving or Christmas in that people used the holiday time to visit their families all over the country, sometimes walking for days. Farther down the mountain on the way to Nuntala, we encountered revelers dancing and singing, adorned with marigolds. The song was very repetitious punctuated with the words "doe shoe ray," and the dancing seemed freeform, so I joined in, to the revelers' delight. Requesting donations to be placed in a basket with marigolds was an integral part of the dance. We thought the request for donations was for religious purposes, but when we asked our guides, they said the donations were probably spent on *chang*, the local intoxicant. In fact, some of the assistant guides had started celebrating early, and no one had seem them for several days.

When we reached Nuntala, the entire town was partying. Many in our group wanted to spend the night in town, as we were the first of our group to arrive, and it was already late afternoon. The decision, however, was to push on for Dudh Kosi (Milk River) before stopping for the night. After a tricky, steep, and rocky descent from Nuntala, we stopped at a farmhouse just as the sky turned dark. The rest of the group had to finish the trail in darkness, aided by flashlights. Because the porters had no light, Baburam ran down the trail to borrow our flashlights to help light the rocky trail for the porters. Even so, Bill's sleeping bag did not arrive until about 10:30 p.m., and some of the assistant guides never made it till morning.

On our seventh day, we left Dudh Kosi and headed for Surkhe up a fairly steep section of the trail and then down again through Khari Khola, a village lovely with flowers. In the next small town, more celebrators approached us, and before we could stop them, they put marigolds on our hats. We knew the routine, but as we didn't have any rupiya small enough, Kurt gave them a one-dollar bill, wondering what adventures they might go through to change it and what it would be used for. In another town, a man dressed totally in white jumped on the trail whirling around and around, but he did not ask for money. We stopped in Bupsa for lunch, and when a family curious about us came close, I showed my pictures and we conversed in my broken Nepali and the young boy's excellent English. While I tried to sun dry laundry, a monk came by asking for donations to restore the *gompa* (Buddhist monastery) there.

In the afternoon we hiked through a jungle area inhabited by many monkeys. The very steep uphill climb made us all thirsty for a cold drink, but we could get nothing until we reached an inn at Pulyan. The trail then descended sharply from the ridge. On this part of the route, the trail was comparatively new, in many places narrow and exposed, especially where it had been blasted out of a vertical rock wall. At one point there was a collection of logs and shrubbery, creating a false sense of security, for the trail actually crossed a rock face above a precipice. In another place, a huge shale rockslide had impacted the trail. Two young men stood on the far side of it, making hooting calls of various kinds. Sherri was hesitant to go first, for after the large slide area, the trail climbed a stone staircase with no guardrail. I didn't know if Sherri was afraid of the exposure on the trail or the hooting fellows, so I went first. When the two men saw that the approaching trekker was an *aama*, instead of a young woman, their hoots suddenly changed to a polite and friendly, "*Namaste, aama.*"

Crossing two streams on wooden bridges, we reached Pulyan at about 9,000 feet, where we waited for the porters, once more getting cold and colder as twilight came on. Finally we were invited into the inn and went to the upstairs bunkroom, where we talked about all sorts of things while waiting. When the fumes from the kerosene lamp started making me sick, I went to a window for some air. Outside I saw another group of celebrators. One fellow wore a wooly coat and crazy sunglasses while his partner–another man–was dressed as a woman with a towel over his head to simulate hair. They wanted money for their dance, and when Patti and Shirley said no, the dancers gave them the finger. Finally the tent-carrying porters arrived, and camp was set up in a field across the road from the inn. But the porters carrying our food were again so late that the cooking crew once more shared their food with us and we ate in their tent. It was after 10:00 p.m. when the final two duffel bags and the last sleeping pad arrived.

Leaving Pulyan the next morning, we enjoyed a pleasant hike on another beautiful day, passing wonderful *mani* walls painted brilliant colors. The trail dropped to Surkhe, a village situated at about 7,500 feet. From there, on our way to Phakding, we passed through an entry gate to a small village. All kinds of Buddhist paintings adorned the walls and ceilings of this entry gate. Lunch was near a large farmhouse just past an area where caves under overhangs had protective rock walls partially closing up their entrances. These spaces were used as shelters for animals: *dzopchuks* (a mixed breed of yaks and domestic cattle), goats, or cattle. We ate lunch at a spot from which we could see the trail to Lukla. Not long after we finished, Ellen and Harvey Friedman, the Los Angeles trekkers, joined us. Baburam and an assistant guide, Baadu, had left early from Pulyan to meet the newcomers in Lukla and to hire *dzopchuks* and yaks for carrying our gear the rest of the way. These strong, shaggy animals could be used only now because they were uncomfortable at lower altitudes and warmer temperatures.

Having just arrived by airplane, Ellen and Harvey looked wonderfully clean to us. We'd been walking for a week already and felt pretty grubby despite morning and evening washups. From the trail, which had many ups and downs on the way to Phakding (9,000 feet), we often saw platforms in the cultivated fields we passed. According to the guide book, people slept on these platforms so they could jump up and chase bears away from the crops.

After a precipitous stone staircase going downhill, the trail climbed steeply to the first hotel in Phakding. The area and the trail were subject to avalanches from Ama Dablam, and portions of the trail had been washed away, making us detour somewhat. Because we were early at Phakding, we watched newly arriving Japanese tourists marching along precisely, carrying identical packs, and wearing identifying armbands, all sparkling clean. There was much activity here with many Nepalis playing around on the high suspension bridge over the river, which we would have to cross in the morning. Harvey expressed his fear about crossing the bridge as well as his uneasiness about using the *charpi*. Having no mercy, we all told him he'd have to face those fears if he wanted to do the trek.

From Phakding, on our ninth day of walking, we saw our first snow peaks up close, revving everyone for the hike from 9,000 feet at Phakding to 12,000 feet at Namche Bazaar. I was concerned about making it, as I hadn't been able to shake an annoying bronchitis-like cough, and my voice was sounding worse and worse. Because Patti had experienced something similar when she arrived, she insisted I take some of her erythromycin. Fortunately that took care of the problem. Crossing the very long and high suspension bridge, we made sure the yaks crossed first. Amazing animals, the massive *dzopchuks* and yaks could balance quite delicately on stones on very steep trails while carrying heavy loads. We felt that if they made it across the bridge, we could too. As we crossed, we enjoyed fabulous alpine views.

After a very pleasant scenic walk to the National Park Service area in Jorsale, we were frustrated by a long wait during which we were repeatedly questioned about video cameras. The charge for bringing one in was $100. Finally the guards realized that we had no video cameras, and we continued up through a beautiful pine forest to a lovely lunch spot by the river. More nuns in burgundy robes were there–also having lunch. We then crossed two more bridges and continued steeply up the side of a hill to reach another very high suspension bridge built by the Swiss. It was very sturdy, but the approaches were difficult for the animals. The trail was steep and very narrow with a precipitous dropoff. It made a very sharp bend just as it reached the bridge. The massive animals had difficulty moving their bodies and four legs around the sharp uphill bend. They could do it, but only very slowly. Once on the bridge, they were all right, but getting on and off took time. On the steep uphill trail beyond the bridge, we met men carrying as many as ten twelve-foot-long boards on their backs. Carrying such loads, they had to rest frequently. One yak we passed was panting so hard that I thought it might collapse.

On the way to Namche, we stopped for the view at Everest View Tea Shop. From the window, we marveled at the superb vista of Mt. Everest, Nuptse, and Lhotse. Many people ascending and descending cluttered the trail, and many greetings were exchanged. We drank a lot of water, moving along the trail which was now not quite so steep, and suddenly we were wandering into town through narrow streets. As we looked around, we heard shouts from a second story window. This was Aanu's lodge, the place we'd been looking for, so we hurried to the upper floor where we drank tea and stayed warm until our gear arrived on the backs of the *dzopchuks* and yaks. Aanu Sherpa was Journeys' representative in Namche Bazaar. He and his wife MingMa were known by or related to almost everyone in the town. Aanu was also the chief guide for the Journeys' group that was taking the shorter trip. They would fly to Lukla and make a round trip trek from there to Gorak Shep and Kala Pattar and back, avoiding the strenuous, but fascinating week of hiking most of us had used to acclimatize ourselves.

This second trekking group also camped in the lodge's yard. From Lukla at 9,100 feet, these trekkers had hiked for only one afternoon to reach Namche at 12,000. Two groups sharing the yard space in addition to yaks and yak herders created quite a close fit. One trekker in the new group had a 104-degree fever and was very sick. Some girls in the new group were already doing laundry. In our group, Ellen, who had hiked one day, wanted a "hot shower." Water was heated in a kettle, a bag was filled, and then the water was gradually poured from a spout onto the person showering. We didn't bother.

Namche was a major town with many hotels, shops, and even a bank where money could be changed at certain hours. Prayer flags flew from the tops of many homes. We bought a flashlight and toilet paper, surprised at the variety of materials available, including items from Tibet. Everything had to come at least from Lukla, but probably from Jiri on either a person's or an animal's back. From bottled beer and canned goods to cokes and candy bars, everything was available, and prices were not outrageous. The town had electricity also, but only from 5:00 to 10:00 p.m.

After a full week of walking through small villages beside terraced fields and meeting only local people on the trail, we were amazed by the number of tourists and the crowded city streets. There were no automobiles, of course, but lots of people and animals milled about, some drunk and arguing.

Surrounded by high peaks on all sides, Namche provided a perfect setting for our tents that night, as the towering, sharp snow-covered peaks picked up alpenglow. At last we felt we were truly in the Khumbu. We fell asleep to the gentle sounds of bells as the yaks jostled each other, changing positions, and to the whisper of sleeping bag and tent zippers opening and closing as trekkers settled in for the night.

Historically, Sherpas were herders and traders. Namche Bazaar was the staging point for expeditions over the Nangpa La into Tibet with loads of manufactured goods from India. On the return trip to India from Tibet, Sherpas brought wool, yaks, and salt. Even though some Sherpas tried growing barley, potatoes, and a few vegetables in the barren fields of the Khumbu, the Sherpa economy still relied heavily on trading. Each Saturday at the important weekly market, lowland people came to Namche to sell corn, rice, eggs, vegetables, and other items not grown in Khumbu. During the trekking season, butchers usually slaughtered two or more buffaloes each week. From villages six to ten days' walk from Namche, porters carried their loads to sell their wares directly. Sherpas from all the neighboring villages came to purchase food and to socialize, exchanging money they had received from trekking for goods they required.

Before we embarked on the second part of our trek, Aanu and Baburam discussed the planned itinerary with our group. Originally the two groups were at this point supposed to travel in tandem. But the group that had just flown in was in poor shape and needed more time to acclimatize. Our group was eager to go, wanting to have more time at the higher elevations. Ellen, who had just joined our group, wanted Aanu and Baburam to change the itinerary so that on the return trip the groups would be in Tengboche on one of the days the monastery there celebrated Mani Rimdu. She knew quite a bit about this yearly ritual and said it was one of the main reasons she had joined the trek. Aanu told her he would do what he could, but it would depend on exactly when the ceremony took place.

It had not, he said, been offered as part of the trip. Ellen was very upset about this. We said nothing as we were totally ignorant on the subject. That night when I read about it in our guide book, I wished it could have been included.

Early in the morning before breakfast, those who wanted a short hike visited the National Park Museum with Aanu for fantastic views of the snow-covered mountains: Nuptse, Everest, Lohtse, Ama Dablam, Kantega, Kusum, and Tham Serku. In the foreground was the sacred Khumbila Mountain, which had never been climbed. All dark rock, it had no snow on it. We were told that when Sir Edmund Hillary attempted to climb Khumbila, he felt a heaviness preventing him from continuing beyond a certain point. Supposedly he gave in, saying, "Some mountains should be left unclimbed." Way off in the distance on top of a foothill, we could see the monastery, Tengboche, one of our destinations. The museum's exhibits on Sherpa life and native animals were absorbing. We had breakfast at about 8:00 a.m. after the walk. Many people were taking showers, but we concentrated on changing money and giving tips to the three porters who were returning home: the "kerosene" man, his son Schumann, and a third man.

Although the day was intended for acclimatizing, we started off for the Everest View Hotel (12,740 feet). We reasoned that as long as we felt okay, moving around at these higher elevations would make us better prepared for what was to come. The way up was steep, through city streets, then past a row of many prayer wheels, which we gave a whirl as we went by. Finally, just twenty minutes from the hotel, we reached Shyangboche airstrip. The views of Ama Dablam and Tham Serku were thrilling and a striking contrast to equally dramatic views into the very deep, green valleys below. Through binoculars we could also see Tengboche Monastery, our designated stop on day eleven, and the brown-colored town of Phortse which we would visit near the end of our trip.

I was very hungry and cold when we reached the hotel but quickly recovered after consuming wonderfully delicious potato-and-chicken soup. A Japanese couple sat at a nearby table, accompanied by two oxygen tanks. For an extra fee, the hotel offered either oxygen or a pressurized room to accommodate its guests. As we were leaving, the Japanese man approached to ask Kurt's age and was impressed that Kurt at sixty-five had hiked up from Namche. Because he'd asked us, I asked for his age. He was sixty-seven and had a heart condition. But he had wanted to see Everest before he died, so he and his wife had flown to the nearby airport and then walked over to the hotel, but they had to use oxygen.

The next morning, with all our gear being carried by *dzopchuks*, we left Namche Bazaar heading for Tengboche Monastery. Because it was market day, we spent some time observing the incredible variety of people and expressive faces as well as the goods being exchanged. Quite a lot of toilet paper was for sale, as well as huge stacks of eggs, sodas, sides of yak meat, clothing, almost anything. Some villagers were involved in bargaining. Others sat on rooftops watching the action below them.

After we passed the museum again, the trail continued above the Dudh

Kosi, tracing a beautiful traverse across the hillside. The weather was gorgeous, the views superb. We stopped for a few minutes to take pictures with Mount Everest in the background, then moved onward through beautiful forest. The grade was easy, and everyone was having a great time. The dust, however, was horrendous, stirred up by the *dzopchuks* and hundreds of people now using the trail. Hoping to filter out the dust, I wore my bandana over my nose and mouth like a bandit.

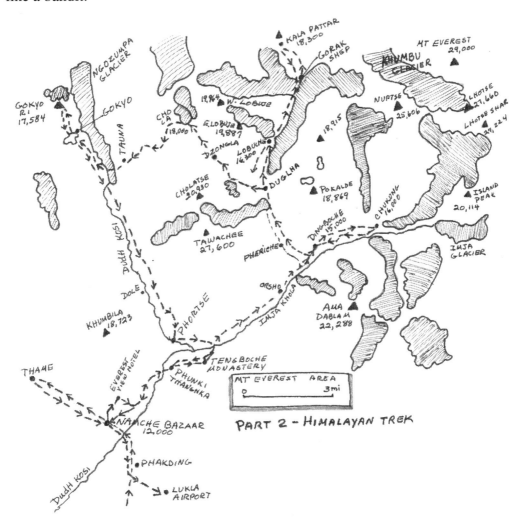

PART 2 - HIMALAYAN TREK

We were surprised when the lunch stop was at a farmhouse prior to the river crossing. But the location was very clean, the floor of the *charpi* had lots of pine needles, and the blue tarp was spread on a grassy area just below a stunning view of Ama Dablam. After lunch when we reached Phunki Thanghka, we saw many other trekking groups crowded together at this standard lunch stop area. I much preferred our stop at the farmhouse. An unusual sight at Phunki Thanghka was the row of large prayer wheels which had been positioned in a stream so that they were turned by water wheels, offering continuous prayers without manual effort.

Before dark we had reached Tengboche, a fantastic place. Monks were busy rebuilding the monastery that had burned in 1989. We watched them painting the inside, where there were several guardian dragons, then had some drinks in a teahouse to pass the time, because only three of our eight *dzopchuks* had arrived. The going price for one of these animals was ten-thousand rupees, about $250. Lovely creatures, these male half-breeds were both strong and docile.

As soon as the sun went down, I felt rather cool. When the wind rose, some of us huddled in the cook tent until the animals carrying our food arrived. While we waited for dinner to be prepared, we visited the monastery to hear the monks chanting as the sun began to set. In order to enter the building, we had to remove our shoes or boots.

The lama sat at one end of the building, near an altar, ringing a bell every once in a while, snapping his fingers and then making a prayer sign. In front of him on either side of a walkway sat two rows of monks, repeatedly chanting or reading the sacred verses. A drummer beat a very rhythmic, almost marching, sound that kept the chanters together. When this stopped, the lama would mutter a few sentences, perhaps directions, and the drums would start again. The drum or gong beats would be single at first, but would develop into a drum roll. At certain times, the long alpenhorns would be blown. Their low-pitched sound reverberated throughout the whole room. At the same time, other monks blew clarinet-like instruments, and some played ramshorns and cymbals. It was a wild aural sensation, capable of transporting one out of oneself. One monk went around lighting candles, carrying incense, and giving the other monks rice or wine. At one point yellow hats were distributed. The monks put these on for a certain part of the service. The hats were tall with a curved top and resembled the yellow feather hats worn by Hawaiian royalty.

Behind one row of the chanting burgundy-robed monks, a novice sat. A Westerner, she wore red with a white prayer scarf. Although the novice did not chant, she prostrated herself at certain times.

On a table in front of the lama were several peacock feathers in a vase. Every once in a while the lama would fling out a black cloth. Near the end, a monk closed the last open window in the monastery. A similar ceremony would be performed just before sunrise when a single window would be opened to welcome the new day.

Our very tasty dinner included yak meat in soft wontons. We ate a lot and slept very well despite noisy laughter nearby. Although the yard of the monastery resembled a tent city because so many trekking groups were stopping there, I was still entranced by the beautiful sight of the full moon passing near Ama Dablam.

The twelfth day on the trail, November 1, began at 4:30 a.m. when we were awakened by drumming and gongs that continued for a long time until the horns started in. By 6:00 a.m. our morning tea arrived, then wash water. We packed up and then made a pre-breakfast trip to the monastery to see the giant Buddha. The statue was two stories high and still in progress, surrounded by many smaller guardians or perhaps other manifestations of himself. It was curious to see a Buddha being made, as it was all in clay. Later the statue would be gilded.

Breakfast was great: cereals, toast, two omelettes, and then we were on our way, picking our path through frost-covered tents and rhododendrons whose leaves were tightly curled against the frost. They would open when the sun shone on them later in the day. Downward we walked for a very short way to Devuche, then up through Pangboche. There I stopped to ask directions when it looked as if I were heading directly into town, instead of bypassing on the main trail.

Near Orsho I talked to a yak driver who wanted to know where I was going, how the trail was over which I had come, and how long it had taken me. All this was in Nepali. Whew!

Higher and higher the trail went until finally it began a traverse over very bare alpine terrain. In gorgeous weather, our efforts were rewarded with constant magnificent views of Ama Dablam, Lhotse, and Dabuche. Because there were no trail signs, I almost took the trail up to Pheriche, but I happened to see Lakpa below me on another trail, and I also questioned a guide coming from that direction.

Pangboche, about 13,000 feet high, was primarily a gray town. The buildings were made of stone, and enclosures for animals had stone walls. Near town, large groups of black birds with red beaks swarmed right in my face-- reminding me of the scary Hitchcock movie *The Birds*.

Our stop for the night was Dingboche, a small village at about 15,000 feet elevation, used primarily in summer. Sherpas with homes lower in the valley own small stone huts in the higher regions and occupy them only in summer while their herds of yaks graze in the surrounding pastures. A few crops, especially barley, are also grown in these high fields. The scenery here was magnificent, but we had to wear all our clothing to keep warm. Hot lemonade also helped. Lunch of grilled-cheese sandwiches, french fries, and baked beans was served inside an inn. It tasted marvelous, but that might have been because high altitudes always make me ravenous.

After three of our *dzopchuks* arrived, two tents were put up in the large yard adjoining the teahouse. By 2:30 p.m. all the animals had arrived, a very pleasant surprise. After dinner we went to bed as it was cold and getting dark. Some people were becoming tired and wished the trek were over.

Each night that we stayed in Dingboche and at higher elevations, our water bottles were filled with boiling water before we went to bed. It was important to have drinking water available at all times, but we also put them inside our sleeping bags to give us some warmth and wore all our clothes inside the bags to remain comfortable. In the morning hot tea and warm water for washing helped get us up for breakfast despite very frosty temperatures. Once the sun rose, however, the temperature became quite pleasant, and we gradually could shed some of our many layers as we hiked along. This was another time when wearing a skirt came in handy.

To get us used to the higher altitude, a walk to Chukkung at 16,000 feet was planned for day thirteen. We would return to sleep at Dingboche. Severe digestive problems had troubled me the night before and sapped my energy, so I moved very slowly on the way to Chukkung, but still it took me only about two hours to get there. Some of us decided to walk beyond Chukkung to see how high we could get, but it soon became clear that we were reaching the current limit of our acclimation. First Patti turned back, then Ellen and Shirley, then Kurt. Baburam, the chief guide who asked us to call him "Babu," went back to get the camera from Kurt so I could take some pictures on the higher ridge. Jeff and Babu were heading for Chukkung peak, but Harvey and I decided to go only as far as the ridge where we could get a look into the declivity on the other side.

Arriving at the ridge, Harvey asked if I wanted to eat some lunch. But I knew instantly that it was time for me to turn back. The feeling that I was about to vomit was becoming stronger, and the odor of egg yolks that always indicated imminent vomiting when I was a child was increasing. As we started down, I threw up and was somewhat concerned because the fluid seemed tinged with red. I was convinced that I had altitude sickness or that I might have it. Then again, perhaps we had eaten something red for breakfast, or the night before, but I couldn't remember. I slowed my pace, but vomited again. Harvey was really worried; but I explained that this often happened to me on hikes and that I felt much better as soon as I had thrown up. He thought I should rest, but I knew I could keep going. I also thought the lower altitude of camp at Dingboche would be the best medicine.

We were back by 2:00 p.m. I had some hot tea in the lodge and ate some cookies, but I really felt lousy. I did get up for teatime and ate a lot of cookies and had coffee, but immediately went back to rest. Just before dinner I lost all I had consumed. Popcorn, which I dearly loved, was served at dinner, but I was afraid to eat it--too much roughage. Instead I took comfort in two bowls of yak soup and some rice. Still feeling weak, I needed to go right back to bed. But before I did, I took a moment to marvel at the beautiful mountains now even closer: Ama Dablam, Lhotse, Lhotse Shar, and Island Peak.

In the morning, I felt fine and enjoyed a very good breakfast. The entire camp was moving from Dingboche to Lobuche at 16,300 feet. Everything started out a bit later than usual, which suited me just fine. Kurt had time to talk to a seventy-year-old woman from Schleswig-Holstein, Germany, who had been to Nepal six times.

The sun was out as we bypassed the village of Pheriche and continued on a long traverse, hiking over part of the terminal moraine of the Khumbu Glacier, and finally crossing the glacier itself on a bridge just before a short uphill climb to reach the village of Duglha. We reached Duglha by 10:00 a.m. after only two hours of walking and ate outside in the yard of a teahouse, enjoying the usual cheese, curried potatoes, *chapatti* (freshly cooked flat-bread), tuna, sardines, and lemonade. The *charpi* was very disgusting according to Patti, Bill, and Kurt, the worst they had ever seen. I decided not to use it.

The higher altitude seemed to be affecting all of us in some way. At lunch, Ellen insisted that I had taken her walking stick. When I pointed out that the one I had was probably mine because it had my name carved on it, she found her own elsewhere.

After lunch we followed the trail higher on the moraine. It seemed a steep way to go, and we did not move very fast. When we saw some yaks with balloons tied to them, some jokers said it helped to lighten the load the animals carried. At the pass we saw stone monuments in memory of six Sherpas who died in an avalanche during the 1970 Japanese skiing expedition on Everest. There were close to twenty other monuments for climbers who had perished since then. Most of the monuments were groups of stones, but there were a few carved mani walls. One porter with a heavy load also carried a sizeable stone in one hand. When he reached the pass, he set the stone up and said a small prayer before moving on.

Beyond the pass, the trail was basically a gentle upward traverse with a stream-crossing on rock and snow. Jeff had developed some stomach problems and also felt somewhat weak from his climb of Chukkung Peak with Babu. Patti also felt weak, but none of us was as sick as the folks in the other group, who were now a day behind us.

When we reached our destination, Lobuche, by 2:30 p.m., most of the tents were already there. An hour later when the wind came up, it seemed very cold. Tea and biscuits in the afternoon tasted good, but after dinner I had diarrhea and also began vomiting. The malady continued throughout the night. Whenever I opened my eyes, I saw bright flashes of light, but I didn't know where they came from or what they meant. I was afraid they might be connected with my sickness. Fortunately, in the morning they were gone.

Meanwhile, Shirley had become very sick with a severe headache. We all had mild headaches, but these could be somewhat controlled by Advil. Hers was another matter. She could not eat or drink and simply stayed in her sleeping bag in her tent.

The next day, I also decided to stay in camp and rest, hoping to recover from whatever I had picked up. Only four from our group left to hike to the Everest base camp by way of Gorak Shep. Kurt came back first about 10:30 a.m. He could not make it even to Gorak Shep. Ellen came next. She had reached Gorak Shep, but then turned back. Finally about 2:00 p.m., Harvey arrived in camp, having turned back when his knee gave out. Only Jeff kept going, but even he did not make it to the Everest Base Camp. He said he would have made it if Harvey hadn't tried to keep up with him. Our group spirit was definitely suffering in the high altitude.

My condition improved during the rest day, and I was able to enjoy both breakfast and lunch. To pass the time I tried to wash my skirt in an icy stream, but it froze stiff before it dried. It was hard to appreciate the magnificent scenery with all the sickness. But it was still a thrill to be sitting at Lobuche at 16,000 feet.

The Gokyo extension of our trek depended on whether Cho La (Chhugyuma Pass) was open or not. Kurt and I had been worried that it would be closed and we wouldn't be allowed to take that route to Gokyo Ri. When we first learned that the pass was open, without ice or treacherous deep snow, we had been delighted. Now we worried whether we could make it physically. The pass was at 17,615 feet, and the way up and down involved a very steep scramble on large boulders.

On our second day in Lobuche, the other group we had met in Namche Bazaar finally joined us. Their experience had been quite different from ours. While we had enjoyed surprisingly varied and very delicious meals, they claimed they had eaten *dhal bat* (lentils and rice) every night. On the other hand, their chief guide, Aanu, was excellent. Knowledgeable about this part of Nepal he had given them a great deal of information. His assistant guides also respected him.

Baburam, our chief guide, rarely answered questions directly. At first, we thought it was just a language problem. But when he didn't even know the names of some of the peaks we were looking at, we believed he was simply inexperienced. He had been on previous treks, but only as an assistant guide. This was his first trip as a chief guide, and the tension between him and his assistant guides was obvious. The behavior and availability of these assistants improved considerably, once Aanu was on the scene. Someone suggested there was a problem because Baburam was a Hindu and the guides were Buddhist, but he had no such problems with the cooking crew. In fact, we often relied on the cooks and their helpers when no one else was around. Though Baburam had difficulty managing his assistants, he did show considerable concern about the well-being of his charges. In order to make sure that we were comfortable, he often expended an enormous amount of personal energy trying to make things right that had gone wrong. These extraordinary efforts would not have been necessary if he had been a better manager. A very likable fellow, Baburam wasn't quite ready to be a chief guide.

Four trekkers from Aanu's group were turning back, either from sickness or because they were simply tired of trekking, even though they had only started in Namche. In our group, Shirley was still very sick. She had not eaten anything for two days, had a devastating headache, and was becoming dehydrated. Although she had her heart set on reaching Kala Pattar, she wouldn't be able to do it. She decided reluctantly that she had to return to a lower altitude. Patti, her sister, and Bill planned to leave with Shirley in the morning. My concerns about sunburn on my hands and face, despite wearing a broad-brimmed hat and seeking shade, seemed minor in comparison.

On November 5, we had been walking for sixteen days. The daily routine and the daily walks had almost become a way of life. Because I felt fine, I started off with the rest of the group who were going to Gorak Shep. Lying at 16,770 feet, Gorak Shep had been the base camp for the 1952 Swiss Everest Expedition.

We moved fairly fast and were there by 9:30 a.m. With time to spare, I had some noodle soup at the Yeti Tea House and then started up the trail to Kala Pattar slowly, so as not to be gasping for breath. Kurt decided he didn't want to go any farther than Gorak Shep. The trail to Kala Pattar began steeply up the grassy slopes west of Gorak Shep to a shelf at the foot of Pumori. Standing on that broad shelf, I could see the entire south face of Everest as well as the pass between Nepal and Tibet. From the top of Kala Pattar, the peak of Everest was quite visible and awesome, rising an additional 10,000 feet above us. I was almost to the top of Kala Pattar (18,300 ft.) when Babu showed up, saying he'd go with me the rest of the way. Although I was not having any problems, he hovered nearby. Kala Pattar is a small peak at the end of a ridge extending from a lower slope of the conical peak Pumori (23,273 feet), a snow-covered beauty that towered overhead. The views of Pumori, Everest, Nuptse, and the stunning Khumbu icefall were truly spectacular. And I rejoiced in knowing that I had actually reached 18,300 feet. The descent to Lobuche and camp was easy, but it seemed endless because there were many uphill climbs. I had to rest as soon as I got back and wasn't too perky even by dinner time. But I was glad I had made it. From our group Jeff, Sherri, Ellen, and Harvey also reached the top of Kala Pattar.

Having reached the farthest point on the planned itinerary, most of the guides, cooks, and trekkers left in the morning to return to Lukla and the airport there. Jeff, Kurt, and I were joined by Alan and Mike from the other group for the five-day extension trek to Gokyo.

From Lobuche, as a large group of people took the trail downwards, we five with a cook, two guides, and two young female porters began a traverse to Dzongla where we would be able to pick up the trail to Cho La. On a somewhat barren plain, we stopped at noon for lunch, but then our guides decided that we should spend the night there before attempting the pass. Our revised schedule now included two days at Tengboche for the Mani Rimdu festival, a spectacular fall ritual performed by costumed monks, and a day side-trip to the monastery in Thame, in addition to our time in Gokyo on the other side of Cho La. We were surprised but quite pleased that Mani Rimdu, the event Ellen had wanted to see, was now included, even though we hadn't asked for it.

As we approached the pass, the terrain became very rocky. The trail seemed more like rock scrambling than like walking. Jeff was in the lead and thought he'd found the trail. I followed him, climbing straight up a ten-foot-high boulder, using cracks and crevices as handholds and footholds. One of the guides wanted to give me a boost on the first step, but he was not sure whether it was proper to touch my rear. Finally, he did it anyway and I moved to the top. Kurt was starting to climb the rock wall below me. Jeff motioned and yelled to go back, that it wasn't the trail after all. Suddenly I heard a yell and a moan and looked back to see Kurt crumpled over in pain. A guide on top of the rock wall had reached down and grabbed Kurt's hand, trying to help by pulling him upwards. Kurt was facing the wall, looking straight ahead, not upwards. He had only raised his arm above his head to feel for the next good handhold. He wasn't prepared to move his body upwards with the pull, and his shoulder slipped out of place.

We had almost reached the pass where the snow lay thick, but after that we knew we would have a long way down to Gokyo. On the other hand, we knew it was quite a long way back the other way, too. I asked Kurt what he wanted to do. We thought it was best to go on, if he could stand it, since once we were over the pass, he and I could follow a well-marked trail on our own down to the Kunde hospital, and this would not prevent the others from going on to Gokyo. We made a makeshift sling out of my long underwear--not much else was available-- and started moving slowly across the snow. I took Kurt's camera and tried to take as many pictures as possible, since he was in no condition to do anything. The pain was excruciating even when he didn't move. And he had to keep moving to reach a safe place before dark.

As we crossed the snow, we met several parties going the other direction. One group told us to go back the way we came, but they had not been over that part of the trail. They knew that the part we were coming to would be rough, but we knew going back would also be difficult. Another man in a group from Boston said his wife had frequently dislocated her shoulder, but she had been able to get it back in place by leaning over and moving it a certain way while he pushed against it. He gave Kurt some codeine, and Kurt tried the suggested method to no avail.

The snow crossing was not a big problem as it was fairly level until the end where it slanted towards the rocks and was wet from melting. Kurt managed that all right, despite the horrible pain. The rocks that followed, however, were very difficult for him because the way down was very steep and broken up. Jeff walked in front, bracing his feet against Kurt's so Kurt wouldn't topple over. I followed behind to make sure that Kurt did not topple backwards. Slowly, very slowly we made our way down the steepest part of the trail. Some of the guides went ahead to prepare lunch in a more or less level spot. We ate some hardboiled eggs and tuna fish but didn't stop to rest. Lunch was already later than usual. After lunch, Alan and Mike went ahead with one of the guides.

When Kurt, Jeff, and I had descended to about 16,000 feet from the pass (17,615), we met a large French group. Two of them came running up to us and almost forced us to swallow the pill they gave each of us. They said they were a paramedical group; one man claimed to be a doctor. Because we moved slowly, they were certain that we had altitude problems. The doctor kept examining Kurt's eyes and making him breathe. Finally we were able to convince the man that the only problem was the dislocated shoulder. For that they could do nothing, they said. The doctor fiddled around with our makeshift sling, but didn't improve things. The group advised us not to stay the night with them but to continue down somehow as it would be very cold. We had never intended to stay with them and would gladly have continued down sooner, but they kept us there with their constant useless examinations and hovering. Finally they did give us some tea and cookies which helped a little.

Unfortunately, from where we left the French group, we had to ascend and cross some hills to make sure that we descended into the correct valley for Tauna and the shorter trail to Gokyo Ri. Psychologically it was very disheartening to go up again, when we knew we'd have to descend whatever altitude we gained. Just as the trail became indistinct and we were trying to decide how to proceed, we met a man who had been with Outward Bound and was now living in Nepal and leading treks. He was heading towards the pass, but when he heard Kurt's story, he stopped to help. Fortuitously we met him near a rock that was about waist high and as large as a table. The man offered to work on Kurt's shoulder and had Kurt lie face down on the rock, with his arm dangling at the side. He next gave Kurt his camera bag to hold, as he massaged the shoulder and spoke softly to Kurt, trying to get him to relax as much as possible. All at once we heard a small cracking sound, the shoulder was back in place, and the pain was gone. We could hardly believe it. Of course, Kurt was exhausted from the pain and the procedure, but we knew from previous experience that we would not have to go to the Kunde hospital after all.

We moved on slowly. Already exhausted, Kurt tended to stumble, and then the growing darkness slowed us even more. Because my flashlight wasn't working, we tried to stay close to Jeff, who at least had a headlamp. After a while, the one remaining guide left us on our own, saying he was going for help so they could carry Kurt. At that point we didn't really care whether the guide stayed or not. Even though the trail was not well marked, we knew that we could get down the hill somehow, especially when the rising full moon somewhat improved visibility. We were surprised when three guides returned without a stretcher, but they explained they intended to carry Kurt on their backs in turn. After Kurt declined their offer, one led the way while the other two walked beside Kurt, gently supporting him so he wouldn't stumble.

At last, a long way off, we saw a light in a farmhouse and were most grateful for it. We did not expect to have anything to eat, however, because we had been expected to reach Gokyo in time for dinner. Instead of carrying supplies with us over the pass, other porters had been sent to Gokyo with our food over a less demanding trail from Phortse. What a wonderful surprise it was to learn that our treasured cook, Ekraj, and his helper had already made arrangements for us with the farm owner. Our tents were set up in the farmyard, and Ekraj had even purchased and cooked some greens and rice so we could have what to us was a very delicious meal. Mike and Alan were glad to hear that

Kurt's shoulder was back in place. They were afraid we all might have to turn back.

Even though it was only 8:00 p.m., we immediately went to sleep, thankful that the shoulder was back in place, that we'd been fed, and that we had a tent in which to sleep. We had been hiking since 6:00 a.m. without our usual two-hour lunch break, and we'd traveled at very high altitudes over difficult, treacherous terrain with Kurt suffering excruciating pain and Jeff and I concerned and worried about him and about what would happen next.

Up fairly early the next morning, we reached Gokyo by lunch time. Kurt, still worn out from his ordeal, moved very slowly, falling behind everyone else, but all went well, even though Alan screamed and yelled at the guides because he thought one of them should be walking with Kurt, in case he had trouble. On the way, we crossed the moraine and then the endless gray crust of the Ngozumpa Glacier. We saw very few crevasses, and the snow and ice were so dirty that we had trouble believing it was actually a glacier we were crossing. We threw rocks on some frozen ponds we passed, but the ice was so thick that our rocks just stayed on the surface.

After intersecting the trail that went downwards to the village of Phortse, we arrived at a small lake with high, snowy peaks in the background--a beautiful sight. Next came a very large lake on which Gokyo was situated at 15,700 feet. At Gokyo, we met Ang Tsering who was guiding a trip for Mountain Travels Sobek. He had previously climbed to the summit of Everest, but despite this claim to fame, even he was having porter problems and asked if we had met any porters on our way to Gokyo.

Instead of our scheduled full day, we had only the afternoon in which to climb Gokyo Ri, a peak of 17,584 feet towering above the lake. Still exhausted from the trauma of the dislocation, Kurt could walk only as far as the lake, where he had to rest. Jeff had already taken off for the summit on his own. Mike and Alan insisted that a guide must go with them, so Angawas did. I thought the trail, though steep, was pretty obvious, so I went by myself. I wasn't sure how far I would be able to go. My pace felt very slow, but I had no trouble breathing and I never had to use the rest step, a technique often used on high altitude climbs. After stepping forward with the right foot, the hiker does not continue forward with the left foot, but only brings it up even with the right. He then takes several deep breaths, exhaling explosively before moving the left foot forward and repeating the same process. Progress is slow but steady, and a sufficient supply of oxygen is maintained.

Thinking I might not make it to the summit, I took many pictures on the way up. Then, just as I told myself that if I didn't reach the top in the next twenty minutes, I'd turn back, a hiker going down informed me that the white pole I saw, not far off, was the summit. Soon I could see that I would make the ridge. Once there, it was only a short way over more or less level rock piles to where the prayer flags and white pole marked the summit. The views were fantastic. Snow-covered monster mountains formed a perfect circle around me. Cho Oyo, Everest, Nuptse, Lhotse, Kantega, Solatche, Duboche. Ama Dablam, so impressive from one of our lunch stops, looked like a baby mountain in comparison to the big guys. I met Jeff on top. Two trekkers planned to stay on the summit for sunset, but during my hike up, clouds had rolled in below us filling the Gokyo Valley, and I was concerned how that might affect visibility. I took the most direct way down, noticing some shortcuts I'd not taken on the way up. Still it was a long, steep way to go. After I passed below the clouds, a beautiful scene appeared below me–the lakes at Gokyo with the village beside them and high mountains behind.

Angawas, who had guided Alan and Mike to the top, stayed with me on the way down, chatting as we walked. I tried to use as much Nepali as I knew, but he was much more fluent in English than I was in his language. He was twenty-five years old, had been married for one year, and had climbed with a British/Norwegian group on Ama Dablam in October, when the snow was almost waist deep. Angawas asked about my family and wanted to know when I had learned Nepali. He complimented me for learning a lot from just one visit.

That night in Gokyo, a Sherpa party in the lodge went on and on. It would have been fun to go to watch the dance, but I was tired out from the day's trip and just lay in our tent. After the repetitious music accompanied by the drumbeat stopped, I heard lots of giggling from the tent where the two young female porters and the handsome, young male kitchen helper were staying.

On our twentieth day of hiking, November 9, we began a long day's descent to Phortse, after a curious incident at breakfast. The five of us had taken all the pancakes we wanted, and only one was left. If we had wanted more, the cooks would have made more. Jeff took the last pancake, just to avoid waste. Immediately Alan called him on it, saying he should have asked if anyone else wanted it, or it should have been divided into five parts. When Jeff said he didn't think it was a critical issue, Alan challenged him to step outside the tent to settle it. Jeff didn't move and Alan left. I thought Alan must be having either an altitude problem or a control issue.

Although the trail was generally downhill, there were also a surprising number of uphill segments. Along the way, we saw several beautiful *chortens* (mini-*stupas*) and stopped for lunch by an impressive waterfall. When the porters still had not caught up with us after a fairly long wait, Kurt and I decided to go ahead as he was moving more slowly than the rest of the group. Finally we reached Phortse, where we had tea and dinner inside a very prosperous farmhouse, though our tents were pitched in the farmyard. Carefully passing by the cattle on the lower floor of the farmhouse, we climbed the stairs to the family's quarters. The kitchen area contained several huge copper kettles, a sign of wealth. We sat in one part of the kitchen where our dinner was cooked while one of the guides tried to get a lantern started. The dinner of roast potatoes, macaroni, and pizza made from Swiss chard and yak cheese was delicious.

Nearby, the family prepared potato pancakes for themselves, rolling bits of dough into long strings and then cooking it. The farmer was a friend of the father of Baadu, one of our guides.

When it seemed warmer in the morning, we ate breakfast outside where we could watch three adorable baby yaks. The farmer's young son was very curious about us. Because he had been very helpful and was fascinated by my chapstick, I gave it to him along with a pen.

After a very steep downhill, the trail traversed a rather exposed hillside, crossed the river, and then again went very steeply uphill amidst bushes and trees to reach Tengboche monastery. Quite a bit of progress had been made since our earlier visit. The windows had been painted, and the monastery had a more finished look. Many people selling items were already gathering in preparation for Mani Rimdu. Tents were crowded together on the flat area outside the monastery, for quite a few trekking groups planned to stay for the ceremonies.

. Mani Rimdu, the most spectacular ritual event of Tengboche Monastery, is performed once a year by the monks during the ninth month of the Tibetan calendar (late October or early November). Originally performed only in Tibet, it first came to Tengboche in the 1930s. After the destruction of Tibetan monasteries, the dance was now performed only in the Solu Khumbu region of Nepal. Because it concurs with the post-harvest lull, Mani Rimdu provides an opportunity for Sherpas to meet with friends and relatives as well as to obtain spiritual blessings. It is primarily a religious observance performed for believers. Tourists are permitted to watch and at one point in the dance sequence to participate. Westerners, primarily trekkers, probably made up only ten percent of the audience. Most people were Buddhists who had traveled from near and far to be there. In contrast to the more solemn, restrained daily evening ritual we had observed earlier, Mani Rimdu was noisy, loud, and lively. If the previous chanting resembled a conservative Roman Catholic or Episcopal service, Mani Rimdu was more like a Pentecostal revival meeting, a valid but more extroverted and energetic mode of religious expression.

Four major components of Mani Rimdu are the mandala–creating sacred space, the *rilbu*–creation and distribution of spiritual medicine, the dances–a visual drama, and the fire ceremony–disintegration of the mandala. The thirteen religious dances of Mani Rimdu recreate legendary events concerning the introduction of Buddhism to Tibet by the omnipotent patron saint, Guru Rinpoche. Throughout the dances, symbolic demons are conquered, dispelled, or converted to benign powers as the forces of order and righteousness clash with those of chaos. We were privileged to see the rilbu distribution and the dances.

From reading our guide-book, we had a general idea of what to expect, but we didn't learn the significance of what we were seeing until I later bought an explanatory pamphlet in Namche Bazaar on our way back to Lukla. Some actions were fairly obvious, but others were too obscure to guess correctly. It was hard for us to recognize the fearful-looking demons as agents for good. But later we learned that many of these fierce devils had been converted into powerful protectors–a clever way of dealing with fears and anxieties. Furthermore, these former practitioners of evil would be great protection, as they would have inside information on how best to defeat any new evil demons that might appear. So vivid were all the dances that they were unforgettable, but I still took many notes so that later I could try to make sense of what I had actually seen. Kurt's photographs were stunning.

On the morning of November 11, the low tones of the long horns continued for quite a long time, as if announcing something. Then conchs were blown alternating with clarinets, and finally the horns began again. The monks making the music were inside the monastery, leaning out of the windows when they blew the horns. Crowds of tourists and locals were everywhere trying to see everything. A pathway had been laid out, marked with white chalk. A stately procession came through the monastery doors, went down the steps, and followed the pathway to a pavilion set up outside. All of the monks wore the yellow curved hats that resembled the hats of Hawaiian royalty. The donors, wealthy Sherpas who had made or indicated their intention to make large donations to the monastery, carried prayer flags. One person wearing a dragon mask appeared. Another wore a mask depicting an old, Caucasian man. The lama and the monks all moved to a small pavilion while the Nepalese faithful assembled themselves on carpets. Monks were served tea from huge pots sitting on copper braziers in which coals were burning. Rice was thrown in the air while packets containing a rectangular block of something, a white prayer scarf, and an airmail envelope were given to each monk in no apparent order. Some of the youngest monks didn't get envelopes but got cash instead.

Next, handsome Nepalese women wearing fur-lined, brocaded hats with ear-flaps, prostrated themselves in front of the lama, bowing three times, after which they went up to the lama for blessings. When they came back from the pavilion, they gave money and scarves to the monks. Some older women who apparently hadn't seen each other since the last festival were showing off the newest grandchild in their family to each other. People, mostly women, tried to give each other money. We couldn't tell whether they were paying off debts or just trying to give each other gifts.

After tea was served by the monks, fans were put into the spouts of the large tea kettles. A monk went around carrying a small container with feathers on it from which he poured what resembled holy oil into people's hands. He approached the oldest people first. Sometimes the recipients tasted it, then put it on their hands and heads. The sanctified *rilbu* pills were given out to people sitting on the carpet, and this was followed by *truh* (holy water) which symbolically cleanses the body of physical and spiritual impurities. Devotees believe the pills empower them with the courage to follow the path of unselfish wisdom. The pills were also said to temper the body against the harsh physical realities of Sherpa life. Next *chang* (barley beer), intended as a long-life blessing, was distributed. The monks also distributed wrapped candies and something resembling potato chips to the worshipers. At the conclusion of the *rilbu* offering, the monastic procession left for the monastery courtyard. No westerners participated in this part of Mani Rimdu, though we were allowed to watch, and many tourists took photographs of the activities.

By nine the next morning, a large number of tourists and Nepalese people had already gathered in the monastery courtyard. About ten, a helicopter landed, making the yaks go wild. When the long alpenhorns and the conchs started sounding, we knew something would be happening–eventually, so we followed the crowds inside.

In the center of the open courtyard stood an altar holding *torma* (ornately sculptured butter and barley) offerings. The altar faced the stairs going up to a platform from which one entered the monastery. It was on this platform that some of the musicians stood wearing the feathered yellow hats. On the left side of the stairs was a balcony with a shade drawn in front of it. As the horns continued, a procession escorted the lama, the current Rinpoche of Tengboche, from inside the monastery to his seat in this balcony on the north side of the courtyard. Directly below the lama were senior monks and monks who played drums and cymbals to establish the rhythm of the dances.

When the dance began, the drawn shade in front of the lama was pulled up. Crowds of spectators circled the open square area looking for seats. Some bleacher-like benches had been set up under the first floor overhang, and there were spaces upstairs. We found a good spot surrounded by villagers who had come from far and near for the celebration. People were squeezing in every-where. Tourists with huge cameras were shoving themselves rudely into the best places for photos. When they blocked another photographer's view there were protests. Most Nepalese people at least said the equivalent of "excuse me" as they stepped over or on you trying to find a spot. A group of nuns with shaved heads and wearing burgundy robes sat together on a blanket in the front. As the music began, two players alternated on the long horns so that the deep sonorous tone was continuous, a never-ending Om. Above this sound and the constant drumbeat, the double-reeded instruments swirled intricate, but repetitive melody.

A few conch blasts heralded the arrival of the first dance: the dance of the golden nectar. Several monks dressed as *Ngak-pa*, wearing black hats crowned with one skull to portray the impermanence of life, descended single file into the courtyard, preceded by an escort of monks playing cymbals and gongs. *Ngak-pa* are benevolent beings who work at dispelling demons and who are able to directly invoke deities. Each black-hat dancer held a silver chalice which was periodically filled by the *Chor-pen* (ritual master) with a *chang* offering representing *duh-tse*, the nectar of life. Then *chang* and rice were thrown skyward as an offering to *Gyalwa Rig Nga* as well as to all the other Buddhist gods. The dance concluded with a symbolic sharing of *chang* by the performers and spectators. This ritual is similar to an invocation and is used to ensure the success of the endeavor. It offers thanks to the gods and welcomes them to the performance.

In the second dance, four energetic performers, representing *King-pa* or couriers of *Guru Rinpoche's* essential wisdom, descended into the courtyard. *King-pa* are lower level deities. Two dancers representing males carried cymbals and wore red and white masks. The two representing females carried drums and wore green and blue masks. Three flags representing the Buddhist trinity topped the masks. The lively dance and its symmetry heralded the entrance of *Guru Rinpoche*, a bodhisattva responsible for introducing Buddhism to Tibet. Each year the monks create, decorate, and paint new paper mache masks for the event. The costumes of rich brocaded fabric were also quite colorful. Some dancers wore traditional Tibetan boots with turned-up toes, but under some long skirts the latest Nikes or Reeboks could be seen.

In a spectacular entrance heralded by a full contingent of reverent monks, *Guru Rinpoche* made his appearance in the wrathful form of his demon-fighting manifestation--*Dorje Throlo*. The dancer, wearing a black mask crowned with five skulls, slowly descended into the courtyard to the accompaniment of drums and horns. A third eye on his forehead denoted omniscience. His ivory apron indicated essential power. He circled the altar three times, attacking the origins of human suffering (greed, ignorance, hatred). The dancer held a *dorje* (thunderbolt) and *pur-ba* (symbolic dagger). After he sat down, he was given an offering of gratitude consisting of *chang* and *tso* (edible *tsampa*). *Tsampa* is a thick moldable paste made from roasted and ground barley. The horns sounded again, and he slowly ascended back into the monastery.

Next six dancers representing *Ngak-pa* descended single file into the courtyard. This time each *Ngak-pa* wore a golden hat and played a small drum while proceeding clockwise about the central pillar. These costumed monks then reentered the monastery in pairs. This dance commemorated the conversion of the demons into protectors of the faith.

Announced by the blowing of *Kang-ling* (thigh bone trumpets), two skeleton figures representing *Thur-dag* or "lords of the universal cemetery" appeared in the courtyard. Following a short dance, two more *Ngak-pa* entered. Through a mystical invocation from which no demon can escape, they lured evil spirits into a small human figure made of *tsampa* (a thick paste made from roasted and ground barley). After symbolically dispelling the demons with daggers, the *Ngak-pa* reentered the monastery. The Skeleton dancers then searched the courtyard for *pam-ro*, a rag doll representing a corpse whose soul had been reborn in another body. When they found it, they abused and mocked the doll while dancing clockwise around the central pillar.

Supposedly a comic interlude, the next dance featured a decrepit old man who entered the courtyard and bungled through a ritual white-scarf-offering to the head lama.

For us, the high point was the seventh dance. Whirling slowly, the grinning masked demon wearing a brightly colored wide-sleeved tunic, an apron of ivory, and a necklace of carved miniature skulls lunged towards his counterpart, displaying in one hand a symbolic human heart, in the other Brahma's sign of power, the thunderbolt. Announced by conch shell trumpets, the low rumble of twenty-foot-long horns, and the steady throb of drums, five more creatures swirled into the monastery's courtyard, banners waving above their huge, grotesque heads. Some had only one eye. Some had oversized fangs. Brandishing daggers, dolls, ropes, spears, cups, bows and arrows, hooks, a mirror, and an iron wolf, all weapons or symbols in the celebration of Buddha's triumph over the powers of evil, the masked dancers hopped in slow circles to the right, then to the left, as the hypnotic chanting rumble of burgundy-robed monks rose and fell, punctuated by gongs and cymbals. Originally these creatures were *Bon* or pre-Buddhist deities who tried to prevent the establishment of Buddhism in Tibet. After defeating them, *Guru Rinpoche* offered them a choice between becoming protectors of the new religion or inevitable self-destruction. Since then, they have worked tirelessly as protectors of Buddhism.

In the eighth dance, two black *Mi-nak*, henchmen of the god *Zur-ra*, descended into the courtyard, furiously battled negative forces with ritualistic sabers, and reentered the monastery. A dancer representing the god *Zur-ra* then appeared, preceded in elaborate pageantry by seven monks. Following a short dance, *Zur-ra* seated himself. The two *Mi-nak* dancers reentered the courtyard, this time with black ropes to symbolically incapacitate hindrances to the religion.

Next, five dancers representing *Khan-dro* or the five spiritual families danced clockwise about the central pillar three times, each carrying an hour-glass-shaped drum and a bell with a *dorje* handle. To complete the dance, they formed a line on the north side of the courtyard facing the head lama and offered a prayer.

Dance ten was another comic interlude. Called "The Yogi and the Novice," it was a long improvisational act, full of derisive scenes. Originally the novice had been played by a monk wearing Sherpa clothing who sat in the audience. When we were there, however, the yogi began by playing innumerable tricks on the audience. Pretending to give blessings, he then threw dirt or yak dung on the spectators. When he tired of this, the yogi, using gestures, managed to convince a tourist from the audience to be his assistant or novice. The assistant, however, was always tricked in some way and then beaten for his mistakes or dirt was thrown on him. The audience and the monks found this slapstick hilarious. The victim had to continue in this role until he found another person to take his place.

The first "volunteer" was a trekker to whom Jeff from our group had been talking. After a few minutes, he persuaded Jeff to be the second volunteer. Jeff at times would tease the monk in return or make fun of him, though Jeff didn't want to push it too far, because he wasn't sure what would be deemed offensive. The outline of the action was that the yogi was trying to teach his

113

apprentice the proper way to do things related to ritual, but no matter what the apprentice did, the yogi deemed it incorrect.

In the next dance, two dancers representing minor deities entered the courtyard from the eastern gateway. After dancing around the pillar three times, they picked up some *torma* offerings from the altar and said a short prayer. They then danced, threw the offerings outside the courtyard, and exited into the monastery.

Four dancers next moved clockwise about the altar while reciting a short prayer. Each carried a sword to dispel symbolic demons within the *ling-ka* (a human figure made of tsampa) by mutilating the figure. Following a short dance with swords, the performers reentered the monastery.

In the next dance, two *Ngak-pa* danced a half circle and then performed a prayer. The ritual master took one of three special *tormas* on the altar and threw it out the eastern gateway of the courtyard while the *Ngak-pa* began another short dance. The other two special *tormas* were then given to the dancers who threw them outside the main gateway.

For the grand finale, all the dance participants in various costumes entered the courtyard, formed a circle, and performed a short dance. A footed bowl was then carried around the altar to gather demons and other enemies. Next it was flipped upside-down imprisoning the demons under a symbolic mountain. A *dorje* placed upon the container represented the final destruction of the demons underneath the bowl. After a dance of celebration, the bowl was brought to the lama who placed some rice in it as a blessing of purification.

Though somewhat incomprehensible at the time and lasting all day long with some repetitious parts, the colorful dances as well as the ceremonies taking place on the first day of Mani Rimdu were an incredible experience, like nothing we had ever seen, giving us a fascinating glimpse into Nepalese culture. The irony was that Ellen Friedman, who had desperately wanted to rearrange the trekking schedule so that she would be in Tengboche for Mani Rimdu, had already flown back to California. On the shorter trip she had chosen, she passed through Tengboche five days earlier than we did. We had been totally ignorant about the ceremony, but happened to be there for these amazing sights because our schedule had been rearranged to make it possible. We never knew whether the guides would have done this on their own or whether it happened because Ellen had brought it to their attention.

During a break for lunch, I noticed that one of our girl porters had a large tear in her sarong. I made signs that I had a needle and thread and would sew it. She and I went into a tent and she unrolled it enough so I could repair the tear. As I finished, before I could stop her, she put her head on my feet, showing the ultimate sign of respect. I was quite touched by this gesture.

After our two-day stay in Tengboche, we felt rested and ready to go on. Now we hiked back on a familiar trail to Namche Bazaar. We had lunch at the same farmhouse with the nice toilet and the great view of Ama Dablam and passed once more the water-driven prayer wheels. In no time at all, it seemed we were at Namche. This time we tented in the yard of another inn, as Aanu's place was taken up with other trekkers, or maybe they just spread the business around. We ate our meals in Aanu's Inn. In the afternoon we went to Khumbu Lodge for tea and talked to some Australians and a Californian who were going to Kala Pattar. From street vendors, we bought cymbals, a yak bell, and a silver belt buckle, such as married women wear instead of wedding rings.

A six-hour round-trip to the village of Thame and its monastery was scheduled for the next day. Branching off from the Everest View Hotel trail, the Thame trail curved around the hillside on a lovely forested path, really pleasant hiking. The guides carried Kurt's pack and were good at pointing out birds, mostly pheasants. We went through several villages, passed a nunnery, and hiked up a steep hill and then down again. Just before crossing a high bridge, we saw a huge waterfall at the side of the trail. In vivid colors, fantastic paintings of two *Rinpoches* adorned a huge boulder wall near the bridge crossing. Water had eaten holes through some rocks creating a very spectacular area. The hike was fairly strenuous, and we were getting tired even before the switchbacks up to Thame where there was a reservoir. We'd seen electric poles without the wires all along the way and learned later that a project was underway to bring electricity to Thame. After pausing briefly at the reservoir, we trudged up the steep hillside to the monastery and walked by a very long mani wall. From the Thame Monastery, built into the hillside, we had terrific views of the surrounding countryside. Mani Rimdu is also celebrated at Thame, but only after the spring full moon. Although we carried lunch with us, when we reached a teahouse below Thame, we enjoyed wonderful, invigorating soup and milk tea while talking to other trekkers--a doctor from Germany and a woman with a slightly French accent who wore a red lace blouse, tight velvet Capri pants, espadrilles, and a forest-green floor-length cape. We saw ceiling-high stacks of stored cow dung on the first floor below the lunchroom. It would be good fuel when winter weather arrived. We had used such fires for warmth at higher elevations and were pleasantly surprised to learn that the dried dung really didn't have any odor when it burned.

On the way back to Namche, we saw two deer-like animals. The male made a sort of whistling sound to attract the female. Earlier we had seen a *kasturi* or musk deer. Light snow flurries fell in one of the higher villages, but stopped at lower elevations. Kurt was last in our group, but as a result he saw two pheasants. One ran across the trail right in front of him. Dinner was inside the inn above the yard where we camped. Across the dining room we saw a stack of various carcasses, but the room itself was nice and clean, we hoped.

Hiking down from Namche Bazaar to Lukla by way of Phakding was fast. By 10:30 in the morning of the second day, our tents were set up on the lawn in front of the Panorama Lodge, owned by relatives of Aanu, our host in Namche Bazaar.

We spent most of the day looking around Lukla, located on a nearby hill. Unlike the small, pretty villages we'd seen on the trek, Lukla was rather grungy. It existed primarily to provide services for the airstrip, to fly people in and out, and to keep them housed while they waited for flights. But the view of mountains we had left behind was beautiful. On our walk up to town, a child kept pestering me, begging for various items. Finally, I said in Nepali, "It is bad manners to beg." He was stunned that I spoke in Nepali and immediately took off up the trail.

Inside the lodge, we enjoyed a festive dinner: chicken, potatoes, rice and dal, carrots, cabbage and a cake with five candles, one for each trekker in our group. One of the guides danced for everyone, but others were too shy. They offered us *rakshi*, the local intoxicant, but we feared its potency at high altitudes. I showed the girl porters my photos. They loved to look at the one of our daughter and her fiancé. Powan, the host, showed us photos from his visit to Seattle, Arkansas, and Louisiana to study forestry and reforestation techniques. After so many days of walking, it was hard to believe that we wouldn't be trekking anywhere the next day except to the airport. We had been walking for twenty-seven days, for at least six hours each day and had traveled from 3,000 feet at Kathmandu to around 18,000 feet at Kala Pattar and Gokyo Ri, with many extremes of ups and downs in between. Because all the rivers in this part of Nepal flow south from the glaciers, the trail had to climb to the ridge that separated two rivers, then descend to the river itself before ascending to the next ridge. Adding together all the uphill climbs from Jiri to Kala Pattar would amount to almost 27,000 feet of elevation gain. In addition, we had climbed up to an 18,000-foot pass, descended somewhat to reach Gokyo and from there ascended to around 18,000 feet at Gokyo Ri. How many miles or kilometers we traveled, we never knew. Once the pavement ends, these distance measurements are not used in Nepal. Distance is measured primarily in terms of time. What's important to know is whether your destination is a three-hour or a three-day walk away.

At breakfast we heard a rumor that there were only two plane tickets available. Supposedly ours had been reserved, and we were to pick them up from someone named R.K. Having learned earlier on the trek that things are not always as expected, Jeff, Kurt and I took off for the airport, along with Lapka, Baadu, Ondi, and the kitchen help who carried our gear. In town, over fifty people were trying to get on the waiting list for the thirty-five-minute flights to Kathmandu. Mike and Alan had their tickets, but they hadn't been stamped. Consequently they had to pay again and then try to get a refund from their travel agent. R. K., the magical R.K., had our tickets. We actually saw them and they were stamped. No planes had arrived, but it was still early. The day before, the first sixteen-passenger plane for Kathmandu did not leave Lukla until almost 10:00 a.m. Our reservations were for 1:26 p.m. I would gladly have taken an earlier flight, but there were many standby passengers. We didn't know whether we took precedence over them or not. We also did not know which of the two airlines: Royal Nepal or Nepali Airways would show up first.

Some people had been in Lukla for five days waiting to get on the plane. Some had missed flights from Kathmandu to Bangkok as a result. The day was beautiful in Lukla, with a perfectly blue sky, but we didn't know conditions in Kathmandu. On the day we left Kathmandu on the bus, it had been very foggy in the morning, but later the fog burned off. I could now understand why we had seen the long line of people at the airport yesterday. We had become part of that same scene.

The so-called airport was a frantic swirl of people trying to get on various planes. One girl in line had absolutely huge eyes that were super-wide-open all the time. I had to wonder if she was on some kind of drugs. People normally blink or lower their eyelids or something. She also had the very latest fashionable haircut. As departure time drew nearer, everyone was told to go back behind the gate and enter through the building. There we had to go through an individual security check in a curtained area with men on one side, women on the other. When the guard inside simply waved me on, I exited and was back where we had been before--in a long line of people waiting to get on the plane. We were gradually advancing: each plane took only sixteen passengers for the thirty-five minute flight.

Finally a Nepali Airways plane landed, and Mike and Alan were taken on board. Our tickets were for Royal Nepal Airlines which should have been the next plane arriving. After a very long wait and what appeared to be some confusion, we heard an announcement that all flights for the day had been canceled. No reason for this action was given and nothing seemed obvious.

Jeff was quite upset because his flight for Bangkok was in two days, and he could not afford to miss it. If we could get on a plane in the morning, he would be okay, but otherwise his plans would be ruined. We went into town to put our name on the list for flights leaving the next day. This line was quite long, and we learned that even though we had had reservations for Tuesday, we would not be taken first in the morning. We would get on only after all the people with reservations for Wednesday had been flown out. We could envision being stuck in Lukla for at least five days. I thought about walking back, but then we'd have to get a bus from Jiri, and it would take us more than five days to get there. The only constructive thing to do was to find a room for the night as close as possible to the airport. Our cooking crew and guides had already left for Jiri. They thought they would be in Jiri in three days. Certainly they walked faster than we did, and they had nothing to carry as they planned to eat and sleep in teahouses.

Most "hotels" in Lukla also had dormitories to accommodate the many trekkers stranded there. We would have been grateful for any space, but Kurt was offered a room that was quite lovely with rugs on all the benches. Then I noticed the altar in the room and realized they had given us their prayer room or shrine. Every Buddhist home usually has a room where a statue or painting of

117

Buddha is kept along with other revered objects and where morning and evening prayers are said. Since the proprietors of the hotel lived on the premises, we assumed this was their personal prayer room. We suspected it was offered to Kurt because he had a white beard. Age is greatly respected in Nepal. Jeff found a place in the dorm, and we three went next door to have some soup and to bemoan our fate. The food was good, but we still didn't know how or when we would be leaving Lukla.

Hearing a helicopter, we thought a trekker with an injury or illness was probably being evacuated. Someone joked about getting out of Lukla by faking illness, but it would cost $2,500, each. We casually watched out the window and noticed that two people from the helicopter were running towards our cafe. When they came through the door, we recognized Aanu Sherpa, who said, "Hurry, this helicopter is for you." We were dumbfounded, but left our soup, paid, and hurried to the inn next door to retrieve our bags. Aanu had porters with him, who grabbed our bags, and we ran to the copter. There was just enough room for the pilot, the three of us, Aanu, and one Japanese trekker, who was happy to pay an exorbitant fee in order to leave. Aanu told me that I should act ill when we got off the helicopter in Kathmandu. The forty-five-minute flight over all those hills and valleys which had taken us a week to walk was magnificent. We flew low enough to distinguish villages and to see the monasteries we'd visited–remarkable!

Pemba, the Kathmandu co-founder of Journeys, our tour company, met the helicopter, and we were whisked away to the Malla Hotel where we had our first real shower in a month. I soaked in the hot tub for a really long time; then to make sure I was clean, I showered after that. What luxury! At dinner, we heard the full story.

When Mike and Alan had arrived in Kathmandu, they had told Pemba that three of us were still waiting; then they heard that flights were canceled. An official had misread the wind velocity and reported eighteen instead of eight, triggering the cancellation. Because Pemba felt responsible for getting us back to Kathmandu, he called a friend with connections who owed him a favor. The entire Nepali Air Force has only four helicopters, so we felt honored and fortunate that one of them had come for us. I had always wanted a helicopter ride, but didn't think my first one would be in Nepal.

Our day tour of Kathmandu began in the next morning. Swayambhunath, the monkey temple, was aptly named. Monkeys were everywhere. Another interesting aspect of this temple area was that Hindu shrines to various gods and the Buddhist *stupa* shared the same space without incident. A huge *dorje* or thunderbolt was also on the premises. Offerings of fruit to some of the Hindu gods did not last long. We saw agile monkeys squeeze between the protective bars and behind the statue of the gods to grab the fruit.

This was also our shopping day. At the Tibetan refugee camp where rugs were woven, we could afford only a very small one. Fabulous metal and carved wood items tempted us, but we had room in our packs only for a carving of Ganesh, the Hindu elephant-headed god of good fortune.

Our last stop was Patan, the second largest city in the Kathmandu valley. Most of the buildings in Durbar Square were built in the seventeenth century. Here we visited several temples and admired another golden entry gate. Within the beautiful courtyard of the Shiva temple we saw not only beautifully carved statues, but also some intricate erotic carvings on the roof support struts. In front of the Krishna temple, a large stone carving of the mythical man-bird Garuda stood on a pillar. The beautiful Buddhist monastery with an astonishing gold-plated roof was built in the twelfth century. In the monastery courtyard, a richly decorated three-story temple contained an image of Buddha.

In the evening, all the trekkers were invited to dinner at Pemba's home in a very up-scale area of town. Drinks before dinner were plentiful and relaxing. A delicious buffet included tandoori chicken, dal, and rice–all quite tasty. We were given a tour of the house, including the family prayer room. Pemba was in a talkative mood and had quite a bit to say about his family and about Journeys, the company he co-founded and represented. The most amazing story he told was of his close call with an avalanche. That experience had convinced him it was time to stop guiding the climbing expeditions to the high summits and to get into another kind of business.

We began our last full day in Kathmandu by meeting Patti and Bill Bright, who were still in town, Jeff, and Babu for a late, huge breakfast of waffles with yoghurt at Mike's. Mike is an American living in Nepal who provides American-type food for homesick tourists. A sign in the restaurant advertized an up-coming Thanksgiving dinner.

Jeff left for the airport, we made plans to meet Patti and Bill for dinner, and then Kurt and I visited nine-story Basantapur tower inside the Royal Palace. At the entrance, a statue of Hanuman, the monkey god, had been touched and daubed with red paint so often that its features were hardly recognizable. From the top of the tower we had excellent views over the city and into other courtyards. When we left to find the shrine for Ganesh, two little girls jumped up to put *tikas* (good-luck red spots) on our foreheads. Then they asked for rupees.

On the way back, we stopped to see Freak Street, famous for drug activity in the 1960s. In 1992, it appeared no different from any other street. Watching some schoolgirls jumping rope, I noticed that they didn't turn the rope as we do; they just raised the rope up and lowered it. Participants jumped in and out or jumped over the rope or whatever they wanted to do.

When we stopped for toffee-coffee ice-cream, Babu caught up with us and asked me to mail two letters for him in the United States. Then he asked us if we remembered bettris. For a while we thought he was referring to a trekker named Bettris, as his English was heavily accented. Finally Kurt realized Babu was asking for repayment of 600 rupees for the flashlight batteries purchased for us before we left on the trek.

Back at the hotel, we picked up our passports and airline tickets for our early morning departure. We were wondering about pickup time for the airport, when Pemba called asking us to meet him downstairs. He said that the Malla Hotel was very interested in having our room. They offered to upgrade us to the Hotel Everest, a five-star hotel that was closer to the airport. Kurt wasn't that interested in packing up again, or perhaps he didn't quite hear what was said. We had made plans to meet the Brights for dinner and had no way of getting in touch with them about our change of plans. Our slight reluctance led the hotel to sweeten the deal even more by adding complimentary dinner and breakfast and an offer to contact our friends, telling them where we were and why.

When Patti and Bill called us later, they said they would be happy to scope out the Hotel Everest. So we had drinks, appetizers, and excellent seafood for free. The hotel lobby was quite impressive with dark-paneled wood walls, huge chandeliers, and plush furniture tastefully arranged in a spacious area. Our junior suite had a huge bedroom plus a sitting room where a large vase of flowers welcomed us. The only drawback was that electricity in that part of the city was shut off for five hours every Wednesday to conserve power. Of course, we were there on a Wednesday. That's Nepal, you just get used to it--even in the midst of five-star luxury.

In the morning, we left early for New Delhi, thrilled one last time by the majesty of the incredibly beautiful Himalayan peaks we could see from the airplane window. Already the trip began to take on a dream-like quality. Had we really walked so many days? Had we really made it to Kala Pattar and Gokyo Ri relatively unscathed? How could we have been so lucky with the weather? So many thoughts, images, and emotions filled our minds and hearts that it was hard to stay focused on any one thing. We were very pleased to have fulfilled our grandiose boast made so long ago. And, indeed, the experience had lived up to and exceeded our expectations. The natural beauty of that part of the world, the people we'd met, the different customs and culture we'd been introduced to, the routine of trekking--all would remain vividly with us for years. We'd also learned more about ourselves, our limitations and our strengths. My pre-trek anxieties about malaria and high altitude sickness turned out to be baseless, and even though Kurt now describes the day he hiked with a dislocated shoulder as the worst day of his life, he still feels the trip was one of the best he'd ever taken.

Mt. Whitney Trail in June

Grossglockner View from Johannesberg

Crossing the Crevasse on Mt. Rainier

Austrian Alps

Faith on the Rocks

Mani Rimdu Musicians

Squaw Valley, California

Terraced Hillside -Nepal

Cortina, Italy

The trail above Duglha

PERSISTENT SKIERS

Canadian Deep Freeze

Colorado Sampling

Jackson Hole, Wyoming

Utah Warmth

California Dreaming

The Austrian Alps

Cortina in Winter

PERSISTENT SKIERS

We didn't ski until we were over thirty, and then only took it up as a way to make winter months tolerable. But we became addicted, persisting through pain, injuries, and frustration when warm winters produced no skiable snow. In the beginning, we skied in Maryland and Pennsylvania on weekends. Vermont and New Hampshire offered economical, instructional family ski weeks. Finally we graduated to skiing in Canada, the Western States, and Europe. Now that Kurt is past seventy, his lift tickets are free at many Colorado resorts. We have no intention of quitting.

CANADIAN DEEP FREEZE

The winter we tried to ski Sugarloaf Mountain in Maine, we woke the second morning to pouring rain. Instead of giving up altogether, we drove five hours farther north hoping for snow-covered hills at St. Anne de Beaupre, north of Quebec City. We were rewarded with three days of uncrowded skiing before rain, spring thaw, and floods drove us home.

Another year, hearing rumors of great skiing at Mont Sutton and Owls Head in the Eastern Townships, an area south of Montreal, we took Alan with us to investigate. Home from college for Christmas break, Karen preferred to stay there, sleeping during the day and partying most nights. It was a wise choice. Conditions were mediocre (not enough snow) until they turned frightful the day we left. The temperature reached minus forty degrees Fahrenheit, accompanied by a howling wind. Only Canadian cars with block heaters and new batteries were self-starters. The rest of us waited (inside the motel, of course) until a local mechanic arrived and without gloves performed some adjustment that got everybody going and heading south. We were glad it was our last day, not our first.

Thinking we'd just been unlucky with the weather, we were pleased to obtain a time-share week at Mont Tremblant a few years later in 1992. Our original plans to ski Mont Tremblant in 1972 had drastically changed just a week before our departure. Because our daughter, then nine years old, was not coming to Canada with us, Kurt had taken Karen skiing at a nearby Pennsylvania resort. When he stopped on the slope to watch her turns, a reckless, out-of-control skier crashed into Kurt's back, knocking him down and cracking one of his ribs. With my mother already scheduled to come from Cleveland to stay with the children, we couldn't waste the opportunity to get away. Instead of skiing, we explored Puerto Rico. Now we looked forward to skiing Mont Tremblant at last, but we were unlucky again.

Unknowingly, we had chosen the coldest January week of a very cold winter to visit. What we did shouldn't be called skiing. Hand and feet warmers and cups of hot chocolate before and after each run helped. I wore so many layers I looked like the Michelin man or the Pillsbury doughboy. Amazingly our Toyota started each morning even without a block heater or hair dryer. Before that week I'd always said it was insane and impossible to ski at minus twenty-eight degrees Fahrenheit. Each morning I'd ask Kurt if we really had to ski that day. But because we'd purchased a week of lift tickets in advance, he always replied, "It's already paid for," and we skied. Reflected heat from the snow and no wind on top made it almost tolerable, but we left a day early, having finally skied the runs at Mont Tremblant.

Eventually we decided to give Canada another try. Skiing Banff and Lake Louise for two weeks in January was magnificent: good snow, breathtakingly beautiful Canadian Rockies scenery, and improved skiing techniques. We'd expected below-zero temperatures, but the unusually warm winter gave us perfect skiing degrees. From our two Australian ski instructors, visiting Alberta for the winter, we learned once more to ski tough moguls, after a wrong turn another day had taken us onto terrain we wished we'd never seen. Rocky Mountain Resort (a time-share exchange) provided a Christmas tree, exercise room, indoor pool, outdoor jacuzzi, indoor sauna/steam room, and hot cider every night. BBC/TV offered evening concerts of classical music. About half the skiers were from Japan, where lift tickets cost $100.00 a day and the lift line wait is at least an hour. These Canadian ski resorts had no lift lines at all, the exchange rate was great, and some resorts even had Japanese-speaking instructors, so the area was a very desirable destination for Japanese skiers.

Banff had grown, becoming a modern city with malls, since our summer visit twenty years before; but herds of elk and buffalo still grazed near town. Some elk, however, preferred the tender leaves of shrubs in town, stopping bus and automobile traffic and startling unsuspecting tourists taking an after-dinner stroll. An art museum featured Western and Native American artists along with artifacts, art, and fables about fictional Exceptional Pass, where people have disappeared and from which cryptic messages have come.

On our day in Calgary, on the way home, we caught glimpses of a Scottish wedding: the men in kilts and the procession led by a bagpiper, in one section of the huge public greenhouse that covered the entire fourth floor of a commercial building. That night we devoured superb steak in a walnut-paneled room with stained-glass windows.

A week later, skiing at Whitetail, a small but attractive ski area ninety minutes from home, I slipped and slid down an icy slope, managing somehow to fracture my heel. No bruises were found anywhere else, but repair involved surgery and wearing a cast for two months.

Whistler/Blackcomb, a ski area about one hundred miles north of Vancouver, British Columbia, was our Canadian ski destination in 2001. Though the tops of the coastal range reach only 8,000 feet, because they lie so far north, spectacular alpine scenery and heaps of snow impress the visitor, even in late March. The ski season doesn't end until June. The temperature was ideal, but morning fogs were deceptive. On the mountain's lower runs, swirling fog made it difficult to follow the trails, unless a skier familiar with the run passed nearby. By afternoon, the snow had turned mushy, grabbing and slowing the skis, making us work hard. Soon we learned the mountain's secret. High above the fog, the sun shone brilliantly on the summit and miles of beautiful snow-covered trails. Down below buying a day's lift ticket without knowing the extent of the fog bank took courage and faith. At the end of the day, instead of trying to ski the heavy, wet melting snow below, we rode the gondola down, as did most intelligent skiers.

Our best move was to show up for the free orientation tour offered by volunteer hosts. Other groups were just leaving as we arrived, so we lucked out having a very experienced guide all to ourselves. After we told him our skiing level, he took us to trails we would never have tried on our own, showing us shortcuts to the runs with the best snow and recommending runs on other parts of the mountain that he thought we would like.

The location of the time-share condo was ideal: five minutes from the slopes, with a grocery store nearby in one of the attractive plazas that make up Whistler Village. But no trip is without its glitches. Arriving in Vancouver at noon, after a very pleasant, smooth flight, we had plenty of daylight for enjoying the dramatic views of mountains, rocks, and gigantic evergreen trees, as we traveled by bus for almost three hours along the waters of Squamish Bay to Whistler Village. A minivan took us from the bus stop to check-in to condo. While congratulating ourselves on how easy getting there had been, we suddenly realized that Kurt had left the backpack containing his ski boots on the bus, which by then was returning to Vancouver. We called the bus company with details. They said they'd work on it and would call us back. After waiting for some time, we called them again. The pack had been found, and it would be delivered at midnight. Since it was complicated to get into the condo itself, Kurt asked the company to deliver the pack to the lobby of the Holiday Inn, which seemed to have a connection with the condos. The desk clerk, who left before midnight, promised to leave a note for the late-night clerk who would replace her. At six the next morning, Kurt dropped by the lobby. Because the late-night clerk had not found the note, he'd sent the pack away. We hoped it hadn't traveled back to Vancouver again. Frantic phone calls followed as we tried to find out where it had been sent. There would be no skiing that day. Once we learned it was still in Whistler Village, we offered to pick it up. The company insisted on delivering it. Finally at two that afternoon Kurt met the delivery man in the lobby and returned victorious.

We lost another day because it snowed too much, but we still had plenty of skiing time during our ten-day visit. Named Burnt Stew, a long, relatively easy trail meandered from the summit down a gentler side of the mountain through vast expanses with photogenic sharp peaks like Black Tusk in the distance. Above the tree line, the trail was identified only by waist high green markers on wands spaced along one side and orange markers on the other, a necessary aid in case of white-out. But no one was restricted to skiing on the trail, if a skier had the nerve and desire to ski something else in between. Only a skier passing outside the resort's boundaries was on his or her own. A trail of intermediate difficulty followed the ridge line before descending through a moguled chute to join Burnt Stew close to the lift line of skiers waiting to go to the top again. In the other direction at the top, a narrow trail led to the saddle, where anyone wanting to descend had to negotiate a tricky, steep, and crowded slot between two huge boulders. This trail led across a snow-covered glacier and eventually gave access to other lifts, creating the possibility for an exciting and challenging round trip. High-speed quad chairlifts at the edge of the glacier took skiers up to summits for other destinations. On the glacier itself, only T-bar lifts could be placed, because the solid foundation needed for the chairlifts could not be reached through the glacial ice.

Certain areas were designed for families and for snowboarders. The terrain parks and half-pipes give skilled snowboarders places to demonstrate their abilities and tricky maneuvers, providing many thrills for viewers watching the boarders perform aerials and awesome jumps. We switched between the two adjacent mountains each day, always discovering new sections and trails not tried before. A trail named Jersey Cream had snow so smooth it felt as if we were skiing on whipped cream. Seventh Heaven offered five or six intermediate trails with varying degrees of excitement, thrills, and beauty. Occasionally we'd catch a glimpse of skilled skiers traversing and enjoying extremely steep slopes we didn't dare to try. About the time we had worked up our courage and our ability to ski on one of the other glaciers, it was time to return. It was easy to see why Whistler/Blackcomb has become so popular among skiers all over the world. Its reputation is well-deserved. For us, the only problem is that it's so far from home.

COLORADO SAMPLING

On our first ski trip to the western United States, we visited Summit County, home to five ski resorts, all connected by a free county-run shuttle bus. We rented a room in Breckenridge, a former mining town, now a four-season money-maker with art galleries, cafes, and the inevitable vendors of tee shirts and other kitschy souvenirs. Two snowstorms created great skiing at Breckenridge,

Copper Mountain, North Peak, Keystone, and A-Basin–all about seventy miles west of Denver just off Interstate 70. Frostbite warnings at every ski lift made us shiver the day we arrived, but later temperatures rose to a more comfortable twenty to thirty degrees. Almost every day was sunny, our skiing improved, and we skied powder. There were no injuries on this trip, and I participated in a Nastar race, winning a bronze medal. World Cup Free Style competitions in ballet and inverted aerials amazed us. We laughed at Ullrfest–a three-day festival with an ice-sculpture competition, a parade (unbelievably skimpy costumes at ten degrees), and a bonfire–mostly old Christmas trees–on which happy celebrants sacrificed old skis (some with bindings), to Ullr, god of snow: but it did snow the next day.

Snowshoeing by moonlight up and over the top of 11,000-foot Keystone Mountain in Colorado with daughter Karen and son-in-law Bret was the high point of a recent January return to the Summit County ski areas. The low point was when Kurt dislocated his shoulder at the top of a ski run. He did take it easy one day, but tried snowshoeing the next day, and then skied, cautiously, but against doctor's orders, of course. When the orthopedist at home told him no skiing for thirty days, he started counting. On day thirty-one, while skiing in New Hampshire, we learned Kurt's skis had delaminated, perhaps the cause of his earlier accident.

Another favorite Colorado ski area to which we've returned is Vail-Beaver Creek. Relaxing after a day of skiing in the heated outdoor pool, as snowflakes swirled gently from a leaden sky to melt on the water's surface, then scurrying from the pool through the nippy air to a comfy couch, where we sipped mulled cider in front of a blazing fire, the lighted ski slope visible through the window opening onto our balcony–this was Vail. The first day was a tough one. After trying out our skis on easy runs in the morning, we joined separate free "meet the mountain" tours in the afternoon, led by volunteers. As I waited for Kurt at the end of the day, a ski patrol sled with a familiar passenger came to a stop in front of me. Not yet adjusted to the high altitude, Kurt had become overtired and had somehow badly bruised his leg. After helping him limp back to the condo, I returned for his skis. Next I took our empty packs and caught the bus to go grocery shopping in West Vail, as Vail itself had no necessity stores: no grocery, no drugstore. The pseudo but charming alpinesque architecture housed only the significant things: painting and sculpture galleries; several shops selling fur coats, diamonds, designer clothing; and numerous upscale restaurants. By the time I returned to fix dinner, using some of my purchases, I had a roaring headache, another altitude victim.

Everything looked better the next day when our altitude symptoms disappeared. Kurt had the evil-looking bruise checked out at the local clinic and spent some of the day in galleries, museums, and the library. Gradually the bruise disappeared and he skied the rest of the two weeks. The huge area's varied terrain has something for everyone. There were so many different trails to try, we never repeated ourselves.

Worried about being delayed by possible snow or sleet in the pass between Vail and Denver, we reserved an early-morning airport van pickup. But when he stopped for his last passengers, the van driver miscalculated the slickness of the side road, and we slid across it. Only the trees and shrubs at the road's side prevented us from rolling down into a deep ravine. Fortunately, only the van was injured, and a replacement was requested to rescue us. It arrived forty-five minutes later. Though grateful to be alive, we started to be anxious about getting to the airport in time, despite perfectly clear weather in the pass. As we raced through Denver, dreading the sound of a police siren, the driver never stopped talking. Only after some passengers screamed that we'd missed the airport turnoff did he finally look around, hit the next cloverleaf for a u-turn and deposit us in the eternally long check-in line. I grabbed an attendant and told her our flight number. "They're boarding," she said. "Run to the gate." That wasn't so easy with suitcase, boots, and skis, but we made the flight.

When we returned to Colorado several years later, we spent one week at Winter Park, a ski area slightly closer to Denver, and one week at Vail. These resorts gave us the most fabulous skiing ever and our first real champagne powder–up to our thighs. I had begun to believe such powder was the stuff of legends, despite the advertising photographs that always feature it. Skiing the light powder felt as if clouds or cotton candy were underfoot. In order to move at all, we had to ski the steepest slopes. Changing from one resort to the other without a rental car, however, was no fun at all. No regularly scheduled van or bus service existed between the two ski areas. We could either hire a private driver at an astronomical price or for a more reasonable, but still painful expense, we could spend an entire day riding to the Denver airport in one van and out again in another.

Back home, we were delighted to find enough snow locally for cross-country skiing in our neighborhood stream-side park. We learned, however, that skiing our local golf course was now prohibited, when park police came to cart us away. Seeing that the offenders were mostly a motley group of senior citizens, they let us off with a warning.

For years we wanted to ski at Steamboat Springs and Aspen, but time-share condos at these Colorado resorts were always booked. When we finally arranged for ten days in January 1998 at steamboat Springs, it snowed every night. It also snowed many days, killing visibility and piling up heavy snow to make our calves ache after only a half-day of turns. Taking a day off, we hiked to the sulphurous hot springs, bubbling in various parks in town, visited the Victorian-era historic home and history museum in town, and enjoyed the art show in a converted railway station. We also spent extra time in the motel's hot tub.

Our unit at Snowmass, near Aspen, was comfortable, convenient, and included breakfast. It was only a short walk to the ski runs, and a bus ride to town. Then we stayed for three extra days at a hotel situated on the slope. No schlepping of skis! From the ski lockers on the lower level, skiiers step out on the slope and ski down to the lift. The last run of the day ends at the entrance to the ski lockers. It was nice to do this once, but carrying the skis is healthier–for one's strength and for one's wallet. Good snow, good weather, good company, good food, and no injuries–a great trip! No weight loss, though, as cookies, coffee, and cocoa were available free on the slopes every morning and at the end of the day.

High winds delayed our plane's takeoff until it unloaded some of its fuel. The pilot explained that we'd have to land briefly at an airport farther west to refuel in order to make it to Minneapolis. Of course, we didn't make our connection to Maryland. We might have spent the night in Minneapolis if the airline had paid for it, but "acts of God" and weather didn't qualify for any compensation other than a free long-distance phone card to let the folks back home know we'd be arriving five hours later than expected.

JACKSON HOLE, WYOMING

When the time-share exchange offered us Jackson Hole for the first week in April, we took it, knowing that we'd had summer snows there. Snow there was, but the ski area's lease with the Forest Service required the resort to close April 3, no matter how deep the snow cover. We had one day of skiing at Jackson Hole's Rendezvous Mountain, an overcast day with fog and light snow. At least Targhee Resort was open; so Kurt, Alan, and I drove forty miles each way over an 8,000-foot pass into Idaho and back into Wyoming for several days. And there was powder (but heavy powder). More accustomed to using the edges of our skis to turn on the often icy slopes in the East, we needed to learn a new technique in order to ski anything more than green-marked beginner trails.

Tiring of the daily commute across the pass, we decided to try local cross-country skiing. The day began beautifully: blue sky, a trail through new snow over frozen streams, amidst tall, dense evergreens and low shrubs at the foot of spectacular snow-capped 13,000-foot Teton peaks we'd hiked and climbed many summers ago. A lone log cabin on the distant horizon completed the picture-postcard winter fantasy. After a granola bar lunch, Alan's headache and altitude problems led us to take the less strenuous road back to the car. We had barely left the Jenny Lake Rescue Cabin when the lowering clouds engulfed us suddenly in a blizzard. At thirty degrees Fahrenheit, the temperature wasn't that bad, but biting, furious winds and blowing snow made the walk back in a total whiteout seem endless. Finally reaching the car, we stowed our skis and hopped in. Suddenly the snow stopped.

Eight years later in 2002, we returned to ski what we had missed at Jackson Hole. A week in early January assured us that the ski area would definitely be open, but we worried that temperatures might be below zero then. Instead, many days were very comfortable with highs in the forties. The January thaw had arrived early and was welcomed by locals after three weeks of extremely low temperatures. We were finally able to experience what Jackson Hole was really like. The snow was good, though somewhat used. Although we skied plenty of intermediate/advanced runs, we also stared from the cable car window in fear and awe at many other runs and cliffs negotiated by fabulous skiers. For us, it was really cool to ski with 1960s Austrian Olympic star Pepi Stiegler. He offered a free ski tour with tips Monday through Friday at 1:30 p.m. In the valley, his restaurant offered Austrian cuisine, tempting but a bit pricey.

The downside of the relatively warm temperatures was that they created icy conditions and dwindling snow. During sunny days, the surface of the remaining snow melted. At night when temperatures dropped to the teens, the surface froze, creating extremely slick runs, unless they were groomed. To groom a slope, specialized machines break up the icy top layer, crushing it into fine granules which become skiable as the sun warms them. The day we decided to try Snow King, the in-town ski area, the manager advised us before we bought a ticket that most of the runs were extremely difficult because of icy conditions. That day became our "rest" day.

Jackson Hole had grown quite a bit since our last visit and now had even more art galleries and motels. A very positive addition was the START bus system that runs all over town and out to Teton Village where the Jackson Hole ski area is located. On our "rest" day we took the bus to the National Museum of Wildlife Art, a collection of paintings, photographs, and sculptures of wildlife by various artists. One room was dedicated to the bison. A special exhibit featured the history of the cowboy, as told through paintings and sculptures. Another room emphasized the sport of fishing.

A combined ticket for the museum and the Fish and Wildlife Service's Elk Refuge sleigh ride was well worth it. Located across the highway from the museum, the Elk Refuge is the winter range for thousands of elk. Our sleigh was pulled by two massive Belgian horses named Dot and Dash, controlled by a young woman's soft voice and skillful handling of the reins. For an hour we rode from one area to another for closeup views of many mature elk with handsome racks of antlers. We also saw a few elk cows. When it becomes difficult for the elk to get at the grass under the snow, alfalfa pellets are provided by the humans. In the spring, the elk return to their summer range at higher elevations where the calves are born.

We were pleased that not everything had changed in Jackson Hole. The blueberry pancakes and the ribs at Bubba's were just as delicious as we remembered, and Bubba's was just as popular. It was also fun to celebrate a successful skiing day with ale at the Silver Dollar Bar where the barstool seats are saddles and where the neon cowboy on the facade of the building has waved his lasso for at least forty years.

Twice we took the bus to Targhee Resort, traveling through a bit of Idaho and back into Wyoming. The day we took lessons, we were the only two in our group–a real bargain. Kurt got help with his new parabolic skis; I got a refresher on skiing medium-sized moguls. With the instructor picking the path, it was an exhilarating run. As advertised, the snow really was better on the western side of the Tetons, and the views of Mount Owen, the Grand Teton, and the Middle Teton peaks were spectacular. Targhee had a superb novice run, worth taking just for the scenic views. A new area, opened in 2002 at Targhee, offered some lovely intermediate runs. When one of them ended in a steep, but fortunately short mogul field, I was grateful for the practice I'd had on our first day at Targhee.

Back at Teton Village, I decided to try the "meet the mountain" free orientation tour, figuring the group might be taken to some areas we hadn't skied yet. Kurt wanted to practice elsewhere. When no one else showed up, the volunteer hostess offered to take me anywhere I wanted to go. Following Tilly, I skied runs off the cable car from the top of the mountain. Originally from Melbourne, Australia, Tilly was an excellent telemark skier and also a travel addict. As we rode the lifts up before zooming down yet another run I hadn't had the nerve to try alone, it was great fun talking about places in Melbourne we both knew and about other splendid areas of the world we had visited. That night at a restaurant specializing in northern Italian cuisine, we enjoyed dinner and conversation with Tilly and her friend Sally, a nurse practitioner who was recovering from a recent dog bite that had required surgery.

While skiing a run called St. John's, Kurt made the wrong choice when the trail split. He knew it was wrong when he had to negotiate a long section of very large, icy, crunchy moguls. I waited for a while at the chairlift, then went up and skied the run again. I went to the edge of that trail, saw the moguls, and didn't want to ski it, unless I knew for certain Kurt was on it and needed help. By then, I thought we'd just missed each other and that he might have gone to a restaurant on another part of the mountain, where we often had lunch. I skied over there, but no Kurt. When I finally went to the base lodge, intending to ask the ski patrol to look for him, there he was. He'd been working his way down the mogul field the entire time, but he made it safely with no injuries.

On our last day we were stunned to see two moose in a clump of bushes close to a ski run. They were visible from the chairlift as well. We thought they'd just stopped for breakfast when we saw them munching the branches in the morning. But they spent the entire day there, kneeling down in the snow to rest and digest for a couple of hours, then returning to eat some more. Hardly anyone could resist watching them from a safe distance. But one woman dared to crawl near them on her hands and knees to get a closeup photo. Not a very smart thing to do. Although they generally don't attack humans, moose are very unpredictable.

Good weather, good snow, and no injuries made for a very good ski trip. Even when I was randomly selected for extra scrutiny at the Jackson Hole airport, I didn't mind too much. The young, good-looking security guard allowed me to keep my boots on, but wanded the soles. When he asked me, almost timidly, if a patdown was all right with me, I had to restrain myself from replying, Oh, yes! I'd read the signs warning us not to joke about security matters, but I regretted the missed opportunity to make someone blush.

UTAH WARMTH

Thinking a ski trip in March was well within the bounds of the West's endless ski season, we planned a trip to Utah. Staying in Park City, an old mining town like Breckenridge, but smaller, we skied three areas there and took the bus twice to Alta and Snowbird, world-class ski resorts. Each day was warmer than the last. College students on spring break skied bare-chested in jams–the guys did, anyway–when highs reached fifty to sixty degrees. Optimum conditions only lasted from eleven until two. Overnight freezing created superfast icy surfaces for two hours each morning. Each afternoon we skied mashed potatoes. At day's end, skiers had to ride the lifts down, over dirt run-outs. One ski area closed for the year. We had fun, but it wasn't quite what we'd expected. Neither was our flight to Utah. Because the airline had assigned our seats to someone else as well, we were forced to fly first class: filet mignon, wine, silver not plastic flatware, cloth napkins, before- and after-dinner drinks, and more space–very nice, but not worth the usual price.

Although we knew better, when we were offered two weeks' lodging free in March of 1993, we returned to Park City. This time we skied eight different areas, including Sundance, home of the Summer Film Festival. The local grocery store's fabulous fresh fish, fruit, and frozen yogurt kept us from losing any weight. The snow was excellent, though mush at mid-day. The day we took off to visit Salt Lake City, the high was near sixty degrees. Kurt skied all the slopes with no problems, but an icy step on the way in to change out of his ski boots sent him sliding across the cafeteria floor until he hit the edge of a table, gashing his earlobe. The cut healed in three days, aided by a butterfly bandage from First Aid. Then on the next to last day, he slipped carrying his skis to the parking lot. Landing on his boot, which dangled from a shoulder carrying-strap, he cracked a rib. The rib belt we found at the well-stocked local drugstore helped make the trip home tolerable. We usually carry our own luggage at airports, but this time we paid a skycap.

CALIFORNIA DREAMING

Forgetting that we had scheduled a week of skiing in New Hampshire, Kurt accepted two weeks in the same month at a Lake Tahoe resort. So, in 1991, we skied for almost three consecutive weeks without a break. Only rain and losing a lens from my glasses sent us home a day early from the January ski week in New Hampshire. With new glasses and clean laundry, we flew to California the next day for a two-week stay.

Unfortunately the snow conditions in California weren't much better. Famed Squaw Valley was practically closed. Skiing at Alpine Resort and on the Nevada side of Heavenly was good, but not what it could have been with better snow. It was cold enough for the resort to make snow, but drought and water restrictions limited snow-making at Heavenly. We soon grew tired of skiing the same run repeatedly. Desperate, we rented a car for a weekend elsewhere–about the same price as lift tickets for three days.

Death Valley's sunlight, sand, and mountains possessed an unusual beauty that made us forget the long drive to get there. We toured Scotty's Castle and stayed at Stovepipe Wells Motel, two places we'd previously only passed in the night, trying to avoid summer's intense daytime temperatures. On the way back, near Lake Mono with its eerie mineral formations, we were impressed by Mammoth ski area and sorry we didn't have our skis with us.

Back in Tahoe, we visited the casinos each night, not to gamble, but to see every fabulous show worth seeing–most with spectacular special effects. But for excellent skiing, we were in the right place at the wrong time–the one disadvantage of planning ahead. Two months later Tahoe received a huge dump of snow, but our vacation was over.

Unlike our first trip to Lake Tahoe, when we returned in 1997, we found plenty of snow. We skied from California to Nevada and back again and slid down many other exciting many slopes as well. On a sunny day, the view of the shimmering intense blue of California's deepest lake from the top of the ridge was breathtaking.

Then came our week at Squaw. Don't go without a rental car! Because the regular Northshore "Squaw bus" was already full, we had to take the Lake Lapper from South Lake Tahoe to its stop on the highway at Tahoe City on the north shore of the lake. After we waited an hour for a connecting bus just to ride the next five miles, we still had another wait for a resort shuttle to take us to Squaw Resort three miles off the highway. The numerous changes were hassle enough, but add to that a windy, sleety day in which we waited with suitcase, skis, and boots for connections--Ugh! Worse yet, Squaw village had no real grocery store. Skipping a day of skiing to get groceries in town via bus was less attractive than existing on macaroni and cheese and other minimal food. Since we were staying in a condo with a kitchen, we refused to eat out at high resort prices, although once we did do pizza. Yes, we are crazy. The skiing, however, was fabulous on the sunny days. On the broad top of one peak, a tall tower-like structure offered bungee jumping, but no one dared to do it while we were there. The resort where we stayed was very attractive and hospitable, with a heated outdoor pool surrounded by snow-covered peaks.

On our last half-day, we tried snowshoeing along a beautiful stream. We had no problems on flat terrain, except for getting used to the awkward stance necessary to avoid catching one snowshoe with the other. It was strenuous going up slopes, and the snowshoes' metal teeth, so helpful on snow, tended to hang up on thinly-covered rocks. Maybe it just takes more practice or a better trail.

THE AUSTRIAN ALPS

Bitter cold met us at the Munich airport in 1982 when we arrived during Fasching week. Icy winds kept many revelers off the streets and forced us to pretend interest in the merchandise of any store open, at least long enough to warm up, so we could face the wintry blasts again. Back at the hotel, the steamy swimming pool felt wonderful.

Cats, ghouls, and other monsters, however, skied the slopes of St. Anton on Mardi Gras, as the temperatures moderated under brilliant Austrian sunshine. Skiing was challenging, the best snow being high near the glaciers, the scenery vast and spectacular, the village picture-perfect. We found a Hungarian restaurant we really liked, and another with a yodeler, but passed up the discos, crammed with visiting young and noisy Swedes. Attractively decorated with Austrian farm implements and antiques, our home for the week was complete with the expected "featherbed' comforters. We joined other outlanders for the local schuhplatter performance in the high school gym, converted for the night to a beer hall.

Our second week in a very small village, Stuben, gave us access to Albonagrat, Lech, and Zurs. You actually <u>can</u> ski from one village to another for lunch and ski back by another route using long trails and connecting lifts. A super sensation! On another trail we were almost the first to follow the snowcat packing down some newly fallen snow, but this wasn't so great. All went well until near the end where the trail became steep and narrow. One ski tip caught in deep snow as did a pole, and Kurt was immobilized with a dislocated shoulder. I saw him sitting, seemingly chatting with other skiers, from where I waited at the bottom of the lift. After his companions skied down to tell me what had happened, he was rescued by the snowcat. An ambulance carried us to the sports clinic in St. Anton, where after x-rays, one doctor pushed and the other pulled until Kurt's arm popped back into place--no painkiller, not even a sip of schnapps! Kurt didn't ski that afternoon or the next day, because he had to be rechecked at noon. By then, amazingly healed, he was allowed to ski but only if he wore a chest harness to restrict his arm. The following day he was back on the slopes, with no more problems despite some lingering soreness.

When it rained one day, we rode the train to Lake Lucerne for sightseeing, coffee, and pastry. Another day when visibility was poor, we took a lesson, skiing behind a native-born instructor. We couldn't believe the leisurely lunches many skiers took on the slopes. Some people seemed to ride the lifts to the restaurants at high elevations just to improve their tans, stretching out most of the day on "beach chairs" catching all that reflected heat and light. We discovered "Jagertee," an alcohol-laced hot drink.

Our train back to Munich was late, and the warm rain we now encountered a total contrast to our arrival weather. The flight to Frankfurt, early the next morning, seemed too long. Then the pilot announced we were landing--- in Bamberg, not Frankfurt--for refueling, since circling while waiting for the fog to lift had consumed the gasoline supply. Shortly thereafter, the fog lifted, but we arrived ten minutes <u>after</u> our scheduled United States departure. We ran to the gate anyway. The steps were wheeled up to the plane's door once more; we entered, sat down, and the plane took off. Just like the movies.

CORTINA IN WINTER

Inside the immense, impressive Palazzo Ducale, marveling at its art, then dazed by the magnificent Basilica di San Marco, its dome and walls glittering with golden mosaics, we didn't mind the mid-January fog and mist. Romantic Venice overflows with museums full of paintings, sculptures, and history, along with dazzling eighteenth-century mansions, elegantly furnished. Everywhere one looks, the view deserves to be drawn, painted, or photographed.

In Campo del Ghetto Nuovo, the world's oldest ghetto, powerful bas reliefs surrounded by barbed wire honor Italian holocaust victims. Opposite this memorial, the Museum of the Hebrew Community is the meeting place for touring three historic synagogues: the German, resembling a baroque theater, the opulent French Synagogue, and the Spanish Synagogue where one marble tile, misplaced on purpose, disturbs the floor's geometric pattern to demonstrate the belief that only God is perfect. We rode the vaporettos and walked a lot, as it was too cold, damp, and expensive for gondolas. But strolling anywhere in Venice is a pleasure, especially just before Carnival, when shop windows are crammed with exotic masks and fantastic costumes.

Would rain in Venice mean snow in Cortina? We had come to Italy primarily to ski and were beginning to worry. When our train from Venice reached the end of the tracks in Calalzo, there were flurries. As the Dolomiti autobus twisted ever upwards on a narrow road, banked with snow, we congratulated each other for not renting a car.

Cortina's reputation is well deserved. Spectacular sharp dolomites jut skyward above the clouds. Gondolas and cable cars rise between crags even extreme skiers would bypass, unloading skiers at a broad flat summit. From this terminal, several ski runs descend, and a connecting lift can take skiers to even more ski areas. Free shuttle buses running between the various areas comprising Cortina gave us a new choice every day, once we knew where to wait for the bus. One day a combination of lifts and runs took us to Rio Gere. After crossing the highway, we rode another lift to the Son Forca area at 2,215 meters. From there we skied back down to a lunch of panini and vino at a Rio Gere trattoria, then took a four-mile run back to Cortina. Though the trail was often obscure, with bumpy patches, thin snow, and grass, it was a good afternoon.

Another day in clear, sunny weather, we skied an eleven-mile corkscrew run of "medium difficulty" from the top of Lagazuoi at 2,778 meters down the mountain's backside past an enormous frozen waterfall, its ice, misty blue and pale lime, glistening in the sun. Farther down the trail, friendly shouts and laughter came from many skiers who had stopped for food and drink at Scotoni's popular rustic restaurant set in the trees. When the trail flattened in the valley about a mile from the village of Armentarola, a German-speaking Italian wearing a Loden jacket and Tyrolean hat waited with his team of horses hitched to a wagon. Behind the wagon stretched two long ropes, each containing ten or so loops. For about one dollar each, we grabbed a loop along with many other skiers and enjoyed being horse-towed, frantically trying not to become entangled in each other's skis.

We had skied into the Alta Badia area of Sudtirol where German language and culture predominated. Sitting on a large deck while occasional light snowflakes decorated our hair, we relished delicious goulash soup and coffee with whipped cream, served by the waiter at the village's four-star restaurant and inn. Getting back by bus might have been a problem, because only one more bus left Falzarego Pass for Cortina that afternoon, and we still had to get back to the pass. The cost for a taxi was prohibitive, but sharing a van with others was well worth the fare.

That night in Cortina, we joined others in a pre-dinner stroll of the city streets. Two women wrapped in luxurious furs gazed longingly for some time at a shop widow containing several fur-draped mannequins. Were they comparing their own coats to those in the shop or thinking about buying a new one for next season? Even men wore fur coats, but the fur was on the inside, next to their skin. The only other place I have seen so many fur coats walking around is at the zoo.

Taking the autobus to Bressanone, we discovered a town where the preserved central square and surrounding buildings from a medieval past are treasured. Twisting narrow lanes between high walls of tan and gray buildings opened into the spacious ancient plaza. Vescovile, the Bishop's Palace, now a museum; majestic cathedrals; unusual sculptures and frescoes; stained-glass rose windows; and ornately decorated baroque organs transported us to centuries past. So did the cold and damp, making us grateful for the modern convenience of an inviting deli tucked into a corner arcade. When Kurt ordered "due cappuccini," the man behind the counter gestured towards me, asking if I was the wife.

Puzzled by this direct question, Kurt assured him that I was. "Bene, bene," he replied. "So seldom are they these days."

Old and new mix readily in Italy. Women dressed entirely in traditional black, including black head coverings knotted beneath their chins, wait for buses or shop in the markets. On the ten-minute cable-car ride to Faloria, fashionable ski-jacketed Italian businessmen on holiday pulled miniaturized cell phones from their pockets to negotiate deals while they rode.

Traveling in Italy never fails to reward us with something unexpected to appreciate and enjoy. On our first winter's visit, we discovered much more than the ski trails we'd come to explore.

GETTING WET

Baptism at White Horse

Getting it Right

New Jersey Pine Barrens

The Tuckahoe, Bull Run, Nantahala, and Ocoee

Floating the Buffalo

Ozark Riverways

Exploring our Boundaries

Two Weeks in the Grand Canyon

GETTING WET

*After twenty years of hiking in the Washington D.C. area, we knew most
of the trails very well and began thinking of some way to enjoy the countryside
from a different perspective. Kurt claimed experience canoeing. I'd been in a
canoe only once, on Lake Elliott in Washington State, where I did nothing but
enjoy an elegant picnic supper with wine while being serenaded by the guitar-
playing artist I was then dating. Our first trip together was with our son Alan, in
the Adirondack's lakes. Renting a canoe, we paddled across one lake, did the
short portage to the next, and paddled again to another. With three in the canoe,
it was a breeze. The scenery was lovely, the peace and quiet serene. Maybe
canoeing was the answer.*

BAPTISM AT WHITE HORSE

Once back in Washington, the two of us ventured farther. We rented
canoes at local boat houses, paddled around Roosevelt Island in the Potomac,
paddled again in the Potomac near Seneca Creek, where there were some riffles,
and then made our mistake. Visiting an outfitter near Harper's Ferry to rent a
canoe, we asked for a recommendation, explaining that we were good in flat
water and maybe riffles, but otherwise inexperienced. "Oh, the water level's low;
you can do the Needles with no problem." We were given PFDs (personal
flotation devices), which we wore, and told where we would be picked up and
that was that.

As we began the trip in water that looked like a lake, we noticed another
couple who could not keep their canoe in a straight line. Round and round they
went, both paddling on the same side of the canoe. We cut a straight line
smoothly through the water up to the remains of a broken dam. Some chutes of
water may have been passable, but we felt safer carrying the canoe over rocks at
the shoreline. The next section was fun, finding passages to thread our way
through the rock garden known as the Needles, as the current picked up. We were
having a fine time, making good choices and learning. When we reached
Harper's Ferry and the Potomac, we confidently picked a chute that we thought
would bypass the rather frightening-looking White Horse Rapids nearby. From
the back of the canoe, Kurt told me not to paddle. He'd steer the boat through.
For a moment we were okay. The next thing I remember is screaming for Kurt,

because I did not see him at the rear of the upended canoe. He was the stronger swimmer, and I was not sure I could rescue him. Though sputtering, I was glad to see that I'd actually done the right thing when dumped--hung onto the canoe. Kurt was attached to the canoe as well, but only by the rope he'd caught as the canoe went past him. We walked the canoe to the shore where we dumped the water out and watched one paddle, two jackets, and my hat floating away. My extra pair of glasses were somewhere on the river bottom. I'd also lost the glasses I wore. Though safety-wise in the mountains, we were totally green on the water and had not tied anything in. We didn't know about kneeling in the canoe to lower the center of gravity, and I hadn't thought to secure my glasses either.

Back on the river, with one paddle, we retrieved the jacket and hat, which we saw floating nearby. Luckily, we also found the second paddle washed up on an accessible rocky spot. Then we saw the inept, circling couple that we'd worried about earlier. They smoothly negotiated the same rapids that had done us in. It must have been dumb luck. Before we reached the takeout, we were trapped by two rocks, and the canoe filled with water, slowly sinking to the river bottom. In that spot, the river was shallow. We could stand up safely, but the water-filled canoe was too heavy for just the two of us to lift. Fortunately other canoers helped us empty it, and we finally safely reached our destination. Though I was happy to have survived, I promised myself and warned Kurt that I would never go anywhere in a canoe again until after I'd had some professional instruction.

GETTING IT RIGHT

Two summers later, we had completed the basic canoe class and were enrolled in the intermediate whitewater level. On the first of two weekends on the Potomac River not far from home, we learned peelouts, eddy turns, ferrying, and other ways to make the river's current work for, rather than against, us. With guidance we ran some minor falls (No, not Great Falls) without mishap. But if we wanted to graduate, we had to face running Shenandoah Staircase, managing a tricky spot over Bull Falls, and making it through White Horse Rapids, the same rapids that previously dumped us into the river. The day of our test, a scorcher, hundreds of tubers played in the Potomac near Harper's Ferry, trying to cool off. Avoiding people in and out of inner tubes added yet another challenge. We did the Staircase, and with good directions and lots of adrenaline, we cruised over Bull Falls. Suddenly we saw White Horse Rapids ahead! I dreaded the rerun, but I was prepared this time, having tied everything in and my glasses on. Determined to survive somehow, we faced our nemesis! It was nothing; we barely recognized the spot and breezed right by. Was the water level so different? Had our skills improved? Or was it good luck? Maybe all of the above. It also helped to see the route other class members took through the rapids.

In the fall we continued to explore Maryland and Virginia waterways. The best trip was on a cloudy October day, paddling with another couple on the Pocomoke River, portions of which become a maze-like swamp, complete with bald cypress trees, knees, and Spanish moss. Our reward on that achingly long, but hauntingly beautiful day was an incredibly delicious fresh crabcake and imperial crab feast in tiny Crisfield, Maryland, right where the crabs are harvested.

NEW JERSEY PINE BARRENS

When we learned that my newly discovered second cousins, Donna and Floyd, were experienced paddlers, we begged them to join us in an exploration of the New Jersey Pine Barrens. We'd read that the dark rivers of the area were swift flowing but without rapids. This would be an ideal way to enjoy a weekend and get better acquainted.

We drove there together but in separate cars, because we had to set up a shuttle to avoid having to paddle upstream. Leaving the women and the canoes at the put-in on the Mullica River, the men drove two cars to the end point of the trip, left one car there and drove back. We led out with the cousins following. At first there were no problems, but when the waterway narrowed and then followed a very twisting course, we lost them. After waiting a while, we finally started paddling back to check on them. They'd taken a turn too fast, and the canoe had bumped into a bank with enough force to tip over, flinging both of them into the thigh-high water. Their dry clothes were in the car at the end of the trip, so they gamely wrung out as much water as they could, climbed back in, and paddled on, drying out in the sunshine, not wanting to miss any of the great scenery in this unusual area. A beautiful blue sky and bright sun enhanced the contrasting beauty of the tannic-stained waters running beside white-barked maples whose bright red helicopter seedpods resembled fruit. Red-bellied woodpeckers visited our picnic at Batsto State Park. Except for the spill, a lovely trip.

THE TUCKAHOE, BULL RUN, NANTAHALA, AND OCOEE

An afternoon and all-night rainstorm on the first day of a Canoe Cruisers trip on the Cacapon River sent us to dry out in a motel, though the Girl Scout troop with us stayed in their tents. The next morning's look at the debris-laden, swollen, racing river convinced even the foolhardy that taking a chance for a second day of canoeing wasn't worth the risk.

Then, because we'd offered to lead a trip in return for all those we'd enjoyed as followers, we asked cousins Donna and Floyd to help us scout the

143

Tuckahoe on the Eastern Shore. Though not really whitewater, the Tuckahoe had been a pleasant, fast-moving stream when we'd run it with our son, Alan, several years before. One of the locals warned us, when I asked, that we might have some carrying to do, because the winter ice storms had brought down an extraordinary number of trees. We needed a portable chainsaw! Our river run became a river walk; mosquitoes enveloped us, biting the vulnerable mercilessly. At first the way was relatively clear. When it became almost impassable with fallen trees and entangled branches, we thought the way would probably open up just after the rough patch we were in.

By the time we seriously considered turning back, we were (we figured) more than halfway and didn't relish paddling upstream and re-portaging what we already knew was bad. Seven hours later we had covered the seven miles to the car. This was fun? Okay, so the last three miles were on an open, wide marshy part of the stream as it nears the bay, but by then we were almost done for. Can you believe the cousins didn't disown us? They're just always busy when we mention a joint trip somewhere.

Because the Tuckahoe was so hopeless, we decided to offer a trip on Bull Run, a local stream, instead. But when a prolonged dry spell caused water levels to drop, we worried whether Bull Run would be runnable. We should have canceled our guided trip altogether, but some potential followers called wanting to do it, even after we explained they might have to drag their canoes through the shallows. So we waited in the parking lot, and waited, and finally hiked the trail when no one showed up. We had canoed that run too many times to make it really fun, despite the numerous herons and Canadian geese that hang out in the area.

Our July 3 "ducky" trip on the Nantahala in North Carolina began well on beautiful clear water, with warm temperatures and a sunny sky. We quickly caught on to the ways of these inflatable kayaks, as we traveled through pleasant class I and II rapids, the current doing most of the work. Our job was more steering than heavy paddling. But the trip became a bit too exciting when Kurt's kayak flipped into the river not far from the class III rapids. Floating on his back, with his feet downstream in the approved manner, he might have made it to shore safely, but while being "helped" over slimy, slippery rocks by a Good Samaritan, he was hit between the eyes with a paddle. We were prepared to walk the short way to the takeout, but when two guides with space in their rafts offered, we rode over the rapids with them. Then to first aid and dry clothes.

All went well the next day on our wilder, but safer, guided raft trip on Ocoee in Tennessee. Although the Ocoee is a dam-controlled river, recreational releases by the TVA create a thrilling half-day ride through class III and IV rapids. The most terrifying moment for me was before we entered the river. The bus dropped us and the rafts at the end of Ocoee Lake created by the dam. I could see a huge drop to the river below, but no road to the river. Surely we weren't supposed to slide down the face of the dam? Only when we carried the rafts to the dam's edge did I see the steps at the side which led down to the river's edge. Rafters were given thorough safety instructions and directions about paddling. These warnings, though necessary, always give me second thoughts about going, but so far I've never backed out of a trip. We tried to attach ourselves to a guide who looked experienced, hoping we'd made a good choice. Everyone wore helmets and PFDs. A guide with each group of six barked commands from the back of the raft as it bucked and plunged through the fourteen rapids. Some rafts overturned and stranded paddlers on rocks in the middle of the river. Because we had an excellent guide and a great crew, we were able to rescue some strandees, taking them into our raft until we could re-assemble at the shore to prepare for the last bit of bouncy river before the takeout and a great dinner.

FLOATING THE BUFFALO

By mid-May you can forget the first 20 miles of the Buffalo National River from its start to Ponca, but the rest of the undammed 155-mile river is eminently floatable. The 34 miles we "floated" (the Arkansas term for any kind of boating) was mighty fine. Swift current, riffles, and absolutely clear limestone-tinted pools beneath high rock bluffs adorned with mini waterfalls and maidenhair fern clusters invited many paddlers of all ages.

The various groups at the put-in soon spread out, and we and our two friends, who live in the Ozarks, had the river's beauty to ourselves until Waterfall Rock, a trap for the unwary. The safest route was on the left. But low water had narrowed the passage by the side of this massive, eight-foot-high boulder, over which a fast stream of water poured. When the narrowed and swifter current pushed paddlers too close to the boulder, the waterfall fell directly into their canoes, causing some unexpected swims. We sneaked by, but our friends weren't so lucky. "Wrecking Rock" was something else. It posed no threat at all, downgraded by the river's changing course.

Some class III water had been predicted, but we found only swift current with class I and II sections. On the first day from Ponca to Kyle's Landing, where we camped, whitewater sections were fairly continuous, giving us lots of practice; but as we floated downstream, the quiet pools grew longer, and there were fewer rapids. Characteristic were long gravel bars separating the flow into as many as four channels. Choosing the perfect path to avoid getting stuck or swept into overhanging branches and stumpwads challenged us. The aluminum Grumman ran aground a few times; even our yellow Explorer got stuck once.

We camped at primitive Steel Creek and Kyle's Landing and finished the trip at Ozark with flush toilets and potable water, but gravel-bar camping is favored by many. One couple we met planned five days on the river. Their gear included lawn chairs and a table with a roll-up top as well as the usual. Camping was comfortably uncrowded until Friday night when weekenders from Little Rock, Arkansas, and Springfield, Missouri, arrived. Tent city rose in the overflow area--one Boy Scout troop had eighteen canoes. But we didn't hear much noise, and because we headed out Saturday morning, we missed gridlock on the river.

In addition to magnificent bluffs rising straight up from the water, some 500 feet high, the lush, velvety greens of conifers and deciduous trees and bushes, and a delicious peace and quiet, the Buffalo offered hikes up side canyons to caves and waterfalls, to a picturesque weathered farmstead from the 1800s, and to a summer-use Boy Scout camp where the limestone-faced dining room had stained-glass windows. Birdsong was continuous, but most birds stayed hidden in the leaves. After 150, we quit counting turtles. Floating the Buffalo feels and looks like wilderness, as the national park consists of the river and a green strip of varying width along its entire length. On our last river day, we saw only one other paddler all day long--except for our friends.

The previous night, while shuttling, Ken was warned of a "killer stump" lying in wait three pools after the group of long ledges just barely under water on the left. Having swum the first day, Ken took no chances. We scouted every blind corner after passing what we thought were the ledges. My question, "Are we past the stump yet?" drew only a disapproving look from Ken who continued to theorize about the stump's position for the rest of the trip.

Now a National River that flows undammed from near Boxley for 155 miles to its confluence with the White River (a river heavily dammed as at Bull Shoals), the Buffalo was saved from dammation when local conservationists won a 1960s epic struggle with the Army Corps of Engineers. The National Park Service (NPS) has improved access from nearby highways (via dirt or gravel roads) and built campgrounds about every ten miles.

A guide, *Buffalo National River*, is available from NPS. The first twenty miles of the river are floatable by canoes only after sufficient rain. But you just have to put in somewhere once you've watched the video *Peace like a River* at the visitor center at Pruitt, which also sells detailed maps and an excellent paperback photobook, *The Buffalo River Country,* by Ken L. Smith.

If you don't want to bring your own canoe on the two-day drive, as we did, you can rent one for about $30.00 a day at several access points, where shuttle service and advice are also available. The best time to float is April-May after which only the lower two-thirds of the river has reliable water levels. But paddlers can enjoy fall colors in October, if there have been early fall rains. Midweek trips are best for avoiding crowds and securing a campsite and a rental canoe.

On our way home we checked out the Ozark Riverways in southeast Missouri, near U.S. Highway 60. The Jack's Fork and Current Rivers, mostly class I and II, are administered by NPS. The Forest Service takes care of the

Eleven Point River. Facilities and services seemed similar to those available at the Buffalo River. We decided to save them for later.

OZARK RIVERWAYS

Our return to canoe the Missouri rivers was a washout. We expected high water in Indiana, but hadn't heard how bad it was in Missouri. When high water closed the Jack's Fork River, we tried the Current, putting in at Cedar Grove to avoid stumpwads, debris, and strainers upstream. That day was really terrific. We looked into Cave Spring; enjoyed the general scenery, though it wasn't quite as good as the Buffalo River; and were impressed by our fabulous paddling prowess--we did seventeen miles in three hours without even working very hard. Pulltite (our chosen campground) was neither crowded nor deserted when we arrived at 2:00 p.m.--perfect. Several birds performed courting rituals right before our eyes, and bunny rabbits munched the grass at sundown. This was living!

In the morning, we woke to a terrifying cloudburst, lightning, thunder, and hailstones. We huddled cringing in the tent, thankful we hadn't pitched it beneath any really huge trees. The storm ended about breakfast time. After eating, we packed our gear and dragged everything down to the put-in just as the park ranger arrived with the "River Closed" sign. The storm had hit earlier upstream, dumping several inches on rivers already at crest stage.

Once this surge passed, the ranger said, the river would drop fast and might be open the next day, if it didn't rain. We hung around for the day, hoping to paddle the rest of the way to our car. We didn't want to pay yet another shuttle fee. Now it was hot and humid, steamy from the storm, and even hiking was not much fun. As we stared glumly at the flooding river, we noticed a dog that seemed to be drowning. Though struggling, with his nose barely above the water, he eventually swam across the chocolate, rising river to the shore. Waved in by the ranger, the dog's owner beached his canoe, claiming the dog loved swimming so much it was impossible to keep him out of the water.

The next day, the river was open, but only to Round Spring, where we would again be stuck; the ranger offered to drive Kurt to Eminence where he could pick up our car. Though the Current was now closed and likely to stay so; strangely, the Jack's Fork was now open. When we and the canoe got back to Eminence, we checked out Alley Spring, thinking we'd arrange a shuttle in the morning. A new storm arrived that night and sat directly over Eminence, knocking out electricity in the little café in town, downing huge trees on the highway to Blue Spring, and crushing our hopes for canoeing. We could see the Current was very high, obliterating the alternate trail to Blue Spring; so we warned my sister-in-law in Quincy of our earlier and longer visit with them. We stopped at Meramec Caverns in the rain, seeing the Meramec River also rising, partially covering the parking lot, and paused at Hermann, Missouri, to buy some Hermanhof wine for our hosts.

EXPLORING OUR BOUNDARIES

"Either an island or a point. They make the best campsites." My cousin Donna yelled our instructions from the canoe behind us. "And fill the water jug from the <u>middle</u> of the lake, before you pull in."

"Okay," I called back confidently, desperately studying the trail map in the bottom of the canoe, hoping the slight bump on the left shoreline was actually the "point" on the map marked by a campsite's red circle. Who could tell? I was new at this. The island campsite we had wanted was occupied; it was already 4:00 p.m., and we were in the middle of Minnesota's Boundary Waters Canoe Area Wilderness (BWCAW).

As we paddled closer to the bump, a vacant fire circle became clearly visible. Now we had only to negotiate a good landing on the rocks, drag our packs out of the canoe, set up two tents and a rain tarp, cook dinner, and locate the latrine before dark. Some days were like that. We'd paddle from portage to portage, taking turns carrying the canoes over rocky and root-covered trails to the next lake. Then we'd carry our packs over, load them in the canoes, lash them down, and paddle some more.

For years I'd heard about the beauty of the Boundary Waters, but fear of mosquitoes had kept me away. One summer my cousin, a former Minnesotan, suggested going after Labor Day when cooler weather would diminish insect numbers, and I agreed to give it a try.

Donna had paddled and portaged these waters often in years past, but her last visit was eleven years earlier. She wanted to celebrate turning sixty-two by returning to her scenes of glory. She was also almost six feet tall, and her thirty-five-year-old friend, Paul, towered above us all at six feet four. We are little people: Kurt is five feet eight and I'm five feet two. But we were relatively strong for sixty-nine and sixty-two and had spent a month earlier in the summer hiking and backpacking in the Southwest. Because Donna could take only a week's vacation, she and Paul flew to Duluth, where we met them with our combined gear and their metal sixty-five-pound canoe. We planned to rent a kevlar canoe, weighing only forty-eight pounds.

In-line skaters and walkers shared the wide shoulder of scenic Highway 61, which hugs Lake Superior's shore north of Duluth. The car stopped twice before turning off at Tofte: once for smoked whitefish and again just beyond Two Harbors at Betty's Pies, a small place crammed with people who knew about pie.

The road from Tofte was fairly decent, even paved for a short while, but we soon hit three miles of construction, where slippery mud required the driver's concentration. Soon enough we reached Sawbill Canoe Outfitters sitting at the edge of Sawbill Lake. Here at the beginning of wilderness, everything can be rented including canoes, vests, paddles, tents, packs, sleeping bags, pads, chairs, tarps, axes, cooking kits, rain suits, carriers, stoves, lanterns, first aid kits, camp hammocks, and bear ropes.

Showers were also available for $2.50, or $3.00 with a towel. A sauna with shower and towel was $5.00. Maps, fishing licenses, dehydrated food, fresh food, and BWCAW Travel Permits could also be purchased. A nearby Forest Service Campground at $9.00 a site was a good place to check out our gear and to fill water jugs and bottles one last time from a well, before we left semi-civilization.

When a gentle rain started, we crawled into our tents, assured of a good night's sleep. We woke to cool, dry, gorgeous weather, picked up the one canoe we were renting and drove for forty-five minutes to Kawishiwi Lake, our starting point. Several canoes moved through the waters; some people were fishing; others had set up camp. As we entered the marshy passage supposedly leading to Square Lake, a solitary black-and-white loon came close, as if to inspect the new intruders.

Square Lake was smaller than Kawishiwi, but though its shape was roughly square, the sides had numerous indentations. One of these was a stream leading to a portage to Kawashachung Lake, but after exploring several dead ends and walking a short portage to yet another lake, we realized we'd passed the entrance early on. Paddling back towards our entry point encouraged us to improve our map-reading skills. On my cousin's last trip, the portages had been marked by wooden signs, and on long portages, logs positioned high between two trees gave the portager a resting spot for the upright canoe. We quickly learned that this trip would be more challenging and adventurous as both of these aids had been removed.

Forty rods was the stated length of the first portage, but the root-encrusted and rock-strewn trail went up and then down before reaching a muddy creek with a questionable amount of floatable water. I carried the canoe farther on, but finally had to rest. Putting the canoe on the ground in a grassy area, I returned for my pack. Paul had carried some gear even farther through very rough terrain, and I wasn't looking forward to that. Just as I returned, we saw canoers coming toward us, still water-borne. We put our canoe into the water right there. Paddling or even poling beats carrying any day.

The next portage, a rocky eleven rods, pinched off the meandering stream, but we managed without unloading everything we'd just loaded and lashed down, by doing a four-person carry for each canoe. From the other side, a narrow, clear passage bordered by water lilies and lily pads took us into Kawashachong Lake, where we found a beautiful campsite, boiled water for the next day, used our "bear rope" to hang all food and garbage twelve feet off the ground, dangling between two trees, and listened late at night to the haunting call of the loon.

Wispy tendrils of fog hovered around the tent flap, encouraging us to stay inside our cozy sleeping bags. Knowing that we had two long portages today before our next campsite didn't energize us either. But once the fog burned off, we ate a leisurely breakfast surrounded by the silent comfort of the north woods. The lake lapped gently at the rocky shore; tall evergreens, maples, and birches stood watch over us, only a hint of their fall brilliance showing on the highest limbs. Sunlight bounced off the lake even as it warmed us. Who would want to leave? Only those who want to see what lies around the next bend. Only those who want to see where the river leads.

At the portage we met a group of three going out. They told us a story of bears carrying off packs that had been left unguarded at portage points, so we rethought our plans. Leaving the canoes, we carried the packs over the 190 rods. This also gave us a chance to evaluate the problems in the trail before we had to carry the canoes. Kurt agreed to stand guard, as a knee was beginning to give him some grief. Back to get the canoes, my cousin and I traded off carrying the canoe and carrying an extra duffel bag and the water bottles. Paul carried the sixty-five-pound canoe on his own. After all that, crossing the next lake took about fifteen minutes, followed by a 95-rod portage. Was this really fun? I was beginning to wonder.

One problem followed another. When Paul's water filter clogged just at dusk, we had to boil all drinking water, rapidly depleting our fuel supply. But after we cleaned the water filter, its efficiency allowed us to conserve stove fuel. Then my stove quit, leaving us dependent on one burner. Still, the fabled hordes of ferocious mosquitoes had not put in an appearance. During the week, I did get five new bites, but I can get that many in ten minutes in my backyard at home. Of course, I stayed completely covered up, and when I saw a few mosquitoes flying around, I even covered my head with a net.

One day, heavy rain in the morning surprised us after a dazzling starry sky the previous night. Breakfast was cooked under the tarp that had been quickly strung up in the downpour. Later we dried things out before moving on. Just as we reached Lake Koma after three portages (They were somehow becoming more bearable.), heavy clouds, thunder, and lightning developed. Up went the tarp with our tent groundcloths forming sidewalls. We huddled inside our shelter, building swales with gravel and digging out small side streams to divert the water running down the trail where we crouched with our gear and overturned canoes. When we thought the storm had passed over, we paddled furiously to a campsite, cooked dinner, pumped water, and went to sleep.

After breakfast, we noticed previous campers had left a rope and carabiner high in a tree, luring me into climbing an adjacent tree and using a paddle to wiggle it loose. I felt like a kid again. We camped there two nights and spent one day exploring. On the map we could see an ideal day trip. One short portage, now without packs, would take us to Lake Malberg. From there another portage would give us access to a circle route on the Kawishiwi River, returning to Malberg.

A late start and threatening weather kept us from completing the Kawishiwi Circle, but Lake Malberg was itself quite beautiful, and we walked over to where the river began, saving the Kawishiwi River circle route for another time. We arrived back at our campground just in time to hunker down under the tarp during a torrential downpour. A break in the storm allowed us to cook dinner in the open before another downpour.

On our way back to Kawishiwi Lake, where we'd started the trip, we found other lovely campsites and met congenial folks who invited us to share afternoon soup with them. A group of twelve mergansers swam past our campsite just at twilight. Early one morning a beaver explored the shoreline. Bears never bothered our food, and though we saw evidence of moose residents, we never saw the animals themselves. One night we thought we heard wolves. When the heavier canoe slipped and pinched a nerve on Paul's shoulder, we women were by then strong enough to carry it in turns. Once we stopped early, had tea and snacks, then read, slept, and wrote in our journals as our damp items dried in the relaxingly lazy afternoon sun.

We arrived back at Kawishiwi Lake, loaded the two canoes on top of the car, and reached the outfitters right on schedule. Fresh salad at the deli in Tofte was more than welcome after our freeze-dried week. So were the hot showers at the motel near Duluth. We'd experienced and survived the Boundary Waters; we'd seen no motorboats, very few mosquitoes, and days of beautiful lakes and woods. We had learned that one can get used to almost anything--including portaging. I know it builds upper body strength even in seniors like us; it probably builds character, too.

TWO WEEKS IN THE GRAND CANYON

Seeing people rafting the Colorado River as we hiked the Kaibab trail from the rim of the Grand Canyon made us want to try it. Twelve years later we did. We knew there were rapids to be run, but a friend who had taken the trip told us there were mostly long peaceful floats in between short periods of frantic action, and the scenery was unbelievable. Hooked on the idea and suppressing our fears, we plowed through numerous brochures, trying to find the perfect trip. Rejecting motorized trips outright narrowed the choices. When we saw a sixteen-day "hiker's special" that offered a daily choice of paddle or oar raft, we sent in our money. The oar raft is large enough to carry gear in the middle on a deck; a guide who uses two very long oars to direct the boat propelled by the river's current; and up to four life-jacketed passengers, who sit on the inflated tubes, two in front and two in back of the oar deck, clutching the safety rope which encircles the raft. The smaller paddle raft rides closer to the water, carries no gear, and has a guide in back who controls a rudder and yells orders at critical moments to the six life-jacketed paddlers using standard canoe paddles. There are no real seats for any of the passengers. Six guides looked after our group of eighteen. Our three oar boats could only carry a total of twelve riders, so each day, six of us had to choose to paddle. The last two guides rowed the garbage raft and the food raft.

We'd done some whitewater rafting in West Virginia, so we knew how to sit on the tubing and cram our feet under it. On the New River we'd done one class V rapid, wearing life jackets and helmets, with a guide in the raft barking instructions. When I heard we'd be doing class IX and X rapids and would not have helmets, my submerged fears rose to the surface. Guides assured us that the higher rating was based on water volume not technical difficulty, and that we should think of a X as a V with lots more water. This was comforting? We wouldn't need helmets, they said, because there weren't many rocks, and there was such a volume of water that we would be more likely to have other kinds of problems first. It was then too late to get any kind of refund if we bailed out, so we stayed. This trip had the potential for being an absolutely fabulous experience or a total disaster.

On the first day, Kurt tried the paddle raft, as we enjoyed beautiful scenery and medium-sized rapids from the put-in at Lee's Ferry. We watched as the top layer of canyon rocks, the tan-colored Kaibab limestone, gave way to the Supai formations, their beautiful red color almost glowing. At Mile 8 of the 221 miles we would eventually travel, our first short hike took us to a fossil of a Permian reptile: padded paws and claws embedded in rock. That night we feasted on chicken cacciatore, salad, and blueberry cobbler. So far so good!

Each morning after breakfast, mesh bags, waterproof bags for gear, and sleeping bags were stuffed and piled along with foam sleeping pads near the shore. Though helping out was optional, most of the eighteen passengers joined the bag brigade, tossing gear along the line to reach the guide on a raft who lashed everything to the oar deck. This was followed by the "morning blather" usually a brief assessment of the previous day's activity and a description of what was planned for the day ahead with advice and suggestions from the very impressive and attractive female lead guide. At night the process reversed. From the pile near the shore we'd grab our gear and a foam sleeping pad and hunt for a desirable sleeping area. One guide would set up the unusual but practical toilet and handwashing station in a secluded spot–sometimes including a lovely view. Before long we'd be devouring delicious gourmet wilderness meals seasoned with voracious appetites heightened by an active, strenuous outdoor day on the river.

Temperatures the last ten days of May were very pleasant, though one morning dark clouds and sleet surprised us. When we reached Mile 20 and a series of rapids called the "Roaring Twenties," passengers on one raft were given pearls and elbow length gloves to wear. Hiking up Rider Canyon to see Anasazi cave paintings, Kurt slipped on mud into a neck-deep pool. The sides were slick and totally vertical. Without help, he'd still be there.

Other hikes took us clambering up a rope, then swimming through four pools to beautiful Silver Grotto; up creek beds to trails that led to the tops of buttes with incredible views; to moss-covered waterfalls; to the throne room (three mammoth natural stone formations resembling seats for giants or gods); to a geological fault with twisted, alien-looking rock strata; and through chest-high Thunder Creek, where the water flowed so swiftly that only forming a human chain kept us from being swept away. At Redwall Canyon, a huge overhang created a cave-like protected beach site, perfect for a fossil talk and a wild volleyball game after lunch.

Where the Little Colorado flows into the big one, we wore our life-jackets like diapers, with legs through the armholes to protect our behinds from the rocks in the rapids we happily floated through. We visited Anasazi ruins and saw from afar caves that had been used for granaries.

Very quickly running the rapids became more fun than terror, and we grew adept at bailing water out swiftly. Riding the front tube of the raft like a figurehead, while clinging to the rope, was like riding a lively horse bareback. When an unexpected big wave pushed me back to the bottom of the raft, the guide worried until I yelled, "Get me up, I want to catch the next one." I spent half the days paddling, though I was also proud of maneuvering our oar raft through a class III and a class V rapid, but that was really hard work. In our first class IX, Hermit Rapids, one wave crashed right on our heads, and the raft was almost vertical–amazing to see it right itself. Crystal Rapids, a class X, slammed our raft against a rock, but we hung on as the raft bounced off safely through exciting high waves.

At Mile 88 we visited Phantom Ranch to mail postcards to be carried by mules to the Grand Canyon's rim, to eat ice cream, and to take a look at Cottonwood Campground, where Kurt and I had camped on our previous visit to the Colorado River. Here the dark primordial Vishnu schist layers of rock are revealed, changing once more the character of the canyon. Admiring the high suspension bridge over the Colorado River, we waved to hikers ascending Bright Angel Trail.

Quiet times held their own wonder. At one lunch stop, a very young canyon wren, just learning to fly, landed on Kurt's shoulder for a moment. One young man often played his flute when we stopped for lunch in echoing canyons. Some evenings guitars played as we drifted off to sleep under the stars. One day of sunshine followed another, and we are forever indebted to our Arkansas canoeing friend who told us about bag balm. A medicated ointment normally used for softening cow's udders, it was the only effective protection and restorative for the cracked skin of hands and feet that had been underwater for too long. We became very popular among fellow sufferers.

153

Besides hearing about the geology of the canyon, we learned to recognize many specialized canyon plants and were thrilled to see spiny lizards, families of bighorn sheep, marmots, chuckwallas, and tall black-necked stilts with long red legs. We were not so thrilled to hear about the small rattlesnake one camper found on her sleeping bag. Though we had all been sleeping in our bags under the magnificent starry sky, we moved into tents that night.

Just as we started through class V, Tapeats Rapids, the last one before the campsite one night, the paddle-raft guide joked that she would push Kurt out in the rapid so we could practice life-saving skills. We entered the rapid just fine, managed a few waves, and then hit a big wave straight on. Two paddlers were thrown together, bumping heads, and Kurt went overboard, though not pushed by the guide, who was horrified. Not seeing him in the back of the raft, I almost jumped in the river to find him, but realized there would then be two people needing rescue. Kurt stayed calm and floated on his back through the rapid to our raft, holding his paddle in the approved manner. Worried about him, we all forgot to paddle, and the river swept us past the campsite before we got to the shore. Once there we had to pull the raft back upstream to camp.

As we reached Mile 157 and the end of May, daytime temperatures soared, making the daylong stop at Havasu Creek, where many stream crossings led to a travertine pool large enough for swimming, very welcome, enjoyable, and refreshing. So many people wanted to paddle through Lava Falls, the biggest rapid on the river, that we had a lottery. I loved paddling, but feeling uneasy about Lava Falls, I did not put my name in, much to everyone's surprise. Instead, I drew out the lucky names. Concerned about possibly dislocating his shoulder, Kurt joined me in an oar raft. Though of fairly short duration, Lava Falls Rapids were extremely intense. We scouted them first, while the guides described procedures in detail. The frothing, swirling, foaming water, resembling the turbulence in a giant washing machine, convinced me I'd made the right choice.

Our raft went first–a very fast, crashing, thrashing run through mighty waves. Once it looked as if we were headed straight into a huge wave. A towering wall of water totally submerged us as the raft bucked one way, then another, almost folding itself in half. We gasped for air. Then a second wave hit us, as we clung fiercely to the safety ropes, and we were out safe. A second guide and his raft full of passengers came through fine. Next was the paddle boat. We saw it enter the rapids, just a shade too close to the bubble line. Our guide told us then to keep our eyes on one person each. The raft and its passengers rode up one side of a huge wave. They paddled furiously, but as the wave crashed, the raft was dragged down into a hole, its back flipped up, tossing all passengers out. Continuing down the huge water slide, the raft disappeared, but eventually was found downstream. Four swimmers headed towards us; two sharing a paddle between them. After we pulled them exhausted into the boat, we saw that the three others had made it to the shore. All were safe, but their experiences while under water were very frightening, and most of them were bruised in some way and shaken up, though very grateful to be alive and out safely.

When our third oar raft joined us, we learned that Pauline, a retired nurse, had lost her grip on the ropes and been thrown into the air and then down on the oar deck. She'd been unconscious for a few seconds, as the raft contorted and buckled through the waves. Rowing the rest of the rapid with one oar while holding onto Pauline, Krista, the guide, had kept quizzing Pauline, trying to bring her around. Now Pauline felt fine, but she agreed to the guide's request that she be med-evacuated and checked out at the hospital. Our entire group floated a short distance downstream to the helipad where we began setting up camp. Contact was made with a plane flying overhead, and about twenty minutes later the helicopter arrived for Pauline. "This flight is an exciting first for me," Pauline said, promising to meet us for dinner in Flagstaff.

Constant water fights on the last full day on the river made the intense heat in the lower canyon on the first of June bearable. That night around a campfire we listened to local folklore and exchanged comments and feelings about our trip. Despite a wide range of ages, abilities, and interests, all members of the group were very congenial and considerate of each other. Many people marveled that Kurt, at almost seventy, did every hike offered. Everyone was impressed by Dave, twenty-eight, who participated in every activity, despite being blind. On hikes he'd walk behind a guide, resting his hand on the guide's shoulder. He'd laugh off occasional scrapes. Sometimes he needed help with the gear or with choosing what he wanted to eat for dinner, but his amiability and courage enriched the trip for everyone. The moon rose late, but it was almost full.

We loaded the rafts in the morning at 5:00 a.m., then floated silently to the landing where a fantastic brunch awaited. After unloading and deflating the rafts we said our good-byes and headed back to Flagstaff, where we had dinner with a rested Pauline and others who didn't have a plane to catch, ending what turned out to be a fabulous and unforgettable experience.

Boundary Waters

Havasu Canyon Hike

Floating the Buffalo River

Boundary Waters Portage

Lava Falls   Colorado River

Bay at Noosa Head - Australia

Katherine Gorge
Australia

Volcanoes National Park -Hawaii Island

Milford Trek - New Zealand

Wallaby & Joey -Tasmania, Australia

PART II — A WORLD OF WONDERS

ISLAND SURVIVORS

Puerto Rico

Hawaii Snapshot

Grand Bahama Island

Fiji

Dominican Republic

St. Thomas and St. John

New Zealand

Australian Adventure

ISLAND SURVIVORS

Although we have different opinions in several areas, when it comes to vacations, we have never had to face the choice between mountains or beach. Even before we met, we were both mountain lovers. Having spent early childhood on the California coast, I liked going to the beach occasionally, jumping the waves, beachcombing, and flying kites, but an entire vacation spent on the beach had no appeal. We always chose a mountainous destination, looking for hiking or climbing opportunities. Tropical islands we planned to save for when we couldn't do anything else. In 1972, a reckless skier cracked Kurt's ribs, preventing him from taking a planned ski week in Canada. This was a time when Kurt couldn't do anything else, so we took our first island vacation, in Puerto Rico. It would be sixteen years before we returned to another island, this time because a scientific conference was being held in Hawaii.

PUERTO RICO

Modern high-rise hotels located on the beach in the Isla Verde and Condado areas of Puerto Rico were very expensive and weren't of much interest to us. Instead, we stayed in historic Old San Juan, for a reasonable price, in a restored Carmelite convent built originally in the 1600s. The white stucco facade with arched entrances, balconies, lots of dark wood beams, heavy doors, creaky hinges, and wrought iron captivated us. El Convento's restaurant was located in its central patio, where candlelit tables surrounded a charming fountain adorned with flowering tropical plants--a very romantic setting. And the food was good, too.

We could walk to El Morro, the famous fort perched on the rocky edge of

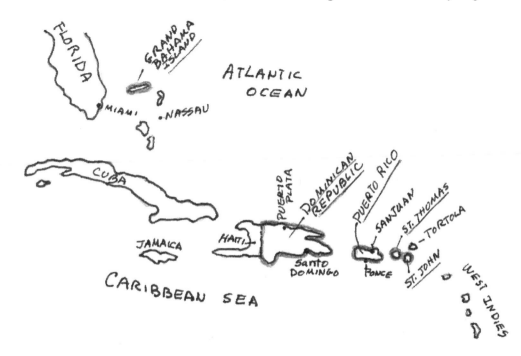

the island. Completed in 1589, the fort rises 140 feet above the sea. Its 18-foot-thick wall is studded with small circular sentry boxes called *garitas*. Found only in the forts of Puerto Rico, these *garitas* have become a national emblem. The fort, a national historic site, covers seventy-four acres and is the largest in the Caribbean. It gives the visitor spectacular views of the sea. The National Park Service tour guided us through the maze of tunnels, dungeons, barracks, outposts and ramps. In 1595, Ponce de Leon was able to prevail over Sir Francis Drake with the help of Castillo San Felipe del Morro. San Cristobal, El Morro's partner in the city's defense was built in 1634. This fort covered twenty-seven acres, but was fascinating because it had five independent units, each connected by moat and secret tunnels, and each fully self-sufficient, should the others fail. We learned a lot about fortifications that day.

In contrast to these imposing structures were the lovely gardens surrounding La Forteleza, built in 1540 as a fortress, but remodeled in 1846 to palatial splendor, appropriate to its role as the official Governor's Residence. These gardens offered an oasis of quiet and tropical beauty in a slightly run-down part of town. Another enchanting spot was the Plazuela de la Rogativa, where a bronze sculpture by Lindsay Daen memorializes a religious procession of a bishop and women who carried torches and chanted prayers for deliverance when the city was attacked by the British in 1797. Thinking that the flames and noise were local reinforcements arriving, the British left the city unscathed. The figures of the sculpture have elegant elongated shapes resembling sculptures of Giacometti.

After three days in San Juan, we rented a car to see more of the island. Our first stop was the Bacardi rum plant, the largest rum distillery in the world. The tour of the plant was interesting, but we really appreciated the free rum cocktails offered to each guest.

Near Ponce, we stopped at the Indian ball park, where remains of seven ball-fields can be seen. Some are outlined with large stones on which petroglyphs are visible. On one of the two dance grounds, stones line up with the sun during the equinox and solstice–Puerto Rico's pre-Columbian Stonehenge. We couldn't resist taking a photograph of the Parque de Bombas, a flamboyant, red and black striped wooden structure, built in 1882 for an exhibition, but used as an active firehouse when we were there. The pleasant town of Ponce was founded in 1692 by the great-grandson of Juan Ponce de Leon. Although Puerto Rico was first discovered by Europeans when Columbus landed in 1493, the first European attempt to settle the area did not occur until 1508 when the King of Spain granted a charter to Ponce de Leon.

Our next stop was at Luquillo beach–a beautiful, crescent-shaped beach with leaning palm trees and many lovely picnic spots. Our time at the beach and the room at the parador almost converted us to beach lovers. The next day we hiked up El Yunque through a very misty tropical rain forest. Palms, giant ferns, banana trees, bromeliads, and a large number and variety of colorful flowering shrubs and wildflowers we couldn't identify surrounded us. A waterfall over mossy rocks was an added attraction. The view from the top was hidden in clouds, but the way up through lush and overgrown greenery was an experience to remember.

HAWAII SNAPSHOT

Every high school girl I knew in the 1950s wished for a Hawaiian honeymoon. Besides collecting linens in a hope chest, girls saved money for that magical trip, even before they were going steady. I wasn't interested. The hype in the brochures I read was too much. No place could be that beautiful, idyllic, fascinating and, well–perfect. Besides, lying around on a beach was not my favorite activity. I spent my honeymoon backpacking in Colorado. Much later, when my husband had a conference in Hawaii, we learned how wrong I was.

In addition to the fascinating and peaceful mix of peoples and cultures, the tropical vegetation, clean air, pleasant temperature, afternoon rainbows, and ever-present trade winds convinced me that Hawaii's reputation as an island paradise is well-deserved. Unexpected was the incredible taste of really fresh, ripe pineapple, and the hiking. It is impossible not to relax in Hawaii--at least somewhat.

We wanted to see and try everything, but our time was limited. Surfing the waves looked like tremendous fun, but doing it well requires more time than we had. Near Diamond Head, which we hiked for the views, expert wind-surfers became airborne on perfect waves, but off Maui at the county beach near the airport, flailing beginners showed us there's more to the sport than meets the eye. Instead of surfing, we tried snorkeling, a new experience for us. Getting the mask to seal well on Kurt's mustached, bearded face was not so easy. The sensation of swimming in the midst of brightly-colored fish of varied sizes and shapes, however, was a thrill which we looked forward to repeating.

Bishop Museum on Oahu captivated us with its rooms of rare polished calabash bowls, dog's-tooth ankle bracelets, feathered cloaks of the nobility, tapa cloth, and other curiosities. Outside, I posed between two women touring from Japan, agreeing to their sign-language request. With no other common language, I couldn't explain I wore my thrift-shop muu-muu just because it was comfortable. So I smiled for the camera and bowed in answer to their "arigato," no doubt memorialized in someone's photo album as an "authentic Hawaiian native."

Downtown, the 1820s mission houses, the church built of coral rather than stone, and the unusual symbolic state capitol clustered near the gold-dressed statue of Kamehameha the Great. At the aquarium, live chambered nautiluses (or is it nautili?) and baby cuttlefish looking like small horseheads were unique among the varieties of tropical fish. Enormous banyan trees in the zoo fascinated us as well.

Everywhere the scenery is dramatic: sheer drops from steep green-covered peaks at Pali Heights on Oahu and Iao needle on Maui are breathtaking. Cliffs fall sharply to the crashing surf, where floating on the clear aquamarine or deep-blue ocean, picturesque islands nestle in coves along the coastline drive. At Byodo-In, fat goldfish leap out of the water for the tourists feeding them, while birds come in answer to a Buddhist monk's whistle, to eat hand-held breadcrumbs in front of the pagoda-like temple, which stands, as if protected, beneath the towering spires of a deeply-ravined mountain range.

Demonstrations, history, music, and dances by friendly Pacific Basin students at Brigham Young University's Polynesian Cultural Center set us dreaming about future trips. Their evening show begins with a tableau of torch-lit war canoes gliding by an exotic backdrop which includes a waterfall. Vigorous ritual dances from various island cultures follow, culminating in a dramatic sword and fire dance.

Waimea Falls Park, on Oahu's north shore, offered cliff diving (like Acapulco) into the pool below the falls, a performance of the ancient hula (even men dance), and a beautiful hibiscus garden. A talk about recent archeological findings and early native life was given by a park employee who had graduated from our local Maryland high school.

On Maui, Haleakala's crater, a moonscape of cinder cones, inner craters, and hardened lava, is accented by its rare silverswords, plants that grow only in lava rock at high altitudes, and the nene geese, nearly extinct large birds, who live on berries and vegetation in the dry uplands of Hawaii.They do not require ponds or marshes like other geese, for they have adapted to the habitat and drink very little water. In perfect weather, we hiked Sliding Sands Trail down 3,000 feet from the 10,000-foot summit of the cone and for almost twelve miles before we climbed out again in mist, clouds, and light rain, up the never-ending switchbacks to reach the road. Then Kurt hiked six more miles up the road for the car, while I took the packs and headed down--but I got a ride from a park ranger.

We stayed in Hilo, on Hawaii Island, near Volcanoes National Park. The Park is a place of wonder, with sulphurous fumes, steaming vents, and glowing, molten rock oozing from the earth's core. The most dangerous and active areas of the lava flow were roped off to prevent accidents to over-eager thrill seekers. As lava cools, it forms a brittle, fragile crust that often conceals a hot molten mass several feet thick. Visitors unfamiliar with this aspect of lava might be tempted to walk on the crust which appears to be totally solidified, before it is.

Where we hiked across Kilauea Iki Crater, remnant of a 1959 eruption, ferns and other small plants were returning in areas that received sufficient water. We walked through the curious Thurston lava tube, located in a magnificent prehistoric fern forest; but the most spectacular experience was seeing living lava. Recent lava flows had closed off two miles of highway near

164

the visitor's center. There park rangers permitted small groups to walk swiftly over still-warm lava to a safe spot close enough to watch and photograph the molten rock, which looked like thick, but gray, hot fudge on a sundae, until a new lava surge broke through the quickly-forming skin to send its glowing orange-red tongue over another rock or into another crevice. Where lava flowed over vegetation, plants burst into flame and smoke billowed. Where it reached the sea, giant steam sprays shot up into an incredibly blue sky.

Parker Ranch on the same island, surprisingly the largest cattle ranch in the United States, originated from cattle that Captain Vancouver gave King Kamehameha in 1795. Foothills of gigantic volcanic ridges, when irrigated, provide lush grazing, resulting in an extensive Hawaiian cowboy tradition on Big Island. Farther down the coast, we drove past old lava flows on both sides of the highway. Without water, the crusted lava creates a barren, waste, and inhospitable landscape. With water, the same terrain produces an abundance of orchids, coffee plants, anthuriums, macadamia nut trees, and gardenias.

On the other side of the island, close to the black lava beaches, lies the haunting Lava Tree State Park. There, living trees were encircled by a lava flow. After the trees burned out, the lava trunk molds remained, creating an unearthly landscape.

Spectacular and abrupt are the contrasts in this fabulous land. We learned to say "Mahalo" and ate Japanese food so often even Kurt became proficient with chopsticks. Apparently Hawaii affects everyone: even McDonald's serves saimin, a noodle soup, and guava along with more traditional orange juice.

GRAND BAHAMA ISLAND

Cruises had never appealed to us, but the postcard offered an amazingly low price for a vacation to the Bahamas, including four days on Grand Bahama Island and two days in Daytona Beach, Florida. Suspicious, I checked with the Better Business Bureau, but there were no complaints about the company making the offer. I grilled the agent on the phone and crossed my fingers and toes, hoping I wasn't being totally suckered. We would have preferred to visit Nassau, but the offer was for Freeport.

As we suspected, the cruise to the island was not much more than slow transportation. The only activity on the ship other than gambling was drinking or sitting on a deck chair. The pool, about the size of three bathtubs combined, wasn't open. The dinner was abundant, but not particularly delicious or remarkable.

We learned almost immediately upon landing that Freeport was not just the name of a historic town, but that the town had been developed fairly recently as a free port (hence the name) to sell duty-free liquor, perfume, watches, and jewelry, and to provide a gambling casino.

Having no interest in such attractions, we tried to find out more about the island's flora, fauna, and natural beauty. The National Park trail emphasized the altitude-dependent ecological progression from sandy beach to mangrove and pine hummock and led us to two grottoes with deep pools, one inhabited by bats. The Garden of Groves, visited by colorful native birds like bananaquits, Cuban emeralds, and Greater Antillean bullfinches invited wandering. Its twelve acres, filled with lush foliage and over 10,000 plants, included orchids, a fern gully, a hanging garden, bougainvilleas, and citrus groves.

Snorkeling was on our list of things to do, but the reef was accessible only by hired boat. We enjoyed being amidst the vividly hued fish and beautiful coral formations, but the water was very choppy that day and made staying calmly afloat a chore, rather than a pleasure. The next day was calmer, but we had used up our snorkeling budget, so we wandered on the beach where we found two beautiful conch shells we cleaned ourselves.

Particularly memorable were some of the island's specialties. Our most delicious meal was sweet and sour fish, steamed the island way, with rice and beans and johnnycake. We sipped Bahama Mamas, liked conch chowder, and enjoyed the Yellowbird nightclub show. Also fascinating to watch were the precise but graceful dance-like signals of the colorfully uniformed traffic policemen. Being an obvious ethnic minority in this country where the Queen's, not American, English is spoken was a new experience. The locals were friendly and helpful, but because lying on the beach soaking in rays, gambling, and shopping are not our idea of fun, four days was more than enough.

FIJI

Fiji (a collection of 300 islands) was our last stop on the way home from an Australian visit. We actually visited only one of the many--Viti Levu. Grabbed by an agent at Nadi airport, we were whisked away by taxi to a nearby inexpensive resort for the night. It had a pool and a restaurant, both closed when we arrived, but we slept in a bure, the romantic, traditional thatch-roofed building with a ceiling fan. At the bus station in Nadi, we saw that the public buses had no glass in their window frames. When it rained, a piece of canvas would be lowered. We were advised to take a minivan, just then loading up for Suva. We'd read these were faster than buses, but crowded, hot, and not as safe, but took a chance. Careening around sharp curves and generally speeding on this five-hour trip, the minivan sometimes stopped to pick up additional passengers waiting at the side of the road. Sometimes it passed them by. Just before we entered a prison compound where there was a guard, the driver put on his seat belt. Some passengers were delivered, and two were picked up. As soon as we were out of sight, the seat belt was removed. At a rest stop, flies swarmed on the waiting food. We drank bottled water and stayed hungry.

In Suva, the capital, the Thurston Botanical Gardens and the history museum with dugouts and ritual cannibal forks were highlights. The museum outlines the fierce Fijian culture and how it has been influenced and changed by outsiders who generally exploited the Fijians and their resources. The earliest contact with outside was with men seeking the valuable and now rare sandalwood. The forests were devastated. Next, an intense harvesting of sea slugs (used as an aphrodisiac in China) thrived. In the 1860s the foreigners visiting the island were less materialistic. Some of these missionaries gave their lives in their largely successful effort to stop the practice of cannibalism and convert the islanders to Christianity. Subsequent industries in Fiji were whaling, gold, copra, and sugar cane. To harvest the cane and work in the mills, hundreds of Indians came to Fiji as indentured servants. With them came their Hindu religion.

Today handsome, sulu-wearing men carry cell phones; cappuccino and latte are readily available; and this main island has two McDonald's restaurants. Still, many people are on foot, weeds at the roadside are chopped with machetes, and open-air markets are crowded and busy. We saw several fully-booked upscale high-rise hotels in Suva, but we stayed in a nearby hostel instead. Our attempts to get a closer look at the president's (or governor general's) home, or at least close enough to take a picture, were foiled by a guard in a jagged-edge skirt or sulu who was not allowed to speak. When I asked if we could walk up the road to take photos, he simply shook his head "no." When I asked if I could take his photo, he nodded "yes." Trying to approach the building from the other side, we soon encountered an area of shabby shacks, feral dogs, chickens, and pigs.

Though most tourists go to Fiji to vegetate at an isolated resort on one of the less populated islands, we wanted to see real Fiji. Warily we walked before dawn to the Suva bus stop to catch an early long-distance bus that circled the island once a day. Though the northern part of the island is very dry, it almost always rains in Suva. In the interior, lush green grasslands in the valleys between steep hills support cattle grazing. Because it was election day, we saw many villagers walking to polling places and standing patiently in long lines. Fiji, for ninety-six years a British Crown Colony, became a self-governing nation within the commonwealth in 1970. In 1987, however, a military coup declared Fiji a republic, and it ceased to be a member of the Commonwealth. Fiji re-entered the Commonwealth in October 1997. At the time we visited, there was some friction between the Fijians who make up 51 percent of the population and who live primarily in the South of the main island and the 43 percent of the population who are Indians, living in the north. This has since escalated.

Many villages in the north of the island are primarily Indian and Hindu because so many Indians came to work in the sugar mills and stayed. In Lautoka, where we spent the night, we were surprised to learn that the enormous tan pyramid standing near the ocean was raw sugar. It looked like sand. We took a local bus from Lautoka to Nadi, where we had a marvelous soup-like dish called Vakalolo, made with all kinds of seafood steamed in coconut milk. There was just enough time before our plane left to visit and marvel at the largest Hindu temple in the southern hemisphere.

Bula! is the universal greeting in Fiji. The answer: Bula!

DOMINICAN REPUBLIC

Free rum drinks for tourists waiting to pass through Dominican Republic customs made us think we'd come to a place that had its priorities right, though the signs in four languages warning of dire consequences for anyone changing money outside an official bank were somewhat disconcerting, as were the armed guards patrolling the gates of the lovely tropical resort, Talanquera, our time-share exchange for the week. Beautifully landscaped and maintained with two large swimming pools, plus a beach club on the Caribbean, the resort offered luxurious buffet breakfasts; daily activities, including Merengue lessons; friendly staff members; a disco at night; and a gourmet French restaurant that was never open, to our knowledge. Bottled water and ice were provided because the tap water was not drinkable, but only the bedroom was air-conditioned: an environment of unexpected contrasts.

Boca Chica beach with its lovely palm trees and its huge, absolutely clear blue semi-circle of shallow water created by a long reef about a mile from shore was a good spot for snorkeling or people-watching. Many amply-endowed German women pampered themselves by having their already well-oiled bodies vigorously massaged. Family groups picnicked on the beach as they do anywhere. Peddlers and vendors insistently hawked their bargains to usually disinterested tourists, until beach police encouraged them to move on. Price haggling was a game everyone played. And of course, when we parked the car on a side street near the public beach, someone immediately offered to stand guard against thieves. Nonetheless, the day at the beach was a good one, and the car was okay when we returned.

Santo Domingo's colonial sector (Columbus discovered Hispaniola in 1492; his son Diego became viceroy in 1509) offered many restored buildings: some are museums, some art galleries. Built before 1512, the Alcazar palace was the home of Columbus and his family for three generations. Ozama Fortress with its six-foot thick walls stands guard over the entry to the Ozama River. In 1500, it was the tallest colonial structure and became the first home for Diego Columbus and his wife, Maria de Toledo. One museum housed Trujillo's (now the republic's) impressive collection of armor and weapons from all over the world. We paid again to protect the car, but managed to avoid the countless "guides" offering their services. Undeterred by our repeated *"no, gracias,"* they could be avoided only by going inside somewhere. When cousin Floyd, whom they particularly liked, threatened to report them to the police, they offered to guide him to the station--for a price. Similarly pestiferous were the illegal money changers who offered fabulous rates for American dollars--but we'd read the signs and weren't interested in consequences. Some of this frantic behavior made more sense when we later learned that the average wage was two dollars per day.

Some of Santo Domingo's other attractions were not quite what we expected. The botanical garden, so large a miniature train is the best way to see it, especially on a hot humid day, included the largest floral clock in the world and the strangely incongruent, but beautiful Japanese garden. The orchid collection, however, was privately owned and not open to the public. The zoo was undergoing renovation. Most of the enclosures were the depressing old-fashioned type, but the new African savannah exhibit was spacious, realistic, and moated. Animals that share a habitat were grouped together or were separately near each other in the case of prey and predator.

Several museums are conveniently clustered around the appropriately named Plaza de Cultura. Until we visited the natural history museum, we hadn't realized that the Dominican Republic has no native animals and that the twenty-one native species of birds are all approximately the same size and color. The iguanas, however, were plentiful. The Museum of the Dominican Man displayed fabulous costumes used in *carnaval* and gave us some insight into Dominican folklore, customs, and history.

We drove on principal highways also used by trucks, cars, buses, horses, mule-drawn carts, bicycles, anything with wheels, all rolling along together until reaching gridlock on one or all three of the bridges that cross the river to the city's center. Once we were waved down for speeding. The inner lane permitted the speed we were driving, but we were in the outer lane where the limit was twenty kilometers lower. In Spanish, the police officer pointed this out while insisting that a "fine" had to be paid. When we asked how much, he replied, "Whatever you wish," and after we coughed up something, he explained with a gorgeous smile that he'd use it for beer and snacks. Once we were waved down for nothing. This time we pretended we didn't speak Spanish. After a *"Buenas Tardes"* and *"Buen Viaje,"* we were waved on again.

One of the most beautiful, though artificial, spots on the island is Los Altos de Chavon. Built in the 1970s, with an Italian movie set designer as architect, this artists' colony and cultural center exists for the super rich who stay in nearby Casa de Campo, home of designer Oscar de la Renta. An entire fourteenth-century village, complete with crumbling church and bell tower and other old-looking buildings constructed from artificially weathered stone, Los Altos sits on a steep promontory overlooking the Chavon River far below. The museum contains early actual archaeology of the area and information about the Taino Indians and their curious sacred stones called *"trigonolitos."* A huge open-air amphitheater showcases classical as well as rock concerts for capacity crowds. A curious place, Los Altos had the most complete *supermercado* we found anywhere.

Los Tres Ojos, a national park near the beach on the way to Santo Domingo, was the other curiosity. At the bottom of a twisting rock stairway in grotto-like surroundings lies the first of the "eyes" (extremely deep pools, one of them sulphurous). After a similar second pool, we entered a very dark cave to be punted across the lake for an extra charge, of course, to an outside lagoon, supposedly bottomless, surrounded by steep vine-covered cliffs, reminiscent of the sacrificial pools in Yucatan. A short walk past the third and deepest "eye," its wall displaying the most enormous wasp's nest I've ever seen, and we were back on the superhighway. I'll spare you the story of the mysterious windshield that suddenly disintegrated as we drove along the highway, the delayed luggage coming and going—and "customs" in the Miami airport—the worst yet! We had only one week in June for the Dominican Republic, but it was enough.

ST. THOMAS AND ST. JOHN

Discovering a totally free week in May 2001, we flew to the Virgin Islands. Ever since I had heard about the underwater snorkeling trail on St. John Island, I had been waiting for a chance to try it. White sails on clear blue water dotted with emerald-green islands: the beauty of the Caribbean was abundantly available even in low season, when for only four days of the week, only two cruise ships stop. High season must be a wild, congested, and profitable time for all.

After checking into Bluebeard's Castle, our time-share exchange for the week, we walked to downtown Charlotte Amalie. Because it was Sunday afternoon, all the shops were closed and even the sidewalk vendors were packing up their goods. When a friendly woman asked if she could help us, I suspected it was the usual hook used to bring tourists into a particular business. But it wasn't. Her recommendation of the Greenhouse as a good place for reasonably priced drinks and food was legitimate. My frozen strawberry daiquiri and Kurt's beer put us in a great mood for the conch fritters and jerk chicken salad that followed. These dishes, though a little spicy for us, were very delicious. We next looked for a grocery store, but as we approached Market Square, we realized we had left the tourist area. The area began to look rather shabby, and the small grocery stores we entered had more liquor than anything else. There was nothing fresh, and the small amount of frozen meat and fish looked unappetizing. A few shelves had staples in large quantity burlap sacks and some canned goods. I suspected Market Square might be more attractive on market day, whenever that was. But appearances may be deceiving. In addition to the unsavory loiterers with their bottles of something in brown paper bags, we saw some very well-dressed people on their way to evening church services.

Many residents speak a creole-type language to each other, and their English has a lovely island lilt to it. They have probably heard everything and seem to remain calm no matter what. In the morning, when a woman standing near the door of the hotel asked if she could help us, Kurt asked her, "Are you a taxi?" Perhaps she wondered what foreign country he came from, but she didn't blink, just said she'd be right back. She was the taxi driver and a great source of information about the island. Because there are no lakes, waterfalls, or streams on St. Thomas, the people are totally dependent on cisterns catching rainwater. Wells, which were used formerly, have all been closed. Everything must be imported from the mainland which increases the cost. She explained that the shops are mainly open for the convenience of the cruise ships. When the cruise ships are in, the shops remain open even on Sunday until 1:00 p.m. When I asked if the wooden shutters on the buildings were for hurricanes, she confirmed this and said there were also hurricane shelters to which people could go. But the shutters were also used by upscale shop owners in the downtown area to discourage burglary. Both government and private schools are available on the island, but all children wear uniforms to school. Our ride from the resort to the Red Hook ferry dock cost $16.00, but it was good way to experience the twisting roads and steep topography of the islands. Driving follows the British system, but since all cars are made in the United States, the drivers sit at the edge of the road rather than at its middle. I wondered if this was meant to give the driver some protection in crashes, or so the drivers could see how close they were to falling off some precipitous curve in the road. We were certainly glad we'd decided not to rent a car or jeep.

For many years Denmark ruled these islands, and some buildings such as the Danish Lutheran Church date from that era. The Danish parsonage was built in 1725. Fort Christiansted, now a museum, told the history of the island through exhibits. It also had some furnished rooms and a dungeon. Children from a Montessori school were touring at the same time we were. Their screams, when their teacher closed the door, told us they really enjoyed the totally dark dungeon. Not much could be seen at the unicameral legislature building, painted a lovely pale green, but the receptionist gave us a booklet on the history of the building and of the legislature. At the Governor's Office Building, we could visit only the first floor because the Governor was using his office. At Historic Hotel 1829, only guests renting a room could visit more than the bar. The nearby synagogue with its small museum was not only attractive, but also unusual. The floor was covered with sand. Some sources claim the sand was there as a reminder of the time when Spanish Jews were forced to convert. The "converted" Jews continued to meet in secret, but used sand on the floor to muffle their steps. The other explanation was that the sand was a reminder of the exodus from sandy Egypt.

St. Thomas had the time-share, historic buildings, Coki Beach (good snorkeling) and Coral World, where we saw baby seahorses and I fed and touched a stingray. St. John had the National Park to which we ferried most days.

Adding a touch of color amidst the palms, cacti, and other semi-tropical plants were the open-air "taxis," with room for sixteen passengers. The canopies that offered some protection from the brilliant sun were usually red and white or green and white stripes. But some canopies were orange and white and even purple. Not many people tried the fascinating, but hot and sweaty hikes which led us by termite mounds in trees, bromeliads, wild pineapples, lizards, hummingbirds, mongooses, petroglyphs and sugar mill ruins.

We rode the Center Road public bus to the stop for the Reef Bay hike to the mill ruins, but didn't have a schedule for the return to town. As we trudged wearily towards Cruz Bay, a jeep stopped. The driver, who was taking his dirty clothes to the laundromat, told us his favorite jokes as he drove to Cruz Bay. When I asked if he'd lived in St. John all his life, he answered, "not yet." He was a photographer, originally from Winter Park, Colorado, but he'd lived on St. John for twenty-two years. We rewarded ourselves with expensive malted milkshakes at a fruit stand he recommended.

Snorkeling was an attractive alternative to hiking in the heat. We are not much for lying on the beach. The famed underwater trail at Trunk Bay was so much fun I did it twice. The water temperature was perfect. Markers resting on the sea bottom not only pointed the way, but also identified fish and the various corals that could be seen. Schools of small, colorful fish swirled past me. It felt as if I were one of them swimming in a huge aquarium. Because I had burned earlier at Coki Beach, even with sun-screen and being underwater, I wore a long-sleeved shirt and lycra tights over my swimsuit. The nude and nearly nude sunbathers on the beach must have thought I was really a weird one.

People were very friendly. When we tried to buy tickets for the Paradise Point tramway, the seller told us that if we waited until the following day at five, we'd get both a free ride and a free rum punch. It was good advice. At the bistro at the top of the tramway, we also ordered a delicious mahi sandwich and mussels in coconut milk so we could stay long enough to enjoy the spectacular view of the islands and the sea at sunset.

Another day at a Cruz Bay snack bar, an aggressively friendly man lectured Kurt because he hadn't responded quickly enough to the man's "Good Morning." Mr. Congeniality rejected Kurt's "poor hearing" excuse. When Kurt finally mumbled a "Good Morning," the man responded heartily, "Well, that's more like it." I call that real friendly!

Enjoying the half-price mango margaritas at the Green House on our last night on the islands, we splurged on fresh fish and lobster tail. We never did find out who had signed our name and room number on a resort restaurant bill for food we never ate on a day we didn't eat there, but the resort believed our complaint and removed the charges. Our week in the Virgin Islands was a week full of surprises.

NEW ZEALAND

Surrounded by darkness, our punt glided silently through the cave's black waters, moving from one grotto to another. Overhead innumerable pinpoints of greenish-blue light glowed from an otherworldly canopy of muted starlight, enchanting viewers with an aura of fantasy. This was Waitomo Cave and its glowworms, just one of the unusual experiences on our three-week New Zealand visit.

My principal worry was the possibility of flash floods and resulting extremely hazardous stream crossings on the Milford Track on South Island, New Zealand. One brochure warned that streams could suddenly rise from ankle-deep to a meter high. I figured that thirty-nine inches was at least armpit deep for my sixty-two-inch frame. But descriptions of rainforests, glaciated peaks, parrots, and fjord-like Milford Sound were irresistible.

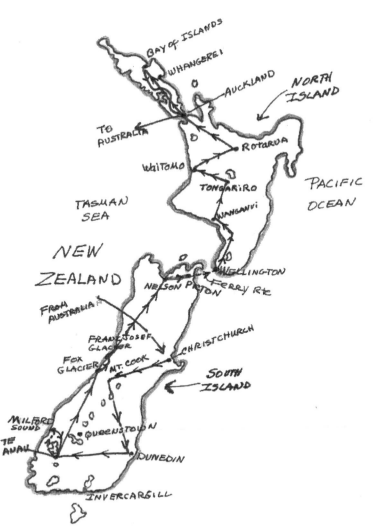

Arriving in Christchurch, as British-looking as it sounds, we devoured the superb Antarctica rooms in the museum and examined physicist Ernest Rutherford's first lab in a nearby ex-college, now craft center. We were awed by the extensive botanical gardens and the immensity of the trees. With ideal year-round temperatures and moisture, plants and trees thrive. Later that same afternoon, we found snow-covered and glacier-laden Mt. Cook and Mt. Sefton inspiring. The complex of peaks between Mt. Cook and the Westlands deserves its title: the Southern Alps. Glacial lakes, moraines, avalanches were all there.

On the east coast, across the Otago plains where sheep outnumber people twenty-five to one, we enjoyed picturesque Dunedin. Valuing the early native population in the South Pacific, Dunedin's museum displayed extensive Polynesian, Micronesian, and Mauri collections. We also stopped in at the specialized pioneer museum that depicted immigrant life in the late nineteenth century. The Otago peninsula was home to an albatross colony and to Lanark castle, a restored mansion serving Devonshire Tea and offering backpacker's lodging in the stables, as well as bed and breakfast in the castle. Queenstown, a former mining town, is now a four-season resort area with skiing, water sports, and parapenting--a cross between hang-gliding and parachuting--available. We rode a jet boat, not realizing the major objective was speed and daredeviltry, not sightseeing. Sudden 360 degree turns while cruising along were lots of fun, if you could stay inside the boat. We also heard about bungee jumping, a horrifying sport!

In Te Anau, headquarters for Fjordland National Park and the trailhead for the Milford Track, we crossed the lake to Te Anau glowworm caves, for a mystic beginning to our four-day "freedom walk." Only eighty hikers are allowed to start the trail each day, so spaces must be reserved several months in advance. Each day, a specific distance is hiked--to the next hut on the itinerary. Forty hikers go with Tourist Hotel Corporation, a company that provides guides, meals (including tea breaks), hot showers, fresh linen, and most of the comforts of home for a price, of course. The forty freedom walkers have no guides, carry their own food and sleeping bags, and stay in a separate, more primitive set of huts, for one-sixth the price. But even the freedom huts had bunks and foam pads, running water, flush toilets, and gas rings. For us, this was luxury. We'd rarely hiked so light--no tent, no stove, no fuel. Only when bunks were claimed for the night were our forty all together, a diverse, friendly group from all over the globe.

After an hour's boat ride across Lake Te Anau, the Milford Track followed a sparkling creek where very large brown trout swimming lazily in groups were easily seen, but not so easily caught. Higher, the beech forest gave way to primitive-looking fern trees, ferns, mosses, and other warm, rain-forest vegetation, and then to sheer rock walls, adorned with rows of waterfalls frisking from ledge to ledge. Hikers tended to spread out, leaving us a pleasant solitude broken only by the twittering of numerous birds fluffing and preening after an early-morning splash in a waterfall. That night at the hut, pesky keas, New Zealand parrots, pecked at a hiker's clothes drying on the rooftop heli-pad, until offered bread and nuts. Then flashing bright orange underwing patches, brilliant against gray-green outer feathers, they sprang into raucous flight.

The switchbacks up to the pass were surprisingly no worse in the morning with packs than they had been the previous afternoon when we'd hiked up to look around and take photos, in case the morning was overcast; but we were equally happy to pause at the top for gorgeous views of lush green valleys and the long trail down to Sandfly Point and trail's end at Milford Sound. A short side trail led to awesome Sutherland Falls, fifth longest in the world. Only on the last day did

174

the mists and rain begin, hinting at the usual eerie beauty the trail displays. We'd had an unprecedented four clear days. Realistically, we were pleased that we'd seen everything without hazard, that my fears of crossing boulder-laden chest-high, icy, out-of-control streams while clinging to cables had not come true. But it almost seemed too easy, and my unslaked taste for adventure stupidly suggested a return trip--this time in the rain! A few other hikers agreed, but we were shouted down by the pragmatists who predictably pronounced: Enough already! Don't you know when you're well off?

With only a few sandfly bites, we headed west, passing farms where deer are raised like cattle, originally intended for the European venison market. Domestic deer, however, lack the gamey taste venison lovers prefer, so the "crop" was now being promoted locally as an alternative to beef or lamb. Franz Josef and Fox glaciers on the west coast, the only glaciers in the temperate zone, were beautiful frozen masses like those in Juneau, Alaska. Rain kept us from more than a yearning look at the track's beginning. On our way to catch the early-morning ferry to Wellington, we bought a few pieces of greenstone or New Zealand jade at a factory. After admiring the National Museum's Maori and Pacific Island culture display and finally finding the live kiwis at the small zoo's noctarium, we drove to Tongariro National Park and climbed one of three clustered volcanoes, marveling at the intensity of the red crater's color, at small emerald-hued lakes, and at the smoke plume from Ngauruhoe's perfect cinder cone. On Ruapehu, ski lodges perched on volcanic pumice, while signs near lifts gave procedures to be followed in case of an eruption. Strange place!

Rotorua's thermal areas were similar to Yellowstone's with geysers, sulphur fumes, silica terraces, bubbly mud pots and steam vents. At the entertaining and delicious hangi (the Maori version of Hawaii's luau) food was steamed over vents in the earth, and a Maori concert of traditional dance and song followed. On the way to Bay of Islands, as beautiful as its name, we admired orange, apricot, mango, almond, kiwi, and feijoa orchards and groves, stuffing ourselves on inexpensive Nashi pears, a Chinese fruit tasting like an apple-pear hybrid. Our day-long cruise to Cape Brett and the exciting passage through hole-in-the rock; a drive through old Kauri forests (one enormous tree was over 1200 years old); and a day and a half in Auckland, a lovely water-surrounded city built on the remains of ancient volcanic cones concluded a fascinating three-week trip.

AUSTRALIAN ADVENTURE

The only island continent, Australia beckoned in 1988, when my husband, Kurt, was selected as his laboratory's exchange scientist. Our fourteen-month stay there gave us almost enough time to explore this incredible country.

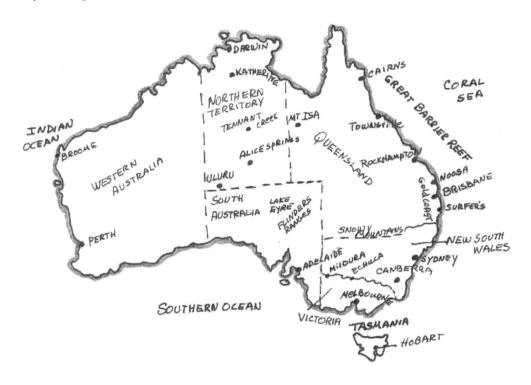

How're ya goin' mates? Yip, we're down under, here in the Land of Oz (as some Aussies call it), enjoying the venue immensely, even though we haven't quite learned to talk "strine" like fair dinkum ockers. It's fabulous country here, full of contrasts and great natural beauty distinctively its own--huge open vistas bordered by tall eucalyptus (gum) trees in some areas and abundant bottlebrush trees and gorgeous flowers elsewhere. Plant and animal life are amazing and the people are welcoming and generous. Learning to buy fruits and veggies at the greengrocers; meat at the butcher shop; and pastries, bread, and meatpies at the bake shop was easy. Driving on the left took a bit longer, and our beer tasting got ahead of our wine sampling, with Foster's, Carlton's, and Victoria Bitter leading the way.

Arriving October 1, after getting on and off several planes, crossing the International Date Line, and reading and sleeping for most of the twenty-one-hour trip, we were met by our cousins and laboratory colleagues. Two weeks later, with the help of the cousins, we were in a rented two-bedroom duplex (one room for the rental piano and my borrowed typewriter), and had filled it with some rented, some borrowed furniture, and a few packing boxes for side tables.

Built in 1925, the stucco/brick house with terra cotta roof came with a lemon tree, rhubarb, and parsley growing in the backyard along with roses, nasturtiums, azaleas, columbines, a ferntree, and other beautiful exotica. Just inside Melbourne, we were twenty minutes by tram to downtown, twenty minutes by tram to the lab, and near anything else that we needed.

By the end of October, even though Kurt worked and I wrote Monday through Friday, we'd seen most of Melbourne's sights: the Royal Botanical Gardens, Old Melbourne Gaol, Queen Victoria Market, the Shrine of Remembrance, Victorian Arts Centre, the zoo with its butterfly house, museums with haunting Aboriginal bark paintings, Mount Dandenong (reached by a train like our Metro), Ferntree Gully Park, Fitzroy Gardens and two cottages transported from England: La Trobe's re-assembled in Australia in 1839 and Cook's built in 1755 for Captain Cook's parents and re-assembled in 1934 to commemorate the voyages of the great navigator. For eleven days in November, we drove a rental car north to Snowy Mountains National Park in New South Wales, encountering our first "wild" kangaroos on the road, just after I'd sneered at the roadside warning sign. (Who ever sees deer cross at home?) But no worries! You just wait until they hop across. Exploring Yarrangobilly Caves and hiking to the top of Mt. Kosciusko, Australia's highest, were the "best of the Snowys" on two perfectly clear beautiful days, even though we hiked through heavy snow (unexpected since there was little snow the previous winter) to reach Mt. Kosciusko's barren top.

Canberra, Australia's capital, was a major stop as we continued our trip north. Outside the city, after passing countless foraging sheep, we visited an exhibition hall where we learned more about different kinds of wool than we'll ever need to know. We found Canberra to be a beautiful city, though somewhat sterile, probably because it was created in 1913 only to stop the squabbling between Sydney and Melbourne over which should be the capital. Laid out on a vast scale to accommodate cars, not pedestrians, the broad avenues were lovely, but distances were long, crosswalks few, and traffic heavy and fast. The High Court's modernistic design was a striking contrast to our classical Supreme Court building; the newly opened Parliament Building was impressive in its use of colors and native Australian woods and wools and unusual in its design; and I was bemused by the National Library's structural resemblance to the Library of Congress's Madison Building, which I'd so recently left. The War Memorial incorporated a huge gallery depicting any battle in which Australians had been involved--a quick history lesson. The National Art Gallery focused on Moderns, but also had a rich collection of Aboriginal works.

We needed more time than we had for seeing Sydney. No building or setting comes near the unforgettable beauty of Sydney's Opera House. Pictures don't do it justice. Because the season was over, we could only take the building tour, fascinating in itself. In the evening a dance school performed Aboriginal and Islander dances along with modern and jazz in a local theatre. Though the whole program was excellent, the native dances were most moving and powerful. Another night we were almost crushed in the crowd trying to see Japan's bicentennial gift--a sound-and-light laser show near the harbor which included an unidentified flying object, resembling a miniature flying saucer. Amazing and somewhat spooky, it wasn't quite worth the effort despite the magnificent fireworks display.

After Kurt injured his toe while doing yoga, we rode the ferries in Sydney Harbor in order to see more of the surrounding area, though he limped gamely through the historic Rocks and Goat Island areas. In Sydney's Darling Harbor, much like Baltimore's Harborplace, we cringed in the clear vinyl tubes of the aquarium as sharks, manta rays, and other denizens of the deep swam above and around us. We stayed near Bondi Beach, well known to surfers and for good reason--the waves are huge and continuous.

Despite his damaged toe, Kurt could not resist visiting the Blue Mountains. He managed by taking a pain pill. Though it drizzled in Katoomba, near Sydney, we still hiked to Bridal Veil falls on a track chiseled out of the stone walls. I wasn't the only one who screamed on the almost vertical funicular near Three Sisters, though all passengers were perfectly safe. On our way back to Melbourne, we drove south along the beautiful eastern coastline, stopping one night at the almost deserted 100-year-old Kiama Hotel for a budget-priced bed and complete Australian breakfast.

Once back in Melbourne, we bought a car, which we planned to sell when we left. Renting almost every weekend was too much expense and trouble. Car shopping was a struggle though, as cars in Australia (old, used, and new) cost two to three times the cost in the states. We christened our twelve-year-old Ford Cortina by visiting Ballarat, a gold rush town of the 1850s. Californians came here after their gold rush dwindled. A re-created digger's village, including a quartz/gold mine at Sovereign Hill provided both fun and information.

Another weekend we traveled the Great Ocean Road, west of Melbourne, for scenery comparable to California's Big Sur, marveling at the curiously-shaped tall sandstone formations standing just off the Port Campbell shoreline in the powerful surf that formed them at the same time that it hollowed out shoreline caves and arches. In Warrnambool, near the site of the volcanic nature reserve, Tower Hill, a cinder-cone island surrounded by a crater lake, we overnighted in an on-site van in a Caravan Park, a concept the United States could well import. Vans and motels here always have tea-making facilities and a fridge--a welcome touch!

At Christmas, preparing for a February trip to New Zealand, we tested our hiking skills in the Grampians, an attractive mountainous area, known for its masses of spring wildflowers, about four hours drive from Melbourne in Western Victoria. Though not very high, the ridges are rugged, with rocky pinnacles and sheer drop-offs jutting out from lower eucalyptus-covered slopes. Views over the vast flat reaches on both sides of the ridge impress, and best of all, most hikes, even from the bottom, where koalas and sulphur-crested cockatoos sleep and clamor in the roadside park trees, take no more than six hours. In contrast, Mounts Bogong and Feathertop, northeast of Melbourne, were all-day treks, building our endurance during the second holiday week. Not far away, Mount Buffalo had something for everyone: tame rosellas (brightly colored parrots), strange gigantic rock formations, waterfalls, snow gums, rock climbers, and hang gliders. In Bright, we found a transplanted Viennese and his wonderful restaurant serving fresh trout and strudel.

Adelaide, South Australia, and the Flinders Ranges at the edge of the Australian Outback were our destination over the five-day Australian Easter break. Here we learned that on Good Friday, everything closes down--even the pubs, which stay open Christmas Day, the only other day in the year museums close. We drove on to the campground near Wilpena Pound, passing homesteads and sheep stations abandoned during the drought years. The Pound, a huge enclosed oval grassy area, is completely surrounded by peaks. Heavy rains the two previous days made the area unusually green and lush, closed some roads, and left some roads we drove partially under water. On a strenuous and enjoyable hike up St. Mary's peak, we met marathon runners and bikers laboriously carrying bikes up the easy back way, hoping for an exciting ride down. The unusual amount of rain stranded tourists outside Alice Springs because the only sealed (paved) north-south highway to Alice was cut in two parts by water. Lake Eyre, a salt pan for the last seven years, suddenly became twenty feet deep and the size of France, permitting use of watercraft and attracting flocks of birds and abundant small animal life. As advised, we carried spare parts for the car, sleeping bags, water, and emergency food, because towns and petrol stations are very few and farther between than they are in even the remotest parts of the U.S. West. Fortunately we didn't need any of it, and though the distance we traveled was much too far for the time we had, we did see another part of that surprising and fabulous country--Australia.

For a few months we settled down to work and to playing music regularly with new friends. Several of Kurt's compositions were performed by these highly accomplished amateurs at musical evenings, and his piece for eight recorders was played and taped by a friend's computer/music synthesizer. Theatre, opera, and many festivals (something was celebrated publicly almost every weekend in Melbourne) kept us moving with half-price tickets to most things. Especially charming was a performance of "Wind in the Willows" in the Melbourne Botanical Gardens: Mr. Toad fell from his yellow boat into the lake from which Otter and son emerged in wet suits, flippers, and goggles. The setting was perfect, and our four-year-old cousin as totally entranced as we were.

On the Queen's birthday, June 12, we went north to get warm and to see the mighty Murray River, then ten feet higher than normal. Restored river cities complete with paddle wheelers and historic re-enactments of a bank robbery and trial added to the fun, but we couldn't find a bed for the night in Swan Hill, as the river forms the border between Victoria and New South Wales, a state where slot machines are legal, attracting hordes of Victorian gamblers to border towns when they want to have a flurry on the "pokies." We toyed with the idea of taking a tent site to have access to toilets and sleeping in the car, but called a hotel in Nyah West, about an hour away. Only because someone had cancelled did we get a room, though we were warned that there was no heat. Lots of blankets and a fire in the lounge fireplace, along with an excellent dinner, made us comfortable. On our way back, Hattah-Kulkyne Park showed us another face of Australia, the mallee: scrub growth, lakes, many birds, and boundless numbers of kangaroos and wallabies.

In August, just as domestic airline pilots went on strike and then quit over a salary dispute, our adult children, Karen and Alan, arrived for a very hectic three weeks. We did fly to Alice Springs, enjoying our Northern Territory camping trip, sleeping in swags under the stars, climbing Uluru (Ayers Rock), and hiking in the Olga Mountains and into and out of King's Canyon. Bush-bashing to collect firewood and having to contribute our drinking water in order to keep a leaky radiator going until it reached a service station added more to the trip than we'd expected. The heart of Australia was truly red, and the largest rock monolith in the world was well worth the trip. We'd expected a more typical desert scene--we did ride the camels, and there were cycads and palms in the valleys where water collected--but the overall landscape was more like our Southwest's Painted Desert with red rocks and scrubby plants. We heard dingoes at night and saw paw prints near the campground; once we saw one dingo from the road. When all airline flights were canceled, we traveled by bus for two nights and a day and a half across the outback from Northern Territory to Queensland. Fortunately we could shift bookings and get refunds. For eight hours on Sunday, after visiting the two mining museums in town, we waited for a connecting bus in Mt. Isa, really the middle of nowhere.

Queensland, on the northeast coast of Australia, nearer the equator, had endless sugar-cane fields and criss-crossing train tracks for the cages that transported the cut cane; but it also offered colorful Kuranda market; the Aboriginal dance troupe; a three-story noctarium; the butterfly house; and the incredible Barrier Reef where we snorkeled to see brilliantly colored fish, many kinds of corals, giant clams, and even a shark at a distance.

Resigned to a forty-eight-hour bus trip to Melbourne, we changed plans when no bus was available, and drove thirty-six hours in a rental car. Even Karen and Alan got to drive on the wrong side of the road and worry whether the large gray lump in the middle of the road was a sleeping or a dead kangaroo. We arrived in time for them to join cousins at a Melbourne disco on Saturday night. Sunday a family reunion followed sightseeing in Melbourne, and Monday with Kurt back at work, the children and I took off for the Great Ocean Road, the Grampians (Pinnacles and Hollow Mountain hikes), Ballarat's Sovereign Hill, and a wildlife refuge where we touched young koalas, patted wombats, saw

Tasmanian devils, and fed kangaroos. Observing Phillip Island's Penguin Parade where parent penguins walked in from the sea to feed peeping young in the nest was a delight. Stopping at Gippsland's Giant Worms, which I mistakenly thought was a hoax, was fascinating. On a frenzied last day we crowded in visits to Queen Victoria Market, the Victorian Arts Centre, and the Old Melbourne Jail.

Although we were scheduled to fly back to the states December 2, we couldn't resist the opportunity to visit one more part of Australia. On Melbourne Cup Day, the first Tuesday in November, when all Melbourne shuts down for a horse race, we flew in an eight-seat plane to Tasmania, the historic island state, once Van Diemen's land, looking more like New Zealand than like the rest of Australia. A tremendous variety of topography is packed into this tiny island--you can drive around it in one day if you hurry, but who wants to? We skipped the casinos, and for six days soaked in history; museums; friendly hospitality; and wild mountain scenery, including the barren wasteland of Queenstown, once a mining center. At Lake St. Clair we fed three kinds of wallabies.

Ten Years Later

A Maori War Chant in what sounded like Yiddish? That's what New Zealand male relatives performed at our cousin's wedding reception in Melbourne, Australia--complete with tongue waggling and other traditional gestures. Earlier that day at home, when her hairdresser collapsed, Maxine, the bride, calmly called 911, while an assistant finished hairdos. A mobile phone call to a seamstress saved the day once more when the long back zipper on the bridal gown opened up during an outdoor photo session. No worries--the seamstress sewed Maxine into her dress. From the beginning, our six weeks stay was wild and wonderful.

We felt we'd come home again, after a ten-year absence. The warm hospitality of our cousins and friends made us easily forget the long flight time. Besides the wedding and surrounding events, including two seders with family, we visited our old neighborhood and favorite haunts in Melbourne. We thought we'd missed seeing our former neighbors, but returning from shopping, they spotted us waiting for the tram and yelled at us to wait. For two weeks we constantly luxuriated in being with family, new relatives, and friends we'd made ten years ago. Musical get-togethers, transportation, housing, everything was arranged for us.

Melbourne's skyline had many new skyscrapers, including a casino with a magnificent foyer, on the South Bank; the Arts Center's tower had reached new heights; and masses of huge flying foxes (fruit bats), formerly seen only in animal sanctuaries, had invaded trees in the Royal Botanical Gardens, screeching and soaring in daylight. Drought had reduced their normal habitat. With our cousins' help, we revisited Wilson's Promontory, a peninsula east and south of

Melbourne, and managed an overnight backpacking trip in this wilderness area. The rosellas, kookaburras, and fairy wrens were plentiful, but we saw no kangaroos, only evidence that they had been there.

Surfer's Paradise is surreal. Huge breakers abound, but so do miles and miles of skyscraper condos, rivaling Miami Beach. Still the clean, sandy beach, accessible to all, goes on and on, and the ocean was warm, even in March, Australia's autumn.

Two weeks of condo time-shares on Australia's Gold Coast let us explore backcountry national parks. Narrow, winding, one-lane dirt roads led to tree-top trails on suspended "boardwalks" that gave us a close-up view of the rain-forest canopy. Hiking up Mt. Warning, a volcanic plug, became very interesting when the trail gave way to a rocky scramble to a storm- and lightning-threatened circle on top. We scurried down after the obligatory panoramic view.

Brush turkeys, kangaroos, carpet pythons, and lace monitors were some of the critters we met on our travels from Gold Coast to Brisbane, where a marvelous exhibit of Indonesian gold and an excellent collection of Aboriginal art caught our attention. We hiked up the easiest of the Glass House mountains, basaltic plugs surrounded by pineapple and sugar cane fields. Using the city catamaran for transport, we got a quick overall view of delightfully temperate Brisbane (A river runs through it.). Our condos were spacious, with ocean views, hot tubs, and indoor and outdoor pools. Our attempts at body and boogie-board surfing in the warm Coral Sea ended with just a few scrapes and lots of sand in our bathing suits and other unmentionable places. Currumbin Sanctuary showed us koalas, tree kangaroos, and an Aboriginal dance group along with other typical Australian flora and fauna, plus an amazing wild lorikeet feeding where swarms of the brightly colored birds plummet from the sky to drink sugary liquid from pie pans held by visitors, sometimes resting on the heads of the unsuspecting humans. We even found timewarp in Nimbin, a 1960s "Age of Aquarius" town, with all kinds of alternatives readily available.

Flying into Darwin from Brisbane, we rented a car and headed for Kakadu National Park, struggling with a manual shift in a heavy downpour. The next day on our way to Bowali Visitor Center, large flocks of brown whistling kites, scavenging roadkill, temporarily blocked the highway. The visitors' center presented a good introduction to this vast wetlands area. Because "the wet" season was slow in ending, some roads were still open only to four-wheel-drive vehicles, limiting our plans. But the beautiful Aboriginal cave art at Nourlangie impressed us as did the escarpment, billabongs and savannah and the horrible swarms of mosquitoes that attacked us mercilessly the one night we camped in Kakadu. These beasts were infinitely worse than those in Alaska: the heat and humidity in Kakadu mean you're fresh meat, no matter how much DEET you wear. If you're susceptible to mosquito bites--don't camp. Eight months later the scars finally faded--from a lifetime high bite count!

From Cooinda, the shuttle bus drove through water at least three feet deep to reach the pier at the Yellow River. The evening boat trip revealed both freshwater and estuarine crocodiles and the Jacana or Jesus bird, so called because it appears to walk on water, while treading from lily pad to lily pad. After a night in a small rented cubicle, air-conditioned and relatively mosquito free, we left for Katherine Gorge.

Here the temperature was pleasant, mosquitoes few, and kangaroos, wallabies, blue-faced honeyeaters, and great bower-birds frequented the campground. The Gorge trip (not quite the Grand Canyon, but good) traversed three gorges connected at high water, but now separate, requiring short walks between each gorge to enter a new boat.

Leaving Katherine, we saw enormous termite mounds, a huge feral pig on the highway, and both black and white cockatoos. A cultural center explained how aboriginal people survived the harsh conditions here and their special relationship to nature and its cycles. We were early at Cutta Cutta Caves (small, but highly decorated with stalactites and stalagmites), giving us time to enjoy three gorgeous waterfalls in Lichfield National Park on our way back to Darwin. Here a perfect tropical sunset closed out a day of touring the parliament building and enjoying the Darwin Museum and Art Gallery's fantastic collection of Aboriginal art and a re-enactment of Cyclone Tracy. At the nearby Northern Territory Wildlife Park, the marvelous noctarium allowed us to see bilbys, strange marsupials resembling a mix of a possum, small kangaroo, and rabbit. A huge area, other parts of the park displayed various Australian habitats and appropriate denizens.

In Sydney we toured the Great Synagogue, heard a concert in the recently restored Victorian City Hall, and enjoyed the serenity of the Chinese Garden (a secluded block in city center) that had been recently constructed. New since our last visit was the 1,000 ft. AMP (Australian Mutual Provident) Tower-Centrepoint, thirteenth highest tower in the world. Basically a telecommunications spire located above a giant shopping center, the tower also contains an observation deck that offers fabulous 360 degree views of the city and of Sydney Harbor. Taking the ferry to Taronga Zoo, compactly arranged on a hillside across the bay, gave us a chance for great photos of the Sydney Opera House and the well-known coat-hanger bridge. Besides upscale shops, the Victoria Arcade housed a life-size carriage made of jade! On our way home from Sydney, we stopped in Fiji, but I've already told you that story.

AMERICA THE BEAUTIFUL

From Sea to Shining Sea

Southward Bound

Michigan's Upper Peninsula

Duluth Surprise

Oregon Odyssey

Southeast Alaska

Alaskan Return

AMERICA THE BEAUTIFUL

Though our country does not have the long cultural history of Europe or as many cathedrals, we have an incredible diversity of people, places, and environments to visit. From Alaska to Florida and in between a tireless traveler can appreciate nature's wonders and humankind's creations, and still not see it all.

FROM SEA TO SHINING SEA

Sometimes being part of a trend is unavoidable. During 1976, families were encouraged to celebrate the bicentennial by using their vacations to see some of the United States. That didn't interest us. Coast-to-coast driving marathons lost their charm for us after the third time we'd made the cross-country trip in order to hike somewhere out west. The layouts of the interstate highways are so similar it's easy to lose track of where you are. Yet the interstates are the most efficient way of getting from here to there. Taking interesting byways, which we have often tried, is more pleasurable, but extends the driving time considerably. But driving was our chosen mode of transportation when traveling with the family. Using the car gave us enough space for camping gear for four and the flexibility to linger at beauty spots along the way and to change plans at the last minute without penalty. For four people, it's also the cheapest way to go, if you camp out. So, without intending to, we celebrated our country's bicentennial by seeing much of it when we drove 8,000 miles during the summer of 1976.

Our plan was to visit some national parks new to us: Mammoth Cave and Carlsbad Caverns; to revisit sites new to the children: Mesa Verde and the Grand Canyon; to visit old haunts, friends, and relatives along the way; to see Disneyland; and to backpack for a week from Onion Valley, California, to reach Mt. Whitney's summit. Our route took us through Kentucky, Arkansas, New Mexico, California, Colorado, Kansas, Missouri, Illinois, and home to Maryland.

We began our circle tour by heading southwest towards Kentucky. The car started making odd noises as we approached Glasgow, Kentucky, not far from Mammoth Cave. We noted with dismay that it was July 4. Thinking we'd lose the entire day because everything would be closed for the holiday, we were happy to find an open gas station. Not only was a mechanic available, but the gas station was on the small town's parade route. While we waited for the work to be done, we watched a fine parade. It had everything: politicians in antique cars, bands, baton twirlers, floats, and horses.

It was easy to see why Mammoth Cave received its name. Though somewhat lacking in the usual cave formations, Mammoth impresses by sheer size. At its highest point, the cave roof reaches 291 feet, the height of a thirty-story building. The rooms are vast, sometimes as wide as two hundred feet; and the trail through the cave is wide and fairly long. The tour lasted about two hours, although the trail is only a small sampling of the more than three hundred miles of known passageways.

Northwest Arkansas was our next stop, where we hiked near the Buffalo River into favorites from our past: lush, green Hidden Valley; Goat Bluff with its narrow trail and frightening drop-off; and Bat Cave, its ceiling covered with sleeping small brown furry flyers. Inside the cave, we crawled in mud up to the edge of the chasm into which a huge and deafening waterfall drops, admiring its power and beauty by flashlight. Disappointed by the renovated and updated downtown square in Fayetteville, we missed many of the old buildings that gave it a quaintness twenty years earlier when I'd been a graduate student and Kurt had been on the faculty at the University of Arkansas. At least the campus was recognizable, though greatly expanded. Old Main, the oldest building on campus, still stood in its place, its chimes continuing to mark each quarter hour. Every returning graduate looks for his or her name sandblasted into a sidewalk that covers more territory each year since the tradition began with the University's first graduating class. I couldn't resist taking a photograph of my name and degree along with those of alphabetically close fellow graduate students I'd known.

At our next stop, the natural beauty of Carlsbad Caverns in New Mexico was overwhelming, surpassing even Cacahuamilpa in Yucatan. Although over-zealous advertising and the elevator entrance made us dubious about visiting, the enchanting formations, some so delicate they looked like flowers and plants, some resembling totem poles, onyx curtains and draperies, and the magic of tiny stalactites reflected in still pools completely won us over. Each room was highly decorated with amazing limestone formations. At dusk we watched for thirty minutes as hundreds of thousands of bats continuously streamed out of a part of the caverns not open to visitors. After feeding on flying insects all night, the bats are said to return to the caverns to sleep all day. We didn't stay around to make sure they all got back.

Fascinated and educated by the Arizona-Sonoran Desert Museum and Saguaro National Monument, we learned to recognize several cacti varieties as well as other desert flora and fauna unfamiliar to us. The museum provided natural habitats for over 200 live animal species, but the baby bobcats were particularly endearing.

In San Diego, we couldn't resist a stop at old town, a six-block area containing many of San Diego's original buildings, some of them restored adobes from the 1820s. We practically lived at the zoo and Balboa Park, site of the 1915-16 Panama-California International Exposition. The charming Moorish- and Spanish Renaissance-style buildings now house twelve museums focusing on art, photography, aerospace, San Diego history, the history of man, natural history, folk art, automobiles, botany, and railroads. The San Diego zoo, a leader in creating animal enclosures simulating natural habitats, had much to show us, as it is one of the largest zoos in the world and cares for many rare and endangered species. Our Marine World visit was all too short, but long enough to get a frozen banana and to wonder at the dolphin and whale shows. We hadn't really believed that everyone enjoys Disneyland. I'd expected simply a giant amusement park: tolerable, but not absorbing. How wrong I was! The mariachis were better than those we heard in Mexico, and it was a pleasure to succumb to the illusions of Jungle Safari and Pirates of the Caribbean. We went early and stayed late.

Nature's wonders reclaimed our admiration in Sequoia National Forest. These ancient giant trees dwarf all around them, invoking a quiet respect from most visitors to the evergreen cathedral created by the branches. Our planned backpacking week on the John Muir Trail with a final assault on Mt. Whitney flopped when Alan, then nine years old, became altitude sick in the first 12,000-foot pass. We had slept the night before at the Onion Valley campground at 9,000 feet, but he needed more time to adjust. After a while, I carried his pack as well as my own, but at day's end developed a migraine headache. It was too risky to chance going on, as the only other descent was at the end of several days' walk. We spent that night camped by glacial lakes on the other side of the pass, where a daring marmot helped himself to some of our freeze-dried ice cream.

In the morning, we descended the way we came, crossed Death Valley by night (an oven, even then) and arrived at the Grand Canyon early. Though we preferred the less crowded and more rustic North Rim, the brooding, changing beauty of the canyon itself was inescapable, despite crowds, heat, and dust. A quick glance doesn't do very much, but the longer one stays, the more the canyon's grandeur seeps into the consciousness.

At Mesa Verde's cliff dwellings, more areas were available for visiting than when Kurt stopped twenty years earlier. The survival skills and the ingenuity of these ancient people is impressive. The four of us followed a ranger-guided tour in a small group. After one explanation about secret rites in which the elders sat around a sacred fire, a young girl from Texas asked, "Where do they see it?" The ranger asked, "See what?" It was hard to keep the giggles down, when the girl explained she wanted to know where the people sat down.

As we drove through Kansas the next day, we were very uncomfortable even with all the car windows open. Later we heard that the temperature had reached 105 degrees at noon. Our friends in Manhattan, Kansas, had a lovely air-conditioned home and served us most welcome cold drinks. In the morning, they showed us part of Kansas that was surprisingly green and hilly–no wheat and no sunflowers.

Heading east, we next stopped to look down on the Mississippi River from the Arch in St. Louis, before crossing the mighty river to drive through St. Jacob, Illinois, a very small rural town, where I went to high school. The town had doubled in size in twenty-five years and now had a population of 800. Our last stop before driving home was for a Bueltmann family reunion at brother

David's in Clinton, Illinois.

SOUTHWARD BOUND

Old Salem Village, North Carolina, an early Moravian settlement, was our first stop on a month-long trip Kurt and I took in September 1991. Here, in restored village buildings, the communal life of these religious refugees is recreated. Nearby, Chimney Rock's impressive views and catwalk trails were fun, even though part of one trail was closed off for filming *Last of the Mohicans*. Hikers gathered at the barrier to watch scantily clad actors running through the rhododendron and pine forest.

On the way to Asheville, we camped and hiked in the Mt. Mitchell area, just west of the Blue Ridge Parkway. With a summit of 6,684 feet, Mount Mitchell is the highest point east of the Mississippi. Driving to the summit, we hiked the crest trail amidst scrubby pines to Mount Craig and Mount Big Tom. Gathering clouds made us turn back, but we still had time for the Balsam nature trail and Craggy Gardens, where fall wild flowers bloomed among the crags.

At the Day's Inn motel in Asheville, a sign stated rooms would not be rented to local residents. Puzzled, I asked the reception clerk what it meant. She told me the policy was in place to prevent prostitutes (male and female) from giving the place a bad name and also to prevent rowdy college students from tearing up the place the way they did in Charlotte. It was a very quiet motel. Asheville's Thomas Wolfe Home was open for visitors, so we learned a bit more about the life of this famous author. The Biltmore Mansion had been vastly improved and expanded since we visited twenty years earlier. Many more rooms were open and beautifully furnished and decorated. More information about the branch of the Vanderbilts who lived there was also now available at no extra cost, something previously missing. The former dairy had been converted to a winery where we tasted five different wines and bought three bottles to take home.

From Asheville we drove twenty miles to Mount Pisgah campground where we planned to hike to the summit and back that afternoon–only a three-mile trip. Chased off the mountain trail by close lightning, thunder, and a heavy downpour of rain, we crouched under a tall rhododendron bush until the rain slackened, then returned to our campsite where we dried out our sopping tent with paper towels.

In Chattanooga, Tennessee, our next stop, we visited the battlefields on Lookout Mountain despite steamy temperatures over ninety-three degrees. The setting of Chattanooga, beside the river at Moccasin Bend with Lookout Mountain at one side was very beautiful, even through the haze that day. Supposedly, one can see seven states from the top of Lookout Mountain when the day is clear. Billboards endlessly proclaimed the magnificence of Ruby Falls, and Kurt remembered being impressed by its unusual setting inside a cave. I had visions of a ruby-colored waterfall cascading to a scarlet pool below so was disappointed to learn that the falls had been named by their discoverer for his wife, Ruby. The height of the falls and the volume of water were worth the admission price, and the colored lights which revolved under the water sometimes made the waterfall look red.

We knew we were in Georgia when we saw a list of workers at Hardees: Linda Adams, Shirley Smith, and Polly Poteet. To reach Springer Mountain, the southern terminus of the Appalachian Trail, we drove through Helen, Georgia, population 300, which hosts a two-month-long Oktoberfest, a Fasching festival, and a Christmas market. These German traditions brought from the homeland and maintained over the years, have transformed the small town into a tourist attraction. Another nearby town, Dahlonega , at one time had a mini gold rush, and mine tours are still given. As a warmup, we hiked a trail on Blood Mountain in hot steamy weather that kept most people away. Though not spectacular like Mount Katahdin (the AT's northern terminus) in Maine, with its knife-edge summit, the Georgia mountains were pleasant and remote with many fall wildflowers in bloom.

Near Atlanta, Georgia's Stone Mountain, containing the Confederate Memorial Carving, is awesome. Heavy rains created instant waterfalls cascading down the carved face of the huge granite monolith just as we arrived, but we still visited the complex of nineteenth-century homes and buildings preserved in the park's Antebellum Plantation. There women in hoop skirts stood at the doors welcoming visitors. The Civil War cyclorama, originally painted in 1885, created a sense of immediacy, and Atlanta Underground was fun with its many shops and restaurants. After stopping at Ocmulgee Indian mounds and marveling at Macon's many mansions, we found the world's largest biscuits and a bathing suit for $8.00 in Waycross, Georgia.

Alligators, pitcher plants, and sundews were numerous in the Okefenokee Swamp. We were fascinated by wild pigs running across the highway and by golden orb spiders that hung upside down in their industrial strength webs on the nature trail we walked. At Tifton's Agrirama, pioneer farms with cash crops of sugar cane, cotton, and turpentine were slightly different from homesteads we've seen in the Northeast and Midwest.

In Gainesville to see Irene Zimmerman, a friend I met years ago on a three-day tour we both took to Chichicastenango, Guatemala, we talked all the way to Cedar Key (on the gulf coast), where we enjoyed a beautiful waterfront view with our delicious fresh seafood dinners. The next day we stopped to see Devil's Millhopper, a large sinkhole formed in the 1800s when the roof of an underground cave collapsed. A path circled the deep hole, but the 221 steps of a wooden walkway led us to the bottom to see plants and animals usually living in ravines farther north in the Appalachian mountains. Payne's Prairie, a large grassy area in north Florida was another surprise. The 18,000 acres contains a fresh-water marsh, hammocks, swamp ponds, and pines. A visitor's center and boardwalk nature trails describe the prairie's history and ecosystem. Have you tried hot, boiled green peanuts? It's an acquired taste, but we found them worth trying--at least once.

In St. Petersburg, we took an obligatory look at the building where our son Alan worked for three weeks while helping map tides in Tampa Bay for NOAA. But we found the nearby Salvador Dali Museum far more enjoyable and fascinating. It was particularly interesting to see how the surrealistic style of this famous, eccentric painter developed from his early, almost normal painting. Reading the curator's speculations about events that may have pushed Dali towards his distortions gave us an introduction to psychoanalysis. The Pier in St. Petersburg, an inverted five-story pyramidal structure located on the waterfront, offered fishing, an aquarium, mini golf, shops, bridges and rest areas furnished with striking sculptures.

The Ringling House in Sarasota, built in Moorish style, is a beauty, and the art museum, newly refurbished, kept us occupied for most of a day. Thunderclouds threatened on tropical Sanibel and Captiva islands, but we still saw many roseate spoonbills, herons, and egrets at the J. N. "Ding" Darling National Wildlife Refuge.

The Everglades had much more water than in 1965 when we visited, and many more alligators. We liked learning about poison trees and varieties of hawks and egrets on the Park Service guided boat trip, but sadly found far fewer anhingas. Snorkeling at Pennekamp State Park in eighty-five-degree water above a reef with colorful tropical fish was not quite Australia's Barrier Reef, but it was very enjoyable. A group of six raccoons made us reconsider eating our sandwiches at their picnic table.

Following a four-day visit to the Bahamas, we started back north towards home. Kennedy Space Center's launching pads, equipment, and "Blue Planet" film followed by St. Augustine's fort, Spanish village, museum, and Flagler College gave us a taste of both future and past. In Orlando we visited relatives before a day at Universal Studios. It's amazing how real the "sets" appear in our slides. The peak experience, however, was Epcot. Our day there was long and busy, but because there were no lines, we saw it all! The setup reminded us of world fairs where corporations sponsor animated shows and demos of technology, and various countries share their beauty and culture while selling food and souvenirs. In addition to displaying the tropical reef community in a gigantic tank, the World of Water cared for a manatee and her baby. In another pavilion, we marveled at new, ingenious methods of growing food. We enjoyed it all; there really is something for everyone there, and we enthusiastically recommend an Epcot visit.

Farther north, we paused at Charleston, South Carolina, with its charming southern architecture and live-oak trees, just long enough to do the historic district walking tour and to visit the market there.

MICHIGAN'S UPPER PENINSULA

At Sleeping Bear Dunes National Lakeshore, located on the northwestern shore of Michigan's lower peninsula, we camped in the D.H. Day Campground and took the Pierce Stocking scenic drive, stopping at various turnouts. Cottonwood trail was a pleasant walk up and over some dunes. From the overlook where daring ant-like tourists scrambled down a very steep dune ending at the lake and then laboriously struggled back up, we had excellent views of both North and South Manitou Islands. A boat departs at 9:30 a.m. daily during June, July, and August for South Manitou Island, where various hikes and campgrounds are available. Visits can be made to the old schoolhouse; farmsteads; a grove of virgin white cedar trees, one existing before 1492; the still-visible wreck of the *Francisco Morazan,* which ran aground in 1960; and the Manitou Passage State Underwater Preserve, where white mooring buoys are used to identify sites for boats carrying divers who want to examine underwater wrecks. The boat returns to the mainland at 5:30 p.m. Our enthusiasm for visiting the island quickly evaporated when we learned that in September there are no trips on Tuesdays and Thursdays.

We had just missed the Maritime Museum's live demo when we arrived in Glen Haven, but we watched the slide show on breeches buoy rescue. Used for rescue during the late 1800s and early 1900s, the breeches buoy consisted of a ring buoy attached to a strong pair of canvas breeches or short pants. When passengers and crew couldn't be rescued in other ways, a cannon-like gun shot a ball containing a line to the stranded ship. Using the line to pull the heavier hawser to the ship, the crew then attached the hawser high on the mast. On shore, the hawser passed over a high structure made of two crossed beams and then was buried in the ground, attached to a sand anchor. The breeches buoy was attached to a pulley that ran on the hawser from the ship to the shore. The person to be rescued climbed into the buoy, sat in the breeches and rode to shore over the pounding surf. The park volunteer standing in the boat shed amidst boats and gear had a hoard of information to share. We learned a lot about the storms, wrecks, and U.S. Life-Saving Service rescues on Lake Superior. Playing in my mind as background music to all of this was the suitably somber modern-day ballad, "The Wreck of the Edmund Fitzgerald."

In Traverse City, crammed with resorts and entertainment, we found wonderfully delicious fresh apricots at a roadside stand, but we passed through too early for the winery tours on Old Mission Peninsula. Farther north along the eastern shore of Lake Michigan, brightly colored masses of petunias lined both sides of Petoskey's main street all the way through the town. From the main highway we could enjoy a few of Bay View's more than 450 Victorian homes.

Our goal for the day was Paradise and Tahquamenon Falls State Park. The lower falls cascade on both sides of an island. During the season, which ended on Labor Day, we could have rowed a rental boat to the island. The upper falls, four miles away, were spectacular, an amber-colored mini-Niagara. But the mosquitoes were everywhere. The day was warm and humid without a breeze, forcing me to eat dinner inside our tent for protection.

In Munising we splurged on the Painted Rocks cruise. It's best to go in the afternoon. That's the way to avoid morning fog and to be there when the sunlight from the west intensifies the colored streaks of mineral deposits on the coastline's sandstone walls. Rust browns, burgundies, yellows, turquoises, and whites stain the walls, as if a child with giant crayons had spent the afternoon coloring a page for Mom. Because the water was calm and the afternoon sunny and clear, we saw bright yellow kayaks cruising the clear lake, darting in and out of the coves and arches projecting from the shore. Just at dusk we hiked to seventy-foot-high Munising Falls; in the morning looking for more great scenery, we visited Miner's Castle Overlook and Miner's Falls, about eight miles from Munising.

We couldn't leave the U.P., as it's called, without sampling pasties, meat- or vegetable-filled dough pockets originating with the Cornish and Welsh miners who emigrated to this area. On our way to Porcupine Mountains Wilderness State Park in the northwest corner of the U.P., we stopped at Gramma's in Negaunee for freshly made, piping-hot tasty pasties.

We were running out of time, so we could only sample the ninety miles of trails at "Porkie" (the park's local nickname). Driving past its small alpine ski area, we parked by the trailhead, taking a short hike for the view of Lake of the Clouds, hundreds of feet below the escarpment where we stood. We could also see Lake Superior and an inviting beach trail. At the summit observation tower we met several backpackers. Later, after staring at a black bear casually crossing the highway, we swayed on the suspension bridge in the Presque Isle River area of the park and enjoyed a twilight look at impressive Manido and Manabezho falls. It was cooler here and there were no mosquitoes.

The Grand Tour of Apostle Islands National Lakeshore drew us to Bayfield, Wisconsin the next morning. Even this late in the season, reservations are needed in order to get one of the fifty seats on the upper deck, which give the best view of these twenty-two islands. On clear days, the three-hour nonstop boat tour gives views of most of the islands and some of the lighthouses, while a narrator relates much of the area's historical background from the days of the fur traders to the establishment of the National Lakeshore in 1970.

On strategically placed islands, six lighthouses, built from 1857-1891, protected ships from missing the navigation routes in the archipelago as they made their way carrying lumber, quarried stone, iron ore, and grain from Chequamegon Bay, once the second-busiest seaport on the Great Lakes. In 1965 the Soo Line ore dock stopped shipping ore from Ashland, ending ninety-three years of ore shipment.

Today the National Lakeshore offers island campsites for boaters and historic sites such as Manitou Fish Camp, where visitors can see exhibits and demonstrations at the ranger station. We saw several small sailboats that were boarding six to seven passengers for personalized tours among the islands.

Madeline Island (2.6 miles from Bayfield) is one of the Apostles not included in the designated National Lakeshore. With a year-round population of about 180, the island has three parks, an Indian burial ground, a museum, rental bicycles, mopeds, and canoes and offers campsites, restaurants, shops, accommodations, and the usual amenities in and around the small town of La Pointe. The island is accessible by ferry from spring breakup (March or April) until winter freezeup (January or February). A windsled provides transportation after the ferries stop, until the ice road is passable. Now that would be a trip!

On the mainland near Bayfield, the Lake Superior Big Top Chautauqua presents a varied schedule of performances and events during the season. Craft shops line the streets not far from charming and attractive bed-and-breakfast establishments.

Because Duluth motel prices would have ruined our budget, we stayed at Amnicon State Park, a secluded haven just off State Highway 35, where in less than two miles through the park, the Amnicon River falls 280 feet, tumbling over the rocky escarpment of the Douglas fault. In the heart of the park, the river separates into two streams, plunging over three waterfalls. A uniquely designed covered bridge and many chirping birds enhanced our overnight stay.

DULUTH SURPRISE

"So what's to do in Duluth?"

We were meeting another pair of paddlers at the Duluth airport for a week in the Boundary Waters Canoe Area near Lake Superior. Because we were driving from Maryland, I figured we might have some extra time in Duluth before the plane arrived. My Minnesota cousin's suggestion didn't sound like much: a lakefront, watching a bridge go up and down. How exciting can that be?

In the morning, after camping in Wisconsin, we crossed the bridge to explore Duluth's delights. Although the French explorer Sieur du Lhut landed on the shore of Minnesota Point in 1679, a permanent settlement was not established until 1852. Built on the sloping ridge that ends in Lake Superior, Duluth vaguely resembles Seattle or San Francisco. Before 1939, an incline railway transported citizens from the downtown waterfront up to the residential area, where large, well-built Victorian mansions offer impressive views of Lake Superior and the shipping activity. Only a deli marks the incline station now.

Our first stop was The Depot, now the St. Louis County Heritage and Arts Center. Built in 1892 as a railroad station serving thousands of immigrants and travelers, the chateauesque-style building, renovated in 1977, now houses three museums: the Duluth Children's Museum, the Lake Superior Museum of Transportation (a world-class collection of railroad rolling stock and artifacts), and the St. Louis County Historical Society Museum. On the fourth floor, the Historical Society Museum features birch-bark canoes, Eastman Johnson's faithful depiction of the Ojibwe people around 1850, Herman Melheim's exotic-looking hand-carved clock cases and furniture, artifacts and photographs about the region's important lumber industry, the story of the fur trade, and an account of Daniel de Greysolon, Sieur du Lhut, for whom city is named.

The train lover will find an overwhelming variety of trains, many of which can be personally inspected, in the Museum of Transportation. Though we were too late for the summertime free trolley rides, we climbed all over a caboose and an electric train and saw two different kinds of snowplow engines, along with a fascinating exhibit on speedy "silk trains" that traveled from Seattle to New York when silk clothing was the latest rage. Our $5.00 ticket was good for unlimited access all day long. The building also houses the Duluth Art Institute, which holds exhibits and four performing arts organizations: The Duluth Ballet, the Duluth Playhouse, the Duluth-Superior Symphony Orchestra, and Matinee Musicale. This historic landmark is very well used.

Watching a bridge go up and down had sounded rather silly to me, but then I hadn't been to Canal Park in Duluth where a 900-ton span rises to nearly 140 feet above the water to permit passage of huge seagoing vessels to and from the twin ports of Duluth and Superior, through which approximately 30 to 40 million tons of cargo are shipped each season. Some of the world's largest grain elevators are located amidst the seventeen miles of channels and forty-five miles of frontage. Minnesota ore, limestone, coal, coke, and salt are among the cargoes handled here. The Twin Ports, 2,342 miles from the Atlantic Ocean and the westernmost end of the Great Lakes-St. Lawrence Seaway, serve nearly two hundred foreign-flag vessels each year, along with an average of a thousand Great Lakes freighters--"lakers" that include 1,000-foot super freighters carrying over 60,000 tons per ship.

Boat-watchers like us line the 300-foot-wide, 1,650- foot-long canal whenever a ship is announced over the loud speaker atop the Canal Park Marine Museum. Inside this free museum, provided by the Corps of Engineers, information about Lake Superior and the history of shipping abounds. Full-sized replicas of ship cabins and a pilothouse can be examined, and an interested visitor can learn more about taconite than most people ever need to know. A hot line for boat-watchers, (218) 722-6489; a free newssheet; and a web site, www.duluthshippingnews.com list ship schedules in season. To landlubbers like us, Twin Ports (Duluth-Superior) gave a fascinating glimpse into a world we'd never known.

The rest of the waterfront park is dotted with attractive sculptures, an indoor amusement center, arts and crafts shops, and eating places. At Grandma's Grill and Saloon, we marveled at the huge mound of Minnesota wild rice served with our grilled salmon--delicious. We skipped the Omnimax Theatre, the Duluth Entertainment Convention Center, Glensheen Mansion and Gardens, and the Ore

Boat Museum this trip because our sightseeing time was running out.

On our way to the airport, we noticed the downtown skywalks, needed in Duluth's snowy winters, then drove the winding Skyline Parkway through various parks and parts of Duluth including the University of Minnesota's campus. Cars parked on both sides of the road alerted us to groups of silent hawk watchers with scanning binoculars. On a clear day, views of Lake Superior and Duluth from flower-encircled Enger Tower in its lovely city park would be spectacular. Haze rose from the lake, as this particular day, even in September, was hot and humid, surprising the newest arrivals when we picked them up at the very quiet Duluth airport.

Surprises continued north of Duluth as well. In-line skaters and walkers shared the wide shoulder of scenic Highway 61, which hugs Lake Superior's western shore on its way to Canada. With a longer stop in Two Harbors, a visitor could explore the five waterfalls of the Gooseberry River in Gooseberry Falls State Park. Spectacularly sited Split Rock Lighthouse, 168 feet above the lake, invites the photographer and lighthouse lover. Sandpaper is only one of the products featured in the 3M/DWAN museum's history of 3M (Minnesota Mining and Manufacturing Company).

Our wilderness week, described in the chapter, "Getting Wet,"was rugged, somewhat rainy, and wonderfully cool with quiet campfires, tall pines, beautiful marshes and clear lakes. At times, the lovely silence was punctuated with the chilling calls of loons and wolves. Because we went after Labor Day, we met only five mosquitoes. I learned a lot about backpacking, portaging, water filters, bear ropes, and why one always carries a tarp; but before we went backcountry, I also learned there's a lot to do in Duluth.

OREGON ODYSSEY

Returning from nine weeks in Austria, we had three weeks at home to do laundry, sort a mountain of mail, and get ready for two weeks in Oregon. We flew free, because we'd voluntarily deplaned on our return flight from a ski trip in California when we were each offered two round-trip flights. We'd used one set of tickets to ski at Steamboat Springs, Colorado, but the other set was about to expire. Oregon seemed like a good destination. In Portland we checked out downtown, the attractive zoo, and the forestry museum and bought camping supplies before heading to Albany for a chicken/salmon barbecue and reunion with friends from Takoma Park and some of Kurt's former colleagues, all now living in and around Albany.

Canoeing the bouncy North Umqua river south of Eugene, we prided ourselves on how well we could follow our former neighbors, Sandy and Steve, who were much more experienced paddlers. Suddenly, the river grabbed us. We had paddled too slowly in one of the rapids. We dried out during a long lunch stop in the surprisingly warm late-September afternoon sunshine. After watching steelhead salmon making incredibly high and repeated leaps to surmount rapids temporarily halting their journey upstream, we drove through thick forests to Crater Lake. Looking like its picture postcard, Wizard Island, actually the remains of a cinder cone, enhances the beauty of the intense blue lake, at 1,932 feet the deepest lake in the world. Hiking up Mt. Scott gave us great views. The drive to the pinnacles, an area of spires and fumaroles, and around the rim of the lake showed us many reasons why the Native Americans considered the area sacred. Strange craggy shapes, volcanic leavings, old-growth forest, volcanic cones, and mudslides indicated this was a very unusual area. From scenic viewpoints, we were enchanted by the phantom ship, a haunting rock formation in the lake. Because the entire area lies at between 8,000 and 9,000 feet, snow closes the rim drive from mid-October to early July. Already in late September we saw a light dusting of snow in the morning.

Oregon's role in the logging industry is well demonstrated at Collier State Park's logging machinery museum, which also exhibits a realistic re-creation of a logging camp's various buildings and furnishings. This educational visit was a pleasant stop on our way to Upper Klamath National Wildlife Refuge. A strong wind made it hard to canoe Crystal Creek and Wocus cutoff, segments of Upper Klamath Canoe Trail, but we saw coots, ducks, a great blue heron, and pelicans. An otter swam unconcerned, passing in front of our canoe. Still bird hunting, we drove through Klamath Falls to Tule Lake and Klamath Lake refuges on what appeared to be dikes separating impoundments of water. Many migratory birds were resting and fueling up there, but they were too far away for identification.

Heading east brought great views of Brokentop, Three Sisters, and Mount Bachelor. The ski area at Bachelor didn't open until November, but it looked very tempting. On the highway, a warning sign "Congestion" was posted in an area that had two buildings. For that part of Oregon, perhaps it was accurate.

Near Bend, we had to investigate Lava River Cave, a lava tube about a mile long with a constant temperature of forty degrees. To see anything, including where to step next, each visitor is offered a lantern. At some places sand had formed shapes and groups of shapes, which had, of course, been given imaginative names. At the High Desert Museum, we learned a lot while enjoying presentations by naturalists on birds of prey, otters, and porcupines. The history exhibits portrayed homestead, rancher, and sheepherding ways of life. Bats, kangaroo rats, burrowing owls, and black widow spiders inhabited the desertarium.

We hated to leave the beautiful painted hills area in the John Day Fossil Beds Park, but there was even more to see. Wonderful fossils had been found near the Sheep Rock Area. In the small town of John Day, we couldn't resist the Wah Chung and Co. Museum where the herbalist Dr. Ing Hay and his business partner Lung On lived from 1880 to 1940. In addition to being a general store, the building held herbs imported from China, bear paws, a Chinese temple, and an opium room offering bunks for anyone needing to chill out for a while.

Sitting on top of Flagstaff Hill, the National Park Service's Oregon Trail Interpretive Center has created a walk-through exhibit demonstrating the hazards and difficulties pioneers faced on their way west. Outside, an encampment, a mine shaft, and the actual ruts left by the covered wagons fascinate the visitor. The area is totally dry, except where it has been irrigated.

Our visit to the Hell's Canyon area of the Snake River was limited to a hike along the shoreline to Stud Creek. The visitor's center at the dam had already closed, and the season for rafting down and taking a jetboat up the rapids in the river was over. We stopped for steak at Pendleton, known for its yearly roundup and the Pendleton Woolen Mills, producer of the elegant and pricey Pendleton jackets and plaid skirts I'd longed for in the 1950s, but never owned.

A clear view of snow-covered Mount Hood raised our hopes that the predicted storm system would dissipate before we arrived. Some skiers were still enjoying the slopes, as we started hiking on a segment of the Pacific Crest Trail at noon. Gathering clouds persuaded us to turn back an hour and a half later as the trail switchbacked farther and farther down the mountain. The sprinkling of rain that started as we neared historic Timberline Lodge became a downpour, encouraging us to look around this magnificent lodge built with wonderful wood and stone craftsmanship by WPA workers in the 1930s.

With heavy rain and high wind in the weather forecast, we left for a drier part of the state. We were amazed at the basalt and tuff palisades cut by the Deschutes, Crooked, and Metolius rivers in Cove Palisade State Park. Nearby, Smith Rock State Park, a favorite with rock climbers, had fantastic tuff and basalt formations and many trails, but our time was too short to linger.

Heading for the Three Sisters and the Pacific Crest Trail near McKenzie Pass, we hiked near vast lava beds, saw several deer, and had a great view of North Sister Mountain before the rains chased us back to the car. Driving in one of the park's remoter areas, we were stunned to see a bobcat cross the road in broad daylight. On the road at dusk, we saw a large buck elk and later a coyote.

Rain the next day convinced us to investigate Oregon Caves National Monument, keeping dry underground while admiring the many calcite white marble formations in this very young cave system. Thinking we'd find the sun in California, we crossed the border to camp in the Smith River National Recreation Area, but woke to rain on the tent in the morning. Rain didn't stop us from hiking in Redwood National Park on a few damp trails. Driving north to the Oregon coast, we wondered at a World War II radar station that had been disguised as a farmhouse. The trail there was littered with colorful banana slugs.

The rain finally stopped that afternoon, so we could enjoy Oregon's spectacularly rugged coast, its sea lion caves, huge surf, and numerous state campgrounds. Simpson Shore Acres Gardens had dahlias, roses, a Japanese garden, and an orchid show. We picnicked at the Umpqua lighthouse and unsuccessfully looked for whales at Depoe Bay.

After exploring the Ft. Stevens Park where we camped, we visited Lewis and Clark's Ft. Clatsop and the Astoria Column, from which everyone should launch a toy balsa glider. We revisited Mount St. Helens, in Washington State, much changed since we last saw it in 1981. The seismic observatory is fascinating; the regrowth of downed trees wonderful. Finally, we drove historic Highway 30 up the Columbia Gorge and back to Portland. We never could find Dungeness crab, but had some tasty red snapper and delicious ribs. In Astoria, seals played in the Columbia River just outside the window of the restaurant while we enjoyed a seafood sampler. We did stop in Eugene, where my family and I lived in 1945, but the old house was gone. Our whirlwind trip convinced us we need to return to this fascinatingly varied state.

S0UTHEAST ALASKA

Escaping the August heat and humidity of the Washington D.C. area, Kurt and I found cooler weather (usually fifty-nine degrees) in Southeast Alaska.

Following two days at Vancouver's 1985 World's Fair (a good one like the 1967 Montreal Expo) and an overnight visit and superb smoked-salmon lunch with Aunt Olive and Uncle Ruben in Seattle, we camped for three unusual sun-drenched, glorious days on the top deck of an Alaska State Ferry, traversing the Inland Passage to Skagway. Cabins existed, but deck passengers (our classification) could travel cheaply, without advance reservations and with equal access to the cafeteria, showers, and bar. Some deck people brought their own food and pitched tents on the deck. We luxuriously slept and lounged on deck chairs, slightly protected by the solarium roof, but still under the stars, in our sleeping bags. Overhead heaters added warmth when temperatures dropped at night. The evergreen-covered islands, so sparsely inhabited, with majestic snow and glacier-laden peaks as backdrops, reminded us of Pacific Northwest areas we'd visited before, the vastness of this land adding another dimension to that wild beauty we find draws us to the West so often.

When the ferry stopped to load and unload at Ketchikan, we visited the salmon hatchery and the totem pole museum like good tourists. At Wrangell we hiked the beach to see Indian petroglyphs. In Sitka, where Russians prospered from the fur trade in the 1800s, the Russian Orthodox church with its onion-shaped dome and beautiful blue color had to be visited. Built from 1844 to 1848, the original church had burned in 1966, but the faithful had saved the treasures and icons, and the structure had been meticulously restored. Nearby, the church graveyard with its distinctive orthodox crosses was unlike usually level and closely-mowed cemetery grounds. Situated on a steep, overgrown hillside, the gravestones were surrounded by evergreens and wild berry bushes, somehow appropriate here, suggesting that even burial has been adapted to fit Alaska's wilderness environment.

Western flowers--lupine, columbine--grew everywhere, encouraged by the cool dampness. Once an elderly, grizzled native Alaskan asked if I was from Alaska (Did I look that tough?), claiming he did so because my pants were the same shade of blue as Alaska's flag! Yes, people were downright friendly. At sea, sighting bald eagles and Dall porpoises during humpback whale watches was the daily routine. Because the route lay within the Tongass National Forest, a naturalist was on board, giving talks and showing movies about the wildlife we could expect to see.

From Skagway we set out on the rugged Chilkoot Pass Trail, part of the Klondike Gold Rush National Historical Park. It's an unusual trail: part wilderness, part history, with artifacts along the path, ruins of buildings, and explanatory photos posted as one goes. An account of this adventure is in the chapter, "Trails to Glory." Once back to Skagway, we rode the ferry to Alaska's Capital, Juneau.

Juneau, accessible only by water, is a stunner! Sharp mountain peaks rise straight up, immediately behind the narrow strip of coastline where the town huddles. From our room in a restored Victorian Hotel (listed on the Historic

Register), we took two trips to see tidewater glaciers and "calving" in Tracy Arm and Glacier Bay. These glaciers were quite different from any we'd encountered before, and calving is an awesome sight. Huge pinnacles and towers of ice split off randomly at the toe of the glaciers, thundering as they crash into the sea, becoming exotically-shaped icebergs, which float away from the glacier, taking on various shades of green and blue. There is no way to predict how much ice will break away from the glacier or when these ice towers will fall. We were lucky. The night we watched "calving" for hours in Glacier Bay, a gigantic section fell, creating an eight-foot swell and evoking many excited squeals from passengers on deck and in the lounge. When it grew dark, and the ship headed back, the bumping and scraping of icebergs against the hull almost nudged us awake. In the icy water, but more often lying on some of the larger floating bergs were hundreds and hundreds of seals of all sizes. Supposedly they choose the icebergs and frigid temperatures to avoid the orcas (killer whales), their predators. Along the way we saw many puffins and other arctic birds, as well as porpoises, spouting whales, and a bear or two on the shore. An afternoon hike through Glacier Bay National Park's young rain forest, just growing up as the glaciers recede, was like a walk backwards in geological time to a continent just after the last ice age ended.

Juneau's museum had the largest collection of kayaks we'd ever seen, some for three or four paddlers. When our friends, the Krugers, unexpectedly appeared in the same museum during our visit, we Marylanders headed for the historic Red Dog Saloon and a celebratory pitcher. Their cruise ship had stopped just that afternoon for a few hours in Juneau. Inside the Red Dog, a honky-tonk player piano was irresistible. With fancy footwork, Mollee and I wiggled and whirled on the sawdust-strewn barroom floor while the guys had a beer. The catchy music continued as I danced out the swinging tavern door. On the street a shabby, toothless prospector grinned and said, "Are you going in?" as he steadied himself by grabbing one of the doors. "On my way out, sorry," I answered, seeing disappointment in his sagging shoulders and listless eyes. Maybe he thought I'd been advertising the good times to be had inside. Our friends never let me forget the kind of guy I seemed to attract in Alaska.

After Kurt and I hiked one afternoon along the side of the mile-wide Mendenhall Glacier, reachable by city bus from Juneau, we completed our Alaskan adventure by stuffing ourselves at a salmon feast at an abandoned gold mine. We panned for gold, finding a few flecks, but the really good stuff was the salmon, smoked on alder--all you could eat.

ALASKAN RETURN

On the horizon, towering granite tors beckoned. Ahead through miles of treeless, spongy tundra turf, not one track but many meandered. No cairns marked the trail, for there were no loose rocks anywhere. We'd been hiking since 9:00 a.m., read the signs warning of a recent bear sighting, trudged on boardwalks over squishy bog areas, and admired the profuse variety of mushrooms, as the well-marked trail gained altitude. An almost cloudless day let us shed a few clothing layers and gave us fantastic views as we rose above tree line, then followed mile signs and painted boulders to the newly built shelter at the edge of a vast emptiness broken by the distant monoliths. We'd seen only one hiker, heading the other way. Retracing our footsteps wasn't an option--we'd passed the halfway point. Now a surreal, sci-fi landscape faced us, where foreboding yet compelling distant shapes called, as the afternoon swiftly moved away. Only after we'd started on two different paths did we notice the odd arrangement of three very long branches. Moving closer, we saw they formed a tripod, surely not accidental; but no other tripods appeared until we were well past the first. Vaguely recalling that the trail description included a tripod section, we followed these markers (reminiscent of a children's story read long ago) to Granite Tors and the comforting mile markers.

The hiker approaching me now asked for information, explaining that his English was poor. "Sprechen Sie Deutsch?" I asked. His grin of relief prompted my next German sentence, one I'd often needed in Austria. "My husband is coming. He speaks German very well." One of the unexpected aspects of this Alaskan trip was the number of German-speaking hikers and tourists we met--the other was the bears we didn't see, despite the numerous warnings. We'd see evidence all right, paw prints and scat. We did wear bear bells to warn them of our approach, and some days I sang every song I could remember, because park rangers said the human voice is a more effective deterrent than bells. Maybe not every human voice--but no bears or other critters came to my portable concerts. Kurt faked fatigue to justify staying out of earshot.

In 1985 we'd taken the ferry from Seattle to Skagway visiting Sitka, Ketchikan, Wrangell, Juneau, Lynn and Tracy Arms, and Glacier Bay, and we had hiked the Chilkoot Trail for three days. Then, in August 1998, we had flown to Anchorage to explore another face of wild and vast Alaska.

We welcomed the cool temperature that allowed us to wear sweaters most of the time, as we admired the spectacular flowers, their vivid, vibrant colors a product of a short, intense growing season with twenty-four hours of sunlight. The excellent museum in Anchorage focused on various life-styles in Alaska and included a very fine art gallery. New to me were the Native American strength games (Contestants "walk" using only their knuckles and toes.) and storytelling by using a story knife in sand. In a store selling Russian icons, the prices ranged from $600.00 to $1,300.00. I assumed these icons were authentic, for they were just the ordinary icons lying around. The really splendid ones were locked up. I didn't ask the price. Rooms were also expensive, but we found a spartan lodge that included a simple breakfast and supper for $65.00.

Two city buses took us to the end of the line, where we walked the long road to Glen Alps, passing a mother moose and calf having lunch in a ravine. Flattop Mountain was a bit of a scramble, but very popular, despite threatening clouds; for it rewarded hikers with a great panorama of Anchorage and Cook Inlet. On our way back, we just missed the bus, seeing it drive by the stop. Our forty-five minute wait was enlivened, though, when three runaway horses pounded down the highway, which already carried car and truck traffic. About fifteen minutes later, three people came running out of the woods, asking if we'd seen horses. Later we saw them each walking a horse back home. From the bus on our way to town, we saw our first bull moose, munching grass near the airport.

After impressive Earthquake Park and an impromptu backstage tour of the Performing Arts Center, decorated with evocative masks, we were delighted to find space in nearby Eagle River Campground. Then the rains began. On our hike to Thunderbird Falls, I even used an umbrella. We ate soup and corndogs in

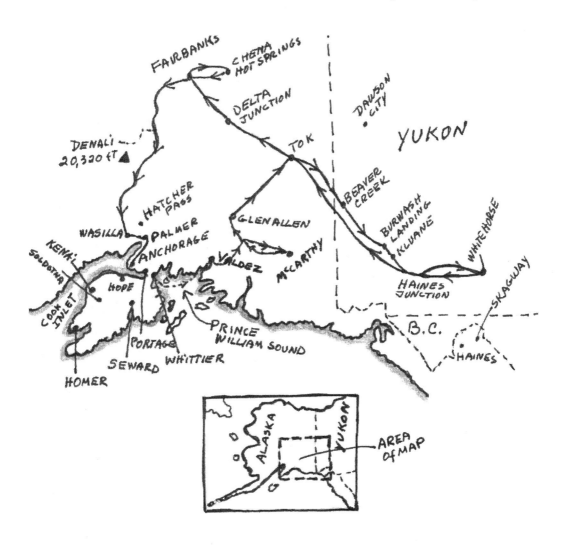

a bar in Palmer, where the huge cabbages are grown, then visited Wasilla's Iditarod headquarters with its slideshow and memorabilia. It was the first of many places in Alaska claiming to be the Iditarod's home.

As the spawning season progressed, more and more salmon were entering the streams to seek the places where they began. Fisherman crowded the highways and stood side by side in the streams to catch the salmon, an unforgettable and bizarre sight. Despite rain, we enjoyed the swimming puffins in Seward's Marine Life Center and hoped one day to see the peaks hidden by the low cloud cover.

Still in rain, we drove back north, taking the Glenn highway to the fascinating Musk Ox Farm where we saw young and old oxen and learned about qiviut, the angora-like undercoat of the animals. We camped near Matanuska Glacier and caught glimpses of several other massive ice flows before we visited Independence Mine in Hatcher Pass where at 3,500 feet, the August temperature was forty-five degrees. Pink and fuchsia fireweed brightened the otherwise gloomy day. We'd exhausted our options and had to drive into the Kenai peninsula, rain or not. On the way we saw the famous tidal bore, a breaking wave up to six feet high rushing ten to fifteen miles per hour with an incoming tide. Just after an extreme low tide is the best time to see a tidal bore. A timetable for the appearance of the bore at certain points along Turnagain Arm is available, so potential viewers can arrive at the vantage points just in time. Many years earlier, we'd observed a similar phenomenon on the east coast at Canada's Bay of Fundy. When we stopped for the night in Bird Creek State Campground, friendly though scruffy-looking neighbors offered us firewood and freshly caught salmon. If only we'd brought a skillet large enough!

After a week of wet, we woke to blue sky and a glorious day at Portage Visitor Center where photogenic icebergs floated on a lake formed by glacial melt. From newly renovated Williwaw campground, we hiked to the foot of Byron Glacier. Camping on Kenai Lake at Primrose Campground gave us a good start on the Harding Ice Field hike the next morning. Exit Glacier, its foot or toe as tall as a house, pours out of Harding Icefield three miles above. The parking lot was full of RVs and cars, the small primitive campground already filled. Most people walked to the foot of the glacier to marvel at its size and the enchanting bluish glow within its crevasses. But there were many hikers on the steep, rocky trail, which gained three thousand feet in three miles. Hikers walked carefully around volunteers carrying boulders and digging dirt to repair damage from rock slides and erosion. As we reached the snowfields, we were astonished to see eleven mountain goats lying on a snowpatch. Later they moved to a nearby lush meadow. In the clear and amazingly warm day, peaks surrounding the glacier sparkled magnificently. The icefield was a fabulous snowy expanse from which glaciers flowed in many directions and only the very tips of giant mountains poked out, looking like islands in a sea of snow or ice. Although carpets of spring flowers bloomed, many snowfields remained. These grew tiresome after awhile, convincing us that because we could already see most of the icefield, we didn't need to traverse every last snowfield, or at least it convinced Kurt, who persuaded me to head down to look for a campground. We found one in a wildlife preserve that served as a base for a couple of good day hikes.

Hoping to see whales, we next camped in Captain Cook State Campground on Cook Inlet where a ranger gave a talk on dog mushing, a popular, but expensive activity in Alaska. Stopping at an old Russian village on our way to Homer, we saw a family riding as they exercised their sled dogs by letting them pull their ATV. Even in Alaska there's not much snowfall in summer. Homer's Salty Dog Saloon can't compare with Juneau's Red Dog, but the charter fishing business was very active. We never realized how big halibuts were until we saw some being cleaned, ready for flashfreezing and packaging for the clients. In and around a nearby nature trail, the art museum had staged a whimsical exhibit which was truly surprising and magical. Constructed webs hung between branches; mythical creatures peeked from behind shrubs, collections of painted stones enchanted while pointing the way. The museum also housed an excellent exhibit on the Valdez oil spill and showed live footage from video cameras trained on a nearby island's rookery--fascinating!

Rain the next day sent us to a "shelter" at a fishing camp on Resurrection Bay where boats were launched and retrieved by roadscraper snowplows, something I'd never seen before. When the sun shone in the morning we hiked fifteen miles to Lost Lake, enjoying our first view of chocolate-colored lilies and iceworms. From Portage we had perfect weather for our train-ferry ride across Prince William Sound. Cars are driven onto flatbed rail cars and transported through a tunnel under snow-covered, glaciated peaks, emerging at Whittier's ferry dock. The ferry captain veered off his normal route to give us a closer look at the magnificent Columbia Glacier and its numerous icebergs and some sea otters. Valdez's small museum, focusing on history and pioneer life, included a reconstructed bar, along with detailed information on the 1964 earthquake, the moving of the entire city to higher ground, and, of course, the oil spill.

In Thompson Pass, when we stopped for a great view of the impressive glaciated Wrangell mountains, a bald eagle swooped down to the highway an arm's length away--a thrilling moment. Surprised and awed by its beauty, I didn't think about my camera, until the eagle soared away.

Driving to Whitehorse in the Yukon Territory, I was intrigued by the stunted black spruce, called taiga, a Russian word for "land of the small sticks." Living on the permafrost severely restricts growth. Fabulous fall yellows and reds of aspens and birches infiltrated the various greens of the wilderness undergrowth around us. At Snag Junction campground, we saw loons in the lake, and a snowshoe hare came to our camp. The Burwash Wildlife and Native American Exhibit was very well done, including appropriate woodland and animal sounds for each realistic diorama. We hiked along the Yukon River around Miles Canyon; saw the longest wooden fish ladder in the world; and enjoyed Beringia

Museum, featuring fossils, flora, and fauna of the land area once linking Alaska and Russia across the Bering Sea.

About midnight we woke to sounds of pounding on the door of our somewhat shabby hotel room and a loud voice shouting "Open the door." "No," I yelled back. "You've got the wrong room. Get out of here." I'd heard some other roomers drunkenly quarreling earlier and thought this was one of them. But the voice went on demanding that we come downstairs because we hadn't paid. I couldn't get rid of the persistent beast. Finally Kurt woke, went downstairs, and more or less got the night desk clerk, an old crotchety guy with a Scots burr, calmed down. It was bizarre; we'd charged the room, then decided to stay another night and told a female desk clerk, but the place couldn't handle it. When we left in the morning, the night screamer apologized. Next time we'll stick to camping!

Otherwise it was fun in the Yukon where we found a very challenging hike up a "route," distinguished from a trail in that you can sometimes find the way and sometimes not. We turned back from our original goal, hoping to reach camp safely before dark. We did see some Dall sheep on this gorgeous day. The state campground was closed to tents because a bear had been marauding, but the private campground a mile down the road was open and safe enough. It provided great scenery on a lake, with peaks surrounding us and hot showers available. On another clear day, a ten-mile hike on a cross-country ski trail showed us several forest fires in the distance, but also many snow-capped peaks and great fall colors.

Heading back to Alaska and Fairbanks we stayed in a log cabin with no electricity or running water in Delta Junction. We did have a kerosene lamp and a roof over our heads. Showers and a flush toilet were a short hike up the hill. In Fairbanks, the university museum featured natural history and an emphasis on various native ways of life throughout Alaska. A special exhibit told of the Aleuts, who had been forced to leave their homes and traditional fishing areas around the Aleutian Islands during World War II, when Japanese invasion was feared. Families were given no advance notice, were forced to leave and were relocated on the mainland in crowded, substandard buildings that lacked adequate heating and plumbing. Food supplied them was also insufficient. Many of these "refugees" became ill and died as a result. Their requests for better living conditions were ignored, and they were essentially imprisoned in this area, although their only "crime" had been to have lived on land that the U.S. military wanted to occupy.

Sandhill cranes and geese migrated through Creamer's Field Migratory Wildlife Refuge, formerly a dairy farm. Early arrivals seemed to call to flocks overhead inviting them to join in the banquet on the ground. It was thrilling to see the large sandhill cranes come in for a landing. We had all the grilled salmon we could eat at Alaskaland, where a mining town had been re-created with historic buildings relocated from the center of town. Some were like museums; others housed boutiques, shops, and places to eat. Most impressive was the full-size paddle wheeler formerly used on the Yukon River. Northeast of Fairbanks we camped and did the Granite Tors hike described earlier. When we discovered a flat tire at the Chena Hot Springs Resort where we'd driven our rental car for breakfast at the end of the road, workers there put on the doughnut spare. In Fairbanks, instead of replacing the tire, the rental folks said, "Just take another car."

Now September, it was nippy in the mornings, with frost at night; time for our Denali Park visit. Wild animals highlighted our eight-hour bus trip to Elieson Visitor Center: three bears (gold, brown, black phases), Dall sheep, caribou, marmot, eagles. Most exciting were two bull moose starting to butt their racks of antlers to impress a nearby nonchalant female. Occurring on the highway, this action stopped all traffic, giving photographers a heyday. We were lucky to be in the first bus and don't know if those behind us saw anything. At the Center, a good portion of Mt. McKinley was visible in the distance. Later, driving to Anchorage, we had better views of both of McKinley's peaks from viewpoints in Denali State Park. While in the National Park, we also hiked up Mt. Healy, but dark clouds gathering, along with fierce, cold winds forced us back to camp after we had taken in various views along the ridge. On the way back, we had time to visit the kennels in the park and watch rangers exercise the dogs they use for patrolling the park once the snows come. Visitors were allowed to pet the huskies in cages if the dogs came close enough signaling they wished to be petted. Caught in the Northwest Airlines pilots' strike, we were rerouted through Seattle and Dallas instead of Minneapolis. It was too early to call Seattle folks at 5:00 a.m, but we got a great aerial photo of Mt. Rainier on our way home.

Darwin Sunset - Australia

Sydney Harbor - Australia

Alaskan Glacier

Ship Island - Crater Lake, Oregon

Cottonwood Campground -Alaska

Cluj, Romania

Holland

Greek Olive Groves
Kurt and Karen

Finisterre, Spain

Segovia, Spain

EUROPEAN EXPLORATIONS

Romanian Ramble

Getting around in Great Britain

Austria, Switzerland, and Italy

Scandinavia

We Couldn't Tiptoe Through the Tulips

No Rain in Spain

Revisiting Some Favorites

Vienna and Budapest

Poland, The Czech Republic, Germany

EUROPEAN EXPLORATIONS

*A scientist with an international reputation, my husband Kurt was
frequently invited to speak at international symposia and conferences or to visit
overseas laboratories. We always tried to make the most of these trips by joining
him. In 1964 the Romanian Academy of Sciences invited him to visit for two
weeks and to give lectures in several cities. He agreed to come if he could bring
his wife and two-year-old daughter. We three traveled for four additional weeks,
stopping in Paris, Vienna, Greece, and Italy. Two years later we spent a month in
England, Scotland, and Wales, where the highlight for our four-year-old
daughter was being invited to dance with the troupe of Scottish dancers
performing at the symposium banquet. Some years when Kurt couldn't find an
appropriate conference or symposium, we had to pay for everything ourselves.
Then we would find other ways to economize in order to make a trip possible.
For us, traveling had become a necessity.*

ROMANIAN RAMBLE

In an effort to establish themselves as having some autonomy and clout
within the USSR, the Romanian government in 1964 initiated some cultural and
scientific contacts and exchanges with the West. Soon after Dr. Murgulescu,
President of the Romanian Academy of Science, visited my husband's laboratory
in Washington, D.C., Kurt was invited to visit Romania for two weeks to give
lectures at the Academy of Sciences in Bucharest and at the university in Cluj.
Our daughter Karen was then two years old, and we were aware that for two-
year-olds a separation from parents was extremely traumatic. The Romanians
answered Kurt that they would be delighted to have the rest of us as their guests
as well.

Our plan was to fly to Paris, where Kurt scheduled another scientific
meeting. Then on our way from Paris to Bucharest, we'd stop for two days in
Vienna. Before we returned to Paris, we'd stop in Greece and Italy. We would be
traveling for six weeks with a two-year-old.

Although Karen was already toilet trained, she was still a toddler and
treasured a soft baby blanket called "pinkie" which needed to be held close
before going to sleep. We created a traveling "pinkie" by cutting up an identical
blanket into manageable sizes, simultaneously creating replacements when some
of the little pinkies were left behind. After Karen learned to sing "Frere Jacques,"
and a counting song I'd adapted to German: "Ein kleine, zwei kleine, drei kleine
dinos"we were ready to go. Karen was already fascinated by dinosaurs, so she
liked the song, repeated it endlessly, and could soon count to ten in German.

While Kurt visited a laboratory outside Paris, Karen and I went to the
Louvre. As we walked up the steps, she sang "Frere Jacques" impressing the
other tourists. Inside the gallery, Karen was very interested in looking for

paintings that included animals. I was allowed to snatch a few glances at other sculptures and paintings on our way to another "find."

My French was minimal and poorly pronounced, but we did not experience any of the legendary snobbishness attributed to the French. As we waited in line for the bus, several people asked Karen's age and had something good to say about her, or at least I thought it was good. At that time, she would drink milk only if she could use a drinking straw. My dictionary gave two words with that meaning. Of course I chose the wrong one when I asked for a straw. When the employees behind the counter laughed, I did too, as I provided the other word.

When Kurt joined us the next day, all three of us looked for Quasimodo in the magnificent Cathedral of Notre Dame, paid to sit down in a city park, and had a snack in a sidewalk café on the Champs Elysee. To my eyes, the white domes of Sacre Coeur were even more beautiful in real life than in pictures. We three quaked with fear as we ascended the Eiffel Tower to a viewing platform. The elevator wasn't too bad, but the stairs within the narrowing iron legs that swayed slightly were a bit unnerving. The photographs Kurt took of the city far below are impressive reminders of the grandeur and elegance of Paris.

Karen enjoyed the ornate furniture and the famous hall of mirrors at Versailles, but eventually she grew tired of walking. In the beautifully manicured gardens, Kurt carried her in a child carrier on his back. The carrier could also be used as a car seat. Fairly common today, these packs had not yet become popular, especially in Europe. Karen and her dad were always an item of interest to other tourists. As Karen rested and Kurt carried her that afternoon in Versailles, we were approached by four Japanese tourists who asked in sign language if they could take photographs of us. Fascinated by the child-carrying pack, they gave us a lovely Japanese hand-painted scarf as thanks. I hoped they didn't think they were photographing a uniquely French custom.

Karen stayed with our English-speaking friends the evening we went to the Opera Comique. It felt strange to see *The Mikado*, a British operetta about Japan, performed in France. Such a mishmash of culture.

Our next stop was Vienna, where Kurt had lived until he was thirteen. St. Stephen's Cathedral with its magnificent patterned-tile roof and ornate interior was a must-see. We also planned to see Herta Jäckel, a family friend and the manager of the Stern family business in Vienna. Kurt's father, a chemist, had owned a small company which produced various items connected with shoes and leather: polishes, dyes, finishes, tanning solutions, glues, and waxes. These products, based on formulas Kurt's father had devised, were sold to other companies who needed them. When the business was taken over by a Nazi in 1939, Herta, a non-Jew, was the only employee remaining who knew enough to keep the business going. Totally ignorant about the business he'd seized, the new owner relied heavily on Herta's knowledge. After the war when Austria passed restitution laws, Herta, at considerable risk to her own well-being, took the necessary steps to see that the business was returned to its rightful owner. She continued to run the business, carrying out instructions she received by letter and phone call from Kurt's father.

Now a plump, middle-aged woman with apple-red cheeks, Herta was delighted to see Kurt again and to meet Karen and me. Not only had she found us a very convenient hotel room, she had also managed to obtain two tickets to Verdi's *Masked Ball* at the Vienna State Opera, a magnificent palace-like building with crystal chandeliers and gold-leafed decorations. Once more we had a taste of cultural fruit salad. An opera set in colonial America, written by an Italian, performed in Austria! The performance was excellent, but I was equally awed by the elegance of the furnishings and surroundings. Although the building had been badly damaged during the war; it was one of the first buildings to be restored, being regarded by the Viennese as a symbol of their cultural interests. Herta, who adored Karen, offered to look after her. But Herta knew very little English and Karen's only German was the dinosaur counting song. They must have managed somehow, perhaps by playing games and drawing pictures, or what Karen then called pictures.

It was the Arlberg not the Orient Express that took us to Bucharest, but the trip was an adventure. The train left Vienna late in the afternoon to arrive in Bucharest by morning. We had reserved a sleeping compartment, but didn't plan to go to it until it became dark outside. We wanted to look at the passing scenery, and we also enjoyed trying to converse with other travelers. In some sentences each word was from a different language. Everyone somehow understood a little bit of what was going on and contributed a word when it was possible. By the time we headed for the compartment, it had been given to someone else because we had not claimed it. We three would have to sit in the crowded coach all night. But when Kurt spoke to the conductor while holding some dollars in his hand, another compartment suddenly became available. Unfortunately, it was adjacent to a very smelly WC. In fact, the smell was so bad that Karen refused to use the toilet–remarkable holding power for a two year old.

We also didn't realize that the dining car was only temporarily part of the train. When we were ready to eat, there was no place to go. We suddenly understood why so many people had brought picnic baskets and string bags full of food. The ever-helpful conductor offered to find a bottle of soda we could purchase, but the drowned fly floating in the bottle made us reluctant to drink it. A few saltine crackers I carried as emergency food for Karen only increased our thirst.

None of us slept well next door to the smelly toilet, and we were very hungry and thirsty by the time we arrived in Bucharest. When four grim-faced men wearing black hats and long black raincoats knocked on the door of our compartment, I was certain that the communists had come to take us away to a secret prison, and we would never see our relatives again. In reality, the Academy's welcoming committee had come on board, when we didn't exit

213

immediately, because they were worried we had missed the train. Kurt's colleague happened to be in London giving a lecture at a symposium, but he had assigned these men to look after us.

We were driven to Academy headquarters, located in an imposing marble mansion. I couldn't help wondering how many people had been killed or sent to a gulag so that the government could have use of the building. The first thing Kurt did was to ask for some water. We waited and waited as one official kept trying to organize our two weeks' stay, asking us where we wanted to go. They needed to know immediately in order to make arrangements. We were most interested in seeing Transylvania, but they insisted that we had to visit the Black Sea resort of Mamaia of which they were very proud. Still we waited for water, and little Karen was getting very upset about it. I began to think again that this was another part of their plot and that we might never get any until we had agreed to almost anything. When the water finally came it was served from an elegant silver pitcher that rested on an equally beautiful engraved silver platter. They had not wanted to use an ordinary pitcher to serve such honored guests.

Before the itinerary had been completely worked out, a man came in and said we had to leave immediately. We were then driven out of town to an elegant country mansion, passing run-down shacks and many drab-looking fences. Lunch, which began with a bitter-tasting soup, was served in a very formal dining room. Next, we were told to wait in the sitting room. This room had lovely brocade furniture, a ceiling-high yellow ceramic tile stove used for heating, and tall windows through which we could view a peaceful meadow edged with birch trees. Although Kurt had seen these beautiful heating units as a child, seeing a ceramic stove was entirely new to me. The stoves maintain a constant moderate heat, once they warm up. The circular part that reaches the ceiling has bench-like sections on each side of it. At last I understood what I'd read about in Maxim Gorky's play *The Lower Depths*. Now it made sense that giving someone a space on the stove was an honor rather than a punishment. Just as I was beginning to enjoy the lovely surroundings and to feel more comfortable and relaxed, we were once again whisked away–this time to a nice-looking hotel in downtown Bucharest where we spent several nights.

Again, I had certain expectations for what a hotel in a communist country would be like. In retrospect, I think my odd ideas came from watching too many old movies. Whatever the reason, I expected the beds to be either cots or hard, convertible sofas. The sheets would be either washed-out blue or khaki. Not at our hotel. It was comparable in every way to fine hotels in any county of the world. What a disappointment!

While Kurt gave his lecture at the Academy the next day, an English-speaking scientist's wife took Karen and me for a tour of the city We observed that only a few older people entered the Romanian orthodox churches. School children wore navy blue skirts or slacks and light blue blouses or shirts, adorned with a red scarf. Many buildings displayed the red flag with the yellow hammer and sickle on it. In the afternoon when Kurt joined us, our guide drove us around the city, pointing out the new concrete high-rise apartment buildings While we looked for remnants of historic Romania, the Romanians took pride in everything that was new. We realized that the need for housing had been severe, but from the outside, the apartment buildings were very ugly.

Other sections of Bucharest were quite beautiful. Classic European-style mansions were adjacent to parks with trees, ponds, and birds. A new exhibition hall, where we examined agricultural products being displayed, was architecturally striking, resembling a huge circular space module. In other parts of the city, more modest housing was quite charming with stucco and wood exterior walls and terra cotta roofs.

We were fascinated by the Village Museum, an open-air park at the edge of the city where more than three hundred houses, churches, and mills from all over Romania could be seen. Many of these were made entirely of wood with thatch or straw roofs. This gave us a glimpse of how people lived in other parts of Romania.

Karen loved the Romanian circus we attended one night. I also preferred it to American circuses because it had only one ring where all the activity took place. We could see everything. American three-ring circuses had always frustrated me. I was certain that while I was absorbed in watching an act in one ring, I was missing something absolutely fabulous that was going on elsewhere. One ring was much more satisfying, and the acrobats were superb.

During the two-week stay we were never invited into anyone's home. We weren't sure whether entertaining guests at home was simply not their custom or whether fear of some kind of surveillance or retaliation prevented this from happening. Kurt did have an official lunch at the Academy where typical food was served, along with seemingly endless toasts of *slivowitz*, a plum-based vodka. For most of the time, we were taken out to restaurants for dinner and encouraged to order steak and french fries. Partly, we thought, it was their way of showing us they could provide what Americans really wanted. Although we were more interested in eating local foods, we did not want to insult their generosity. We ate more steak and french fries in Romania than we ever did at home.

An English-speaking scientist, Constantin, had been assigned to us for the two-week stay. We suspected that Constantin had his instructions for keeping an eye on us as well, but he was pleasant company, and eventually we convinced him to show us the Romania we really wanted to see. We were also assigned a driver who drove a huge Russian-made car and did not speak any English. He had tried to personalize the car by decorating the inside with live flowers, a homey touch. Constantin was fascinated by Karen, especially when she learned to mimic his "*Cum te chiama?*" (What is your name?). It was Constantin who explained that Romanians were descended from the Dacians, a people sharing a common ancestry with the Romans. He said the Romanian language was closely tied to Latin, and that any ugly sounds in the language were "slavic" imports.

Many people did look somewhat Italian, including Constantin, but there were also many faces that had slightly Asian or Mongolian features, particularly the high cheek bones. I found both types attractive, but Constantin looked down on those he called the invaders. Later we heard that the first peoples in what is now Romania were Thracian tribes, whom the Greeks organized into a state called Dacia. Dacia was conquered by the Romans in 106 A.D. Even today controversy remains about the origin of the Romanian language.

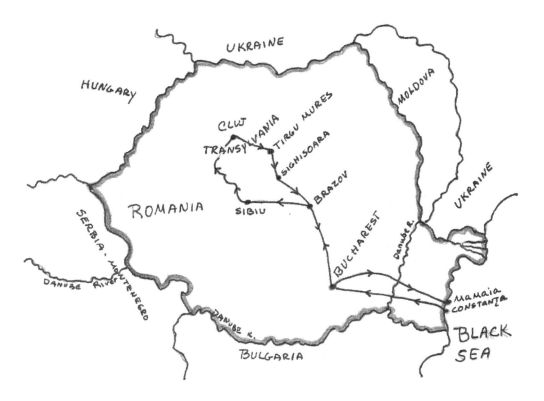

Snow had closed the road to our chosen destination in the Carpathian mountains, so we were taken instead to some other lovely parts of Transylvania which were mountainous and heavily wooded. In Brasov, a Saxon medieval town, we stayed in a very up-scale hotel. On the table in the suite we were assigned, a large vase full of handsome red gladioli made us feel like visiting royalty. But when we learned the hotel had no heat, we three huddled under the covers in the afternoon, waiting for a hot supper to remove the chill. The cold weather had come earlier than expected, and heat was an expensive commodity.

In another Saxon medieval town, Sighisoara, we wandered through narrow alleys and climbed the 172 steps of a covered stairway to reach a fourteenth-century church at the top of the hill. The church was all right, but the tunnel covering the steep stairs was much more photogenic.

Not far from Brasov, we took a look at unfurnished Bran Castle,

216

originally built in 1212 by Teutonic knights. It was further extended in 1377 by King Ludovic I de Anjou and was used to protect Brazov against the Ottoman empire. An imposing fortress, the stone and stucco castle sat high on a hill. Both square and round towers and many turrets could be used as lookout stations. The atmosphere in this castle reminded us that feudalism had lasted much longer in Romania than in other parts of Europe with the Renaissance reaching the country only in the eighteenth century. Today there are plans to popularize Bran Castle as Dracula's home. Vlad Tepes (Count Dracula) did occupy the castle for a short period of time, but the actual castle of Count Dracula lies in ruins in a more remote site.

Almost as impressive was Peles Castle, the summer residence and retreat of Romanian royalty, situated near the city of Sinaia in a thickly forested area. Built in 1873 by Carol I, King of Romania, this handsome half-timbered building was filled with beautiful carved wood paneling and wooden and bronze sculptures as well as handsome chairs and settees upholstered in red velvet. It was a very costly and elegant royal hunting lodge.

When Kurt learned that Cluj, a city in the north, was in a German-speaking area, he decided to give his lecture without an interpreter. It was the first time he'd ever given a lecture in German, but the students at the university had no trouble understanding him. A very old city, Cluj had many buildings with the pointed towers and dark turrets we associate with fairy tales.

Because our visit coincided with a tour by the Russian Ballet Company, hotel rooms were hard to find. Although our reservations had been made early, we obviously didn't have the status of the Russians, and we were kicked out of our hotel and taken to another one. Our small room had no regular double bed, but only a couch that opened up into a bed and–it had blue muslin sheets. Now we were seeing the real Romania, just as I'd imagined it. Constantin had even lower status than we did. He spent the night trying to sleep on a row of three chairs that had been lined up to create a sleeping surface. And none of us got to see the ballet!

From Cluj we traveled to Tirqu Mures, a town where many Hungarians lived. A large statue of the Hungarian-born king Matthias sat in the courtyard of a church which featured a typical Hungarian decorative ceramic-tile roof.

To reach Mamaia, we passed again through Brazov and Bucharest, then crossed the Danube river on a ferry. In Mamaia, a Black Sea resort, high-rise tourist hotels towered above the beautiful beaches, reminding us of the Miami, Florida, coastline. The Romanians sought to attract an international clientele to these hotels by providing staff who were fluent in the language of the guest. Each hotel had a designated language, since there were not enough staff people who were fluent in all languages. A casino and nightclub nearby had been created solely for the tourists. Only dollars were accepted as payment, and native Romanians were allowed to enter the building only if they were guests of a foreign tourist. Not being gamblers, we weren't very interested in going, but

Constantin was desperate to get in, so we all went. The meal was all right; the wine was not so good; the floor show consisted of what appeared to be members of a high school gymnastic class performing their exercises, wearing gym suits complete with navy blue bloomers. We couldn't understand the great attraction. We'd hoped to see some ethnic dances or folk customs, but Constantin said that sort of thing was not very popular, or perhaps it was frowned on by the government as somehow decadent. It was always hard to tell whether the explanations Constantin gave were the real explanations or whether they were what he was required to tell the tourists.

Although the beaches were uncrowded, we didn't go in for a swim. By October, the Black Sea was quite cool, and the skies were often overcast. Far more interesting was nearby Constanta where excavations had uncovered ruins of a Roman wall; foundations for buildings; Roman columns; and a statue of Ovid, the poet, who had been exiled to the city when it was known as Tomis.

For our last night in Bucharest, Constantin finally got the message and dared to take us to a student hangout in the University area for dinner. We had the local fare: fat pork sausages, sauerkraut, and beer. I even saw a man wearing a khaki trench coat with his collar turned up.

From Bucharest we flew to Athens to begin our five days in Greece. As we left our hotel room, we saw Greek soldiers in red jackets and traditional white pleated skirts parading around the main square. Heading for the Acropolis, we took a short side trip to see the Olympic stadium built in 1895 for the first modern Olympic games. For lunch we stopped in the oldest quarter of the city, the Plaka, at the base of the Acropolis. Many small homes were crowded together, along with many tavernas which served typical tasty Greek dishes. The path from the Plaka led through the excavation site of a Roman Agora, where the most interesting building was the Tower of the Winds. An eight-sided tower, the structure had been identified with the hydraulic clock of Andronikos erected in the first century B.C. A symbolic face representing one of the eight winds was carved on each side of the tower.

At the Acropolis reality matched what my imagination had dreamed. The hill was laid out with many temples and altars, but the Parthenon, built between 447 and 432 B.C., the glorious symbol of early Western civilization and culture, possessed a majesty and superb artistry even in ruins. We were fascinated to see the marble columns, gray and blue under cloudy skies, change to a yellow-orange on a clear day as they reflected the sun. Thanks to an intensive and fascinating unit on Greece I had enjoyed in the sixth grade, I could identify the three major types of columns: Ionic, Doric, and Corinthian, as we wandered among the temples.

Most of the decorative friezes and many of the free-standing sculptural groups could be seen only in the Acropolis Museum, where they'd been placed to avoid weathering and vandalism. Standing out in the open, however, were the six female statues which take the place of columns holding up the cornice of the attractive Porch of the Maidens, just one of many small cult buildings with graceful porches which make up the Erectheion.

On the south side of the Acropolis, we examined the Theater of Dionysus, built in the sixth century B.C. Here the first drama was presented in 534 B.C. by Thespis. Our word for actors, *thespian*, is derived from this dramatist. The open-air auditorium's seating capacity of fourteen to seventeen thousand includes sixty-seven throne-like seats of honor.

From Athens we drove about forty miles south to Cape Sounion to see the famous Temple of Poseidon standing on the summit of a promontory. Because the cliff plunges sharply to the sea on one side, I held Karen's hand tightly to keep her from wandering off. From the temple built in the second half of the fifth century B.C., fifteen slender Doric columns still stand. In contrast to the busy acropolis in Athens, there were not many people here to enjoy the magnificent view of the setting sun on the sea. We hurried back to Athens in time for a sound-and-light show on the Acropolis and a delightful folk-dance performance in the open-air theater.

The next day we planned to see Eleusis and Delphi. Eleusis was particularly interesting to us because it is one of the oldest communities in Attica and was the center for the Mysteries of Eleusis. These mysteries, explained only to the initiates, had to do with explanations regarding the afterlife--what one might expect in Hades or in the Elysian Fields. The cult worshiped Demeter or Ceres and Persephone. Two caves along the sacred bath were called the Sanctuary of Pluto and represented the spot where Persephone entered and emerged from Hades when she was abducted by Pluto. Ruins of buildings, altars, and triumphal arches remained.

On the way to Delphi we passed Mt. Parnassus. To the Greeks this mountain was sacred to Dionysus and the Maenads, but Latin poets made it the home of Apollo and the Muses. From what we could see, it was a very high, arid mountain. Only goats could find enough scrub to nibble. As we passed by Thebes we thought about Oedipus and the Sphinx, but there were no ruins or excavations related to the dramas we knew.

The Sanctuary of Delphi is known as the second most impressive sight in Greece. We walked the sacred way, which had once been paved with marble slabs, past many votive monuments and the various treasuries, built by competing towns to house the donations from their citizens. The Temple of Apollo was built between 370 and 340 B.C. Within this temple, the Pythia presided. She had a special chamber where, bending over the Omphalos, a sacred stone, she inhaled sacred vapors which brought about a prophetic trance. Numerous rulers, generals, and commoners in ancient times consulted the Oracle at Delphi to hear Apollo's advice, often confusing or misinterpreted, given through the Pythia. In the Delphi museum, we were captivated by the sculpture of the bronze charioteer of Polyzalos, whose eyes still retain their inset colored stones, and whose pose is the essence of elegance and calm. Of the many sculptures there, we particularly liked a winged sphinx and the acanthus column.

Continuing west through olive groves, we crossed the Gulf of Corinth by ferry to reach Patras, a busy port city. Its ancient acropolis is crowned by ruins of a Byzantine castle. Now in the Peloponnesus, a large peninsula, we especially wanted to visit the excavations at Mycenae, where King Agamemnon ruled during the time of the Trojan War. Agamemnon was the brother of King Menelaus, whose wife was Helen of Troy. The ruins of Mycenae were excavated by Schliemann from 1874-1876. Several types of tombs could be seen, but all had been entered and looted before Schliemann arrived. The hill has been occupied since the beginning of the Bronze Age around three thousand B.C. During the late Bronze Age (1600 to 1500 B.C.) royalty were buried in shaft graves in what is called the Royal Circle. Most interesting were the beehive tombs in which royalty were buried between 1500 and 1300 B.C. The term "beehive" refers to the shape of the interior of the burial chamber. These circular tombs were in part cut into the earth or rock and in part constructed with cut blocks of stone. The gigantic lintel stone of the chamber entrance was usually about at the level of the natural slope of the hill. Above the lintel stone a distinctive triangular space was built to relieve the pressure from the many rows of large stones stacked overhead..

Clytemnestra's tomb, constructed in 1300 B.C. had been completely restored and was approached through a stone corridor and entered through a gate covered with three enormous lintel stones. The other impressive beehive tomb was that called the Treasury of Atreus or Tomb of Agamemnon. It, too, had a vast corridor and a monumental gate. The lintel of the tomb consisted of two enormous blocks, one of which weighed at least 120 tons. We also marveled at the huge encircling wall of the fortress which was made of very large stones. It was thrilling to see these places and to think that these people really had existed and were not simply mythical figures depicted in the Iliad and in the Greek tragedies.

Our next stop was the famous theater of Epidauros, built in the fourth century B.C. On the stage, only the foundations of the buildings that had created the set remained. The orchestra, where the chorus danced and sang, was a full circle of hardened earth. The left-hand section of the semi-circular open-air auditorium had been restored. Originally there were seats for fourteen thousand spectators We couldn't resist testing the excellent acoustics. A whisper on the stage near the altar can be heard from the highest tier. Nearby was the Sanctuary of Asclepios, the god of healing. According to legend, he was born on a hilltop in the area and was nursed by a goat.

We drove to the southern tip of the peninsula hoping to spend a couple of hours on a nearby island, Spetsae. Through sign language we understood that there was only one more boat going to the island that day and that if we took it, we would have to stay overnight. We didn't have that much time to spare. Somewhat disappointed about that, we drove through Corinth to Piraeus, another famous port, where we saw octopuses draped over a clothes line to dry. We had a delicious seafood dinner including calamari before returning to Athens.

Another vivid memory is the wine festival we visited at Daphni and the terrible taste of the retsina we tried there. Although many Greeks prefer this resin-flavored wine, it would take a long time for us to get used to the taste. We'll never forget the perfect and stereotypical image we had from one vantage point: small blazing-white stucco houses were clustered all over the hillside enhanced by the brilliant blue of the Mediterranean sea glistening below.

Gradually making our way back to Paris, we flew to Rome. Kurt, who had been there before, gave as a two-day whirlwind tour. We did the antiquities first: the ruins of the forum, the Palatine Hill with its ruins, and the Coliseum, where I imagined Christians, lions, and gladiators as we walked among the holding cells and through some of the rows of tiered seats. Finally we roamed through the fascinating baths of Caracalla, mostly red rock ruins with some statuary fragments. We made the expected pilgrimages to the Spanish Steps and the Trevi Fountain, but skipped going to the grave of John Keats, the English poet.

At Vatican City, we climbed stairs inside the dome for a fabulous overview of Rome. Kurt carried Karen in the backpack up the seemingly endless stairs, but near the top of the dome, the ceiling of a winding ramp lowered, forcing him to bend over. Karen didn't like lying on her back looking up at the ceiling, so she got out and walked the rest of the way on her own. We admired the famous paintings in the Sistine Chapel, bending our necks back and thinking about Michelangelo lying on his back to create the works on the ceiling.

I hated to leave our spacious hotel room with its huge armoire, floor-to-ceiling windows with deep burgundy drapes over sheer curtains, and large and comfy double bed, but it was time to drive north in our rental car. We were heading to Florence, but were delayed when Kurt couldn't avoid hitting a bale of hay sitting on the highway. Though he thought he had driven over it gently, we ended up with a flat tire and a dented wheel rim. No problem for the Italians. Using a crowbar, the mechanic beat the wheel rim into shape and put on a new tire. There was little English spoken, but they figured out the problem. I didn't know the word for bale of hay, so I mumbled something about "piedra grande" which I hoped they would understand as "large stone."

As a result of the delay, we spent the night in Siena, a walled medieval city with narrow winding paths, striped bell towers, and the large piazza where the famous horse race *Palio dele Contrade* has been held annually since 1656. We couldn't stay as long as we liked because we wanted to see some of Florence and Ferrara.

In Florence, Karen wondered why the statues didn't wear any clothes, and as before, she looked for animals in the Uffizi Gallery and the Pitti Palace. Because the light was just right, we got some great photographs of the biblical scenes on the famous carved doors of the baptistry. In Ferrara, our next stop, our friends made sure we saw the magnificent frescoes in Este Castle and sampled the Municipal Museum in Schifanoia Palace before we raced on to Venice. Karen liked feeding the pigeons in San Marco Plaza until too many of them became rather demanding. She let her Dad finish the feeding. We took a *vaporetto* (public passenger ferry) to Murano to see Venetian glass blowers, and of course brought home a tiny glass animal. Because Venetians ate dinner around 9:00 p.m., we had a difficult time finding a restaurant that would serve us a meal before Karen's bedtime.

From Venice we took a fast road to Genoa, then drove the coastal highway to Monaco, where we admired the yachts of the rich and famous nestling in the harbor. We drove the breath-taking corniches cut into the steep hillside, but were disappointed when we were refused entry to the casino. Did they know we weren't gamblers, or did we look too shabby? We were never quite sure, but we think we couldn't enter because Karen was with us.

Before driving north towards Paris, we savored the taste and flavor of Provence, home to many famous artists. The afternoon light in Aix-en-Provence created a glow on every building, which even ordinary humans could notice and appreciate. We hunted out a three-star restaurant, Les Baux, for a superb gourmet meal, willing to spend a little extra as we neared the end of our trip. The attractive setting among large boulders in hilly terrain was a lovely surprise. We were reminded by the Roman amphitheater in Arles and the arena in Nimes that France had once been part of Roman Gaul. In Avignon, we stood by the picturesque twelfth-century bridge and sang the nursery rhyme: "Sur le pont d'Avignon..."

A longer-than-expected travel time to Chartres, allowed us to view the magnificent cathedral in late afternoon sunshine. The low-angle light created wonderful definition for all the carvings on the outside and intensified the deep colors of the famous stained-glass rose window.

For a final splurge we had lunch on a sunny afternoon at a three-star restaurant and inn which had been a country estate. When we ordered noodle soup for Karen, the waiter inquired whether "*la petite mademoiselle*" preferred vermicelli or broad noodles. Karen said, "vermicelli," imitating him. As it turned out, she liked them. To accompany our delicious meal, the waiter recommended a vintage wine that was so heavenly we agreed that the restaurant's three stars were well deserved. It was a memorable finish to an unbelievable six-week tour.

GETTING AROUND IN GREAT BRITAIN

Two years later a symposium in Aberdeen gave us a month to look around the British Isles. On the way we stopped for a fascinating twenty-four hours in Shannon, Ireland. The medieval tour began with a three-hour, sixty-mile bus ride through the lush green and misty Irish countryside. We visited Bunratty

Folk Park and had tea in an Irish thatched cottage, roamed the ruins of twelfth-century Quin Abbey, enjoyed an Irish step-dancing display by children in an old hotel, and had a taste of stout in an Irish Pub. That night, we hired a baby sitter for Karen, while we participated in a medieval banquet in Bunratty Castle. Lit only by torches, the stone castle was a perfect setting for the evening. Greeted by costumed wenches who offered us mead made with fermented honey, we were soon joining in the hearty songs that accompanied the very ample dinner. A roasted turkey leg and potatoes were served, not on plates, but on a circle of bread. The only utensil was a knife. Wine jugs circulated freely. It was sometimes difficult to hear the Celtic harp that accompanied some music played by recorders and sung by costumed performers, but everyone had a boisterous and enjoyable time, enjoying the pretense and re-enactment of what might have happened. With only an hour's nap between our flight's arrival in Ireland and the beginning of the fascinating, non-stop tour, we suffered from more than jet lag when we arrived in London.

Located in the Belgravia section of London near Victoria Station, our bed-and-breakfast establishment gave us convenient access to everything. Days were devoted to visiting the famous sites such as Westminster Cathedral, where we admired the architecture and stained glass and easily found the poet's corner, burial place of many of the writers I'd studied. St. Paul's Cathedral, designed by Wren, was austere in comparison, but from its roof it provided wonderful views of London. Having seen the movie *Mary Poppins*, Karen sang "Feed the birds, tuppence a bag," as she looked for an old woman with a bag of bread whom she expected to see near St. Paul's. We heard Old Ben chime the hours as we gazed at the magnificence of the Houses of Parliament.

Orators ranted and raved in Hyde Park to anyone who would listen. A few minutes of that sent us hurrying on to the fabulous London Zoo where Karen enjoyed an escorted ride on a donkey for a few pence. Pomp and ritual were central to the Changing of the Horse Guard ceremony we watched at Buckingham Palace. At Nelson's column, near Charing Cross, pigeons surrounded Karen as they had two years before in Venice. This time the experience was much more fun for her.

Kew Botanical Gardens were sumptuous with native and exotic plantings and an astounding palm house modeled on the Crystal Palace at Brighton. From Kew we took a bus to Hampton Court where we toured the magnificent castle Cardinal Wolsey built for himself in 1514, which was a royal residence from 1525 to 1760. Henry VIII and six of his wives lived here. We were intrigued by the indoor tennis court where Henry had played. It had a protected area for spectators to watch the game. King Henry also held jousts on the spacious grounds which were now beautifully landscaped with both formal and informal gardens. At the edge of the gardens was the River Thames. From the dock we returned to London by boat, enjoying the views of historic places, famous buildings, and pleasant villages on both banks of the river.

Another day's outing took us to Cambridge to see the splendid stone carvings and Gothic architecture of King's College Chapel. We were thrilled that we happened to be there just as the choir was rehearsing. The many architectural styles visible at the university, founded in 1284, would inspire anyone to deep thoughts, but Karen had noticed the small boats on the water, so after admiring the architecture for a while, we rented a boat, and Kurt punted on the Cam river, just as many Cambridge University students do.

Back in London we stood in line to enter the Tower to view the crown jewels. Not far from the Tower Bridge was the Royal Observatory in Greenwich where we stood on the Greenwich meridian from which our time zones are reckoned.

London Bridge had not yet fallen down, despite the nursery song, so it required a visit. So did the British museum. We had to inspect the Elgin marbles, statues and fragments from the Parthenon in Greece brought to England by Lord Elgin. The Egyptian room of the museum had a fascinating collection of antiquities, including mummies. I managed to get a quick look at the British Museum's circular reading room on which our own Library of Congress reading room had been modeled.

Most nights after dinner, all three of us were ready for bed, but one night the landlady entertained Karen till her bedtime while Kurt and I treated ourselves to a Royal Ballet performance at Covent Garden. *The Lady and the Fool* and *The Two Pigeons*, ballets new to us, comprised the program. The dancing itself was spectacular, but everyone gasped in amazement when at least twelve white doves were released from the stage as part of the final dance.

From London we drove southeast to Canterbury to see the great cathedral with its graves and carved likenesses of Edward the Black Prince and other nobility who were buried inside the edifice. Canterbury is one of England's oldest and most historic cities. Chaucer's *Canterbury Tales*, written around 1300, relates a fictional pilgrimage to the shrine at Canterbury of St. Thomas a Becket who was murdered by knights of Henry II in 1170. The tomb and shrine were destroyed by Henry VIII, but some thirteenth-century stained-glass windows remained.

Because I had just finished taking doctoral exams in the field of English Literature, I was very interested in seeing every literary site I could squeeze in. Kurt was interested in historical sites, and sometimes we had to do something that was fun for little Karen.

Driving past the white cliffs of Dover, we realized that we would only get the full impact if we had been arriving by sea. But Dover was on our way west to Cornwall, and so was the site of the Battle of Hastings where in 1066, William of Normandy became William the Conquerer. By the time we visited both Winchester and Salisbury Cathedrals where archeological excavations were taking place, we were beginning to have trouble keeping the cathedrals separated in our minds.

Located near Amesbury on the Salisbury plain, Stonehenge enthralled us. At the time there was no barrier, and we were allowed to walk among the awesome gigantic monoliths. As it happened, we were there on June twenty-first, midsummer's night, and we saw many celebrants arriving wearing wreaths on their heads and wrapped up in what looked like white sheets. We left before the celebration got under way.

Dartmoor was bleak, a fitting scene for all the crime novels set there. We hoped we wouldn't meet an escapee from Dartmoor prison. The coastal scenery at Torquay and Plymouth was dramatic. High cliffs fell sharply to the sea below. One sunny day we climbed a hill to enjoy the view to the sea and gorge ourselves on very delicious strawberries and Devon clotted cream. Knowing Gilbert and Sullivan operettas, we had to stop at Penzance. We stood at Land's End, just because it was there.

Turning north, we soon reached Tintagel where we walked out to the ruins of legendary King Arthur's Castle. Though little remained, the scenery and the setting on a rocky headland set our imaginations remembering tales of the Knights of the Round Table and the search for the Holy Grail. Nearby we roamed over the ruins of Glastonbury Cathedral where King Arthur and Queen Guinevere are said to be buried.

Bath was our next stop. I wanted to see Bath because some of Jane Austen's novels, satires on eighteenth-century social customs, were set there. We did admire the Georgian style of architecture preserved in Royal Crescent, typical of the eighteenth century when Bath was the vacation spot for the wealthy. But it was the entire street of gaudy half-timbered, white-washed homes side by side, but leaning in many directions, that captivated us. Never had we seen that many structures of that type all in one place. Bath's Roman ruins were a genuine surprise. First discovered in the late nineteenth century lying twenty feet below street level, the Roman baths are among the finest Roman remains in Britain. Colonists longing for the warmth of home built large pools to take advantage of the curative hot springs they found.

Wordsworth's poem "Tintern Abbey" was the reason we made a slight detour to see this ruin which inspired the poet, before we spent two days in the charming Cotswolds. This area consists of many small villages with names like Stow-on-the-Wold, Chipping Campden, Moreton-in-Marsh. Most of the dwellings are made of a yellow-orange stone which is much cheerier than the gray stone often seen in England. Sometimes the villages are only a mile apart. Karen was delighted with the complete one-to-ten scale model of Bourton-on-the-Water. The model houses were just her size. Because the model is complete, it contains a model of itself which is one to one-hundred scale.

Quite a contrast to these small villages was the town of Oxford and the gray gothic towers of Oxford University. We saw students in caps and gowns exiting what looked like a church. Nearby was one of England's "stately homes." Given time and money considerations, we decided we could do only one of these tours and settled on Blenheim Palace, birthplace of Winston Churchill. The British nation had given the large estate and stately palace to John Churchill, the first Duke of Marlborough for his victory over the French at the Battle of Blenheim in 1704. We gawked at the plush furnishings and heavy draperies, but also realized that tours were being offered only because the current noble owner was having difficulty raising funds to pay his taxes. How the mighty had fallen!

We drove north to Shakespeare's town, Stratford-on-Avon. We didn't have time to see a play there, but there were many restored buildings to visit, including Anne Hathaway's cottage with its easily recognized overhanging thatch roof. In one cozy half-timbered shop we ate cucumber sandwiches, with the crusts cut off the bread–the British way of making sandwiches. In general, we found breakfasts unusual with fried tomatoes, baked beans and cold toast. One host at a bed-and-breakfast thoughtfully provided cornflakes for his foreign guests, but they were the limpest cornflakes we've ever eaten. The brewed tea we found everywhere was really delicious, and we enjoyed lots of fish and chips, with malt vinegar instead of catsup on the chips. We loved scones that were served at Scottish high tea, an indulgence we allowed ourselves only once.

Although we knew the legend of Lady Godiva, in Coventry it was the cathedral built in 1954 that captivated us. Incorporating the ruins of the fourteenth-century cathedral, destroyed by Germans during World War II, the cathedral was a stark reminder of the Nazi destruction. Because Coventry was a center for heavy industry, the entire center of the city, including the cathedral had been heavily bombed. We couldn't pass by imposing Warwick Castle without making a stop. A well-preserved medieval fortress, it contains some sections built in Norman times, and is still inhabited. Furniture and armor collections were displayed in the state apartments.

Traveling for a month, we encountered all kinds of weather. Even when a day began with sunshine, there were often unexpected showers, when clouds suddenly appeared and just as suddenly blew over. This wasn't much of a problem, though, because there was always some cathedral, abbey, or museum close by to engage our attention until the rain ended. As we drove narrow roads with hedges above stone fences, we admired the trees and other vegetation, which for some reason, seemed more tame, more civilized than the trees we were used to in the United States. We loved the many well-tended flower gardens that adorned almost every house or small cottage. Because Karen already knew the poems of A.A. Milne about Winnie the Pooh and Christopher Robin and friends, when she became bored, we read from Kenneth Grahame's *Wind in the Willows*, stories set in the English countryside about the numerous adventures of Mole, Ratty, and Toad.

A side trip into Wales allowed us to visit the enormous thirteenth-century Caernarvon Castle where the first English Prince of Wales, Edward II, was born in 1284. The investiture ceremony for each new Prince of Wales is held at this castle. Our primary interest, however, was to see Mt. Snowdon. From Llanberis, a steam locomotive climbs about five miles to the top. Because the day we arrived was clear and beautiful, we decided to hike to the top, if we could find a baby-sitter for Karen. When the owner of the gift shop, where we inquired, offered to look after Karen, we were on our way. The approach to the ridge was steep, but once it was reached, we had fantastic views in all directions as we walked the ridge line to the summit at 3,560 feet. We felt very virtuous for having expended the effort to make the climb as we watched the train arrive at the top disgorging its passengers. Back at the gift shop, where we purchased a stuffed animal for Karen and an angora scarf for me, we learned that Karen had not even missed us. She had made friends with the owner's son, who was also four years old.

From Llanberis we crossed a bridge to Anglesey Island and another to Holy Island in order to reach Holyhead. I had thought it was a sort of Land's End, the Welsh island farthest west in the Irish Sea. Perhaps I thought there would be a steep drop-off or a dramatic headland. I knew I had read something interesting about Holy Island in a guidebook, but there wasn't much to be seen beyond a ferry dock and the sea itself. For once, I had to agree with Kurt that it had been a long drive with very little to show for it. Later I realized I had confused this Holy Island with Holy Island in Northumbria, England, where the Lindisfarne Gospels were created at the Monastery St. Aidan founded in A.D. 635.

Driving east, we returned to England to investigate Robin Hood country: Sherwood Forest and the town of Nottingham. We toured magnificent Lincoln Cathedral with its 365-foot spire, before stopping near Leeds at the town of Keighley to visit a family friend. Kurt had last seen Jo Telford in Vienna in 1939. They had a grand reunion at her small, white-washed stone cottage, built half-way into a hill to conserve heat. We made a day trip to see the great cathedral at York and learned that the Yorkshire dialect sounded almost like a foreign language. For lunch we ordered Yorkshire Pudding, not realizing that it was a kind of soggy popover covered with gravy and served with beef, in place of potatoes.

We were too late for the daffodils Wordsworth contemplated in the English Lake District, but we found many beauties to admire and enjoy in the lakeside villages of Kendal, Windemere, and Grasmere. Forested hills led to sub-alpine summits as the road snaked through shadowed valleys far below. At Ambleside, we toured the home of Beatrix Potter, author of *The Tale of Peter Rabbit, Squirrel Nutkin,* and other favorite childhood books Karen had heard read to her. The quaint illustrations in the books came to life in the cottages and countryside we saw around us. Dinner at the well-known Ambleside inn, restaurant, and pub, The Drunken Duck, was another memorable splurge, though the name did not originate from the technique of filling a duck with wine before roasting it, as I had imagined. Apparently a barrel of beer had burst and the contents had seeped into the ducks' regular drinking ditch. Finding the ducks seemingly dead at the crossroads, the owner started to pluck their feathers in preparation for the oven. As she did so, she discovered they were not dead, merely dead drunk.

Before entering Scotland we visited the ruins of Hadrian's Wall. Built in A.D.122, the seventy-three-mile-long, mostly stone structure marked the northern limit of the Roman empire at that time and was built to keep barbarians out. Although the political border actually lies along the Cheviot Hills, Hadrian's Wall is often considered the dividing line between Scotland and England. Running from Solway Firth to Tynemouth, the wall spans all of England at its narrowest width.

Ruins of the medieval abbeys at Jedburgh and Melrose were romantic stops in what is essentially Sir Walter Scott country. Having grown up on his novels, we had to tour Abbotsford, a handsome mansion which contained his mementoes, collections of rare books, armor, and weapons.

A gray, overcast day was a fitting backdrop to the dramatic turrets and towers of eleventh-century Edinburgh Castle, which seemed to brood over the city from the heights of Castle Rock. Located in Princes Street Gardens on our way to the castle, the large floral clock, first of its kind to be built, was quite beautiful. Farther down the street was the graceful gothic spire, 200 feet high, which encircles a marble statue of Sir Walter Scott. On the castle tour we saw the Scottish regalia, older than the English crown jewels, and the royal apartments, including the birthplace of James VI of Scotland who became James I of England after the death of Elizabeth I. We walked the Royal Mile between the castle and Holyroodhouse, a sixteenth-century palace associated with the Stuarts, taking in the sights of Edinburgh's oldest part with its narrow, crowded buildings, many stories high. In this section of town, buildings were mostly either gray stone, weathered wood, or dark-colored because of pollution.

We bypassed Glasgow, stopping at mighty Stirling castle, perched on a high crag. In the geographical center of Scotland, it also has seen much Scottish history. Two kings were born in the castle and Mary Queen of Scots was crowned there. Nearby was the famous Bannockburn field where Bruce defeated Edward's army in 1314. A few miles farther on we stopped at Loch Lomond, singing the song remembered from childhood, "By the bonny, bonny banks of Loch Lomond." As the sun suddenly shone through the clouds, the lake glittered at the foot of forested green banks which were truly bonny. A beautiful drive along Loch Fyne led us to Inverary, where the Duke of Argyll's Castle could be toured and where I bought a 100 percent worsted-wool stole in the dark green-and-blue Black Watch tartan.

Farther north on the Firth of Lorne from the harbor of Oban, ships left daily for visits to Staffa and Iona islands, traveling around the Isle of Mull. We knew Mendelssohn's *Hebrides* Overture inspired by Fingal's cave on Staffa, and I remembered some of the legends about Fingal. A basaltic mass that has been eroded by nature, Staffa houses a myriad of fantastic forms, the most famous being the great colonnade of lava pillars which rise from the depths of the ocean and which are pierced by gigantic caves. Passengers could visit Staffa and enter the most famous cave (at their own risk and weather permitting). We could hardly wait to leave the dock. Weather, however, did not permit. The sea was rough and rain threatened, making walking on basalt too risky. The captain tried to get close enough to give us a view inside, but everyone was disappointed. The ruins on Iona were some consolation. On this island, St.Columba with his followers had landed in A.D. 564 and founded a monastery. From this center of Celtic Christianity, he gained converts in what is now Scotland. Without this outpost of Christianity, along with the monastery on Holy Island in Northumbria where manuscripts were saved, Christianity might not have survived the Dark Ages. Although the Danes burned this early monastery, a Benedictine abbey was later established on the same site. The island did convey a feeling of peace and quietness.

About twenty miles farther north, we reached Ben Nevis, at 4,406 feet the highest peak in Scotland. We didn't intend to reach the summit, but we hoped to spend a day hiking the trail upwards. The weather wasn't the greatest when we started out, but we dressed as warmly as we could. Kurt carried Karen on his back and we started up, along with several other hikers. We hiked for about forty-five minutes and were making good progress under a cloudy sky. As the trail made a switchback to gain more altitude, a cold sleety wind blasted us. When small hailstones pelted us, we decided to turn back. We'd save Ben Nevis for another day. Glencoe, the site of the massacre of the Macdonalds by the Campbells of Argyll by order of King William of Orange is as dark and shadowed as the deeds that took place there. The soldiers who carried out the murders had accepted the hospitality of their hosts for two weeks before they suddenly turned on them. This violation of the sacred law of Highland hospitality was what gave the event such notoriety.

To reach the Isle of Skye and its famed climbing mountains, the Cuillins, we drove a small road to Mallaig and took the ferry from there to the landing at Armadale. Most of the roads this far north were the infamous single-lane roads with sighting rods to indicate the wider spots known as passing spaces. The best technique we found was to pause slightly in a passing space, check if the road was clear to the next space, and go for it as fast as possible. We didn't relish having to back up towards a passing space, if we should happen to meet someone on the road about halfway.

Driving from the port at Armadale in the very late afternoon, we stopped at the first town we came to, Broadford, where we learned that no hotel space was available. The woman at the tourist information center offered us a room with breakfast in a private home. We were relieved to have any place to stay as the weather had turned cold and rainy. Inside the cluttered, but cozy kitchen, the gas heater put out a welcome warmth, but we noticed our room upstairs was quite chilly when we deposited our suitcases there. The room did have a small wood stove, though, so we thought we'd only have to ask for some kindling and chunks of wood.

The stout hostess offered us a cup of tea, so we joined her and her toothless husband in the kitchen. They were very friendly and asked us many personal questions. Then they began talking about previous renters. Laughing, the wife said to us, "Can you imagine? We had two maiden ladies from the United States who stayed here, schoolteachers they were. They were so silly, they actually tried to start a fire in the little wood stove that hasn't worked for years. We told them the stove pipe wasn't connected to anything, but I guess they didn't listen. Too smart for their own good. Almost burned the place down." We were glad we hadn't asked for matches or kindling. The woman was extremely worried that Karen might wet the bed and added a waterproof layer to the bedding, despite our assuring her that Karen, now four, had not had an accident since she was two years old. We stayed talking in the warm kitchen as long as possible, then raced upstairs, took off our shoes, and slept in all our clothing. In the morning, breakfast consisted of greasy fried eggs, strips of bacon, and fried bread. We hoped the fat would keep us warm.

A constant drizzle stayed with us as we drove towards the famous dark Cuillin mountains. Heavy, dark clouds threatened a serious downpour but also made the scenery dramatic. A forlorn ruined castle stood alone at the edge of a marsh. Trying to see as much of the island as we could, we drove both loops of the one highway that could be driven, awed by the many lochs surrounded by high peaks of bare rock that towered over them. Dunvegan Castle was as imposing a fortress as any we'd seen. Some places we saw the old "blackhouse" a white-washed stone one-story building with a dirt floor and a thatched roof held down by stones to keep it from being blown away. In most places, more modern cottages had replaced these primitive dwellings.

Late in the afternoon we caught a different ferry from Kyleakin to cross Loch Alsh to return to the mainland. A second ferry was needed at the town of Strome Ferry. We were trying to reach Kinlochewe near Loch Maree, but the distance was longer than we could drive that night. There were not many possibilities for spending the night or even getting a meal along the desolate road, surrounded by lochs, fishing streams, and three-thousand-foot peaks.

When we saw a huge red-brick and stone building with a tower and many bay windows, I urged Kurt to stop and inquire whether they rented rooms. Unknowingly we had reached fabulous Loch Torridon Hotel. Officially it was an upscale resort hotel catering to fisherman, but they let us stay. A sentence from their brochure read "The Sport includes salmon and sea trout fishing on two rivers and two lochs, also numerous brown trout lochs. Sea fishing from our own motor boats. Stalking." For an extra charge, dogs were permitted in their owner's bedroom, but not in public rooms. We had a very nicely appointed room with a private bathroom. After a very delicious dinner, salmon of course, we were invited to compare an impressive number of single unblended malt whiskeys. Though I don't care much for whiskey, these drinks were so smooth that I kept sampling until I could barely toddle to the room. Kurt was in the same pleasant condition. The contrast to our previous night's accommodation was unreal.

In the morning, after a sumptuous breakfast, which included delicious Scottish oatmeal, we drove to Loch Maree. Large enough to contain several small islands, it was a very beautiful spot, though by now we'd seen so many beautiful lochs, it was hard to say that it was, as reputed, the most beautiful loch in Scotland.

Some roads continued north, and even farther north lay the Orkney and Shetland islands, but we wanted to make a few stops on our way to Aberdeen for the symposium. After following a long, tiring, but very scenic circular route that took us farther north and west out to the sea, past more lochs and then back eastward, we turned south at Dingwall and finally reached Inverness at the head of Loch Ness. I wanted to watch for Nessie all day long, but we could only spare her thirty minutes, and when the legendary sea serpent didn't put in an appearance, we drove on.

Scotland has many legends, ghosts, and haunted places. I think we may have come under this influence one night. Preparing for the trip, we had found an excellent article on the inns of Scotland which described the food and drink in detail, made recommendations and gave explicit directions to some of these out-of-the-way establishments. We'd even brought the article with us. But we left it behind in the hotel room when we took a long drive through the gloomy Great Glen and through some villages on a sightseeing day. When we realized we would arrive back at the hotel after the dinner hour, we began looking for an inn. Unfortunately, on that part of the road there were not many small villages, and when we passed slowly through them, only cottages lined the roadside. I tried to remember what I'd read in the article. As we entered one village, the name looked familiar, and I confidently told Kurt that just after he crossed the bridge over a stream, he should turn left and at the end of the road, there would be an inn that was famous for its salmon. There was a road turning left just after the bridge, and though it seemed to go on and on, it did end at an inn, which served us a delicious meal that included salmon. We didn't even care that the service was somewhat slow, we were so pleased to have found the place. It was almost dark by the time we left.

As we drove through a seemingly uninhabited area, I noticed what looked like small fluorescent circles hovering at the side of the road. More and more of them were appearing. The circles glowed with either an eerie blue or a chilling greenish color, and some of them seemed to be moving. It took me quite a while before I realized that the lights from the car were being reflected by the eyes of the many sheep lying in the fields the road ran by. But the strangest experience was yet to come. When I re-read the article on Scottish inns to confirm my great memory, neither the town nor the inn we visited were mentioned at all.

We squeezed in a quick stop at the Cairngorm Mountains where we rode a chairlift for the superb views and attended an afternoon of the Highland

Games, watching various competitive feats of strength and skill including tossing the caber, performed by kilted men. Then we drove by Balmoral Castle and arrived in Aberdeen just in time to pick up registration packets and tickets. While Kurt did science, Karen and I enjoyed various trips planned for the accompanying spouses. We had tea at Haddo House, a stately home built in 1732, visited beautiful gardens, and learned more about Scottish history than I've been able to remember.

The symposium banquet was carried out in high style with exquisite and more than ample food. We were led into the dining room by a bagpiper and drummer. Kippered salmon was followed by *hairst bree*. The name suggested some hideous concoction like haggis, but it was actually a very flavorful harvest soup. Next came lobster newburg. The meat course, braised venison slices with rowan jelly and chestnuts was accompanied by vegetables and potatoes. Dessert was a fresh raspberry treat. Between the numerous courses, several vocalists presented Scottish folk songs. One singer was accompanied by a harpist. We were also entertained by dancers in colorful costumes who enthusiastically performed three sets of Scottish Highland dances. Karen was absolutely enthralled by the dancers, standing on her chair to watch them. Earlier we had purchased a kilt and scarf in the bright red Stewart pattern for her, and she wore them with a white blouse to the banquet. One of the tall male dancers noticed her enthusiasm and came to our table asking her to join them. She imitated what she saw them doing and was thrilled and excited by dancing with grownups. We enjoyed watching our little four-year-old whirling around to a Scottish Reel, as if it were her heritage. It was the highlight of the trip for her, I think.

On our way south to Glasgow we drove by imposing, crenellated Glamis Castle, the childhood home of Queen Elizabeth and Princess Margaret and where, according to Shakespeare, King Duncan was murdered by Macbeth. We spent our last night in Perth and flew home from Glasgow.

AUSTRIA, SWITZERLAND, AND ITALY

When our son, Alan, turned five, we traveled with both children and my mother to Europe. Kurt had a week's conference in Italy scheduled, but we had grandiose plans for before, during, and after. We began in the south of Austria.

Tyrol's flower-bedecked A-frames were beautiful, despite the rain, mist, and fog. Castles and picturesque villages could still be visited. The meadows took on an intense, vibrant green. Few snow-covered or rocky Alps appeared through the clouds, but the snowfall on the peaks surrounding Innsbruck made the children's cable car ride more exciting. While Kurt and I joined a climbing school in the Grossglockner area, my mother and the two children explored Innsbruck for a week. Although my mother knew very little German, the three of them managed to get around to city parks, rode the cable car to the scenic overlooks at Hungerburg and Seegrube (about 6,000 feet high), and enjoyed the free band concerts in the square each night. Our successful climb of Austria's highest peak is described in the chapter, "Getting High."

Rain still pursued us in Switzerland, but we all enjoyed Zermatt, awed by the magnificence of the glaciated peaks of the Matterhorn, Monte Rosa, and Breithorn. From the viewing area at the end of the tram ride from Zermatt to Gornergrat, the panorama of these beautiful Alps was inspiring.

The medieval sections of Bern, Thun, and Luzern were enchanting. According to a fifteenth-century chronicle, when the city of Bern was founded in 1191 by Duke Berchtold V of Zähringen, he agreed with his advisors that the city would be given the name of the first animal caught at the hunt. Because that animal was a bear, the town was named Bern and given a bear as its coat of arms. Since the end of the fifteenth century, bears, kept in a bear pit in town, have been popular not only with visitors but also with residents. One woman of Berne bequeathed the bears a legacy. Of course, we had to visit the bear pit to admire the bears, and both children left with miniature bears on key rings. The town hall square in Thun was surrounded by arcaded houses and dominated by a castle which overlooked a flower-decked fountain at the center of the square.

In Lucerne we walked both the Spreuerbrücke and the Kapellbrücke. These covered bridges are famous for their painted panels. One has a death dance, whereas the other has 110 paintings depicting the history of the town. The bridges were originally built in the thirteenth and fourteenth centuries and have been restored. The paintings dating from the sixteenth century have also been renewed. Another day we visited the famous Lion Monument and the garden of glaciers which contains thirty-two huge potholes formed by glaciers. One pothole was thirty feet deep and twenty-six feet wide.

At Lake Lucerne, Kurt rented a small rowboat and took the children for a short ride. For a moment or two he couldn't figure out why we were screaming and waving at him from the shore. He couldn't see that he was rowing directly into the path of a huge excursion ship coming in to the dock. When he heard the warning toot from the ship, he quickly changed direction, rowing as fast as he could to avoid a collision, and giving the children a bit of excitement they hadn't expected.

At our last stop before Kurt's conference, our friends the Schmieds showed us a moated castle near their home in Nussbaumen, and took us to a performance of a Viennese operetta, *The White Horse*, which I enjoyed even though I didn't understand much of the dialogue.

When Kurt left for Lago Maggiore and his NATO conference, the rest of us began ancestor-hunting in Germany. It was thrilling to find near Bruchsal the church records of my father's grandmother, her parents, and their parents and to see their church, St. Marcellus, built in 1758 in Stettfeld. The Bueltmanns in northern Germany were harder to track, but we finally learned my great-grandfather's first name. The children particularly enjoyed an animal compound near Bielefeld where we drove slowly among free-roaming lions, tigers, elephants, and other wild animals. Buying peanuts was a mistake: the monkeys appropriated the roof and hood of the car, insisting on more nuts after our supply ran out.

My mother had saved money by flying Icelandic Airlines, but this meant that when she left us after a month, we had to deliver her to Luxembourg for her flight home. On the way we drove along the Rhine, taking in views of the romantically situated castles on high promontories overlooking the water, and seeing the famous Lorelei. The actual Lorelei is a cliff towering 433 feet above the Rhine just where the river forms a dangerous narrows filled with rocks. According to legend a siren-like maiden lived on the rock and by her singing lured sailors to their death. From my childhood, I remembered my father singing in German the well-known song based on the legend. At the site, I sang the song for my children.

From Luxembourg, we drove south to meet Kurt in Italy, after his conference ended. Karen at age ten turned out to be an excellent map reader, helping me navigate the large industrial city of Saarbrucken. Luckily we arrived at the small village designated as a car-train stop just in time for loading. Even though taking the train through an alpine tunnel avoided driving some winding roads up and over the mountains, I still had to negotiate some exciting switchbacks in the snow before reaching Italy. The rain continued in Pisa, as we visited Antonio Indelli, a good friend we'd originally met in the States, and his daughter Raffaella. Then teaching chemistry at the University of Pisa, Antonio knew the best restaurants as well as the best items on the menu. At that time visitors were allowed to ascend the leaning tower, an exciting, but dizzying experience. We also admired the beauty of the baptistery dome, which appeared to be decorated with lace, and the marvelous carvings of the life of Christ on the bronze door panels of the cathedral.

On our way south to Bari and another lecture, we stopped in Naples, where a strike by the garbage collectors resulted in unattractive piles of garbage bags in the streets and an aroma which made us question our decision to stop. The guidebook had described the "Old Spacca Quarter" as the heart of old Naples where a noisy, excitable populace swarms in its narrow crowded streets. We didn't notice anything unusually lively or exciting when we walked through the designated area, but on another stroll we accidentally walked through an area crowded with people gesticulating wildly and talking loudly. Children and dogs darted here and there, chasing each other. The children screamed; the dogs barked. Birds in cages were screeching and sometimes singing. On one corner we saw an organ grinder with a monkey begging for coins. On another, someone was singing "O Sole Mio." Every door in the narrow residential street was open. Men in undershirts were seated at tables smoking, drinking, and playing cards. The women served food to their large families who crowded around a table in what passed for a front yard. This, to us, was the true "heart of Napoli," vibrant, earthy, and full of the joy of life.

Taking the hydrofoil from Naples to save time, we were on the Isle of Capri in forty minutes. We were warned that if the water was too choppy, the row boats could not enter the grotto. There would also be long lines waiting for the possibility of going in. Despite a cloudy day, Capri's Blue Grotto was indeed spectacular. The wind quieted as we arrived and not even the crowd of tourist boats waiting to get in could diminish the supernatural quality of the cave's luminous blue pool. We also briefly stopped at Anacapri, the principal town on the island, perched on the side of a mountain with superb panoramic views. Whitewashed houses with typical Mediterranean red tile roofs and flowers blooming everywhere made every visitor feel relaxed and welcome.

Chair lifting to the top of Vesuvius, about thirty miles south of Naples, we walked at the edge of the vast crater and down to some of the still-smoking holes, unable to stretch our imaginations far enough to envision the enormity of the cataclysm that destroyed three ancient cities simultaneously. Our sunniest day was in Pompeii, where new excavations increase the haunting fascination of the sleeping city. The lupunare has been overrated. I'd expected to see licentious or scandalous decorations on the walls, but what I saw was fairly ordinary. Perhaps the licentious section of the Roman brothels was still being restored. In other sections of the preserved town, the beauty of the mosaics and the still-vivid paintings was unforgettable. After a few hours of wandering the cobbled streets, we experienced a strange but wonderful feeling of the immediacy of ancient life and times, as if we had been there. The children were enchanted by the numerous small lizards sunning themselves and darting from rock to rock.

Bari showed us endless olive groves, an octagonal hunting castle, an extensive archaeology museum, and preserved in a gargoyled Romanesque-Byzantine cathedral, the relics of San Nicola, protector of children--the original St. Nicholas.

SCANDINAVIA

It all began because we thought Karen had one last year to fly for half fare. It ended with day-long hikes between glacier-surrounded Norwegian mountain huts; a steamer ride down the Sognefjord to Bergen; and an evening of folk music, dance, and food at Fana. By the time we learned that according to airline standards our thirteen-year-old daughter was a genuine adult, we had made so many plans, seen so many enticing photographs, and were so eager to go there was no turning back. We economized by staying in numerous youth hostels where families were welcomed, as long as they brought sheet sleeping bags and carried International Youth Hostel passes. Accommodations varied from cots in a large classroom without desks to bunks in a lakeside country house with its own luscious raspberries growing in the yard. In Elsinore, our "motel-room" faced that portion of the moonlit North Sea lying between Denmark and Sweden. In one Norway hostel, a *stuga* (log cabin) with kerosene lamp, pot-bellied stove, and no water made us feel like pioneers. At Spiterstulen hostel, surrounded by glaciers and looking at Norway's highest peak, the public areas were luxurious. Not only was there a heated swimming pool, but in the fancy upstairs restaurant, students dressed in traditional costumes waited on the diners. We ate in the cheaper cafeteria downstairs.

We had four weeks. Our three days in Copenhagen were filled with castles and countless archaeological, folk, ethnic, and fine-arts museums. Flowers were everywhere. Tivoli Gardens, an enchanted otherworld, especially at night, captivated our imaginations and mesmerized Alan. But we were devastated when our eight-year-old disappeared. We hadn't realized how much he resembled Danish eight-year-old boys until we scanned the crowds for him. They all had the same "dutchboy" haircut he had. It was closing time, and most people were strolling to the exit. We prayed he would not stroll away with a stranger. Calling his name got no response. Retracing our steps back to a section of the park he had not wanted to leave, we found him enjoying an unobstructed view, since everyone else was gone. We were too relieved to scold him. He claimed that we, not he, had been lost. He had known exactly where he was.

From Copenhagen, we headed north for Elsinore to look at a dubious, but impressive, Hamlet's Castle. The red brick, copper-covered castle full of secret passages and casements was built in 1574-1585, long after any actual Hamlet was haunted by his father's ghost. But early versions of plays based on the Hamlet story were circulating from 1590 on. The impressive castle would be the ideal setting for any play about Danish Royalty to a chronologically unaware playwright. Restored in 1629 after being gutted by fire, looted, bombarded, and occupied by Swedes, the castle is starkly furnished. In the basement sits a statue of Holger Danske, hero of mythology who is supposed to pick up his sword and shield and come to the aid of Denmark when the country experiences its darkest hour. Short distances to the next castle, museum, monument, or Viking ship made sight-seeing in Denmark a pleasure, but we had to hurry in order to squeeze in a restored Bronze-Age village–similar to a Williamsburg but a thousand years older.

Very popular in all of Scandinavia were *Gamle By's* or old towns--open-air museums where buildings removed from town centers were reconstructed, furnished, and peopled for visitors in a park-like setting. We paid homage to Hans Christian Anderson, visiting his restored home in Odense, and stopped in Billund for several hours at Legoland. Here even Mt. Rushmore had been constructed from Legos. Visiting children, including Alan, drove motorized Lego cars in an area with streets, houses, and traffic signals. Each child's car carried a flag indicating the language of the driver, and from a watchtower a voice in the appropriate language reminded the young drivers that they must stop at the red light or warned that they were speeding.

I insisted that we stop in Jelling at the giant rune-stones erected by Harald Bluetooth for King Gorm and Queen Thyre--Anglo-Saxons all. Not far from Aarhus, we stood on the highest "hill" in Denmark to take photographs. Named *Himmelbjerget* (Sky Mountain) the top is less than 500 feet high. Nearby in the town of Silkeborg is a museum we couldn't pass by. Inside the eighteenth-century manor house, the tanned hide of the 1,600-year-old man accidentally preserved in a peat bog created a lasting impression on us all. The body had been discovered in 1950 and was so well preserved that scientists could determine the contents of his last meal: flax, barley, and oats. For our last meal before we left Denmark on the ferry to Sweden, we had a bit more food. We splurged at Hvidsten Kro by eating the entire "Gudrun's recipe": herring, bacon omelet, cold meat course, hot meat course, and koldtbord--cheese, fish, salami, liver paste, bread, and butter. For the less hungry, the half-recipe is recommended.

We were prepared for Denmark's flatness, but Sweden's resemblance to Minnesota and parts of the Pacific Northwest was a surprise. The countryside was beautiful with distinctive red farmhouses centered in endless golden grain fields. Nearby, numerous small and some very large lakes sparkled under clear blue skies. The week-long heat wave--ninety-five degrees each day--sent us gratefully into the lakes several times. The castles of Sweden, while interesting architecturally, were disappointing compared to those in Denmark until Skokloster near Uppsala, where we were overwhelmed with ornate furnishings and various collections. We did, however, enjoy a baroque concert played on appropriate period instruments in the empty castle at Vadstena. Painted wood church interiors in Sweden and the ornateness of cathedrals recalled that although Lutheranism was adopted by Scandinavia, its accompanying austerity wasn't--always.

Stockholm, most cosmopolitan of the capitals, was filled with transient students, steel-and-glass skyscrapers, and establishments advertising Swedish sin. But there were parks of quiet beauty, and the city hall, a modern building echoing medieval architecture, had a power of its own, despite the fact that its gold mosaic room used for Nobel Prize banquets has been called the height of Western decadence. The enormous Norse folk museum housed many very well done exhibits; and the 1622 Warship Wasa, being restored after 300 years of submersion in the harbor, was fascinating. The Milles sculpture garden contained many of the sculptor's figures, some running, some flying, and others reaching for stars--in stone.

A slight detour on our way to the Dalarna lake district took us to Falun and its famed copper mine, which in the seventeenth century supplied the copper for the roof of the palace at Versailles. Visitors wore hard hats and raincoats for a tour through the mine, worked since the Middle Ages. The tour began with an exciting descent of 180 feet and led through old chambers and winding passages.

Dalarna province, considered the most tradition-laden of all the provinces of the country, continues to hold Maypole dancing and fiddling contests. Folk costumes and handcrafts are abundantly available. The Dala horse, a miniature carved wooden figure enameled bright red and thought to bestow good luck on its owner, was displayed in every souvenir shop in Sweden. Our good luck was to find cooler summer weather in this more northern area of the country.

We returned our orange Volkswagen with the denim upholstery in Oslo. An island in Oslo's harbor contained almost every tourist attraction: Viking ships, the Kon-Tiki, polar exploration ships, and a final "old village" or skansen with a stave church and folk dancers. Truly moving were the life-size figures portraying much of humanity's pain, struggle, joy, and wonder in the Vigeland Sculpture Park in another part of town. At the park's restaurant, we observed most people were drinking but not eating. We wondered if liquor was simply cheaper than food, or if, instead, drinking was a Norwegian preference.

By train and bus we reached the glacial area--Jotunheim--where good weather and marvelous scenery accompanied our hiking for three days. Before long the trails led through barren, treeless areas, essentially huge boulder fields left behind by ice-age glaciers. Even for adults who could stride from the top of one boulder to another, it was a strenuous go. For Alan, who had to descend from one boulder in order to climb up the next, it was very tiring. One day we hiked for almost twelve hours to reach the next place we could stay. The last few miles were a chore, demanding many rest stops. We were all tired. We could see the hut in the distance, but we didn't seem to be getting any closer to it. Dinner was almost over by the time we arrived and were taken to the charming sod-roofed cabin where we spent the night. Breakfasts at the hostels were huge smorgasbords, and we ate as much as we could, often taking along some fruit, cheese, and rolls for lunch to avoid having to eat what the hostel provided: pork-liver paste on rye crisp. The unusual eighty-five degree temperature resulted in back-packers' stripping to bathing suits, and many Scandinavians enjoying the sun and the lakes in the nude.

The hostel at Spiterstulen was very modern, more like a hotel, though our room had four bunks in it. Alan chose one upper bunk on which to rest while Kurt and I scrambled up a nearby steep snowfield to a glacier. We returned to disaster. Karen had been reading in her lower bunk when she heard an odd sound above her. She looked out just as Alan's lunch spewed forth. She hadn't been able to open the window, and was very glad to see us. The next day with everyone recovered, after a public bus ride to the dock, we enjoyed a beautiful ride down the Sognefjord, as the ferry stopped at islands and isolated farmsteads to deliver mail and packages and to take on passengers. Steep spruce- and fir-covered mountains edged the narrow, deep blue inlet of the sea, creating dramatic scenery.

In Bergen, a lively seaport where playwright Henrik Ibsen and violinist Ole Bull had lived, we encountered an over-friendly drunk one evening when we waited for our bus. He'd decided Kurt was his best friend and kept hitting him on the shoulder to demonstrate the friendship. He may have been speaking English;

it was hard to tell. Though he seemed friendly, not belligerent, there was no one around to help us, should his mood change. We were greatly relieved when the bus arrived. Other encounters in Bergen were much more pleasant. We tasted reindeer steak and whale-meat, visited buildings remaining from the time of the medieval Hanseatic league, and rode the funicular, a cable railway, to the top of Floien, most famous of Bergen's seven hills, for a panoramic view of the city, neighboring hills, and the harbor. No one should miss the colorful open-air market where flowers and fish are sold. Huge red salmon lay next to enormous bouquets of intense blue and yellow tulips. Colorful dahlias and sweet-smelling stock occupied a stall next to large tuna, whose silver scales glittered in the sunlight. Brightly-colored umbrellas decorated the area as vendors hawked their goods.

Our Fana-Folklore evening began with a visit to the eighty-year-old stone and wood Fana Church. After the organist played folk tunes, we were led by a fiddler to a large hall where we ate bridal porridge and a customary leg of mutton. A traditional Norwegian wedding ceremony and celebration were reenacted. Men wore black top hats, red vests over white shirts, black knickers, and white knee socks. The women wore red-and-black headdresses and white lace aprons over long black dresses adorned with silver jewelry. Dancers in regional dress invited us to join them in performing folk dances. Though obviously prepared for tourists, the excursion still gave us a colorful and romantic view of the old ways in Norway.

WE COULDN'T TIPTOE THROUGH THE TULIPS

In 1987, one of Kurt's scientific conferences was in Maastricht, the oldest fortified city in the Netherlands, with its Roman, medieval, and seventeenth-century remains and restorations. There our turreted room in L'Empereur Hotel overlooked the train station's elegant twelve-foot- high stained-glass windows. Already important in 1000 A.D., as part of the Holy Roman Empire, St. Servatius's Basilica fronts the Vrithof, a huge square where even in mid-September, crowds enjoy the many encircling open-air restaurants. An organ recital, a modern dance performance, and a chamber music concert were some of the evening activities available. While Kurt listened to lectures, I took a day trip to the impressive St. Pietersburg caves, where Jesuit monks left incredible carvings and chalk paintings on the soft marlstone walls. In contrast to the rest of Holland, which is totally flat, Maastricht has one hill.

Only thirty minutes away by train was Liege, Belgium. The old city, huddled below the brooding Palace of the Prince Bishops, resembled a painting when viewed from the Citadel hilltop. We took the 353 steps of the *beuren* (farmer) staircase down, not up. Flowers bloomed in the square between the statue of Charlemagne and a church holding a finely wrought twelfth-century brass baptismal font that survived the French revolution only because private citizens hid it.

Brussels, center for several one-day jaunts, was a world in itself. Grote Markt, a cobblestone square completely enclosed by the gabled, gilded guildhalls unlike anything we'd seen elsewhere, was constantly in motion--folk dancers, mummers, bands, and costumed folk groups parading. At restaurants diners ate *moules* (mussels) prepared in a dazzling variety of ways or *waterzooi* (a thickly wonderful soup), munching afterwards on Belgian waffles. Sunday morning a live song-bird market took place in front of the town hall, which was so ornate we mistook it for a cathedral. Works by early Flemish painters and by both Breughels, along with some Hieronymous Bosch-like paintings were only a few of the Modern Art Museum's treasures. A few stops on the metro took us to an incredible collection of Etruscan, Egyptian, Greek, and Roman antiquities sharing a park with a museum of tanks and World War II aircraft.

Fortified since Celtic times, the citadel in Namur with fabled secret tunnels was a disappointment when we learned, after a healthy hike to the top, that in September the park was open only on weekends. Ghent and Bruges, centers of medieval cloth-manufacturing and other guilds with impressive guildhalls to be visited, offered canal rides, which gave us a different perspective on the two cities. Van Eyck's *Mystic Lamb* triptych in St. Bavo's cathedral in Ghent drew many tourists, as did the gray, grim Gravensteen Castle. Loveliest of all was Bruges, a truly romantic spot with parks, meandering canals, and enchanting buildings. Climbing the 366 spiraling steps to the belfry's summit atop the Halles, we arrived in time to see the hammers striking some of the forty-seven bells of the carillon. Any bats living in that belfry must be totally deaf! The ornate Gothic room in Belgium's oldest town hall, a lacy stone Gothic structure, contrasted strikingly with the twelfth-century Basilica of the Holy Blood where a lovely wood-paneled church sat above a dimly lit grotto (also a church) suggestive of a place where very early Christians might have worshiped in secret.

The painter Rubens's house in Antwerp was jammed with touring groups, but the Brewers' Guildhall, now a museum housing several floors of antique musical instruments and strange paintings, was almost empty. At the Antwerp zoo, unnoticeably adjacent to the Central Railway station, a woman petted and talked to a large caged eagle, which stood quietly, bowing its head next to the bars, seeming to appreciate the stroking.

In Arnhem on the Rhine river, we visited Holland's fine open-air museum, home of a variety of windmills and other historic farm and city dwellings. That evening, a fabulous dinner began with smoked eels, included wild boar and venison, and ended with a special Dutch chocolate concoction for dessert.

Amsterdam, with its canals and distinctive narrow, gabled buildings with top-floor hoists, began and ended our trip. The Rijksmuseum, like our Smithsonian, contains treasures for every taste--room after room of paintings, furniture, jewels, and ceramics and Rembrandt's *Nightwatch* enshrined in its own room. We were touched by the starkness of the Anne Frank house, now a memorial museum. On our trip to North Holland for wooden shoes, windmills, and small fishing villages on the former Zuider Zee, we learned all about dikes and reclaiming land--quite different from the way I had imagined it worked. Delft, Rotterdam, and Madurodam, a miniature model of Holland with miniature moving everythings, completed the afternoon. Though we couldn't tiptoe through the tulips in September, we brought home lace, cheese, delft, and Droste chocolate liqueur.

NO RAIN IN SPAIN

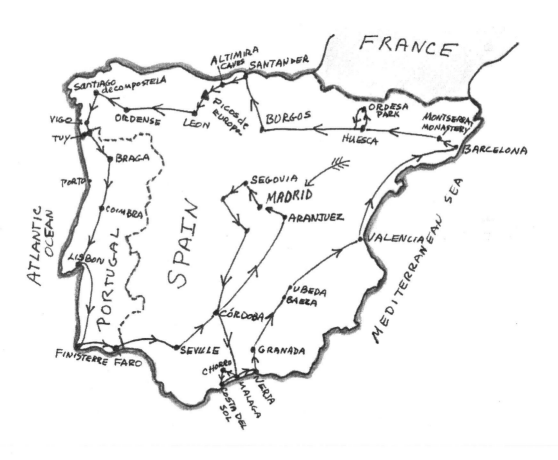

In August of 1981, our big indulgence was four weeks in Spain and Portugal. Flying on Spantax (a Spanish charter airline) and renting a Seat (a small car like a Fiat) from Atesa (a Spanish government-run firm), we hoped to pare down expenses. But the inflation rate soon reduced us to hunting for the simplest accommodations and meals, except for one super splurge outside Seville when we stayed in one of the swanky government-run Paradores--this one, a reconstructed fortress with adjoining Moorish-type swimming pool. Luxurious elegance, Spanish style, abounded, accompanied by the largest number of English-speaking tourists we encountered the entire trip. On our independent and self-planned circle tour of Spain, we tried to include most of the historic, geographic, or architecturally interesting sites, and found most other tourists were either Spanish or European (We were constantly asked if we were French.). Most of the English-speakers were either on the beach at Costa del Sol or holed up at the Paradores--or perhaps there just weren't that many. We found few bargains in Spain--most items costing the same there as at home.

Bypassing resorty Torremolinos, we stopped at the port city of Malaga on our way to the Cave of Nerja, discovered only in 1959 and famed for its fantastic limestone formations. Our daughter's facility in Spanish was very helpful because English was not that readily available. She often served as our interpreter for the totally Spanish guided tours of government buildings and museums we usually found ourselves on, and she competently took charge in those complicated situations that my "very basic" Spanish couldn't handle.

Contrary to Shaw's linguistic exercise, the rain does <u>not</u> fall mainly on the plain. In the month we were there, it rained only once--the day we were trying to explore Los Picos de Europa, high, craggy peaks in northern Spain, part of the Cantabrian range. After the endless dry dust of La Mancha with its interminable olive groves and sunflower fields, the Costa Verde, also in the North and looking much like Ireland, was delightfully refreshing. Montserrat's Black Madonna and the area's odd geological formations were impressive, as were the Pyrenees, still carrying a few patches of snow, despite ninety-degree temperatures in the valley. We were disappointed that the Caves of Altimira, famous for stone-age drawings, were no longer open for public viewing. In order to preserve the paintings, only researchers were allowed to enter. In Huesca, after dark during Fiesta, a wrong turn found us surrounded by student revelers, some sleeping sprawled across the narrow alley we were trying to traverse, others beating on the roof of the car while singing or chanting in Spanish, and one with a wine skin leaning in at the window, promising everything to any female who would meet him in a secluded plaza nearby. Not having celebrated ourselves, we were relieved to find our way out to the main road, unharmed and without harming anyone else.

Spain was a treasure chest of wonders. The Alhambra's famed reputation is well-deserved. Its fascinating beauty had us seeking out Washington Irving's many tales about it. Sitting on a hilltop overlooking Granada and situated to catch even the slightest breeze, the Alhambra is a distillation of the Moslem art and culture that dominated Spain for several hundred years. Begun in 1238, it consists of several parts. Only the outer walls remain of the Alcazaba, a citadel built in the eleventh century. Other parts are better preserved. The Palacios, made up of several highly decorative rooms, had intricately carved, domed ceilings, graceful carved arches, carved columns, charming fountains, sculptures, and bright tiles. Though the Moslem religion prohibits images of humans, the carved intertwining calligraphy and the domed ceilings that seem to have stalactites amaze the viewer. In the famous Patio de los Leones (courtyard of the lions), carved white marble columns support lovely arches. The ground is paved and the walls are covered with brightly colored tiles. The Generalife, higher on the hill, is a fourteenth-century palace noted for its maze of terraces, grottoes, flowing fountains and numerous pools. The mesmerizing sound of flowing water was everywhere, seeming to alleviate the heat somewhat.

In Cordoba, La Mezquita, the strange Moorish-Christian "barber pole" mosque in Cordoba had an unusual beauty and a tortured history. Built by order of the Caliph Abderraman I between 785 and 787, the mosque is a fantastic labyrinth of red-and-white, peppermint-striped pillars and arches. Many of the white marble columns were recycled from ancient Roman temples and Visigoth churches. If the height of the pillar being re-used was not correct, it was made to fit by sinking it into the ground. An expansion in 987 added columns of blue-and-red marble. The mosque contained double arches creating a unique ambience of light and shadow. One set of arches connected the pillars, while the other held up the roof. The Mihrab, a domed shrine of byzantine mosaics, which once housed the Koran, was placed on a side wall, rather than in the center of the building. Another peculiarity: the mosque was not oriented towards Mecca, but towards Damascus. The third largest mosque in the world, La Mezquita is said to have initiated the Arabian-Hispanic architectural style which combined Roman, Gothic, Byzantine, Syrian, and Persian architectural features.

When the Christians re-conquered Cordoba in 1236, they consecrated the mosque to be a Christian cathedral and added the Royal Chapel with its intricately carved ceiling and Baroque choir stalls. In 1523, against the will of the town's administration, the Catholic Church persuaded Charles V to permit them to build a cathedral within the mosque itself. To make room for the many ornate side chapels, dozens of arches and pillars were removed. It is said that when Charles V finally visited Cordoba, he regretted the damage done to the interior of the original building. The mixture of architectural styles, the resplendent artwork and craftsmanship, and the curiously entwined places of worship create a stunning yet disquieting impression upon even the most sophisticated traveler.

Madrid's Prado with innumerable paintings--Goya, Velasquez, Hieronymus Bosch, El Greco--was an unbelievable feast for the eyes and the soul. In the royal palaces and monasteries we saw tapestries and ornately decorative furniture. Cathedrals protected paintings, carvings, jewels, silver, and impressive baroque organs. At Escorial, the solemnity of the royal tombs was

243

alleviated by the opulence of the royal library. In Toledo we bought replicas of old swords and jewelry, but were vaguely disappointed with the so-called "El Greco House." Although the guide book stated clearly that El Greco had only lived in the area, and that the "house" was merely typical of his time, being more of a museum than a place he actually lived, we went anyway. There were several paintings which we liked, the furnishings gave an idea of how he might have lived and what his studio might have been like, but it somehow just didn't seem right that the museum should call itself the "El Greco House." The name seemed a sort of ploy to draw tourists in.

Justly famous Burgos cathedral stunned us with its flamboyant diversity of Gothic architectural styles. There under an octagonal dome lie the tombs of Spain's hero El Cid and his wife, Dona Ximena. In Barcelona we were captivated by the surreal designs of Gaudi, a turn-of- the-century architect who detested straight lines. His La Sagrada Familia, the Church of the Sacred Family, only now being completed, is a never-to-be forgotten visual experience. Also in Barcelona, at the zoo, we saw the world's only albino gorilla. The fairy-tale castle in Segovia, the ancient walls of Avila, the Barcelona naval museum featuring a reconstruction of Don Juan of Austria's ship in the battle of Lepanto (no mention at all of the Spanish Armada!), the constant references to Ferdinand and Isabella and subsequent royalty made it easy to believe, wonder at, and relive some of Spain's past glory and grandeur.

We made two mistakes on this trip. First, we should have flown to Barcelona. Driving long distances on superhighways in Spain is unhealthy. Exhaust pipes on Spanish trucks, placed on the side of the cab, reached only as high as the window level of our rental car. The end of the pipe bent slightly away from the truck, belching irritating fumes directly into the open window of any passing car. I felt sure being subjected to this for hours caused my week-long respiratory infection and wretched cough.

Our second mistake with less serious consequences was arriving in Santiago de Compostela on August 15. We were surprised when no rooms were available in Leon, where we'd stopped for the magnificent stained glass of the Gothic cathedral there. Thinking a larger city would offer more, we drove on to Santiago, only to find a similar situation. We knew August 15 was the Catholic Feast of the Assumption, but didn't realize what an important holy day it was in Spain. Despite the long summer days, it was getting dark when Karen and Kurt left the fourth hotel they had tried. A swarthy, casually dressed man approached them, asking in Spanish if they were looking for a room. I was suspicious when they brought him to the car, but we outnumbered him four to one. At his home we met his family and were shown a room with three beds and a nearby bathroom. On the wall hung his framed university diploma. He'd majored in math. Pushing the beds together, the four of us slept across them sideways. There are some advantages to being short. After coffee and pan dulce in the morning, we paid, gratefully thanked our host, and headed for the cathedral to see a magnificent statue of St. George slaying the dragon and an urn containing relics of St. James, the apostle alias Saint Iago. Although Compostela has been famous as a popular pilgrimage site for centuries, we did not see any recognizable pilgrims that day.

A striking contrast to Spain's heat, Portugal's pleasant temperature along with numerous museums still to be seen in Lisbon made us wish for more than our allotted five days there, despite the language difficulty. Most of one delightful day was consumed by the incredible National Palace in Sintra with its Moorish architecture and marvelous glazed tiles or *azulejos* on interior walls and by nearby Pena Palace with its numerous towers, cupolas, and defenses. At Coimbra, we gave our attention to buildings at the world's second oldest university, founded in 1290. We regretted missing the turnoff for Battle Abbey or *Batalha* where King Joao I and his English Queen, Philippa of Lancaster, daughter of John of Gaunt, lie with their hands entwined. Their son, Prince Henry the Navigator, largely responsible for Portugal's period of dominance on the seas, lies nearby. It was windy and cool enough at Finisterre (Land's End) to bring out the sellers of homegrown, handmade wool sweaters, and three of us brought home treasures. Do not ask about the river crossing by ferry back into Spain or the night four of us tried to sleep in the rented Seat, the Spanish equivalent of the smallest Fiat, unless you have a long time to listen.

REVISITING SOME FAVORITES

Kurt's participation in the 1983 Eu-Chem Conference on Molten Salts held on the French Riviera in May opened the way for the two of us to revisit Europe. He had also been invited to lecture in London and in Leeds. On our first day in London, we miraculously found two seats available, despite sold-out signs, for a Royal Shakespearean Company production of *Henry IV*, *Part 2* at the newly opened Barbican Centre. Although the play is not my favorite, its Falstaff scenes were excellently done, and the pageantry of the royal procession was impressive. Strikingly different was the raunchy, bouncy Donleavy play, *Balthazar*, which we also enjoyed two nights later at the Duke of York's theatre. In London we revisited a few favorite spots, picking up details we'd missed before: a thorough tour of Westminster Abbey, a good look at St. Paul's, and a showery afternoon in Kew Gardens. The tulips and azaleas were still gorgeous in Regents Park, where I finally had a camel ride for ten pence at the zoo.

Following Kurt's lecture at London's National Physical Laboratory while I visited Hampton Court, we took the train to Leeds, a Victorian town, where the gracious hospitality of friends made us feel quite welcome. While Kurt lectured at the university, I explored the town, finding a rare seventeenth-century church full of carved dark Jacobean oak paneling and beams. The exotic bird collection at Harewood House, near Leeds, was fascinating and unexpected. Before leaving

England, we spent two days in the Lake Country, admiring a few remaining daffodils, thinking about the Romantic poets, and finally reaching the summit of Mt. Helvellyn. At the summit, bare and reminiscent of the Norwegian mountains, a sudden strong wind brought mist, fog, and rain. We pulled on every bit of clothing we had, then hurried down the impressive craggy and exposed Strider's Ridge to the lush, green countryside below, where numerous sheep cropped early spring growth. We're now experienced fell-walkers, with a healthy respect for the fells.

A sharp contrast to England's chilly spring was the Riviera's sunny Mediterranean weather. At St. Aygulf, site of the conference, the daily sun tanned its numerous local topless sun-worshipers (This was supposedly a family beach!), but the sea itself still retained enough chill to entice only the Scandinavians attending the conference. Most conferees preferred to spend their afternoon break at the resort's pool, despite or perhaps because of the prevalence there of bi- rather than mono-kinis. The arranged tour to Grasse was ideal for perfume lovers. Home to three perfume distilleries--Fragonard, Galimard, and Molinard--Grasse is a city full of flowers and aromas. We passed fields and fields of lavender. There wasn't much to see on the free tour of the distillery, although it was amazing to learn the large amount of flowers needed to distill a small amount of perfume. The perfumes even at the discounted rate were much too high for my budget, but I did buy some cologne. We found the visit to the ruins of the Roman occupation at Frejus much more worthwhile and interesting. Frejus had been founded by the Romans as a shipbuilding town, and it was in Frejus that Octavius built the ships that defeated Mark Antony and Cleopatra at the Battle of Actium. The Roman ruins are extensive including a theater, amphitheater, and aqueduct.

From Nice, where the conference bus dropped us, we headed for Italy in a rented car, north through the Maritime Alps. In Milan we spent Sunday touring the cathedral and walking on its impressive statue-studded roof with a hometown friend, coincidentally in Italy for scientific reasons. After a struggle with the *gettoni* (tokens) required for Italian public telephones, but not widely available, we relaxed during a beautiful afternoon and evening at a friend's home near Lago Maggiore. In the morning, Kurt lectured in Milan while I took the subway to see the *Last Supper*, along the way giving directions to a Japanese businessman grateful to have found someone who spoke English.

By late afternoon we reached Ferrara where we spent three days with the Indellis, causing my Italian and Anna's English to improve daily. We had originally met Antonio when he taught for a year at the University of Arkansas and had met the rest of his family when we visited Italy in 1964 and 1972. Shortly after our 1972 visit in Pisa, Antonio had given up his position there, preferring to teach chemistry at the University of Bologna, much closer to his ancestral home in Ferrara. The university also had the honor to be the oldest university in Europe, being founded in the eleventh century. On the day that Kurt gave a lecture in Bologna, Antonio gave us a short tour of the old, attractive city with its miles of shade-producing arcades, lovely plazas, decorative fountains, and two leaning towers. During our days in Ferrara, we had time to visit the palaces, monasteries, and museums we'd missed on our previous visits. We had time, also, to renew our friendship, relive old experiences, and relish Anna's excellent cuisine once more, before we left for Austria by way of Padua, where we admired the gorgeous Giotto frescoes in the Scrovegni chapel. Impressed by the sheer crags of the Dolomite area, and now more comfortable linguistically in an alpine region where both Italian and German were spoken, we were only disappointed that we were a few days too early for the summer skiing season at Marmolada, a giant glaciated massif, surrounded by spectacular panoramas. Hiking was out as well, because the rain began just as we returned to the small village inn from our scenic drive. Threatening but tolerable, the weather the next day permitted excellent views of Cortina d'Ampezzo, whetting our not-very-latent desire for a European ski vacation. That afternoon, scrambling around Tre Cima di Lavaredo or Drei Zinnen (a famed area for rock climbers), we explored the lookout caves carved out of the rock, reminders of World War II. This area, a high pass near the Austrian-Italian border, has often been the scene of severe fighting.

Austria was a bargain! Bed and breakfast for two was twelve dollars, half the price we paid in England (a slightly different breakfast, of course). We stayed in picturesque farmhouses and elegant homes in town--all clean, all modern, and all very comfortable. A perfect, warm, sunny day let us thoroughly enjoy the Hochalpenstrasse, which we had last driven in fog and snow in 1972. Built in 1935, and since improved, the high alpine road gives access to the Hohe Tauern National Park and terminates in front of Austria's highest mountain, the 12,547-foot Grossglockner and its largest glacier, Pasterze. On the way, the road passes through every vegetation zone from cornfields to permanent ice. With sixty-seven bridges, several tunnels, and two spurs to lookout spots, the road makes its winding way over hills and treeless alpine tundra before it reaches the high pass to descend to Heiligenblut. This time we had gorgeous views of the Grossglockner, the mountain we climbed on a previous visit. Driving up a side road to the observation tower on Edelweisspitze, we were able to take in a dramatic vista of snow-capped Austrian Alps as well as green valleys far below.

Salzburg's old-city area charmed us, as we made the required pilgrimage to Mozart's birthplace, to the marionette theater for a performance of *Abduction from the Seraglio*, to the Hohensalzburg Festung (castle-fortress), and to St. Peter's, a fifteen-hundred-year-old abbey whose cloisters and treasury were opened to visitors for the first time in history in celebration of that anniversary. Near Salzburg we visited a salt mine, guided by retired miners and riding on the wooden slides built for quick access between levels in the mine. We finally got to ski on June 9 in Tuxertal, a high valley, where skiing on the glacier, midst snow, sleet, sun, and rain was a once-in-a-lifetime experience (Yes, once is enough).

Just to reach the skiing area at ten thousand feet, two lifts had to be taken--one a gondola. It's a weird experience to go from vivid green pastures where cows graze to the world of snow and ice above in just a few minutes. In winter, the whole area is skied. What runs those must be!

In the medieval city of Solbad Hall, a colorful city-wide religious procession took place on our wedding anniversary. It was merely a coincidence that this was also the Feast of Corpus Christi. Near Hallstadt we visited two caves, a mammoth cave similar to those in the states, and an impressive ice cave, unlike anything I'd seen before. All water entering the cave freezes and forms fantastic ice sculptures, as well as coating the walls and floors of some of the chambers.

Following a short stop in Innsbruck, where glissading (sliding with bent knees, but no skis, down steep snow patches) was the latest fad, we drove through the Salzkammergut. Austria's only lakes were ringed solid with body-to-body beach lovers and picnickers. Windsurfers dominated the water. Tiny plots of grass between the highway and the lake were fenced in, apparently owned or rented by families for weekend outings or for summer vacations. Where the space was large enough only for a table, beach chairs were placed in the water.

Generally, we ate very well in Austria. Trout and veal were excellent--especially in some of the simple country gasthofs. We found palatschinken and cevapcici, but our quest for Salzburger nockerln and authentic zwiebel rostbraten, specialties from Kurt's childhood remembrances, was unsuccessful.

When serious rain made us cancel our plans to hike up Wildspitze, we left Austria by the Timmelsjoch pass, facing on the Italian side of the mountain a steep, sinuous, narrow road needing repair. We found the sun only when we reached the Italian plains, stopping for a quick view of old Verona (Romeo and Juliet). After an overnight stop on the Italian-French border, we hoped to hike near Mt. Cenisia, but more rain forced us south. We traversed the Blanchon pass in a summer snowstorm. The pass to Val d'Isere was still closed by snow, and the one we took was barely open. High in the pass, looking like some outer-space expedition, a giant hydroelectric construction project was just getting underway. Thunderstorms chased us from Grenoble to the Maritime Alps, but the sun was gorgeous for our rewarding Grand Canyon visit. This day-long hike, along the floor of the Grand Canyon of the Verdun, began with a steep descent to the river. Later, an unexpected two-hundred-foot-long iron ladder wedged between two sheer cliffs and at least a kilometer of trail through an unlit cave provided a fitting finale to our European adventure, though we did squeeze in a performance of the Bach Choir on the one night we spent in London before our early morning flight home.

VIENNA AND BUDAPEST

We'd thought that Aspen and Australia would fulfill our travel lust for the year, but early in June of 1999, Kurt was offered a free round-trip ticket to Vienna, Austria, an offer we couldn't refuse. Born in Vienna, Kurt attended school there until 1938. A few years ago students at his "high school," Bundes Gymnasium 19, while learning about the Holocaust, wondered what had happened to the students (mostly Jewish) who had been expelled from the school when the Nazis took over. They first placed a plaque in the school, listing all the students. Then with the help of their teacher they tried to locate all those students. Survivors they located were interviewed or asked to write about their experiences. The teacher found these stories so compelling that he wrote a book about the project, including the survivors' stories, photographs, and memorabilia.. This book was to be presented to the public on September 30, and Kurt was invited to the occasion. It was a very emotional and moving experience. Fifteen former students were able to attend. Some still lived in Vienna, one came from Ottawa, one from Buenos Aires, and three from the New England area. Of the 104 who were expelled, 7 had been murdered by the Nazis. The rest had managed to survive, somehow, though some had died recently. Kurt was one of the younger students. Many survivors spoke at the presentation, as did some students, the director of the school, journalists and historians, and the author of the book. The next night a more informal evening was held so that the seventeen- and eighteen- year-old students (ten females, one male) could talk with the survivors. One of the speakers, Harry Kaufmann, was a close childhood friend of Kurt's whom he had not seen since the 1940s. Harry lives in New York, but the two had lost contact with each other. The book had little information on another childhood friend, listed only as emigrating to London, but Kurt thought Tommy Mayer was at Berkeley, California. As a result of some research, Kurt and Tommy were reunited the following November.

Teachers from the school met us at the airport, presenting me with a gorgeous bunch of flowers (an Austrian tradition) and then whisked us off to the charming pension where several of us were staying. After quickly unpacking, we caught a tram for Vienna's Ring area, because tours of the Burg Theater were given only on Wednesday. This was the building where Kurt's great-aunt and great-uncle performed in the early 1900s, a beautifully decorated building with mosaics in gold by Klimt, ornate waiting rooms, grand staircases, and impressive chandeliers.

Melk Abbey on the Danube was our destination the next day. We'd missed this glorious exuberantly rococo church and library on previous trips. Back in Vienna, the Fine Arts Museum with the largest collection of Brueghels in the world was magnificent in itself, never mind the abundance of paintings and sculptures. The next day we thrilled at crown jewels, ecclesiastical vestments embroidered with gold thread, and other treasures in the Schatzkammer, and walked through the Hofburg apartments. Our hike in the Vienna Woods began at road's end near our pension. The trail led towards Hermanskogel, through vineyards up to Kahlenberg, where roast chestnuts were available, along with views of Vienna and the Danube. Sunday, after hearing Mozart's *Coronation Mass* at the Michaeler Kirche with new friends from Buenos Aires, we visited Schonbrunn, avidly listening to an audio tour of the recently refurbished royal apartments and revisiting the small zoo and formal gardens on the spacious castle grounds.

Misty rain added to the foreboding atmosphere we found in Budapest, reached by train on Monday. The castle hill area (Old Buda) overlooking the Danube offered St. Matthias' Cathedral with its stunning patterned roof of colored ceramic tile, the turreted Fisherman's Bastion, history and music museums, archeological diggings of medieval fortifications, a fabulous pastry and coffee shop, a somewhat hokey but fun self-guided walk through cave-tunnels under many of the buildings, and magnificent views of Pest across the river, where the largest basilica in Hungary, St. Istvan, is located. In Pest, the large, double-towered Great Synagogue, which even has an organ, had been painstakingly redone. Mostly unknown to us, Hungary's past vividly came to life at the National Museum of History, filled with many beautiful objects. The ethnography museum, formerly the Supreme Court building, was interesting architecturally with classical statues lining the flat roof line. The museum's exhibits educated us about ancient folk beliefs and ways of living, and the collection of regional clothing from various villages displayed a fascinating variety of styles. The most ornate costume belonged to a pig herder. Perhaps these were his Sunday clothes.

The Opera House tour was well worth waiting for. The interior of the building had been magnificently restored. Similarly, the interior of the Parliament Building with its impressive statues of past rulers was gorgeously decorated. The replica, housed in a glass case and made entirely of toothpicks, was amazing. Though many buildings are still grimy from heavy pollution and damaged from various wars, some exteriors are being cleaned and repaired. The interiors of the most important buildings are incredibly beautiful, gilded, and immaculate. Many were built during the Austro-Hungarian Empire, when Budapest, as a second capital, rivaled Vienna--culturally and architecturally. In Old Buda the next day, we reveled in the Hungarian Painting and Sculpture Museum in part of the castle, avoiding a persistent "guide" by pretending we knew no English. The collection of late-Gothic winged and gilt altarpieces was simply fabulous. In the History of Budapest Museum, another wing of the castle, artifacts from the early Stone Age, the Bronze Age, and from the era of folk wanderings gave way to vaulted chapels in the basement, which were found almost intact during castle excavations and were now reached by tortuous tunnels. On our last day, we took train and bus to Szentendre (St. Andrew), a small village at the Danube Bend, also home to an ethnographic open-air museum with farm and village buildings from various parts of Hungary. A Serbian Orthodox museum was full of icons and other exquisite religious objects.

When our "hostess," who spoke no English, told us in sign language that we'd have to leave because she had a reservation for our room, we returned to Vienna and had the afternoon for the Natural History Museum and its amazing collection of specimens, gathered by royalty as early as 1730, before anything was protected or considered endangered. Fascinating was a 3D show of microscopic organisms under a microscope projected on a screen. Wearing special glasses, we saw these magnified critters move, eat, and almost reach out to touch us.

Bratislava in Slovakia was our final stop in Europe. Kurt's grandmother's family was originally from Bratislava, then called Pressburg. On a gray, rainy day, the old city--what remained of it--showed us cathedrals, baroque buildings, and narrow twisting alleys. The castle fortress housed many museums, one on musical instruments. Across the Danube rose a plethora of concrete high-rises, practical housing built during the Communist era.

POLAND, THE CZECH REPUBLIC, AND GERMANY

Passing over vast chasms and rocky ravines, the gondola dropped us at the ridgeline of the Tatra Mountains, near Zakopane, in southwestern Poland where Kurt's mother had hiked in the 1920s. Warning signs along the exposed and rugged trail marked the Polish-Slovak Republic border. Guards in green uniforms patrolled the boundary, but seemed to enjoy the scenery as much as we did. Though no higher in elevation than New Hampshire's White Mountains, the Tatras, having more recently emerged from the earth's core, are more barren and jagged. From the treeless ridge, sheer dropoffs fall to valleys lying in deep shadows far below. Yet a well- marked trail traverses the crest, offering side hikes of varying lengths and difficulty. On a distant hill, elk or deer grazed. Nearby, a herd of sheep enjoyed the sun. At dusk, just as we left the forest, a fox crossed the trail. Earlier, a group of eight nuns in habits striding up the trail made me think of *The Sound of Music*. But the hikers' greeting here was *Dzien Dobry* (Polish) or *Dobry Den* (Slovak/ Czech) instead of *Guten Morgen* or *Grüss Gott*. We made the most of our time in the Tatras, though we never reached the summit of Giewont with its iron cross, slippery crags, and necessary cables and ladders. Oh, we could have made it, but just ran out of time. (Hmm!) On our third day of hiking, we still had a five-mile walk to Lake Morskie Oko (Eye of the Sea) after the public microbus stopped at the Polana Palenica car park. Horse-drawn wagons were available, but we toughed it out, going on to circle the lake and clamber up to a higher tarn. Fall colors glowed amidst evergreens, strange rock formations beckoned, and waterfalls charmed hikers. There were quite a few of them, even this late in the year. Again the summit was beyond our time limit. If we missed a van back to town, we would have a very long walk. When the sun came out briefly, we had glorious views of the large lake and the lodge beside it. By then it was October 1, and we'd been in Poland for two weeks traveling by train and bus on our own, finding rooms as we went.

Our six-week trip to Eastern Europe began in Warsaw September 19, 2001. Pictures of the rubble that was Warsaw in 1945 made the reconstructed buildings on the main square even more amazing. Without any background information, the casual visitor would assume the elaborate and fanciful facades of the renaissance and baroque buildings had been standing for several hundred years. After a castle tour, we admired the reconstructed barbican (fortifications) and ate at a "milk bar" from an earlier era. Food is ordered from the cashier and dished up from a small kitchen. The dictionary was needed, but the food, though simple, was tasty and inexpensive. The Royal Walk to Lazienki Park, the Chopin statue, and the Palace on the Water, took us past embassies and stately buildings and into the Museum of Ethnography (regional dress and *skopjas*-- elaborate creches), the National Art Museum, and numerous churches. In front of the United States embassy we saw flowers and many notes of sympathy and condolence from Polish individuals referring to the September 11 terrorist attack. Other stops were the Warsaw Zoo, across the street from our hotel, a Polish Orthodox church where services were held underground, the only surviving undamaged synagogue, and the memorial to the ghetto.

Leaving the train station in Krakow, we were immediately invited to inspect a room in a nearby apartment. It was convenient, the price was right, and the hosts quite hospitable. Elzbieta even spoke a little English. Did you read *The Trumpeter of Krakow* as a child? Every hour on the hour a trumpeter plays the *hejnal* (warning call) from the high tower of Kosciol Mariacki (Church of the Virgin Mary) once in each of four directions. The melody ends half way through a repeated phrase, just as it originally did, according to legend, when the arrow of an invading Tartar pierced the throat of the watchman trumpeting a warning of the enemy's approach. Though the trumpeter died, his warning saved the city. A magnificent carved altarpiece by Weit Stoss, and brightly painted medieval angels dazzle visitors inside.

The story behind the two asymmetrical towers is also incredible. The builders were two brothers eager to outdo each other, who competed in erecting the higher tower, even though both towers were on the same church. At their bases the two towers appear to have been planned symmetrically. The first three stories on each tower are identical, having three arches on the facade with the center arch containing a window. All the windows are the same size and fill up the entire height of each story.

The north tower continues with three more stories of the same size. In contrast, the south tower has only two more stories, but they have been elongated. Although the windows remain the same size, they fill only two-thirds of the new stories. Had the construction stopped at this point, the south tower would have been higher than its neighbor.

Not happy with this situation, the elder brother, working on the north tower, constructed two octagonal stories, using a brighter red brick for the walls and accenting the angle where the sections met with a column of white stones. In addition, he added windows, faced with the same white stone, in each of the eight segments. On top of this "new" addition, he placed a circle of sixteen shorter spires whose height raised the top of the north tower above that of the south tower. Then from the center of this circle of spires, a single, slender Gothic spire rises even higher. When he completed the spire in 1478, the builder murdered his younger brother to prevent him from finishing the south tower. Remorse soured the murderer's success, however. After a public confession of his crime, he committed suicide by leaping from a high window of his own tower.

In 1500, a Renaissance dome was added to the lower tower, bringing it up to the height of the crown of spires on the north tower, and in 1666 a golden crown, symbol of the Virgin as Queen of Poland, was added to encircle the gothic spire of the taller north tower. It is from this taller tower, long used as a watch tower, that the trumpeter plays the haunting melody each day. The lower tower serves as the church's bell tower.

Krakow survived World War II relatively unscathed. Besides the Rynek Glowny (Market Square) with its impressive cloth merchants' hall, town hall, and several churches, Krakow's main attraction is Wawel Hill dominated by stunning Wawel castle and cathedral. The castle's tapestries, superbly preserved, have so much gold thread they create a 3-D effect. In one room, the squares of the coffered ceiling contained sculpted heads instead of the usual carved rosette, creating a somewhat creepy effect. I couldn't resist Dragon's Den, a long spiral staircase ending in a cave, exiting to a riverside park where a sculpted dragon periodically belched flames. In Kasimierz, the Jewish quarter, two restored synagogues are now museums and several restaurants proudly served "Jewish food." From Krakow, a local bus goes to the Wieliczka salt mine started in 1200 and operating continuously until 1997. There's still salt, but mining it isn't profitable. Although the mine today also houses an underground sanatorium for allergy sufferers and asthmatics, the real attractions are the fantastic grottos and carvings the miners did in their spare time, especially the huge cathedral with its statues, shrines, and salt chandeliers.

"Przepraszam, czy jest menski bielizna?" Hesitantly, I asked my question, composed on the spot. But... I was understood. Kurt now has several sets of Polish underwear, purchased in Krakow, after he discovered he had forgotten to pack ANY extras. For three weeks in Poland, where English is skimpy, we relied on my self-taught pronunciation, a phrase book, and a dictionary when we couldn't find any speakers of English. *Wejscie* and *Wyjscie* are dangerously similar. With "e" the word means entrance; with "y" exit. Kielbasa often came with *Frytki* (french fries), and *"Nie rozumiem"* (I don't understand) was an easy way out of sticky situations. Sometimes only symbols appeared: a triangle for men, a circle for women. What a challenge! And what a relief to find more German as we traveled farther west.

Family history drew us to Tarnow, where Kurt's mother was born in 1900, to Nowy Sacz, home of her mother who died in 1906, and to Bielsko, the family home from 1914. In Tarnow we found records in the archives and almost miraculously the gravestones of the two sisters who had married Kurt's grandfather, Herman Klein. In Nowy Sacz, the skansen, an open air park displaying old dwellings and a wooden Eastern Orthodox church, gave us a glimpse into Polish rural life and customs.

Ending two weeks of fog and rain, a glorious sunny day graced our raft trip through the scenic Dunajec Gorge. The rafts, controlled by two men, were made by lashing four narrow wooden "canoes" together and nailing boards over the middle. Twelve people sat on the boards with their feet in the coffin-like canoes. This pleasant trip ended in Szczawnica (try saying that word), a small village where Kurt's maternal grandparents, the Kamholzes, had spent summers ninety years ago. Villagers and tourists celebrated the tenth year of the local ski lift with folk songs and dancing, horse and carriage competitions, three parapenters, free rides on the chairlift, and lots of food and drink: bigos, pierogi, smoked sheep's-milk cheese, and...pizza. Our room there in a private home cost sixteen dollars and had a modern private bath.

After the Tatras (described earlier), we visited Wroclaw to see its huge, ornately decorated city hall, its market square, the National Museum, the famous Panorama Raclawicka depicting the battle between Polish peasants and the Russians, and several old churches nestled together on an island. An hour's boat ride on the Odra River gave us a different view of the city. Deciding to lighten our bags by mailing home extra clothes and Polish literature we'd collected, we faced the daunting task of finding boxes to mail it in and filling out customs forms, all in Polish. We were pleased and impressed to find the two boxes waiting for us in Maryland–in perfect condition.

Prague should be visited. Even in October, crowds thronged the main square with its famous and fabulous astronomical clock, the brooding Jan Hus statue, the incredibly beautiful buildings and churches surrounding the main square, and the restaurants. Wherever and whenever you looked around in Prague, something beautiful or unusual could be seen. Very popular with tourists was the Jewish museum, made up of six synagogues in Prague. The Spanish synagogue is a jewel with its Moorish design and freshly painted glowing colors. Hordes of tour groups and independent visitors waited to enter the Royal Castle, to photograph the elaborate changing of the guard, and to wander through the magnificent Prague Cathedral. Artists and vendors sold souvenirs to many tourists from all over who traversed the Charles Bridge stopping to rub the brass dog in the bas relief beneath the statue of Bohemia's patron saint St. John Nepomuk, hoping to have their wish granted. Meanwhile a lively group, called The Bridge Band, played dixieland jazz attracting an appreciative audience. Cultural activities were slowing but still lively with several chamber music concerts, a puppet show, and an opera being offered. The huge statue of St. Wenceslas (yes, the King from the Christmas carol) was a must. A special self-guiding exhibit, "Ten Centuries of Architecture" took us to underground parts of the cathedral and castle, across the moat to a garden and an elegant Renaissance summer palace, and back again. We spent a somber day visiting Terezin, the concentration camp where Kurt's Stern grandparents died in 1942.

Karlovy Vary (Karlsbad) had paved but confusing hiking trails in its surrounding hills. We climbed to the Diana Tower for great views after walking by the amazingly ornate post office building and the colonnades where guests are still "taking the waters," meandering about carrying oddly shaped ceramic mugs designed for sipping the mineral waters of the various springs. This very attractive town had many architecturally interesting structures, strolling areas, shops, villas, and upscale restaurants, along with a beautiful Russian Orthodox church topped by gold and blue domes, near a statue of Karl Marx. Karlovy Vary was a regular vacation spot for the Klein grandparents when they lived in

Bielsko, but the town only boasted about the visits to its clinics by people like Brahms, Beethoven, Turgenev, Pavlov, and President T.G. Masaryk.

From the train to Dresden, we caught glimpses of the grotesque and dramatic sandstone formations of Sachische Schweiz, an area we later hiked by taking daily electric trains from Dresden and crossing the Elbe by passenger ferries. These hikes took us up ladders, over precipices, to Konigstein, a fortress built into the rocks on the top of a hill, and to Bastei, with its spectacular bridges and the ruins of a much older fortress.

Dresden had restored many of its buildings but was still working on its castle. The Zwinger Art Museum had so many Old Masters we couldn't take them all in. The Green Vault, a collection of Hapsburg treasures--jewels, silver, gold, and ivory creations--was unbelievable in its artistry and monetary value. In Leipzig, we listened raptly to a choral concert in Bach's church, St. Thomas Kirche, visited the Bach Museum, and skirted the lively Friday market in the square to drink coffee at the oldest continuously operating coffee house in Germany after we toured the coffee museum.

In Wolfenbüttel, home of the famous Herzog August Library with its 350,000 printed works published before 1830, including the oldest printed book in the German language, we stayed with our friend Hanna Lustig who lived in D.C. when we did. Wolfenbüttel itself has many charming tilted, half-timbered houses, some using decorative slate as siding. In nearby Gifhorn for a two-year internship, our niece, Kim Bueltmann, showed us her apartment and office and the town's castle and unusual windmill museum.

Berlin's new Jewish Museum, part memorial, part Jewish history, remains somewhat controversial, but is definitely worth a visit. On the outskirts of Berlin, our hike in the Volkspark Glienicke on the Havel River with Helga Haftendorn, a friend from the 1950s, took us to the popular restaurant housed in the Russian style Nikolai Blockhouse. The hearty and delicious lunch more than satisfied Kurt's curiosity about authentic Berlin food. In Berlin's center, the famous Pergamon Museum's remarkable archaeological collection of Babylonian, Greek, Etruscan, Assyrian, and other sculptural antiquities, including the stunning Ishtar Gate, consumed the rest of that afternoon. The Museum of Musical Instruments, the Old Masters Gallery, and the Applied Arts Museum, all located near symphony hall, filled an entire day. Excellent weather for a train ride to Potsdam to see Frederick the Great's Schloss Sanssouci, his ornately decorated Chinese Tea House, and the town itself, enhanced another day. Dinner at a new Turkish bistro with Sandra Lustig, an environmental planner living in Berlin, was fun; she really knows her way around town. The Brandenburg gate was being restored, but we could see the Quadriga on top; we were awed by the splendor of the Reichstag's glass dome and its light-catching mirrored cone which funnels the light directly into the legislative chamber, though we disliked the long wait to get in. That afternoon at the Tiergarten, a large modern zoo, the antics of a porcupine family with five babies delighted us. A boat trip on the Spree River, a visit to the

New Synagogue (now a heavily guarded museum) with its gold-decorated domes, and a stroll in Nikolai Viertel, another attractive section of Berlin, kept us very busy on our last day.

When we arrived at the Warsaw train station, after a six-hour ride, a Japanese couple asked me in Polish about the bus schedule. They were greatly relieved when I asked if they spoke English. Because it was almost midnight, we went directly to the airport, waiting there until 4:00 a.m. to check in for the full early flight to Amsterdam and home.

Hall in Tirol -Austria

Budapest Parliament -Hungary

Alan -Vigeland Sculpture -Norway

Skansen -Nowy Sacz -Poland

Courtyard -Feldkirch -Austria

**Kosciol Mariacki - Krakow
Poland**

**Reichstag Dom - Berlin
Germany**

South America

Altiplano Train Stop

Machu Picchu - Peru

SEEING OTHER PARTS OF THE WORLD

Guatemalan Getaway

One Month in South America

South of the Border (Mexico)

It's a Wild Life (African Safari)

Impressions of India

Ten Days in Japan

Coping in China

SEEING OTHER PARTS OF THE WORLD

Ever since I can remember I've loved to travel. My high school Spanish teacher, who spent her summers in Mexico, invited me to join her when I was a junior. I could tell my parents didn't like the idea, but they didn't refuse. They merely said if I could raise the money, I could go. Being fifteen and living in a small town, I had few opportunities to make as much as I needed. Later, neither my family nor I could afford financing a junior year abroad. Instead I worked in the cannery in the summers, and during the school year, ushered at the movies and clerked in the college bookstore to pay for my local tuition. I don't remember how I found the money for my trip to Guatemala. But when this opportunity to visit a country outside the United States arose, I was determined to go. It was the first of many visits I eventually made to explore other countries of the world.

GUATEMALAN GETAWAY

When I couldn't get to Guatemala for her wedding, my friend, Berta Avila, invited me to come for a visit after summer school ended. We'd become good friends the previous year at the University of Arkansas. Berta and two other friends had driven home with me to Illinois for a relaxing spring break. My young cousin who lived with my parents was, at the time, fascinated with the rhyme about the bear named Fuzzy Wuzzy. He repeated it endlessly. Berta wanted to know what the term "Fuzzy Wuzzy" meant, and after we explained that and the pun, she was determined to learn the rhyme to demonstrate her English skills at home. There were only three sentences: Fuzzy Wuzzy was a bear. Fuzzy Wuzzy had no hair. Fuzzy Wuzzy wasn't fuzzy, was he? Because so much of it was nonsense, she had trouble keeping the words in the right order. We all, including Berta, shared many laughs and giggles over Fuzzy Wuzzy. At the end of that year Berta returned to Guatemala to teach English, including Fuzzy Wuzzy, and six months later she was married. Now she wrote that she wanted me to meet her new husband as well as the rest of her family.

While making trip preparations, I was offered a university teaching position in Iowa. Perhaps it was the fever resulting from the required typhoid shot that affected my judgment. Although I also needed money, was momentarily sick of graduate school, and could use a year off. Whatever the reason, I signed a contract. The end result was that I would have only one day after my return from Guatemala to get ready to teach classes.

I'd given up my grad-school apartment, loaded my car with all my worldly possessions, and parked it at a friend's house. From Arkansas, I took a train to New Orleans, where I boarded the cheap flight Aviateca offered to

Guatemala City three times a week.

After picking me up at the airport, Berta and her husband, Felix, took me to a performance of Maxwell Anderson's "Joan of Lorraine" put on by the Guatemala City Theatre Guild. Fortunately for me it was in English. Most of the cast members had some connection with a large English-speaking community in the city. The program was bilingual, so I had a chance to practice my Spanish reading ability.

As we were driving home, several men in military uniform stopped the car and asked Felix to get out. I was terrified. Berta whispered to me not to say anything. As if I could! Felix was told to open the trunk of the car. The men looked inside. The trunk was closed; Felix got in the car; and we drove home. "What was that all about?" I asked. "Just routine, to keep the common folk in line," Felix said. "But there's no point in protesting, as their actions can be unpredictable. It's better just to comply and hope they are satisfied."

The next morning we attended a wedding. Afterwards we drove to the military club for the reception. Here I was introduced to many friends of the Avila family while we waited for the bride and groom, who were having their pictures taken. Although Berta and Felix were bilingual, most of their family and friends spoke only Spanish, so I had a great opportunity to practice the little Spanish I remembered from a high school course. Once the bridal couple arrived, champagne was distributed to the approximately 200 to 250 guests. The couple drank with hooked arms, and then the guests drank a toast to the couple. A marimba orchestra consisting of snare drums, a bass fiddle, and six men at marimbas played a waltz as the bride and groom danced alone. When everyone joined in for the next dance, the bridal couple made the rounds, visiting each table and having a drink with the guests seated there. After another round of champagne and some snacks followed by several rounds of a mixture of whiskey and seven-up, some hot soup was served. These people really knew how to have a party. The soup was followed by a plate of salad, pressed meat, and other delicacies. Then another round of whiskey was offered before the wedding cake was cut and served with coffee at about 4:30 p.m. As the somewhat tipsy groom cut the cake, he made a long speech all about the glory of Guatemala.

Earlier the groom had brought his cousin to our table offering him as my dance partner, if I wished to dance. While the music was going, we were fine. The groom's cousin was good looking and danced well. But once the music stopped, I learned that his English was more non-existent than my Spanish. We managed to exchange names, and I asked where he worked. We told each other the Spanish and English names of food–a thrilling exchange. Another dance partner had more English, and I also danced with Berta's father, a fabulous dancer, despite being sixty-three.

After the reception we drove a short distance to Lake Amatitlan where many city residents go for picnics. This beautiful lake is surrounded by steep mountains thickly covered with tropical bushes and trees in varying shades of dark green. Many Indians sat by small stoves cooking and roasting corn, tochitos, and other food to sell to anyone who would buy. As they waited for buyers, they ate some of the food themselves and women nursed their babies. By happenstance, we met Berta's older brother Victor and his family who were also there for a Sunday afternoon outing.

Berta and Felix lived in the large home of Berta's parents, as did two of her unmarried brothers. Her parents were warm, hospitable people who made me feel very welcome and comfortable despite the language barrier. With her parents and brothers I could have only rather primitive conversations, since my Spanish was limited, and they spoke no English. Their house was built in the typical Spanish style with all the rooms encircling an open patio. I was stunned to see poinsettias that were trees, not house plants. They and other tropical plants created a beautiful and colorful central area. From the street, the interior of the house was completely hidden. The entrance was through a very heavy door in the tall, thick, white-washed wall, topped with broken glass, that surrounded the building.

Monday morning I was up at 9:00 a.m. for breakfast. Most everything was already laid out, and I ate everything the maid set before me. Their custom was to set the table the night before, with the plates upside down protecting the flatware underneath. This was new to me, but seemed a practical way of doing things. Berta had written out instructions for me, along with some critical Spanish words I might need. Berta and Felix both worked, so during most of the week I was on my own. Because most of the family spoke no English, my Spanish vocabulary increased daily, and my fear of speaking incorrectly gradually diminished. I did have a headache at the end of the first two days, caused by trying so hard to communicate.

Toya, the maid, walked me to the corner where I caught a bus for downtown, watched carefully, rang the bell, and hopped out at the National Palace and other government buildings. The palace was built around a lovely patio containing very striking murals on early Mayan culture and current industrial developments. At the Cathedral of Guatemala, a beautiful church loaded with old paintings, the main altar was being repaired, but some of the smaller side chapels contained exquisite carvings and altarpieces. I noticed that petitioners included very well-dressed individuals as well as grubby Indians.

The open market fascinated me with its gorgeous flowers and rather unsanitary meat markets where flies of all sizes hovered on the hanging meat carcasses. Prices were high because haggling was expected. Each seller had a little stall and all were shouting, "Aqui, Senora, Senorita, Aqui." Many sellers had small cubby holes within the market building, or they came at 5:00 a.m. to stake out a claim for a spot on the floor. Others felt that being outdoors on the steps and sidewalks was more advantageous. The market took up an entire city block.

At the very modern public library, I was surprised that there were no females visiting. On the way out, as I stopped to take a picture of a mural, a young man who could speak English introduced himself and walked with me until we saw Berta's father, who had been waiting for me at a pre-arranged spot. Berta's father had been worried about my going about the city on my own. Now his worries were confirmed. He grilled Roberto, and let me know he was upset that I had allowed a young man I'd just met walk with me. Senor Avila was very traditional. Later, Berta told me that Roberto was quite all right, but her father was very protective.

I'd signed up for a two-day trip to Chichicastenango which left on Wednesday, but I wanted to see as much of Guatemala city as possible. The afternoon before I left, I visited an amusement park, the natural history and science museums, and a museum on ethnology that displayed regional dress of various Indian groups.

Leaving the city early in the morning, our first stop was Antigua, a city established in 1566, that still displayed its Spanish Colonial magnificence. The yellow and white church and convent of La Merced were particularly attractive. Touring a textile mill was a new experience for me, and I purchased a few hand towels as souvenirs. One of my companions on the tour, Irene Zimmerman, was a librarian specializing in Latin American bibliography. She knew about the Museo del Libro Antiguo in Antigua and suggested we visit there. Instead of shopping, I accompanied her to examine twelve books written and printed in Guatemala on the first printing press brought to Central America. These included the first book printed in Guatemala which was written in Latin in 1663 by the Bishop of Guatemala, Fray Payo de Rivera. He had introduced the printing press to the country in 1660. After lunch we stopped briefly at Chimaltenango to see an old colonial fountain situated on the continental divide so that its waters overflow on the one side to the Pacific Ocean and on the other to the Atlantic. Breathtaking views of deep-blue Lake Atitlan surrounded by volcanic peaks thrilled us as we descended the hill to the valley and then drove higher again to reach Chichicastenango just in time for dinner at the Mayan Inn.

A well-known tourist hotel, the Mayan Inn was a prime example of Spanish architecture. Each room had a fireplace and opened onto a central patio. Dark wood beams could be seen on the ceiling and at the corners of the room where the white stucco walls met. Furnishings were a mix of Indian and Spanish colonial styles. The waiters and room boys wore colorful Mayan costumes. Although the food was somewhat American, it was delicious. They did serve Guatemalan coffee and had one special Guatemalan dish available.

After dinner, I discovered that I had lost the key to my overnight bag. The manager, Arturo Mendez, seemed eager to help; but one of my travel companions, Willie, was successful in getting the bag open. Although she claimed she had no previous experience, she managed to open it by using a paper clip and a bobby pin. Relieved that I had access to my toothbrush and other necessities, I went out to the patio where the marimbas were playing irresistible music.

Two women seated at a table stopped me to inquire where my reed purse in the shape of a basket had been made. They had recently been to Ecuador and were amazed when I told them my mother found it in Chicago. Unable to read the country of origin label on the bottom, they asked their handsome guide, Victor, for help. Having had a few drinks, Vic replied, "To find out, you must dance," and suddenly I was doing a modified rhumba–apparently to the delight of the observers. Vic was interested in finding out when I would be returning to Guatemala City and informed me that he would be there Friday night also and that we could have a big time. I only smiled enigmatically, trying to follow what I thought was now a samba.

Apparently the manager of the hotel also wanted to dance with me, but he was somewhat shy. Vic helped him out. Arturo was less flamboyant than Vic, but equally charming and good-looking. It was pleasant dancing with him, for his waltz and foxtrot were very good. Vic came back just as the band began playing a jitterbug on the marimba. I, of course, resorted to my favorite dance–the charleston. Although this was new to Vic, he was grand and caught on very quickly. The native Indian marimba players were very interested and amused by the novelty. It was a rather incongruous combination altogether, but good entertainment for the other guests–and, of course, I enjoyed putting on a show. After I danced a few more times with Vic, Arturo returned and Vic danced with Willie. Arturo had asked me to join him for a drink when the dancing ended. Almost everyone had gone to their rooms, so Arturo and I had the bar to ourselves. Over a creme-de-menthe, my favorite drink at the time, we talked in Spanish and English about our families, volcano climbing, music, our plans and goals in life, and inevitably of the inevitable. Arturo had what he thought was a marvelous idea. I should stay with him (no doubt the ambiguity was a result of language difficulty) for several months and teach him English while he taught me Spanish. "And," he added, "you could teach me to loave (love)." But as he was thirty-eight to my twenty-five and Latin, I said that I had heard that Latin Americans were much more skilled in that art than we were. Though he was disappointed I hadn't accepted his invitation, he wanted to write to me. Long distance I could handle.

In the morning in the lobby and at breakfast, many guests at the inn stopped me to ask if I was the girl who had danced the previous night. When I said I was, they told me they had enjoyed my dancing immensely. One woman told me her husband couldn't go to sleep because he liked my dancing so much. Her husband said he thought I had real talent and should be on the stage or in the movies. They introduced themselves as Dr. and Mrs. Max Wolf of Vienna and New York. He was a dermatologist and actually knew some of my current boyfriend's relatives who were also from Vienna and New York. Perhaps they were only teasing me, but at the time I took their comments as a compliment.

After breakfast, Irene and I went through a local ethnic museum before meeting the rest of our group. I learned that in the north of Guatemala, Tikal was the land of tigers. With the others we went to the home of the maskmaker who made masks for Conquistadores and Morales. An Indian dance, which I had learned the night before, was performed in costume. The highlight of the day was the visit to San Tomas Cathedral where food was blessed by a witch doctor and roses were offered and candles burned in honor of both catholic and pagan gods. Many of the devout ascend the stairs leading to the main entrance on their knees as others swing smoky censers and chant prayers. We saw three christenings in which salt was put on the tongue and water on both the head and the back of the neck. At the same time that some people were going to the cathedral, the colorful and picturesque open air market where Indians wearing beautiful costumes were selling and buying was full of activity and sound.

The road back to Guatemala City traversed the edge of the mountainside, with hairpin curves so narrow and dangerous that each driver had to honk his horn to give those coming the opposite way time to find a wide spot in which to stop. We passed several gorgeous waterfalls, saw Indians making charcoal, and were surprised to see a rock wall into which parakeets had pecked small niches for holding their nests.

The next morning I walked to Cerro del Carmen to meet Roberto, the young man I'd met at the library earlier in the week. We walked through parts of the city I hadn't seen, and he took me to a park where there was a relief map of Guatemala clearly showing how mountainous the country was. In the afternoon I shopped for presents and went to an English movie with Spanish subtitles. I had wanted to see a Spanish movie, until I realized that there would be no English subtitles provided in Guatemala. It was fun, however, trying to decipher the totally Spanish newsreels, ads, and previews.

Included in the family outing on Saturday, I saw even more of real Guatemalan life. We drove to a colonial cemetery in Antiqua to see the ornately carved stones, stopping on the way for drinks from a bottle of cognac. Founded in 1560, the old University of San Carlos was now a museum containing art treasures saved from buildings destroyed by earthquakes, dramatic murals, and a model room showing the method and procedure used for doctoral candidates at that time. The candidates had a very rough time, I thought, but the celebration afterwards was worth it. We also visited San Felipe, a cathedral noted for miracles. Its steeple was painted red.

Sunday afternoon our destination was Los Aposentas, a state park, where we swam in frigid water. The single changing room served both men and women, but there were individual stalls. Our picnic lunch was delicious: frijoles, tortillas, noodles, chili peppers, bananas, and *cerveza* (beer). Many Indians were relaxing, wearing only their under garments. Children up to the age of five were naked. After climbing a small hill, we visited Ciudad Vieja, founded in 1527 and destroyed in 1541 when it was covered with mud and water from the crater of a volcano. Haunting were the ruins of the Black Palace, where the governor of Guatemala, Pedro de Alvarado had lived. After he died, his widow, Beatriz de la Cueva, who called herself "*La Sin Ventura*," made certain she was elected as his successor. She thus became the only woman to govern a major American political division during Spanish times. In 1541, a few weeks after assuming office, Beatriz and her twelve maids were drowned by a sudden flood from the volcano, Agua. The dramatic story sounded to me like a good libretto for an opera.

On my last day in Guatemala I found a new key for my suitcase; visited the new University of San Carlos, modernistic in architectural design; and stopped at the local cemetery. The rich were buried in family vaults which looked liked miniature houses or they were buried in niches in the cemetery wall. Only the very poor were buried in the earth with a cross to mark their place. Within the cemetery were separate sections for British, Jewish, Chinese, the war dead, professors, and the fraternity of barbers. Some monuments were quite attractive, resembling abstract sculptures.

I treasured these remarkable ten days in Guatemala. Experiencing a culture somewhat different from what I was used to was very exciting. It had also been a new experience to feel tall. For the first time in my life I walked among many adults who were shorter than I was. At five-feet, two-inches, I am usually not able to see the tops of other people's heads. Although I hated to say goodbye to the Avilas and to Berta and Felix, my time was up. I had to be in Iowa when classes began. Because the airlines had changed the days of the week on which they flew to New Orleans, I lost my one day for class preparation and was also not able to take the train to Fayetteville to pick up my car. Instead I flew to Ft. Smith, where my friend met me in my car. After dropping him off at Fayetteville, I drove thirteen hours without stopping to Wartburg College in Iowa, where I taught my first classes of the semester the same morning I arrived.

ONE MONTH IN SOUTH AMERICA

My obsession with South America began with a fourth grade social studies project, when I lived in California. It was my secret dream to visit one day. When I learned that my husband had relatives living in Buenos Aires, I had another reason to go. In December 1962, I took our six-month old daughter to her grandparents in Chicago, then flew to Miami where I met Kurt. This was the first of many trips we would take together to explore other parts of our world.

Panama

Our Braniff flight from Miami to Panama City was delayed for seven hours. Soon after the plane took off, we encountered a frightening thunder-and-lightning storm. Despite the delay, when we arrived in Panama at 4:00 a.m., a travel agent was waiting to help us through customs. In Panama City we walked to the Balboa statue and to the President's Palace, where egrets adorned a pool in the patio. We looked in on the native market and the church of Carmen with its twin towers and took a swim in El Panama Hilton's pool. Redheaded Blanquita Amoro sang and danced that night at the Portobello Supper Club. Although our room at the Hilton was quite enormous, everything felt clammy and appeared slightly run down In the morning, we rented a car to drive across the isthmus and back. Five miles away from Panama City, we stopped at Old Panama, a city in ruins. At every church we passed, Catholic children were having first communions, the boys in light brown suits, the girls wearing long white dresses and veils.

We planned to stop at the Miraflores Locks, drive through jungle preserve, and then take a look at Colon, on the Caribbean side of the isthmus. We had seen how locks work before, but watching enormous, tourist-filled ocean liners pass through the locks created a different feeling. We thought about all the hard labor and suffering involved in the construction of these locks, which enabled ships to cross from one huge ocean to another without passing Cape Horn and the fearsome weather in that region. The jungle preserve was actually a rain-forest preserve, beautiful with tall tropical trees reaching for the sun and vines hanging from the leafy canopy to the undergrowth. The topography was also unusual. We saw undulating sand-dune-type hills and high vegetation-covered peaks on our way past thatched huts and small villages to El Valle. This resort city was entirely ringed by walls of an enormous volcanic crater. In El Valle, a procession, probably in honor of Mother's Day, celebrated December 8 in Panama, caused us to make a small detour around the band, a group carrying a statue of the Virgin, and the first- communion children.

Ecuador

In Ecuador, we stayed at the luxurious Hotel Quito. Both exterior and interior were very tasteful, but at 9,000 feet, who uses the swimming pool? Leaving immediately to see the town of Quito, we found a park crowded with Indians eating and playing cards, while someone was telling the Christmas story via flannelboard. When the sky grew dark, we headed back through cobblestone streets to the hotel, passing some quite lovely homes and others whose architecture was strikingly odd.

On our way to the Equatorial Monument the next day with a guide, we drove through many Indian villages. We stopped at a home where Indian rope shoes were made from sisal. Here we saw guinea pigs and chickens hanging around the kitchen. The Indians were very cordial, inviting us in to look around.

Standing at the official monument marking the equator, we could see the tops of two mountains where the Incas thought the equator was located. Back in the city, we were fascinated by the collection of musical instruments from all over the world housed in the Casa Cultura. La Compania church was lavishly

gold leafed, while La Merced had many pictures of miracles supposedly performed by the good lady. After walking by a huge mural near the university and the brilliant white American embassy, we were back in time for the plane to Peru.

Peru

Glimpses of Amazon basin country and huge deserts enhanced our flight from Quito to Lima, but the cloud cover obliterated all nine of Ecuador's volcanoes. Our hotel, the Gran Bolivar, was definitely the European type, complete with bidet, antique furniture, and parqueted floor. Quite cosmopolitan, Lima also has many beautiful Spanish Colonial balconies. Nights are very lively, as tea is served from 5:00 to 7:30 p.m. and dinner only begins at 9:00 p.m. Our dinner at Grill Bolivar began with pisco sours, followed by anticuchos and steak chorillones. I asked for a typical Peruvian dessert, but didn't like it much: a thick purple pudding made from purple corn, cornstarch, cinnamon stick, and dried fruit. The floor show consisting of a singer and a small orchestra was much better.

When we visited Lima Cathedral where Pizarro is buried, some men with ermine-decorated capes were holding a service including incense. At the Archbishop's Palace, the beautiful dark wooden carved balconies were being oiled and polished. On the way to Pachacamac, we saw many beaches and a shrine built in the wall over which water drips, seeking the ocean. Pachacamac ruins gave us the opportunity to walk on burial grounds where bones, skulls, hair, and fabric could easily be seen. We also visited Temple of the Moon, Temple of Pachacamac, and Temple of the Sun. The latter commanded a tremendous panoramic view of the ocean and fertile oases made so by irrigation, carried on even in the time of the Incas. Driving through the fantastically beautiful

269

residential section of San Isidro, we saw ancient olive groves. On the outskirts of the city much new housing development was visible.

Lima's art museum had a display on monuments and historical buildings that had been either mutilated or destroyed. The upper floor contained some Inca exhibits and many artifacts from the time of the vice-royalty, including ornately carved wood furniture, dresses, ornaments, and paintings from churches. We admired the fabulously large collection of silver stirrups and a few modern paintings. On our way to find Pueblo Libre, we got on the bus going the wrong direction and went through Rimac, an entire city that seemed to be a slum. Lying across the river from Lima, Rimac contained an eighteenth-century bull ring still in use in 1962. Eventually we found Pueblo Libre and with it the historical museum–a building in which both San Martin and Bolivar lived at various times. Adjacent was a fascinating archaeological museum with an entire room full of trepanned skulls. Several mummies could be seen, as well as carved and decorated stones and many vases. The museum was beautifully arranged with maps, dioramas, and replicas of Indians.

Magnificent views of the snow-covered peaks of the Andes thrilled us on our non-pressurized DC-4 flight to Cuzco, which lies at 11,340 feet, in a narrow valley between two peaks. The flight itself became fairly exciting when we were suddenly told to start using the oxygen tubes that we had been given.

Barely inside Cuzco's main cathedral, we were "guide-napped" by a young man whose English was terrible. He showed us three altars: one carved in wood and covered with gold leaf; the second, beautifully carved in natural wood; and the third in current use, all in silver. An unusual painting of the Last Supper by an Indian showed the disciples and Christ eating a typical Indian meal. Inside the adjacent monastery, we met a French-speaking priest who showed us the Cross of the Conquistadores.

Outside in the narrow streets, we marveled at the stone of twelve angles, with other stones fitted around it. In addition to stopping at several other churches, we visited a home said to be the place where Gonzalo Pizarro had lived during the occupation of Cuzco. It appeared that nothing had changed since that day.

In the afternoon we were taken to ruins of Tampumachay about five miles from Cuzco. Llamas grazed near Pucara, a red stone fortress. To escape a heavy rainstorm, we crawled into a cave that contained several benches, a table or altar, and a labyrinthine passage, close to the ruins of Sacsahuaman with its Inca throne. Nearby was sliding rock, a fifty-foot slide of stone, where Inca children supposedly played. Some of the stones were so immense we couldn't imagine how they had been moved into place without modern machines. Back in Cuzco we saw remains of the Temple of the Sun, a rounded tower in the ruins of a convent. The church and convent of Santo Domingo had been built on the walls of the Temple of the Sun and had used its stones. A 1950 earthquake destroyed much of the church and convent, but the Inca walls including the rounded tower remained. Nearby was a building said to have been a school in Inca times. Snakes were carved on the rocks forming the foundation.

Lovely tilework decorated the Archbishop's Palace. In one place, the 1950 earthquake revealed Inca temples to the moon and stars, previously unknown and hidden under a church and convent. The earthquake destroyed the more modern structure, but the Inca stonework survived intact.

The high point, however, was the visit to the ruins of Machu Picchu. We traveled in the *autocarril*, (buses with flanged wheels run on a regular train track) up over the hills surrounding Cuzco and overlooking the Urubamba River canyon. Waterfalls, snow-covered peaks, terraced fields, footbridges, llamas, moss, ferns, tunnels--the scenery on the trip was marvelous. When the train stopped, we stood in line for a space on the back of a pickup truck that climbed the zig-zagging, hair-pinned dirt road gaining 2,000 feet in elevation in five miles to reach the magnificent ruins discovered in 1911. We walked through roofless, but fascinating rooms of palaces, residences, and temples. We should have allowed more time to hike the sharp peak overlooking the ruins, but we did take a side trip on this clear, sunny day, walking along the old Inca Trail up to the pass indicated by a sort of way station and a tree. The setting in this isolated area was unbelievable and mysterious, raising many unanswered questions. Who actually had lived here? Had it been a religious retreat, a sacred city? Had it been a city where women, children, and the elderly were taken for safekeeping while the men battled attackers? Had it been the last stronghold of a clan or tribe of people? Only the foundations and walls of stone remained. Did the residents abandon Machu Picchu, traveling elsewhere. Had the weather over centuries destroyed the buildings and whatever they had contained? Why were there no artifacts found on the site? Had the city been besieged, looted, and burned? At the time we visited, there were no answers.

That evening back in Cuzco, we attended a program of native folk dance along with the Japanese ambassador and his entourage. The music, though somewhat repetitive, was played by an interesting harp and flute combination. Some of the dances showed Spanish influence, but others such as Dance of the Devils and Rope of Gold seemed to have older origins. Probably the best was Dance of the Jivaros or savages.

On our way to the performance we had noticed a red flag outside a house. In Quito, Ecuador, a red flag had meant that fresh meat was for sale. But here in Cuzco, it advertised that *chicha*, the local intoxicant, was available.

Bolivia

Riding the train from Cuzco to Puno gave us a good view of more snow-capped peaks and the vast altiplano area with its farms and herds of llamas, sheep, and cattle. Women in wool ponchos and derby hats walked near fields of grain. Whenever the train stopped, sellers of llama fur goods and knitted wool hats, gloves, and socks massed beneath the open windows, hoping to make a sale. After tedious customs at Puno and some confusion in the dark, we finally found our cabin on the S.S. Atlanta for our night crossing of Lake Titicaca. Hoping to see a sunrise on the lake we got up at 4:30 a.m., but the sky was overcast. Many birds and native fishermen poling their balsa boats created an unusual scene against a slate-colored sky, streaked with the beginnings of dawn at the horizon and dark, heavy, rain clouds hanging overhead. Snowy peaks in the background added another dramatic touch to this otherworldly view at the highest lake in the world navigable to large vessels. After several hours on the train, we arrived in La Paz, a city situated at 12,000 feet in a bowl surrounded by peaks even higher. The train snaked its way down the dry hill, resembling hills in South Dakota's badlands, to the station. At the highest and coldest levels the poorest residents lived. At the bottom of the hill, where the land is a bit more protected and the temperature is somewhat warmer, the very wealthy had built luxurious homes.

In the main plaza, we saw the Governor's Palace, protected by guards with machine guns. When we arrived at the very beautiful Church of San Francisco, a funeral had just taken place. About ten minutes later as we stood in a nearby shop, a military band followed by a truck full of funeral wreaths passed by heading for the cemetery.

The main cathedral on the Plaza Murillo was quite enormous and more European than any we had seen so far. Kurt's visit to the embassy and AID offices revealed that things were much more optimistic than our first impressions of Bolivia had led us to believe. Agrarian and social reform were taking place.

For our day trip to the *jungas* with an English-speaking guide, we hired a car to drive up from La Paz to a narrow snow- and ice-covered highway at 15,000 feet before descending east and down into semitropical and tropical ravines where coffee, bananas, and other fruit and vegetables were grown and then shipped via trucks over the wild mountain roads. The warm sun at the luxurious resort hotel where we stopped for lunch felt good as did the lower altitude and just being off the road. I was impressed by the host at the hotel, a slim, dark-haired man who looked very Spanish and wore tall leather boots. After a quick trip through the town of Corioco, we headed back over the wild road through rain and snow. Many memorial crosses lined the highway. At each curve the driver honked the horn to warn any approaching trucks. Once I was certain that only two wheels of the car were actually on the highway, as we met a truck on a curve and had to give him most of the road.

Chile

Our two-hour flight from La Paz to Arica showed us snow-covered peaks again, as well as the vast North Chilean desert area containing some very large hills, which were mostly sand. Arriving at noon, we had seven hours to wait for our flight to Santiago. While we were waiting for a bus to take us to town for lunch, one of the Lan Chile stewards asked me something in Spanish. I thought it was in connection with the bus, so I answered yes. But shortly thereafter, the steward returned, asked us to select our luggage from the pile in a locked room, took us to board a different flight, and we were on our way to Santiago almost five hours ahead of schedule. The plane was loaded with children and babies; but lunch was good, wine was served, and we were in Santiago in time to make a survey of downtown. Dinner at the Pollo Durando provided tough steak and excellent folk music and audience dancing. We consumed a whole bottle of wine, which really livened me up and put Kurt to sleep.

Everything seemed cleaner in Santiago than in other cities. After arranging for a 3:00 a.m. pickup in the morning for Puente del Inca, we hiked up Santa Lucia Mountain, essentially a city park, very beautifully arranged. Entrance to the historical museum was two cents. At the University of Chile an exhibit explained divided Germany and the Berlin Wall. On the way back to the hotel, we stopped at the central plaza, the central market and cathedral, and the Palacio Moneda. At San Cristobal, we rode the funicular to see the enormous statue of Christ on top of the hill.

Not many people were out when we stood on a street corner at 3:00 a.m. waiting for our transportation. We were relieved when an ancient British-made Ford picked us up for an exciting ride up to the Andes Mountains and the ski resort, Portillo, where we were supposed to have breakfast. We arrived at 6:00 a.m., but the hotel did not open till 7:00 a.m. An unofficial open door let us sneak in to snatch a forty-five minute nap in the billiard room. From large dining room windows we drank in a magnificent view of the lake and its surrounding peaks while eating breakfast. We held our breath the whole time the Ford drove through a one-track railroad tunnel to the other side of the mountain, hoping the driver knew the train schedule. After customs and passport checks at the border, we passed by gorgeous mountains and arrived at Puente del Inca by 10:30 a.m. Here, unexpectedly, we found a hot spring and spa and a natural bridge spanning the Aconcaqua river. After an "enforced" leisurely lunch, we tried to hike up a nearby mountain, but a strong wind came up, and stickers and thorns were quite bad.

The hotel where we planned to spend the night was federally run, and for that reason was really cheap. Also for that reason, perhaps, we had no hot water and no electricity. The lights worked only at certain hours. In the morning, we were picked up by a station wagon, which carried a French United Nations official and a psychologist and his father from Cordoba. Finally we saw Mount Aconcaqua and other fabulous peaks of the Andes. At the Argentine border, an attractive German girl easily persuaded our driver to take the alternate route via Christe Redentor, so we were able to see the statue of Christ of the Andes at 13,000 feet and participate in a hair-raising ride down and across hairpin curves, some so sharp the driver had to stop and back up in order to make the turn. The face of the psychologist sitting in the front by the outside door turned green, even though he closed his eyes and muttered prayers for our safe delivery.

In the morning, we took a bus to Valparaiso, the chief port of Chile, built on a small plain and on nineteen hills, which rise 1,000 to 1,400 feet behind it. Of course we rode the funicular from the lower part of the city to its heights for the view. We then headed for Plaza Sotomayor, the center of the city, walking through the financial section located on Calle Prat. Vina del Mar, called South America's Riviera, was our real destination. To get there, we caught a local bus at Plaza Victoria and rode to the end of the line. We hadn't realized that the resort town was ten miles away. On the way, we saw a white hearse drawn by two pairs of white horses. We got off at the beach and looked around, but didn't have much time to do anything else because the bus trip was much longer than we expected. We hurried lunch to make the 4:00 p.m. bus back to Santiago. A wild trip through the slums at the top of Valparaiso got us to the bus stop on time, but tickets were sold out until 6:00 p.m. Finally we got a sort of bootleg bus that left when it got enough passengers and picked up more on the way. We were already too late for the Lope de Vega play we had wanted to see, but we did hope to eat out, until we got off at the wrong stop and had to take the long way round to Huerfanos via a ratty bus filled with alcoholics. We had a small sandwich in the hotel and then packed.

Leaving Santiago for Puerto Montt on Kurt's birthday, we reveled in the wonderful views of snow peaks, farms, and the Chilean lakes, as it was sunny most of the way. From Puerto Montt we were driven to Puerto Varas where we spent the night. The next morning we left by steamer, crossing the beautiful lakes, each one a different shade of blue or green, ringed by steep mountains covered with a lush growth of evergreens and aspens. In the distance we could see Mount Osorno and other snow-covered volcanoes. Alternating between bus and boats as we crossed Lakes Petrohue, Todos los Santos, Puella, Puerto Blest, and Nahuel Huapi, we arrived in Bariloche, Argentina, late one afternoon. The scenery rivaled that of Switzerland, Norway and the Canadian Rockies.

Argentina

In Bariloche, we stayed at Llao Llao, a luxurious and scenic Argentine mountain resort comparable to any in the Alps. From there we hiked to the top of nearby Cerro Lopez, where the sun was warm enough to let us linger, despite a brisk wind that picked up late in the afternoon. We had only two days there before we flew to Buenos Aires.

Our relatives, whom I had never met, waited for us at the Buenos Aires airport, even though our plane was five hours late. We celebrated New Year's Eve with Uncle Emil and Aunt Irene and Aunt Balka. Uncle Emil made certain we saw the Casa Rosada; the Colon Opera House; the obelisk on Avenida Neuve de Julio; the Plaza de Mayo, surrounded by important buildings; and the white marble Congress. He knew the best places for *asado* and grilled chicken along the shore of the Rio de Plata. Some museums and buildings were closed for the holidays, but there were wonderful parks everywhere. Despite the intense midsummer heat, Uncle Emil walked everywhere with us, though he kept inquiring whether we needed to rest.

Brazil

Our last stop in South America was the incredibly beautiful city of Rio de Janeiro. We were amazed by the juxtaposition of mansions and hovels near the beach area. The beach at Copacabana was magnificent, and the sand castles built only to be washed away were ornate and impressive. The patterned pebble walkway by the beach was beautiful. Though we knew no Portuguese, we managed to purchase some slacks for Kurt using a nasalized Spanish, which apparently the salesman understood. Our free tour of Henry Stern Jewelers (unfortunately not a relative) resulted in the purchase of an unusually set dark topaz ring. We took the cog railway up Mt. Corcovado to see the enormous statue of Christ with outstretched arms and rode the cable car up Sugar Loaf (Pan de Azucar) for glorious views of Rio's unforgettable bay, dotted with tree-covered islands. This was our last glimpse of Brazil, for though our flight home made a stop in Brasilia, the capital, all we saw were the lights of the city from the air.

SOUTH OF THE BORDER

Mayan culture and pyramids drew our family of four to Yucatan in 1974. Flying to Merida, we were mesmerized by the pyramids at Chichen Itza, Uxmal, and Kabah. Fixed cables, though not absolutely necessary for climbing or descending, helped alleviate the paralyzing fear experienced by many pyramid visitors when they attempted the extremely steep, shallow steps. At one pyramid we felt claustrophobic as we ascended steps in an very low-roofed inner tunnel to see a carved leopard with emerald eyes.

When Montezuma's Revenge laid Kurt low for two days, I explored one of the local historic buildings. What a lift to the spirits when, ignoring the two children by my side, a rather attractive young man lured me, almost persuasively, to try out the hammock with him in a secluded patio. Oh, those Latins!

In Mexico City, Chapultepec Park absorbed us with its fantastic National Museum of Anthropology (overwhelming even when compared to our Smithsonian), the largest roller coaster in the world, the zoo, and museums of history and modern art. Without half trying, we learned much of Mexico's history and its numerous wars of liberation. Xochimilco Gardens were rather commercialized, but fun anyway. Cuernavaca was disappointing. It seemed to be less Mexican than other towns, too modern and American. There were too many tourist-type shops, and the Kentucky Fried Chicken restaurant on one corner of the central plaza seemed out of place. But it wasn't a total loss. Cortez's palace had been converted into a museum and contained murals by Diego Rivera, and at a huge native market, we found the oversized piñata Karen carried home on the plane. Taxco, the silver town, was charming, its setting in mountains impressive, and its cathedral gorgeously ornate. The nearby Cacahuamilpa Cave--a national park--was the most extensive and most filled with formations we had ever seen.

Though we didn't climb either snow-capped volcano, we visited Ixta-Popo park by way of a paved road to 14,000 feet. Pavement was only part of the huge contrast Kurt noticed, having visited twenty years earlier with his brother to climb to 17,000 feet, stopping short of the 18,000- foot summit. A luxurious, large stone lodge and visitor's center had replaced the shabby cabin where they'd spent the night. The wild dogs were also gone.

Early morning gave us beautiful views of the two volcanoes, but before long thick clouds obscured everything. We had to turn back anyway, even before reaching snow, because the children, especially Alan, had altitude troubles. He was very cold, he said. And when we finally paid attention to him, we saw that his face was very pale, his lips blue. He recovered once we were back at about 10,000 feet.

The beach at Acapulco was fun--delicious fresh fruit, high breakers, and inevitable sunburns. We had to watch the daring divers from the cliffs who must match their descent to the breaking surf and tides. The warm temperature of the water took me back to childhood on Southern California beaches. Each afternoon, though, brought fearful storms. Karen's Spanish was helpful; people were very friendly, and once we caught on that Mexico is the veal-eater's heaven, we ate very well. Who can forget mango ice cream? Unexpected were families swinging giant iguanas at the car in hopes of making a sale, the cleanliness and industry of the natives, and the absence of beggars. Instead dozens of children circled selling "chicle" (chewing gum) and we realized the origin of the brand name, Chiclets.

Because it was not a market or feast day, we didn't find much to see at Patzcuaro. On the other hand, the crowded boat ride on Lake Patzcuaro to Janitizio Island was a great chance to mingle with locals enjoying an outing. We saw a few of the lake's famed fishermen using their butterfly nets to catch whitefish. The nets are so delicate they have been compared to butterflies. But the most fun was on the island, ascending the spiral staircase leading to the top of the 132-foot statue of Morelos which dominates the town of Janitizio. On the walkway leading from the dock to the statue, vendors sold everything, including attractive lacquer-ware bowls and trays, paintings on vellum, and beautiful macrame belts.

Guanajuato enchanted us with its brilliantly colored homes built on the flanks of a mountain canyon. Narrow streets, overhung with balconies, were often so steep that they became stairways. Particularly attractive was the Juarez theater, with columns and balustrades. Guanajuato was also a city of parks. Because we stayed too long in Guanajuato, we could only drive as far as Irapuato that night. Although we hadn't planned to stop there, outside town on the highway to Salamanca, we found Posada de Belem. The grounds of the posada were lovely: birds singing in cages, well-trimmed shrubs, bougainvillea blooming, lemon trees, and a large swimming pool. Our room was spacious, with a dark-beamed ceiling, and it was within our price range.

Mexico City's Metro was clean and the underground shopping centers interesting, but the press of the crowds on Metro was unbelievable and scary-- worse than New York City. Archeological findings unearthed during Metro construction made a fascinating exhibit.

Don't mention driving in Mexico City. Just crossing an intersection is an extreme adventure. You'd better move fast. Those drivers do, and they are both daring and merciless. Our one misadventure occurred after a rowboat ride we took in the park. On our way back to the hotel, Kurt discovered that his wallet was missing. Gone was all our remaining cash and our tickets to the Ballet Folklorico. We'd been thinking about going home earlier than we'd planned because all the prices were higher than the latest guide books had listed, but now that became our only option.

IT'S A WILD LIFE

We planned a three-week camera safari in Kenya and Tanzania in August, escaping Washington D.C.'s dreadful heat and humidity for a refreshing seventy degrees in Nairobi. In the National Park at the edge of the city, giraffes; zebras; wildebeests (gnus); ostriches; huge Cape buffalo; and antelopes such as impala, gazelles, hartebeest, and elands share the land. With a face like an eagle wearing a quill headdress, the secretary bird attracted our cameras, but catching a good view of the gorgeous smaller birds like the little bee eater, superb starling, and black-and-white shrikes was difficult. Binoculars were critical. At the edge of the park Masai herdsmen watched their cattle graze, their red tunics splashed against the dry hillside where umbrella acacia and yellow fever acacia trees created the expected scenery we call African. Crowned plovers, vultures, marabou storks, monkeys, hippos, a rock hyrax, and just at dusk a lion eating a zebra completed our first game drive–incredible!

The minivans drove north past coffee, pineapple, and passion-fruit orchards; cloud-obscured Mount Kenya; wheat, corn, and potato fields; an occasional modern tractor; many donkey carts; and people walking everywhere. We saw goats and cattle grazing in the median strip. Stacked at intersections, many oil tins full of recently harvested potatoes were for sale.

The Samburu Reserve, on our way to Buffalo Springs Lodge, showed us two new kinds of antelope: the delicate and lovely gerenuk (giraffe antelope) and the oryx. Baboons and elephants greeted us when we opened our cabin door after lunch. Our afternoon drive found waterbuck; three young male lions; three cheetahs; vervet monkeys; helmeted guinea fowl; yellowneck spurfowl; osprey;

hornbill; and more vultures and herds of giraffe, elephants, gazelles, impalas, zebras, and Cape buffalos. We enjoyed buffet dinner in a beautiful lodge, adjoining a small swimming pool, but slept inside the mosquito netting provided for each cabin bed at this low-altitude site (3,400 feet).

We soon learned the safari rhythm: early-morning game drive, lunch and rest in any shade you can find at noon, late-afternoon game drive. The animals also slept at noon. We camped two nights in tents at El Karama Ranch, where Guy Grant, owner of the 14,000 acres, charmed us around a campfire. Born in Kenya, Guy bought the ranch thirty-three years earlier and grazes about 700 cattle amidst the approximately 3,000 protected wild animals that migrate through the area seeking grass. In the morning we hiked to a high plain filled with zebra, eland, ostrich, gazelles, baboons, and waterbuck, but when we neared, they retreated. On our way back, we found bones of giraffe, zebra, and warthog.

Although it was unlikely that any wild animals would approach the campsite, a guard kept watch all night by a campfire, just in case. Even so, on our second night, we had a very unpleasant surprise. At dusk, when we were all in the dinner tent eating, the guard left the tents for ten minutes to get his plate of food. During that brief time, someone came up from a ravine where they probably were hiding, slashed one of the tents in the back, reached in and pulled out whatever they could get, and ran off. Returning from dinner to their tent, the two teenage girls in our group discovered their suitcases containing most of their clothing, their passports, and their airline tickets were gone. Though Mr. Grant and the police came right away and tracks were found, there was no recovery. The tour guides immediately called the home office in Nairobi and arrangements were made for the passport and airline tickets to be replaced when we returned. Because she was a psychologist, the aunt of the girls, who had given the two cousins the trip as a gift, was able to help them manage their feelings of loss and vulnerability. Fortunately, she also had made a photocopy of the airline tickets which helped immensely in getting them reissued. We all felt less secure than previously, since this invasion was totally unexpected. The guides and Mr. Grant were shocked as well, claiming that nothing like this had ever happened before. Group members shared extra clothing and other items with the girls, but some things such as walking shoes (They were wearing sandals.) and even more importantly prescription asthma medicine had to be replaced in a nearby town.

On our way to the next camping site, we also stopped at the regional police station to make a formal report. The girls and their aunt were interviewed, and the police told them they would be notified if anything was found. None of us thought there was much hope of that happening. The police were not very hopeful either. Though we had the option of interrupting the trip and returning to Nairobi immediately, no one wanted to do that, not even the girls. Later when we parted, the girls said that though it had been a very disturbing experience for them, they felt it had also been good in that it brought the group closer together.

The shared traumatic experience had created stronger bonds between us. I was impressed by this mature observation and by their ability to see a positive side to the experience.

Tawny eagles, hunting jackals, a tiny antelope, the dik-dik, hyenas, and warthogs were photographed on our next drive just before we left for Nakuru National Park, stopping at the equator on the way. Besieged by friendly folks wanting to sell or trade something, we resisted, for this was the usual routine at every rest or lunch stop. These salespeople were extremely skilled at bargaining and enamored of bandanas. Once I traded a bandana for two bracelets, but usually they got the best of it, I'm sure.

Lake Nakuru's spectacular flamingos, dwindling because of pollution, still made a large part of the lake appear to be covered with pink blossoms. Cohabiting the lake, the greater and lesser flamingos feed on tilapia and blue-green algae. New sightings in this park were white rhino, boubirds, caracouls, yellow bishop bird, weavers, augur buzzard, square-tailed drongo, lark, lilac-breasted roller, fisher's lovebird, blacksmith plover, and Egyptian geese. After a late afternoon rainstorm, in front of a euphorbia forest (trees resembling segmented cacti), a spectacular double rainbow thrilled us, despite our futile search for leopards. Suddenly our guide-driver turned up a road to find two female lions, each with four cubs, who played like kittens. Who cared about leopards? The next afternoon, as we turned back for dinner, a leopard crossed the road in front of us. The sky was too dark for photos, so we watched the big cat creep through tall grass stalking a gazelle. Then as a herd of Cape buffalo crossed our road back to camp, we tried to pass, almost separating a mother and her calf. Mom whirled around, furiously coming after us, but our driver sped to safety.

On the way to Hell's Gate, where a geothermal plant supplies twenty per cent of the power needs of Kenya, we saw oranges and flowers growing near the sweet water of Lake Naivasha and learned that leafy branches lying on the road were a warning of a vehicle breakdown ahead. Our hilltop campsite caught the wind, cooling us, while in the plain far below, sixty or more Cape buffalo grunted and grazed. In the morning, we hiked along a warm river to the steam vents of Hell's Gate Gorge. Afternoon tea at Elsamere (home of Born Free's Joy Adamson) and visiting the museum holding her botanical and tribal paintings seemed extremely civilized after our days in the wilderness. Real flush toilets were welcomed by all. That night at the campsite, hyena calls echoed for a long time. In the morning we saw tracks around our campfire: genet cat, hyena, zebra, and wild dog.

Along the fertile rift valley, stands selling carrots, potatoes, onions, cabbages, and baskets lined the roadside. We munched on delicious fresh roasted ears of corn our driver bought from a roadside seller on our way to Loita plains, where we camped on Masai land and hiked through scraggly fields to see wildebeest, impala, zebra, gazelles, hunting ants, and aardvark holes, but no aardvarks. Our lunch of African vegetable stew, veggie salad, and fresh tropical fruit salad with avocado was especially tasty.

The tall, slender Masais we visited were also curious about us. After a group of children sang and were rewarded with bubble gum, a few of us sang for them. They laughed. A donation to the village allowed us to visit, take pictures, and enter a hut. Jewelry and gourds were sold and traded. Both men and women enlarge their earlobes; the beautiful women shave their heads and when married wear long beaded earrings from the top of their ears as well as handmade beaded collars and bracelets. Women also gather firewood, build and repair four-room huts made of wattle and dung, fetch water, give birth, and look after their many children. The children herd the cattle (Some attend the nearby mission school.), leaving the men, who can have as many wives as they can afford, free to carry clubs and hang out in town. Adolescent boys, the warriors (Morans), in red tunics, guard the village and liberate cattle from temporary owners, since the Masai believe all cattle in the world are Masai property. Wealth is measured by the number of cattle a person owns. Wearing red supposedly protects the Masai from wild animals. Homegrown gourds are used as containers for milk to which blood from cattle is added for more protein. Some families also graze goats and sheep, which are killed for weddings and other celebrations. We saw no furniture in the dung-covered huts. Masais sleep on animal skins and sit on the ground. Their huts generally have a central cooking area and four rooms: one for father, one for mother, one for children, and a guest room, with a small storage area where the calves are kept. Because people travel by foot over long distances, and the villages are the only place where one could sleep inside, a room is always available. We declined the invitation, preferring our tents.

That night at dinner we had our second strange and unpleasant experience. Jonathan, one of the guides, came into the dinner tent to share a joke about sacrificing a goat and drinking blood, but no one got the point. Then he starting teasing the Masai young men who had shown us around. "David, how do you like these people?" he asked. "They are different from us. They have white faces and we have dark. Do you like them?" His remarks made everyone a bit nervous, although we thought Jonathan had probably been drinking. He kept trying to snatch the bottle of brandy belonging to one member of our group. "I'm sorry for what happened," he said. "I have your shoes." We weren't sure what he meant, but Helen and Jean, who had been robbed, said that earlier in the day he told them that he knew who took their shoes. He then returned to picking on David, saying that David would perform a Masai ritual for us. Finally when there was no response from anyone, Jonathan said, "I guess I take a joke too far." But no one laughed. Although nothing further happened, his behavior made us feel very uneasy. He hardly seemed to be the same person who the previous day had led the bird walk, identified various plants, and pointed out the unusually large nest made by the hammerhead, a nondescript brown bird with a plume which makes his head resemble the shape of a hammer's head.

On the way to the Masai Mara, the Kenyan part of the Serengeti, we saw smoke from distant fires where grass burned to eliminate tsetse flies and ticks and to encourage growth of fresh grass when the "short rains" arrived in October. An ostrich courting dance was captivating, and for the first time we saw topis, antelopes with charcoal and burgundy abstract art markings. A permanent tented camp, Fig Tree, with its pool and excellent food also had hot showers.

That afternoon after seeing many wildebeests, three cheetahs, a black rhino and its baby, a huge bull elephant, and an elephant herd, we spotted two female lions. As we drove closer, the van got stuck. Keeping the lions in view, we got out and pushed. The lions never moved. Among the numerous birds was a flycatcher with a beautiful long brown tail. An intensely vibrant, deep-orange sunset ended the day. Our last day began with a truly fantastic early- morning game drive: first, three hyenas hesitated to eat because a huge group of vultures hovered over the kill. Finally, one hyena grabbed a leg and ran off to eat alone. In another spot we saw lions mating and several single male lions eating fresh kill. As we left for Nairobi we said *kwaheri* (goodbye) to velvet-eyed, long lashed giraffes and birds named longclaws.

In Nairobi the next day, we walked to the city hall, the cathedral, the mosque, and the parliament building. Most people dressed formally: men in suits, women in skirts. When the newspaper reported that a policeman had been shot at lunchtime the previous day by robbers, on the main street where we had been walking, we were glad to be back safely.

Our week in Tanzania began with a five-hour bus ride, bad roads, a hectic border crossing, and glimpses of Mt. Kilimanjaro. Dinner the first night was a romantic alfresco buffet, candles on the table, overlooking the Tarangire plain. In the morning, the closeness of elephants on the path outside our cabin door surprised us. On a game drive, we saw elephants nurse, mate, and dig for water at the stream's edge to avoid drinking the small frogs in the stream. We counted storks, baboons, love-birds, a monitor lizard, and many other birds. Lunch and a swim in the pool preceded a hellish game drive where stinging tsetse flies besieged us for too long. Gigantic baobab trees with huge trunks and leafless branches, looking more like tree roots, towered over all.

The worst roads we had led to Ngorongoro Crater rim for incredible views of an awesome expanse. Ngorongoro is the second largest crater in the world and home to all kinds of animals except giraffe and impala. We checked in at the lodge and cabins, then drove to the bottom of the crater, where crested guinea fowl, hungry for our packed lunch, gave us a chance for close-up photos. Flamingos at the great soda lake came close. Crested cranes, jackals, sandgrouse, bat-eared fox, three rhinos, and a mousebird thrilled us, as did the many hippos at the pool, egrets, and sacred ibis; lions rested at a distance. Our driver, also a mechanic, towed a stuck landrover and helped get it started, for no one wanted to spend the night in the crater.

Driving towards the Serengeti, we stopped at Olduvai gorge and its small museum for a lecture on the Leakeys' work. Louis and Mary Leakey and their children were remarkable in the large number of fossil and tool discoveries they made and for the vast amount of data they contributed to the fields of paleontology and anthropology. They are responsible for confirming that human evolution began in Africa, and for pushing back the dates for the existence of various species. Louis and Mary had first visited the Olduvai in the 1930s, but political unrest in Kenya interrupted their work. When they returned in the late 1950s the exciting discoveries began. In 1959 they discovered the oldest hominid ever found, *Australopithecus Boisei*, dating back almost two million years. In 1960, Mary and her son, Jonathan, discovered *Homo Habilis*, a separate species equally old. Continuing their work after Louis' death in 1972, Mary and her team found, in 1976, fossilized human-like footprints showing a small striding primate. This was evidence that upright walking was an older trait for hominids than either brain size expansion or modern tooth structure, leading to further questions about what had motivated upright walking. Our inspection of the five layers where excavations took place and the site where the fossils were found left us amazed at the skill the Leakeys must have had to recognize what they found. Pieces of fossils that the local curator showed us looked almost the same as ordinary rocks lying around.

Eating our lunch at the park gate attracted superb starlings, barbets, and rufous tailed weavers. Just past the gate, three lions slept very close to the road. Ostriches, spotted hyenas, hippos, African hoopoe, waxwing, and topi remained on the now dry, desert-like Serengeti; the migrators had moved north for grass. At Lobo Lodge, perched dramatically among the kopjes (rock formations), rock hyrax and baboons abounded. The swimming pool nestled in the rocks with its own waterfall.

Hyenas, many giraffes, waterbucks, a young crocodile, and a cheetah close-up enlivened our long drive to Lake Manyara, which supports quite a variety of wildlife with its lush grass and sweet water. Hippos, numerous birds, blue monkeys, banded mongooses, crested guinea fowl, and a giant forest hog kept our binoculars busy.

I worried about malarial mosquitoes, but got fewer bites in Africa than I did at home. I learned some Swahili, but used it mostly to greet our camp crew and drivers, as their English was excellent. Seeing the animal wildlife in Africa was a magnificent experience. Wildness in large cities is the same the world over. We learned this wish in Swahili: *Amani na Iwepo Duniani*--May peace prevail on earth.

IMPRESSIONS OF INDIA

Although my New Delhi friends were traveling, we used their home to store our sleeping bags and wool clothes, to recuperate from our Nepal trek, and

to reorganize. After buying two small, hard-backed suitcases, a chain, and a padlock for traveling on the train as we had been advised, we reserved two train seats for Agra leaving the next day. In Old Delhi, we were impressed by the massive Red Fort and enjoyed the monkeys loitering there.

The Taj Mahal truly deserves its fame, even though we didn't see it by moonlight. The setting of the Shah's memorial to his wife, amidst long rectangular pools surrounded by trees, creates a feeling of peace- fulness and beauty. The carved marble, the inlaid stone, and the designs mesmerize, evoking quiet meditation and wonder, despite hordes of visitors taking photos. At enormous Agra Fort, the beauty of the octagon room and audience chambers was not diminished by the numerous monkeys clambering over a prohibited area. A local bus took us to a mysterious abandoned city, Fatehpur Sikri, where wonderful marble screens formed a prophet's tomb. During our bus trip to Rajasthan, dancing bears by the side of the road competed with water buffalo, bullocks, and many camels for our attention.

On our first day in Jaipur, most stores closed to avoid problems with a student demonstration. As we strolled in a city park, wondering what we should do next, we were greeted by a young Indian man named Deepak, who asked if we could read a handwritten letter some former tourists had sent him. Deepak said he could read printed English, but had trouble with script. We were never certain whether this was the truth or a ploy. However, Deepak was very helpful, taking both of us on his motor scooter to the railway station, through crowded streets. Three on a motor scooter is quite cozy. On another strike day, when everything in

Jaipur closed again, Deepak offered to take us to the Amber Palace in his car, if we would buy gas. He also took us to the only Hindu Temple that was open. There a half-naked priest immediately welcomed us, placed necklaces of flowers over our heads, and asked for a donation. Deepak also knew a manufacturer who was open despite the strike. We fell for a silk rug, sandals, some sandalwood gifts, and a lacquered box, since prices were reasonable. No doubt Deepak received a commission for bringing us in, but we didn't begrudge it. That seemed to be the way of life in India. Someone always appeared eager to be helpful. But after a few days, we grew more wary of people who began with "Hello, I am your friend," followed quickly by "Come to my art school; please visit my uncle's shop;" or, "I want to show you something interesting." The day we had lunch at Deepak's home, we met his wife Veena and daughter Monica and watched the video taken at the couple's wedding seven years earlier. In turn we treated them to a restaurant meal the next night. I had a lesson in sari wrapping and wore one of Veena's saris to Rambagh Palace to see the view and the lovely grounds. She offered to sell it to me at a good price, because she wanted to buy a new one for an upcoming wedding. According to Deepak, I walked correctly and from the back could pass as Indian. But as he said, there was no way we palefaces could disappear in a crowd.

The hotel we stayed in had once been a palace and had Mughal portraits on the walls. The lounge area, though somewhat shabby, had heavy, ornately-carved rosewood furniture. The arms on the couch were carved in the shape of crocodiles. Amber Palace, its elephants, inlaid silver walls, exquisite marble carvings, and colored glass simulating the semi-precious stones originally used, brought the time of the Mughal rulers back to life in all its splendor In one room, two candles were lighted to show how the ceiling reflected the tiny candles a multitude of times, making it look as if we were surrounded by stars.

Rooms in the Jaipur City Palace and Museum were filled with Rajput carpets and miniature paintings. Navigating through the crush of people in the pink city, as Jaipur is called because many older buildings are that color, was work. Seeing the Jantar Mantar, an outdoor stone observatory, restored in 1901, but originally created in 1728 by Maharajah Jai Singh to study the heavens, was well worth any effort. Although the structures resemble abstract sculptures, each has a special purpose, such as measuring the positions of stars or calculating eclipses. Intrigued by the Hawa Mahal or Palace of Winds, the facade of a building where women could look out carved screens but could not be seen, I insisted we climb the ruin to the top. On the way there, we saw a man playing his oboe-like brass instrument to a cobra in a basket. We were also fascinated by the somewhat old-fashioned Central Museum in Albert Hall. Among its many treasures were miniature models depicting various aspects of Indian everyday life. Other exhibits showed examples of various customs and dress and described the use of henna to decorate women's hands and feet for special occasions. Near the museum, a totally naked man paced back and forth.

The following day as Deepak dropped us off at the train station, he was approached by a woman begging. When he offered her one rupee, she gave it back, insisting that he either give her twenty rupees or nothing–amazing nerve. He said it was her ruse, because she thought he would be too embarrassed to give her nothing, but he wasn't taken in. While waiting on the platform for the train, we were besieged by several begging children who were very aggressive and annoying, until a well-dressed Indian man shooed them away with a phrase he later taught me to use.

Considered the most romantic city in a state replete with fantastic hilltop fortresses, exotic fairy-tale palaces, Udaipur is also known as the Venice of the East. Founded in 1567 by Maharana Udai Singh, Udaipur rivals any of the world-famous creations of the Moghuls with its Rajput love of the whimsical and its superbly crafted elegance. The Lake Palace, covering all of Jagniwas island in Lake Pichola, is the best late example of this unique cultural explosion. Converted into a luxury hotel with courtyards, fountains, gardens and a swimming pool, it is the favored destination of the rich and indolent.

Although we were ready to splurge a small fortune for a room in the fabulous Lake Hotel, hoping just once to be surrounded by splendor and decadence, none were available. We had to satisfy ourselves instead with Udaipur's ornate Vishnu Temple carvings and the City Palace Museum's domes, art, and peacock mosaics, while staying in more modest lodgings. Women singing at the Vishnu Temple urged us to come to the altar. After I made the usual donation, a woman poured some holy water into my hand. Not sure it was water, I sniffed it first, but the woman demonstrated that I was to drink it from my hands, as she did. I wasn't sure that holy water was bacteria-free, so I pretended to drink it, letting it run down my face. She was very pleased, though, and then put more holy water on my hair. A thirty-minute boat ride on the lake gave us great views of the City Palace and the adjoining luxurious Shiv Nivas hotel, previously part of the palace. Sunset at the ruins of the Monsoon Palace, on a hill outside town, was followed by folk dances; in one, a woman balanced water jugs and daggers on her head while dancing on shards of glass.

At the last minute, we decided to try to see the Ellora and Ajanta caves near Aurangabad. We could only squeeze in this extra stop if a flight was available early in the day. The most the airline offered was two places on the wait list. Amazingly, we got seats and were in Aurangabad by noon. That same afternoon we took a car and driver to Ellora caves, about an hour's drive from Aurangabad. At Ellora, three different religious groups had created shrines and monasteries by carving fantastic, larger-than-life stone sculptures of their deities in 600 A.D. On our way back to town, exploring the maze-like Daulatabad Fortress, reached through an unlit tunnel, was a delightful diversion, despite the heat.

The next day, joining an Australian couple, we rode several hours to Ajanta caves for the haunting remains of exquisite cave paintings started in 200

B.C. Besides the admission fee, an optional lighting ticket could be purchased, so that as we entered an attendant would spotlight the paintings. Visitors without a lighting ticket could see very little. Because these were Buddhist temples, the paintings generally depicted scenes from Buddha's life, though many depicted everyday life from that period of time. In one there was a large procession. In another, a monkey could be seen riding a cow. A third showed a ship with many containers on it. Surprisingly, the people in the paintings had dark curly hair, unlike the straight hair most Indians have today. The colors in all the paintings were still vivid, though only fragmentary. Ceilings in the caves were decorated in a stylistic manner with lovely bird and flower motifs.

On the way back, our driver drifted off the road and into a field when the steering wheel became totally disconnected from the rest of the car. He waved down a tour bus, which grudgingly took us on. When the bus driver asked for one hundred rupees, the Australian woman thought he wanted that amount from each of us, and she said that we all refused to pay. The driver refused to drive on, and a lengthy discussion with commentary from other passengers ensued. We had a train to catch in Aurangabad. When she finally realized the amount was a total for all four of us, she allowed us to pay, and the bus moved on. We barely had time to grab a bite to eat before our overnight train to Bombay left.

Only two second-class, three-tier berths were available, in different cars. Many people crowded onto the train without tickets; passengers chained their luggage to the seats while they unsuccessfully tried to sleep amid the sound of vendors hawking food. An Indian family worried that I was traveling alone. My berth was on the top tier right under the ceiling fan. Only a partial metal grill separated me from the next top berth occupied by a gentleman who wished me a pleasant sleep. When the train stopped at one station, five men clambered onto the berth opposite me, and two perched on the end of my bunk, asking me not to reveal their presence. At the next station they jumped off.

Bombay was a city of extremes: many green parks and polluted beaches, skyscrapers and slums. Near the lovely Hanging Gardens was the excellent and beautiful Moorish style Prince of Wales Museum, where we saw a model of the Parsi Tower of Silence. In order to avoid defiling the earth, bodies of the Parsi dead are arranged in a circle on the roof of the tower, permitting vultures to clean the bones in an hour or two. When the bones are completely dry, they are placed in the center core of the tower where they disintegrate. In contrast, Hindus burn their dead and spread the ashes in a sacred river. The eldest son shows honor and respect for his father by lighting the funeral pyre.

A short boat trip from Bombay took us to Elephanta Cave, which housed many carved representations of the Hindu deity Shiva: a huge *lingam* (phallic symbol), the source of energy; Shiva dancing the cosmic dance; Shiva marrying Parvati; Shiva playing chess; killing the demon of darkness; and Shiva meditating; Shiva as one-half woman, one-half man; and Shiva with three heads: destroyer, preserver, creator. We also found one statue of Ganesh, the popular elephant God, son of Shiva and Parvati, who represents wealth and happiness. A rather plump woman carrying three brass jars on her head asked Kurt to take her picture. He thought she just wanted him to send her a copy, but after he took her picture, she asked for money for posing for him. He hadn't even intended to take a picture of her, but now he had one–for a price.

Portuguese Goa, a coastal resort town in the southwest, was tropical with excellent seafood available. On the Emerald Waters cultural cruise, a river boat went first upstream and then returned as four dancers performed traditional rice harvest, canoe, and running dances; and singers introduced us to folk songs of the area. Celebrants of St. Francis Xavier mobbed Old Goa December 3, for a festival, so we visited its ancient Catholic churches the following day.

As soon as we arrived in Goa on December 2, we tried unsuccessfully to confirm our flight to Cochin for three days later. An airline strike had cancelled all flights to Cochin until December 8. We didn't have the time to wait, so decided we'd have to skip Cochin and ride 16 hours by bus to Mysore. At the bus station, we were persuaded to buy two six-dollar tickets on a superdeluxe bus scheduled to leave the following night. In the morning, when we went to collect our refund for the cancelled flight, we learned the pilots were flying again. We could visit Cochin after all.

On December 5, we arrived at the airport at 6:00 a.m. for an 8:30 a.m. flight. After checking in, we learned departure was delayed to 11:20 a.m. We would have quite a few hours in a building with bathrooms, but with no food service. About 10:00 a.m., an official insisted that we go to a nearby hotel, have lunch, and come back at 1:30 p.m. He claimed the airplane had not yet left New Delhi. An Indian journalist going to Cochin for his grandmother's ninetieth birthday joined us for food vouchers and the drive to the hotel. Just as we three were finishing our snack, a man rushed in saying our plane was leaving in ten minutes. When no cabs or rickshaws came by the hotel, a staff person gave us a wild jeep ride to the airport. As we entered the building, we heard that the plane was departing at 12:30 p.m. Running to security, because it was then 12:30, we learned that our plane hadn't even arrived yet. When it finally landed, some very important person got off, immediately entered a waiting limousine and was driven away. We walked out on the tarmac and boarded, wondering what would happen next. Miraculously the plane took off and landed in Cochin an hour later.

The boat tour to Old Fort Cochin; the ancient synagogue and Jewish quarter; the Dutch Palace; St. Thomas Church, where Vasco de Gama was originally buried; and the Hill Palace Museum with its many fountains, thrones, and collection of various means of transportation made us quickly forget about the extra effort and anxiety we experienced to get there. Cochin, in Kerala State, gave us another view of India. It seemed less shabby and more modern than other parts of India, but this also meant more automobile traffic. About half the men wore straight skirts of various lengths. We were fascinated by the Kathikali Dance performance. In this story dance, a costumed dancer pantomimed a

287

narrative that was sung or chanted by someone else. Both performers wore very heavy makeup and vividly colored costumes and were accompanied by flute and drum.

When no direct trains from Cochin to Mysore were available, we were advised to take the Nilgri express, a steam-engine train, to the hill station, Ooty, where we could transfer to a bus. The train took us from palm trees and banana groves, past waterfalls, and through tunnels to tea plantations. From Ooty, we took a bumpy, wild, five-hour local bus ride over the mountains and through a wildlife preserve where monkeys were numerous and we once saw a family of three elephants standing by the side of the road. Arriving in Mysore, we were eager to visit its magnificent Maharajah's palace built in 1907 with incredible stained glass, inlaid marble floors, a gold howdah, and silver doors. In the ceremonial rooms, flamboyantly-colored arches were supported by wildly decorated columns. Taking a bus to Chaumundi Hill outside town to see the ornately carved temple there and a magnificent carving of Nandi, the Bull, we hiked back to our hotel in the suburbs, a former Maharajah's summer guest house, built in 1926. We noticed the traffic on the roads was very light. That night we enjoyed dinner accompanied by sitar music in the elegant dining room. Only in the morning, when we saw there were no taxis waiting for fares outside the hotel, did we learn that there had been riots in town the previous night.

The student demonstrations in Jaipur had been our first exposure to the volatile and unpredictable behavior of some groups in India. On December 5, a mosque had been burned to the ground, just as devotees were preparing to gather there. Hindus claimed the mosque had been built on a site sacred to them. By December 9, newspapers reported that about 400 people were dead, mostly rioters who had been shot by police attempting to quell any violence.

A curfew had been imposed on Mysore. No cars or taxis were allowed to cruise around looking for fares, but the hotel saw that we reached the Mysore train station in time for our train. When we reached Bangalore, we noticed many uniformed soldiers both inside and outside the station. We had planned to look around Bangalore that day, since our connecting train to Madras didn't leave until 10:30 p.m., but were officially advised that it was not safe to leave the station. While waiting there, we met a young American man who had been in India for four months and was on his way home. Stopping in Bangalore to visit Peace Corps friends, he had seen a soldier fire into a group of people because the soldier had seen a burning fire. This incident convinced the American to hurry to the station, hoping he would reach Bombay intact in time for his stateside flight. Several trains were cancelled, but our train to Madras arrived an hour early.

The Madras station did not seem to have an upper-class waiting room. People were sleeping all over the floor area when we arrived at 4:00 a.m. A notice requested passengers to vacate the white tile area from 10:00 to 11:00 a.m. so it could be cleaned. There were many soldiers around. We thought we should wait until daylight to try to go to the hotel. About 5:45 we went outside and were grabbed by an auto rickshaw driver who wanted ninety rupees to take us to the Kanchi Hotel. There the clerk was amazed that we got any transportation, since a bandh or curfew had closed everything for the day. After 6:00 a.m., no transportation was supposed to be available. No restaurants were open, but the hotel staff said we could get bread and butter and tea from room service. Around noon we went for a walk and discovered Connemara Hotel with a functioning coffee shop and a great buffet. We went back for dinner that evening. The police asked if we were looking for a telephone, the only reason anyone would be outside during the curfew. The streets were totally deserted, a phenomenon in crowded India. Many Westerners ate in the hotel's restaurant that night, and by the time we finished our dinner, activities were reaching normal levels.

After buying tickets for our forty-hour train ride to Delhi, we took a city tour in Madras to see the impressive buildings of the High Court and the bazaar. When we stopped at the Madras Beach, I rode a horse for ten rupees. Many people were digging big pits in the sand to collect fresh water. Because the temples still functioned, non-Hindus were only allowed to go into the courtyard, but many marvels could be seen even there. In addition to housing several shrines, these temple complexes in the South Indian state of Tamil Nadu are enclosed by high walls, with several gateway towers called *gopurams*. Often soaring to over 150 feet high, these pyramidal structures are totally covered with intricate carvings of gods, mythological creatures, humans, and animals. The *gopuram* at Kapaleeshwara Temple was crammed full of carved, dancing, writhing figures, vividly painted. At first, the painted *gopurams* seemed too gaudy and Disneylike, but before long they took on a surreal beauty and fascination that dazzled and intrigued our minds. A similar several-story high decorative pyramidal structure crowned the main shrine in each complex, like an echo of the breathtaking, awe-inspiring *gopurams*.

Taking the landscaped marine drive, our city-tour bus drove through some very upper-class areas of town as well as some areas that were quite wretched. Popular with everyone was the snake farm. Our last stop of the day was Volluvar Kottam, a gigantic carved stone temple chariot twelve feet high. It was a memorial to a prolific poet, Thiruvaru, whose works were all inscribed on black marble slabs. Seating 4,000 people, the auditorium at the site is the largest in Asia. We only had time to view the outside of St. Thomas Church, supposedly where "doubting Thomas" the apostle was buried.

Leaving at 6:00 a.m, the day tour to the beach temples passed by the Rajiv Gandhi Memorial on the way. At Kanchipuram, magnificent temples with extremely high *gopurams* and carved, unpainted figures enthralled every viewer. Started in the seventh century, they had later additions and improvements. The temple to Shiva was very ornate with many outside buildings and a pool. Although we were not allowed to go into the most important part of the temple, because we were not Hindus, a beckoning holy man at an altar depicting Shiva as Nataraj, the dancing god, welcomed us. He put a brass cup on our heads and a red tika on our foreheads, said a blessing in English, and asked for a donation. The carved figure of Nataraj was repeated over and over all the way to the top of the high *gopuram*. At the temple dedicated to Parvati, her statue was everywhere. The main attraction there was the gold *gopuram* in the center. Sandal salesmen hovered like flies around the visiting tourists, as did beggars. The third temple we visited was Vishnu's. Inside, a carved turtle on which there was a pedestal, represented the mythic turtle that carries the earth on its back. Even the structural supporting pillars were totally covered with many decorative and symbolic carvings. Some pillars had been made from one block of stone. Vishnu could be seen in his manifestation as a horse; as Krishna; and riding on Garuda, the mythological winged creature that serves as his transport. The side temple was extremely ornate in contrast to its *gopuram*, which was non-representational, with Vishnu shown only symbolically.

Next were the *Rathas* at Mahabalipurim. These were very old, simple temples carved out of monoliths. In addition to the temples, we admired huge carvings of a lion and an elephant. The stone sculptors seemed to let the size and shape of the stone determine the subject matter of their carving. Nearby, bas relief panels showed Krishna milking a cow, playing the flute, and holding up a mountain to save people. Many tourists lingered at the magnificent Arjuna's Penance, which included elephants, deer, two monkeys, and other lively and realistic carvings.

The shore temples were a middle stage between the early monoliths and the *gopuram* types. They were lovely temples in courtyards. After lunch we stopped at a crocodile farm where the focus was to study the effect of the egg's temperature on the gender of hatchlings. The total crocodile and iguana population in residence was 3,056. Huge numbers of marsh crocs lay around on top of each other. The final stop on our twelve-hour trip was VGP Golden Beach, an amusement park and beach resort with many statues and a magic show, in addition to the usual rides. Because most of the visitors were from various parts of India, we were quite interested in seeing what amusements appealed to them.

Before leaving for Delhi on the train, we had time for the Madras Museum. Its bronze gallery, ethnography, and stone sculpture areas were quite good. At the hotel to pack, we peeked in at a wedding reception to see the groom dressed totally in white, wearing a huge turban like a Maharajah. And there was lots of music.

Food on the long train ride was not bad and was supplemented by fellow travelers sharing the extra goodies they brought. On our last day in Delhi, we visited the beautiful tall red-sandstone and white-marble tower at Qutab Minar. There were also many beautifully carved screens and some Hindu carved figures still on the columns, but the face of every figure had been removed by Moslems who, like the Jews, do not permit lifelike representations of the sacred, considering them idolatrous. In the middle of the courtyard stood a twenty-one-foot-high iron pillar, erected in the fifth century A.D. An inscription on it

Africa

Elephant Family

Giraffes at the Acacia Tree

India

The Nilgri Express

Kapaleeshwara Temple Gopuram

Rambagh Palace

China

The Stone Forest

Near Yangshuo

Crane Releasing Pavilion

Starting up Emeishan

Hiking on Huangshan

indicates that the pillar was created elsewhere during the even earlier Gupta period. The pillar has never rusted, but no one knows why. The Bahai Temple of Peace was a very beautiful place with gardens and pools surrounding a nine-sided lotus-shaped house of worship. No columns support the structure. Next we visited Hamujan's tomb, a precursor to the Taj Mahal. From here there was a beautiful view of Chisti Tomb, but we could not visit because it was in a Moslem area that was tense. The Lodi Gardens, a huge green area with tombs and a mosque with five arches, was very decorative inside, like the Alhambra. We next stopped at Safjandan's tomb, the last one to be built. It had quite a few turrets on top and minarets, but was quite plain on the inside. Our final stop at Indira Gandhi's home, now a museum, was quite moving. Mementoes and photos tell the story of her life.

India taught us to expect the unexpected. Never have I seen such masses of people or such extreme contrasts between rich and poor, between beauty and wretchedness.

On our way home we had a three-day stay in Bangkok. Traffic and pollution were as bad as rumored. The floating market was scenically quite interesting, though there were not many sellers of hats and bananas, as had been advertised. We tried the foul-smelling Malaysian fruit, durian, reputed to have a wondrous flavor, despite its odor. We found both smell and taste revolting. I enjoyed a Thai cultural dance and dinner evening, although Kurt felt it was not as intricate or exciting as the one he saw when he visited twenty-five years earlier. We were both overwhelmed by the very large reclining Buddha with mother of pearl inlay on his toes and the soles of his feet. The standing Golden Buddha was modern, but very impressive. Quite attractive with a ceiling and wall of red and gold, the Marble Monastery was also unusual. Carved demons on the windows protected the inside of the building. The Grand Palace/Emerald Buddha complex, practically the symbol of Thailand and Bangkok, was extraordinary; it was both beautiful and exotic with its brilliant, glazed ceramic roofs and upward curving eaves. The huge, grimacing, and almost frightening carved Chinese guardian statues came as ballast when Thai ships returned from China, having taken rice and teak and bringing back silk and tea. The Emerald Buddha, who has several costumes, was wearing his winter gold mesh cloak. People in shorts or other inappropriate clothing were refused entrance to the temple complex. However, for the convenience of visitors, a shop across the street rented slacks and long skirts. No one's feet were to point directly toward the front of the temple. They had to be on the diagonal.

Our last stop was the Vimanmek museum, housed in the largest teak wood building in the world. Built in 1901, it had served as King Rama V's Palace. He preferred Vimanmek to the Grand Palace, claiming it was cooler in summer and a healthier place to live. The inauguration of the mansion in 1901 was held in combination with the top-knot cutting rites for five young members of royalty. Topknots used to be the style for children's hair. When a boy was 13 and a girl 11, a tonsure ceremony was held at which the topknot was cut off, symbolizing the end of childhood.

Hostesses and hosts stationed in the thirty furnished rooms that were shown told visitors how each room had been decorated and used during the time the Royal family lived there. Rama V (King Chulalongkorn), who lived from 1868 to 1910, had been very impressed by Western methods of law and education. He reformed the legal system of Siam as the country was then known, and introduced state education for the masses. Previously education had been the privilege of the rich or available only through monasteries. Although Siam's first king took over in 1238, the city of Bangkok came into existence only in 1782, when it was founded by Rama I, the first King of the present Chakri dynasty. A bloodless coup in 1932 replaced Siam's ancient absolute monarchy, and in 1938 the country's name was changed from Siam to Thailand.

TEN DAYS IN JAPAN

Because it was already cool in Australia, I wore wool slacks and a turtleneck when we flew from Melbourne to Kyoto, Japan, for the fortieth meeting of the International Society of Electrochemistry. Traveling on official business, Kurt had to fly on a United States airline. I saved money by using Singapore Airlines (highly recommended), but I had a twelve-hour layover between planes in Changi Airport in Singapore. The airport was beautiful, with a tall indoor waterfall, free tourist films in an auditorium, and many interesting exhibits. ut the heat and humidity were intense. With no access to the lightweight clothes I'd packed, I looked for something cheap to buy at the gift and souvenir shop. The cotton dress I found for fifteen dollars resembled what the stewardesses on the airlines wore. I didn't care. I had to have something cool, even if it looked a little odd with sneakers instead of sandals. Just before the plane left for Kyoto, a steward stopped at my seat and asked, "Are you serving the drinks tonight?" I smiled and said, "No, it's my night off." I've worn the dress many times since, in Maryland summer heat.

After meeting at our hotel, we didn't even unpack, but used the rest of the afternoon to visit the Higashi-Honganji Buddhist Temple, a very impressive wood building with typical upward curving eaves. In addition to the shrines for various Buddhas, the temple also housed important national treasures.

Our hotel offered two styles of breakfast. Most European and American tourists tried the Japanese breakfast of rice, tossed salad, tofu, soup, pickled cabbage, fish and rolls, and a hardboiled egg marinated in soy sauce. Japanese businessmen all chose eggs, bacon or ham, orange juice, and toast. Kimonos and slippers were provided for each guest at this businessman's hotel, creating a sense of luxury. Our private bathroom, however, was so compact we joked that guests could take a shower, brush their teeth, and use the toilet simultaneously.

Sanjusangendo Temple, our first stop after breakfast, housed 1,001 golden goddesses or boddhisatvas, some with wings, all with halos. The god of thunder, god of the wind, and a group including an underworld figure and two demons were overpowering. Most of the tourists were Japanese. Across the street, the National Museum showed archaeological finds, ceramics, decorative screens, kimonos, tea sets, beautiful bowls, netsukes, musical instruments used in rituals, and sculptures. One sculptural group depicted five scholars or writers who were life-size. Each had a wild and distinctive facial expression.

On our way to the Kiyomizu temple, the street was filled with shops, a pagoda, and an interesting complex of buildings, through which we wandered. Merchants offered free tea to lure prospective buyers inside shops, where little machines made candy or a sweet pancake with a Japanese character branded on it. On the bus going to the Heian shrine, each street and important tourist attraction was announced in both Japanese and English. The buses were very efficient. Passengers entered at the back, picking up a ticket from the machine. As they left by the front and the driver, they paid their fare, based on the ticket they held.

The green glazed tile roofs on reddish-orange buildings and the huge, red entry gate of the Heian Shrine dazzled us, but the site was being repaired, so we couldn't enter. The gardens, however, were quite lovely with pathways and rock stepping-stones to islands where one could meditate amidst the propped up limbs of ancient pine trees. Little arched foot bridges and waterfowl enjoying the pools created a picturesque and typical Japanese view.

Nijo Castle was another incredible place, one of the Shogun's homes. Fearing personal attack, the Shogun had commissioned the nightingale floor to be constructed. Every step made a creaking sound, like a bird chirping, which warned of anyone's approach. In one room, an audience scene with life-sized models had been re-created. Rooms had walls of gold leaf with tatami mats on the floor, but there was no furniture. The castle was surrounded by a double moat.

While Kurt attended meetings, I visited other temples in Kyoto. Eikando, like many other monasteries, had a series of small temples along the path to the primary one. It also had a covered walkway up the hillside to a little shrine. Incense was always burning. In the main shrine, the Buddha was looking over his shoulder, a rather touching and different view from the usual straight-on placement of his head. Small colorful gardens decorated the lower part of the hill.

The ceilings at Nansenji temple were painted with graceful maidens and phoenixes. In the main temple, the gorgeous sliding screens were decorated with gold leaf and painted with green bamboos partially hiding a ferocious tiger. Windows opened to special views. Through one I saw a small, peaceful waterfall. Through another, a piece of bamboo repeatedly sent a single drop of water into a waiting saucer as a little statue watched amidst greenery. Many Japanese maple trees, their leaves still green, surrounded the area.

Along the canal, I followed the philosopher's walk to Ginkakuji, the silver pavilion, to see the two famous raked stone arrangements. One of these represented the sea of China, the other Mt. Fuji. Several times a day monks tend these sites, using wooden-toothed rakes to create perfect wave patterns in the stones. The pavilion itself and the main shrine are off limits to the public because national treasures are inside. But who is to know if this is true, if no one is allowed inside to see them?

At Ryoanji Monastery, everyone lined up to meditate on the fifteen rocks arranged in a bed of raked white stones. For some people, the scene looked like islands in the sea. To others it resembled a sea of clouds with mountain tops poking through. Some saw the rocks as shapes of various animals seeking zen; others saw Buddha and his attendants. Whatever the interpretation, the arrangement invoked some sort of meditation.

Though Buddhism is a primary religion in Japan, the older Shinto religion continues to co-exist. Shinto derives from nature and ancestor worship and is not written down. Its deities include mythological ones such as the sun goddess; historical personages; and natural objects such as rocks, old trees, and mountains. A Shinto service was part of a tour connected with Kurt's conference. The service began with low chanting, then a flute and drum were played. A branch of a tree was offered to an invisible deity. There was quite a bit of rising and sitting. Two girls in white and vermillion danced with bells and branches. Long sticks with festoons of paper were shaken to purify the room and the people attending. Children are taken to a Shinto shrine at ages three, five, and seven, auspicious times for parents to pray for the continued growth and good health of the child.

We next participated in a tea ceremony. The host used a bamboo brush to whisk the powder with a small amount of water to create the frothy, foaming, green tea. Because this type of tea is bitter, it was served with a sweet cake. The rules for the ceremony were described in detail. Participants sit in a circle and drink tea one after another. When it is your turn to drink tea, you are to say to the person on the right, "It is an honor to drink tea with you." To the person on the left you say, "May I drink tea before you." Then you are to look ahead and say, "I drink with respect." The bowl should be turned so that its back faces you to show your humility. You are then to drink in three gulps, making a slurping sound to get every last bit. Next, you should wipe the edge with two fingers and turn the bowl so the best part faces you. It should be placed on the tatami mat, and you are then to admire the bowl. This was considered an informal tea ceremony. The formal tea ceremony lasts four hours and starts with arranging the charcoal, admiring the arranged charcoal, and preparing all the utensils to be used in the process.

Observing women doing four different kinds of Ikenoba flower arrangement included hearing the rules that governed this art form. We also visited a factory where we had a chance to paint a handkerchief with a design, using a stencil. Another fascinating part of the day tour was seeing women weave silk, using only their long fingernails to pull the threads. Our last stop was the Imperial Palace and Kinkakuji, the Golden Rooster pavilion. In an exquisite setting on an island in a large lake, a golden pavilion with a rooster on the very top is admired by all.

That evening we sampled another kind of Japanese cuisine. The evening began with a short performance–two dances by two Maikos (Geisha trainees) at Gion Corner. The kyori ori style meal focused on having everything, including bamboo shoots, artistically arranged in lacquered dishes. For most foreign guests, there was not much "real" food to be eaten. After dinner we visited a sixteenth-century historic building in the famed courtesan area of town. A geisha, her face covered with white makeup and a tiny rosebud mouth painted on her lips, was attended by a servant and two young children. She performed a ritual welcoming of the guests and then demonstrated her skill at performing the tea ceremony. Some women sang and played kotos. After the applause died down, the geisha walked slowly on very high clogs in a procession through the audience before saying, "Okimi," a Kyoto dialect word for "thank you."

In nearby Nara, we visited the sacred deer, the giant Buddha, and Kasuga Shinto Shrine's hundreds of iron lanterns. We took the train to Osaka to see its impressive double-moated castle and the red, steeply-arched moon bridges over waterways. In the train station, when we changed trains, not only did a Japanese man offer to help us, but he also walked us to the place where we should wait, going considerably out of his way to do so.

At a Shinto shrine, we started to leave when we noticed a pregnant woman and a family with a baby conversing with a priest, as we thought they would prefer privacy. The baby's father, however, came running out to the vestibule and through sign language made it clear that he would like us to join them, as long as we took our shoes off. Perhaps he thought our presence would bring good fortune. The ceremony involved chanting, some dancing, and the shaking of festooned sticks for purification. Blessings were then given to the baby and to the expectant mother.

On the next to last day, we took a bus out to the mountains, partly for the scenery, which was exquisite, and partly to see what Japanese do on weekends. Many families go to the woods and rivers to have picnics, just as families do everywhere. Some monks stood near the river chanting, beating a drum, and accepting donations.

The best was Kyoto itself, surrounded by mountains, with 1,600 shrines and temples and lovely Nijo Castle. The abundant conference banquet concluded with excellent performances of dancers and musicians. We visited many of the city's shrines, often set in the hills, always containing rock gardens carefully tended by monks. Whether it's the combination of lush woods, rocks and water, the aesthetic arrangement of objects of nature, or simply the elimination of

295

extraneous distractions, a strong sense of tranquility pervades these places, reaching even the westerners who visit. Beauty was everywhere.

To keep costs down we ate mostly tasty and filling noodle dishes. One hundred grams of beef cost as much as a kilo of beef in Australia. Hot coffee was three dollars in a coffee shop, but iced coffee was available for one dollar from vending machines.

People were very friendly and helpful, and though there wasn't much English around, we could manage. Most younger people wear Western clothes, but the old ways are maintained. Ten days was just enough to whet our appetites for a longer revisit.

COPING IN CHINA

For many years, we had dreamed of visiting China, entranced by the beauty of the scenery depicted on scrolls in museums, by the ancient culture and civilization, and by the uniqueness of the Great Wall. Our interest was further piqued when the terra cotta warriors buried near Xian were discovered. But when we heard that the dam being built on the Yangtze River would change or destroy the scenery of the famed Three Gorges, we had to go at once, before the dam was completed.

We considered taking a package tour, but the offered itineraries never included all the places we wanted to see, and none of them would have allowed us to hike the three sacred mountains that had captivated our interest when we read about them. We also wished to travel less like Western tourists who generally stay in superior class hotels and are somewhat protected and insulated by being in a group with a guide. We prefer totally independent travel, but having heard that getting train and plane tickets on the spur of the moment in China was almost impossible, even if one speaks Chinese, we decided to compromise and use a travel agent to make basic arrangements as our son, Alan, had for his trip to China.

While planning our trip for October 2000, we relied on Alan's experience. Having a long-standing interest in Asia and its cultures, he was well informed about China's geography and history and had studied Chinese prior to his three-week visit in 1998. In three cities he was met by pen-pals or relatives of his friends, but he had planned his own itinerary and used a travel agent only to pre-arrange internal train and plane tickets, transfers, and hotel rooms. Starting with Alan's recommendations of places he had visited and others he didn't have time for, we added a few additional stops at places we had heard of or read about. Allowing for travel time, we saw that we would need thirty-eight days in China just for what we considered basic. We'd already made some hard choices   in order to make the trip affordable.

Kurt and I both took beginning courses in Chinese. Kurt's class, conversational Chinese, focused on what a tourist might need, and it covered material very quickly. In contrast, my class included recognizing and writing the Chinese characters and moved more slowly. Learning to hear and then reproduce the four different tones in Chinese involved a great deal of repetition. Very few Chinese words have any connection to English so building a working vocabulary relied heavily on being able to memorize and remember words. To help myself I made up personal hints. For example, the Chinese word *bu* is a negative. It sounds somewhat like the English expression of disapproval, *boo*. The Chinese word *cesuo* (toilet) begins with the same sound as the word *cesspool*. But Kurt felt some of my elaborate memory aids were harder to remember than the words themselves.

At first I felt very uncomfortable being able only to imitate the teacher's words and phrases, as if I were a toddler learning to talk, but after a while, I could respond to simple questions in Chinese using the correct tone and inflection. Though writing Chinese characters was not a skill I needed for the trip, the physical process itself reinforced the visual and mental recognition of the characters. It was very thrilling to write an entire sentence in Chinese, an ancient language that I had always assumed was so difficult I could never learn any of it. When a Chinese film with English subtitles was shown locally, we could recognize a few spoken words, but not enough of them to do us much good. We had a long way to go. After our classes ended, I borrowed language tapes from the library, bought a Chinese workbook called *Chinese in Ten Minutes a Day*, and tried to spend time studying Chinese every day.

Because the standard Chinese tourist visa allows a maximum stay of only thirty days, we thought we might have a problem getting a visa for thirty-eight days. A longer stay is permitted for tour groups, if the applicants present a letter of invitation with a stamp of approval from the provincial authority in China, but we were not going on a tour. Hima, our travel agent from Asian-Pacific Adventures, a company based in California, arranged for her contact in China to fax us such a letter.

With the faxed letter, which invited our tour group (consisting of two people), a completed visa application, and sixty dollars each, we stood in a long line at the Chinese Visa Office in Washington D.C. to submit our request. Calling two people a tour group seemed suspect to me, and the fax we received was almost illegible. But Hima assured me that her contact had an excellent rate of success in getting these extended visas. She, nevertheless, allowed us to postpone payment until we had our visas in hand, recognizing my reluctance to purchase airline tickets before I knew the approved length of my stay. As Hima predicted, we had no problems, and our passports returned with visas good for sixty days.

From Beijing, our first stop, we planned to take a train south to Ji'nan our base for visiting Qufu, the home of Confucius, and Taishan, a holy mountain. Next we would fly southwest to Xi'an and Chengdu. After spending a night on

CHINA

Emeishan, a holy mountain near Chengdu, we would go farther south to Shilin (Stone Forest) near Kunming. From Kunming, our most westerly city, we would fly northeast to Guilin where we would take a half-day boat trip on the Li River to Yangshuo. We next would fly to Chongqing to begin our three-day cruise on the Yangtze river. From Wuhan, where we would disembark, we would fly to Tunxi for a two-day hike on Huangshan (Yellow Mountain). A five-hour drive to the east would bring us to Hangzhou on the coast. From Hangzhou we would take the train to Nanjing, to Suzhou, famous for its gardens, and finally to Shanghai, the city from which we would fly home. We skipped Hong Kong, since Kurt had seen it before, and we already had a very long list of fabulous places to visit.

At each destination, we were met by a local English-speaking person who held a card with our name on it for identification. He or she was responsible for taking us to the hotel, giving us our plane or train tickets for the next destination, and for taking us to the airport or railway station for departure. All of these "greeters" were very congenial, and though they weren't required to do so, many of them were eager to share their knowledge about the city we were about to visit. The "greeters" were always accompanied by a driver who had a car, and who rarely spoke any English.

298

In addition, Hima had sent us a list of contact persons and phone numbers in China, should any problems arise. We were very impressed by the fact that someone always met us, the tickets had always been purchased, and we were invariably picked up on time. We had learned of Hima from our son, who had been very pleased with the arrangements she made for him, and we, too, were amazed and more than satisfied by the quality of service she provided.

Usually we explored cities on our own, after being dropped off at our hotels, but four times we had guides who stayed with us for the entire day, giving us much additional information. In Beijing, Lulu took us to the Great Wall and the Ming Tombs. Max was with us for two days in Qufu and Ti'an. In Xian, Michelle showed us the terra cotta warriors and the Banpo Neolithic Village, and in Kunming, Stacey took us through the Stone Forest and the Sani Village. Another guide, Little Lee, took us to see the great Buddha at Leshan, after our independent hike up the holy mountain Emeishan.

We had given Hima a list of the places we wanted to visit and told her that where possible we'd prefer to be on our own. As the trip progressed, we were left more and more to our own devices. By the time we reached Shanghai, no one needed to meet us, we found our hotel by ourselves, and we took a taxi to the airport for the flight home.

Because Alan's flight to China had been via Vancouver, British Columbia, I assumed that we would be leaving from there or from Seattle. Departing from the west coast would also give us a chance to visit relatives in Seattle, to attend a class reunion at Pacific Lutheran University near Tacoma, and to visit several close friends who were skipping the class reunion. We used frequent-flyer miles to Seattle which I thought would decrease our total airfare. I e-mailed Hima that we could leave from Seattle or Vancouver on October 8. When our tickets arrived, I was surprised to see that instead of going directly to China from Seattle or Vancouver, we had to fly south to San Francisco and then change planes. Perhaps the San Francisco-Beijing flight was a bargain fare.

We left the reunion party in Tacoma early because we had a 7:00 a.m. flight to San Francisco, but we still weren't in our motel near the Sea-Tac airport until after 10:00 p.m. Trying to set our alarm clock, I noticed the battery had died–a bad omen, I thought. But when I found the right battery in a convenience store within walking distance, I felt less apprehensive.

Our domestic flight was on time, so Kurt and I had no problems making the international flight connection. Then, just as all of us settled into our assigned seats, the pilot announced that passengers could deplane if they wished, because a fuel-loading problem would delay departure for at least an hour and a half. We didn't bother getting off, but became concerned when the plane didn't move even after the fuel problem was finally solved. Then we learned that two passengers had deplaned permanently, and their baggage still had to be removed. These delays, especially the last one, revived my anxieties about bad omens. We were now two hours late, before we had even started. Once we were airborne, however, all the problems evaporated.

Arriving in Beijing, we moved easily through baggage claim and customs and were pleased to see a young man holding a sign with our name on it. Steve, our "greeter," who had been patiently waiting for three hours, led us to the car and its driver. On the hour-long drive to the city, we saw many bicyclists on the road and some shack-like homes beside it. Before long, however, many beautiful lights and skyscrapers in the downtown area convinced us that we had arrived in a major metropolis. Because we went to bed right after checking in, we woke early in the morning, well rested after our long flight, despite my weird dream about going back to the U.S. or being there and suddenly realizing we'd gone back and were missing our whole trip. I was very happy to wake up in Beijing.

Our hotel, quite modern, attractive, and conveniently located, served an extensive breakfast buffet offering both western and eastern favorites. Steamed buns, sesame cakes, cream of rice cereal, vegetable and jello salads, pickles, peanuts, spinach, sticky rice wrapped in bamboo leaves, almond cookies, fruit compote, tofu, and soy milk were some of the Asian breakfast choices.

Now totally on our own, we headed towards the nearby Forbidden City and Tiananmen Square. As we walked by a park, we noticed a group of women who were all wearing light green pajamas, holding red scarves, and performing a graceful dance routine. Later we realized they were actually doing their morning exercises, a popular activity in China.

Luckily, when we arrived, only a few other tourists were exploring the Forbidden City. Home of emperors from both Ming and Qing dynasties, this palace complex was originally laid out between 1406 and 1420, but the wooden buildings we saw had been rebuilt in the late eighteenth century, after frequent fires. The intricately carved, arched marble bridges leading to the main entry were a favorite site for taking photos. Seeing the huge imperial courtyard empty was a momentary shock. We had last seen the courtyard filled with warriors and thousands of people prostrating themselves in the movie *The Last Emperor*. We marveled at the bronze incense burners, their shapes suggesting animal forms. I was also fascinated by the queue of carved mythical animal figures that lined each slanting edge of the roof to prevent the entrance of evil spirits. We learned that the number of animal guardians in such queues was directly related to the importance of the person being protected. Here, because the emperor was being guarded, there were nine figures, nine being a sacred or magical number. We never found more than nine animals on any roof.

More and more arriving tourists wandered about peering into richly decorated throne rooms and shrines or visiting special exhibits on ceramics and bronze creations. A ferocious-looking pair of golden imperial lions was especially interesting. The female lion held a lion cub under her paw while the male lion held down a ball (perhaps symbolizing the globe). Although I'd seen similar lions in front of many Chinese restaurants at home, I had never noticed the sex distinction before.

Another unusual sight was a woman wearing white gloves and a surgical mask as she swept an area in the courtyard. Perhaps her attire offered some protection from the pollution in Beijing and the blowing sand from the Gobi desert. Two symbols of imperial justice, a bronze grain measure and a sundial, also drew our attention. The huge bronze turtle in front of the Hall of Supreme Harmony was actually a *bixi*, the offspring of the dragon, and it symbolized the stability and longevity of the emperor's reign. A removable lid allowed incense to be burned inside, causing smoke to come out through the *bixi*'s mouth. The imperial garden at the northern end of the enclosure was our first classical Chinese garden with rockeries. These grotesquely-shaped, water-eroded rocks, resembling abstract sculptures, captured our interest as we followed interweaving walkways to quiet pavilions.

Crossing the street to Jingshan Park, we hiked up the tall, artificial hill made from the earth excavated when the palace moat was created. Following the path which wound around and up the hill through cave-like rock formations, we were glad to rest when we reached the pavilion perched on top. The pavilion, housing a large Buddha, also provided a great view down into the Forbidden City.

In the park, a young woman guiding three older Chinese ladies who spoke only Chinese, practiced her English by greeting us. I practiced my Chinese by responding that I was happy to meet them. Surprised and pleased to hear me speak Chinese, the older ladies immediately asked how old we were. I was glad that I'd learned Chinese numbers.

Nearby was Beihai or North Lake Park, a huge area containing many gardens, artificial hills, pavilions, halls, temples, and covered walkways. Most interesting of the nine admonitions to visitors posted at the entrance was the seventh: "Decadent songs and behaviors that go against decency are forbidden here." Several young boys following a monk and a very old guru, rushed over to Kurt, waving their cameras and pointing. We finally figured out that they wanted to stand next to Kurt while a friend took a photograph of them. Groups of primary school children on outings with their teachers never failed to say "hello," practicing the English they knew. They were quite surprised and delighted when I always responded with *"Ni hao ma."*

At the top of the White Dagoba (a dome-shaped Buddhist monument usually containing liturgical objects or writings) was a green Buddha. Built for a visit of the Dalai Lama in 1651, the Dagoba's resemblance to stupas we saw in Nepal was not surprising.

Farther down the hillside was Falun Hall, a monastery where larger-than-life statues of the four guardian kings stood, two on each side of the entryway. They were an integral part of many of the shrines and monasteries we visited in China. Representing the kings of the North, South, East, and West, each had a different skin color: white, blue, red, and black. In the main temple we saw three blue-haired Buddhas representing the past, present, and future. Many Chinese people offered incense and prayers to these Buddhas. Across a small bridge we had a snack in Round City, where we marveled at the artistry of the white jade Buddha and an enormous jade bowl supposedly dating from around 1250 – the time of Kublai Khan. In another part of the park, we found the very impressive Nine Dragon Screen, fifteen feet high and seventy-one feet long. Made of ceramic tile, it is one of three such screens that are famous in China.

As we walked to the Lama Temple through narrow streets, we noticed that cars parked on the sidewalk, legally, forcing pedestrians to pick their way around them. The facades of buildings had been made presentable, but looking down alleyways, I saw some very filthy living quarters. Almost all the public toilets were clean, but were the Asian type. Each stall contained a ceramic block on the floor with a center hole and a slightly raised footprint on either side of the hole indicating where the user should stand or squat. Later we learned that a western style toilet with a seat was always provided for handicapped users.

Because the Lamasery was closing when we arrived, we headed back to our hotel, observing the many bicycles, the wild drivers, the masses of people, and the businesses and homes along the way. In addition to traffic lights at intersections, a traffic guard with a flag attempted to control the bicycle traffic. There was only one good method for crossing the street: look both ways and go; do not hesitate; don't even think about changing your mind; dodge and weave when necessary. Automobile drivers were very skilled, but they were also very daring, as were the experienced bicyclists and pedestrians.

There may be many rules in China, but people seemed to delight in ignoring them. To own a pet, for example, a license is required, but we learned that many people don't bother, hoping they won't be caught and fined. All-pedestrian areas, upscale malls near gray, old-style housing, outrageously high platform shoes, mini skirts, McDonald's, KFC, Pizza Hut, and an abundance of cell phones were all evidence of China's swift progress towards capitalism–at least in the city. Generally people were very well dressed, and we saw fewer beggars and panhandlers than we usually see in Washington D.C.

To avoid huge crowds and vendors, we visited the Great Wall at Mutianyu instead of at Badaling. Our guide for the day, Lulu, was a tall, pleasant young woman of Manchu descent, who told us that she was twenty-five years old and had married just three months ago. After an ninety-minute drive, we reached the impressive site. Beijing was situated in a basin, surrounded by low hills, so we were astonished at the many steep, craggy, hills in this area. A chairlift and a cable car had been constructed to help everyone reach the top of the wall. Because it was early, we had the wall almost to ourselves and could easily walk back and forth on it, in addition to examining the construction of the watch towers. I also wanted to walk to the spot where the wall had not been reconstructed, but that round-trip would have taken several hours, an amount of time we did not have.

The Great Wall crosses northern China from the east coast and continues for about four thousand miles to the center of the country. During the Qin dynasty (221-207 B.C.) when China was united by Qin Shihuang, the various fortification walls built by various warring states for self-protection were connected to fend off barbarians. Qin ordered that the wall be six horses wide at the top and eight horses wide at the bottom and that it should be five men high. The outer wall is slightly higher than the wall closest to Beijing, but the wide "highway" filling the space between the two walls is level from side to side. Built entirely by hand using soil, stone, and bricks, depending on what was available locally, the wall averages twenty-four feet high and eighteen feet wide. Over a million people were conscripted to work on the wall, and it is said that the bodies of those who died were thrown in with the dirt and rubble to create the highway. The wall was rebuilt and extended during and up to the Ming dynasty. In some sections the wall is crenelated, having towers and fort-like structures to protect those who were watching or shooting arrows through narrow slots in the towers. The wall often meanders, creating a serpentine path, in order to take advantage of the natural landscape. It usually rides the ridge of high peaks, but at other times it closes off a pass between two ridges, creating a continuous barrier against invaders. Although the wall was never effective in keeping out the Mongols, its enormity and the stories surrounding its construction make it one of the wonders of the world. The Great Wall is the only man-made structure on the earth's surface that is visible from the moon. No longer continuous, it has been assiduously restored in several sections, primarily to serve as a tourist attraction.

On our way to the Ming tombs at the outskirts of Beijing, we drove through a mountainous area and then through villages where soybeans were being harvested. The Friendship Restaurant, a standard tour stop for both western and Chinese tours, offered samples of many Chinese dishes for lunch. In an adjoining shop, workers with agile fingers demonstrated the process of making cloisonne. Browsing in the gift shop was encouraged, but there were no high-pressure salespersons.

Paired guardians of carved stone stood on either side of the Sacred Way to the Ming Tombs. Some of the twelve sets of animals were realistic, some mythical. One pair stood, while the next pair knelt. The mythical creatures with wings, outsized claws, and unexpected body parts from various animals were followed by twelve sets of larger-than-life warriors and civil servants. At the Ming Tombs, where thirteen of the sixteen Ming emperors have been buried, tourists actually descend stairs into an excavated tomb. After passing the coffin boxes and small boxes for jewelry, we reached the coffins. In front of the coffins were three Ming vases and three thrones: one for the emperor and one each for his two empresses. On a table in front of each throne were candles, along with several symbolic items.

Emerging from the tomb, we stopped at the museum containing photographs, artifacts, and details about the archaeological excavation. In an adjacent building, a "free" health assessment was offered, along with a demonstration of Chinese health methods--acupuncture, massage, and qigong. Qigong resembles faith healing in that practitioners try to project their *qi* (life's vital energy) to perform miracles. When trying to help a patient, the hands of the practitioner are held slightly above or next to the patient's body, without touching it. Some patients claim to have been cured of their disease through this method.

Doctors wearing white coats pointed to wall charts during their interesting lectures delivered in heavily accented English. Even the strange electricity demo was fun, giving us a definite buzz, but the free health assessment soon became a high- pressure pitch to sell various pills. Kurt was warned that he had to balance the yin and yang of his kidneys. For only $50 a month for three months, some black pills made from special herbs would help him. I was told that I had a weak liver function and too much heat and that I needed to regulate my metabolism. I also had a weak heart function, an irregular beat, and stringiness of the blood. My blood was too thick for my veins or arteries and had liver fat on the walls. Until I heard this diagnosis, I had been feeling fine. All these problems were found by a "doctor" holding my hands. I needed two medicines and would have to take them for three months. When I said no thanks, two doctors replied, almost in unison: "Take them for only one month, and we promise all speckles and wrinkles will disappear."

The whole procedure became very unpleasant, as the doctors almost threatened me with dire consequences because I did not buy anything. When Kurt complained to Lulu that he found the Health Assessment visit unpleasant and that such visits would definitely leave tourists with a bad impression of China, she claimed this was the first time she had stopped there and that she was shocked at the behavior of the "doctors." Probably feeling a bit guilty about this, she went out of her way to give us helpful hints for the rest of our stay in Beijing when we would not have a guide.

To save time the next morning, instead of walking or trying to figure out the bus system, we took a taxi to the Summer Palace, a complex of temples, royal reception rooms, residences, and strolling areas constructed in the eighteenth century at the edge of the large Kunming Lake. In order to reach the top of the main pagoda there, we had to climb many steep steps, but the view over the lake and the rest of the buildings was superb. We could see pagodas on distant hills, marking other important places. As we started to enter one pavilion, we heard an old man singing, accompanied by a stringed instrument. The Painted Corridor, essentially a covered walkway, continued for almost half a mile, with scenes painted on the ceiling, on supporting beams, and on the upper part of the walls. Many people had come to picnic, enjoy the day, and visit with friends. One of the principal attractions, the marble boat, had been restored in 1888 by the Empress Cixi, using money supposedly reserved for the construction of a modern navy. Very beautiful with inlaid semi-precious stones and stained glass, the structure is totally useless, except for providing a unique dining room at the lakeside. From the deck of the dragon-boat that we took back to our starting place, we could admire the bridge with seventeen arches which spanned the lake.

When we couldn't find the bus that went to the Old Summer Palace, we took a pedicab, but the pedaler charged us twenty *yuan* and only took us back to the entrance where we had started. Our long taxi ride from town was a real bargain compared to this tourist ripoff. We next took a taxi for another twenty *yuan*, but at least this driver took us to the right place. Unfortunately Kurt did not have any small bills and had to give the driver a one-hundred *yuan* bill. The driver was not happy about changing such a large bill for us, and when he gave us our change, he stuck in a counterfeit ten-*yuan* bill.

The woman in the kiosk at the Old Summer Palace refused to take our money when I tried to pay for tickets. I thought she was trying to overcharge us, until she showed me the bill I had presented and another that she had. Then it was obvious that my bill was counterfeit–just printed on regular paper. I apologized and gave her another. Now I understood why I had seen so many Chinese people holding all bills they received in change up to the light for scrutiny before they accepted them. I adopted the same technique, even though I didn't really know what to look for.

Originally laid out in the twelfth century, the Old Summer Palace area contained impressive ruins of palaces from all over the world that had been built by Jesuit architects during the reign of the Qing emperor Qianlong in the eighteenth century. One ruin had resembled Versailles and several others had once had magnificent fountains and statuary. Destroyed during the Opium Wars in 1860, by both France and Great Britain, the buildings were mostly partial ruins, except for a stone pavilion and a stone maze restored by the government. Many Chinese couples wandered along the side paths decorated with pots of bright yellow and white chrysanthemums. A very pleasant place, even in the autumn, the area must be a haven in the hot summer. We made sure we took a metered taxi back to town, fearing another ripoff, and this time there was no problem.

That evening we strolled along Wangfujing Dajie, an attractive modern shopping street. When I asked for "*er*" ice cream cones, the vendor reminded me that I should use *liang*, an alternate word, when requesting two of anything. *Er* was just for counting things. A cafeteria in the huge mall Dong An offered a variety of tasty dishes for dinner, allowing us to point to what looked good. For dessert, we both enjoyed a huge gooey rice or tofu ball covered in sesame seeds.

On the street, two "art students" said hello and invited us to their exhibition of calligraphy and classic Chinese painting. In India this had been a popular way to get customers, so we said we couldn't come now, maybe another day. They were polite enough to move on, looking for other western tourists. Although this part of Beijing was quite modern with shopping malls, escalators, electronics, and stylish clothing, I still saw a woman using an abacus to add someone's bill in a specialty candy store. Maybe her computer was down!

The next day we returned to Yong He Gong, the largest Tibetan Buddhist temple complex in China, outside Tibet. Inside one of the main temples, behind an enormous gilt Buddha carved from white sandalwood was another incredible sandalwood carving that resembled a large mountain with many small figures all over it. These scenes represented various events in the lives of Buddha and his followers. From a historical exhibit, we learned more about Buddhism in China and Tibet. In another hall, we smiled at the erotic Buddhas that were draped with scarves to avoid offense.

Across the street was Confucius's Temple and the Imperial College, where rows of engraved steles (large, upright stone tablets) stood in the courtyard, naming citizens successful in passing the civil service examinations which began during the Han Dynasty around 200 B.C. In the museum of musical instruments, we were fascinated by a costumed group performing on *sheng* (a Chinese koto), ocarina, stones, and *qin* (a Chinese two-stringed violin). In another room, examples of the classic arts such as cloisonne and modern ceramics were displayed.

Instead of walking the long distance from the Temple to Tiantan (Temple of Heaven) Park, we took the subway to have more time at this very beautiful huge park and its three temples lined up in a north to south direction with short walkways between them. From the fifteenth to the seventeenth century the emperor sacrificed animals once a year, praying for a bountiful harvest in the round and richly carved and decorated Hall of Prayers that has practically become an architectural symbol for Beijing. The smaller octagonal Imperial Vault of Heaven was surrounded by the echo wall, where a whisper could be heard on the opposite side of the temple. Each temple was encircled by marble steps. Their roofs, made of beautiful blue tiles and shaped like peaked sun-hats, culminated in gold top-knots. Although no one was allowed to enter the two temples, lines of tourists, mostly Chinese, paused at the entrance to look inside for a few minutes at the bedazzling beauty. Embedded in the designs on the ceiling was a carved dragon holding the pearl of power.

The third "temple," the fifteen-foot high Circular Mound, consisted of white marble stones arranged in three tiers, utilizing the imperial number nine and its multiples. The top tier, a round platform formed by nine concentric rings of stone each containing nine stones, was totally open to the sky. Constructed in 1530 and rebuilt in 1740, the site was used at the winter solstice for ceremonies to honor heaven.

. We also visited the Hall of Abstinence, located to the west of the three temples. Here the emperor stayed for three days and nights purifying himself prior to the annual ceremonies in the Hall of Prayers. Signs in English and Chinese described the rituals that he followed. Outside, strolling photographers were busy, posing their many customers in various imperial costumes. Before returning to our hotel, we hunted out the famed Beijing Duck restaurant, but we were disappointed, having eaten tastier Beijing duck in Washington D.C.

Our last half-day in Beijing allowed us to return to Tiananmen Square. Although the museums there were closed for renovation, we enjoyed the elaborate outdoor floral displays, some with waterfalls, that remained after a competition and festival. We couldn't help remembering the horrible massacre of the students demonstrating for democracy in 1989. Had this site been so peaceful and beautiful then? It was hard to visualize the ghastly 1989 events when all around us happy families picnicked on the grass and Chinese tourists and schoolchildren poured out of buses to mill about and chat with each other while standing in long lines to view Mao's body in his mausoleum. For us the lines were too long and the security too strict. No backpacks, jackets, purses, or cameras were permitted, but there was no secure place to leave these items. We noticed that many of the Chinese visitors just threw their belongings in a heap somewhere, but we were not comfortable doing that.

Despite knowing that we had managed quite well on our own for two and one-half days, we were glad to be picked up by Tracy, a young woman who took us to the train station and found the correct track for us. In the wild rush at the station, we almost missed the train to Ji'nan. When Kurt removed his backpack to send it through a security check, he dropped the ticket that Tracy had given him. Luckily, she retrieved it from the security policeman just as he was about to throw it away. Tracy also helped us move through long lines of crowding people on the platform. Our soft sleeper was very elegant with the seats already transformed into beds, though we'd be arriving at our destination before dark. One of the two men sharing the compartment with us rested on his bunk for most of the trip; the other sat at a small table in the aisle outside. The pear juice and cookies provided were welcome as we traveled for five hours through flat agricultural country.

Waiting for us in Ji'nan were Max, our next guide, and Mr. Ma, the driver. They would stay with us until we left for Xi'an. Our hotel, the Liangyou, was rather posh. In addition to all sorts of amenities, including slippers, our room on the twelfth floor also had a hair dryer. We were taken to another hotel for a dinner, which was served without our ordering it: egg drop soup, beef with tomatoes, tasty mushrooms, wonderful broccoli, and some vile marinated pork-mostly skin and fat. This was followed by cakes and a final soup. Apparently soup is served at the end of the meal to aid digestion. On the way back to our hotel, we stopped for a while to see the dancing fountains in the large central square where hundreds of people were watching a movie on a huge outdoor screen.

An enormous breakfast buffet with all sorts of interesting things (peanuts, pickles, salad, dried fish, steamed buns, cookies, waffles, eggs cooked to order, and sweet rolls) gave us a good start for the drive to Qufu, the birthplace of Confucius. On the way, we saw many people working in the fields, mostly hoeing. Some were harvesting cotton while others walked behind an animal pulling a plow. In one place, however, I saw a man guiding a plow that was pulled by four men instead of an ox. The only time I had seen anything like this was in drawings of life in ancient Egypt. Husked ears of corn created a bright design where they lay on roofs or hung from roof edges to dry so they could be more easily shelled. When we stopped for lunch, I thought for a moment that each table had been supplied with both white and black after-dinner mints. But the playing board accompanying the "mints" made me realize I had been looking at the discs used to play Go, a popular and ancient Chinese board game.

Confucius's forest was quiet and peaceful with many cypress trees amidst the graves of Confucius and all the male descendants in the Cong family. Confucius's wife was also buried there, but his female descendants were buried with the family into which they married. A well-rounded person, according to Confucius, should be skilled in poetry, calligraphy, and music and should show filial obedience, respect, and courtesy to others. Confucius lived and died in poverty, but when later emperors saw that his emphasis on filial piety and respect could be used to control the people, they honored him. In the Song Dynasty, his descendant was given the title of Duke Yansheng along with the power to appoint officials and even to execute wrongdoers. The last Duke Cong left with Chiang Kaishek in the 1940s. Four miniature animals decorated the eaves of the duke's mansion, indicating his high rank, but on the Confucius temple itself there were nine guardian animals, the same as for the emperor in Beijing. Quite beautiful, the temple had octagonal rather than round pillars bearing very deep ornate carvings of dragons and other motifs. When the emperor came to visit, the pillars were covered with silk so that he would not see that these pillars were more beautiful than those in the Forbidden City. Because the emperor was entitled to the best of everything, such a discovery would have had unpleasant consequences. In place of the usual Buddha, the temple housed a painting of Confucius. As in other temples, many devotees burned incense sticks as they offered prayers. The courtyard was filled with thirteen pavilions, each containing a stele standing on the back of the turtle-like creature, the *bixi*, one of nine offspring of the dragon. Supposedly, putting a stele on the unruly *bixi's* back would weigh it down and make it behave. In the courtyard, a colorful group of about thirty costumed musicians carrying flags and wearing long pheasant feathers on their hats paraded, advertising an evening performance on ancient instruments.

Late in the afternoon, as we entered Ti'an, our next stop, we drove through an industrial district where coal was being sold along with vegetables and eggs. People were repairing tinware, and meat carcasses were hanging from poles at the side of the road. At the Dong Fang (East Place) Hotel, we reorganized our plans for climbing Tai Shan. We had hoped to hike the entire route, not realizing how long it would take. Max had planned to take us to the cable car and have the driver wait there while the three of us explored the summit area. After we explained our ideas, Max telephoned his manager, and we agreed to a compromise. Mr. Ma would drive to the cable car station on the other side of the mountain as arranged, but Max, Kurt, and I would take a minibus to the nearby half-way station, hike up to the summit, explore that area, and then after we had lunch, take the cable car down the other side.

The hike up Tai Shan gave us a closer look at Chinese culture. Many examples of calligraphy adorned large stones at the side of the trail. The surrounding scenery resembled a Chinese screen painting. A lovely pine tree with an outstretched branch was aptly labeled "The Welcoming Tree." Souvenir sellers were everywhere. One of the specialty souvenirs sold at the stalls was a peanut-shaped container with three little birds inside. When the peanut was opened, the birds moved around and sang a short melody.

When the trail became steep there were steps, rather than a trail, though quite a few of the steps were being repaired or replaced. Many men carried stones and mortar in old-style wire baskets hanging from yokes on their shoulders. Much of the work was done by hammer and chisel, but some workers had a battery powered hand tool to score the stones, making them less slippery in the rain. We were startled when suddenly two people came running down the steps towards us. Most hikers kept a steady pace whichever direction they were going. We stopped, as did the people behind us, to find out what might be wrong. The running couple pointed upwards behind them where we saw a group of twelve men carrying an extremely heavy piece of machinery needed for repairing the trail. I would never have imagined that such a piece of machinery could be carried by human strength alone, even with twelve men helping. It was an amazing sight to see these men carrying the machine down the steep section of the trail, all the while moving this way and that to keep it from toppling to one side or the other. Luckily, they stopped for a brief rest just before reaching us, and we were able to continue up the hill without much delay.

Along the way, men carrying empty sedan chairs offered their services for a price, as it was a warm day for hiking. Some wearying walkers hired them and were carried to the summit as if they had been emperors. Many people asked Kurt how old he was, and when I told them, they gave him a thumbs- up.

Despite the warm day, at the summit (about 5,000 feet) the wind felt chilly whenever the clouds obscured the sun, and we were glad to have our jackets. Reaching the top of the mountain, we were astonished to see an entire city with hotels, shops, temples, and overlooks. Gold calligraphy covered a huge stone, a poem written by an emperor. Tourists, mostly Chinese, were everywhere. An unusual sight in front of one temple was a huge black kettle covered with padlocks. Lovers have their names engraved on the padlocks which are then locked to a chain on the kettle, symbolically locking their hearts together. Another custom was for the lovers to place a small pebble on a branch of a bush. Supposedly their love will last as long as no one disturbs the stone. Max not only explained all these customs, but he also asked our help in choosing a carved jade charm for his girlfriend, and later asked us to help him improve a love letter he was writing her in English–a fascinating assignment.

As we wandered from one spot to another, a group of people who had actually hired the sedan chair carriers came by enjoying their luxurious ride. The various lookout spots had wonderful names such as "Pavilion for Appreciating the Sunrise."

Lunch for the three of us was a varied feast including shrimp, fish, and many other courses. We had the restaurant almost entirely to ourselves, as most people were eating food they'd brought with them or had purchased from street vendors. Because I had asked about it, Max ordered a cornmeal pancake I'd seen being made on the street. Like a tortilla, it was filled with a scallion and some bean paste, making a nice snack.

The most strenuous part of the trip was trying to reach the cable car station, as Max did not know the way and had to keep asking. After we scrambled down some fairly narrow, steep places, we finally looked back to see the easier, new path. Because we did not hike the entire route, we will not be granted immortality, but Max assured us that our two-and-one-half hour climb up the stairs would result in our living to be at least one hundred.

On the return trip to Ji'nan, Mr. Ma stopped at a Muyu stone factory where free tea was offered. Muyu stone, found exclusively in Shandong Province, is reputed to have great healing powers if you drink tea from cups or teapots made of it. Despite this fabulous claim, we didn't purchase anything. After our large lunch, we thought we'd skip dinner. Instead, we found a convenience store, where I purchased a large bowl of ramen noodles. Our room's electric teapot provided the boiling water we needed. If only we hadn't added the sauce, which was full of chili powder!

Though we'd intended to go only to the airport in the morning, Max insisted we had to see every attraction his home town had to offer. First we were taken to Thousand Buddha Hill, but the only Buddha we saw was an enormous fat gold-colored statue at the bottom of the hill. Max claimed most of the others had been destroyed by the Communists. From the top of the hill, a view of several mountains slightly resembled a profile of a Buddha lying down. Too much haze interfered with the great views into town and into the distance, but reaching the summit did provide a nice scramble up some rocks. Next was the Shandong Provincial Museum, which we visited impatiently, worried about missing our flight. As it turned out, we had misunderstood, thinking the time we needed to be at the airport was our actual departure time. Before driving us to the airport, Mr. Ma handed Max a camera and asked him to take a picture of the three of us.

Checking in at the airport was hectic, because most Chinese simply push and shove to get ahead. One woman, concerned that I would be left behind, helped me get ahead of someone else by gently pushing me forward. At least I thought that's what she intended, so I thanked her in Chinese. There was no sense in not pushing in with the crowd. "When in Rome . . ."

Xi'an, home of the Army of the Terra Cotta Warriors, was our destination. Here our new guide, Michelle, spoke excellent English and began giving us information on the ride into town. Xi'an had served as the capital city for twelve different dynasties, but most of the information we learned was about the Qin, the Han, the Sui, and the Tang dynasties.

Qin Shihuang, who established the Qin dynasty and from whose name the word "China" derives, was the first emperor to unite the country by defeating all the other regional rulers. He was also responsible for beginning the construction of the Great Wall. Discovered when Qin's tomb was excavated, the famed terra cotta warriors were "life size" statues of actual individuals, each with a different facial expression. These thousands of warriors had been made to accompany the emperor into the after-life, assuring that it would be pleasant for him.

Following Qin Shihuang's death in 206 B.C., Liu Pang, a commoner, led a revolt overthrowing the government and established the Han dynasty. One of the accomplishments of the Han dynasty, which lasted for four hundred years, was to introduce civil service examinations for those seeking to be government officials, replacing the hereditary system.

During the Sui dynasty the city received its name. Over three centuries of turmoil and wars had followed the collapse of the Han Dynasty in A.D. 220, so when the Sui dynasty reunited China in A.D. 581, Wen Ti, the emperor, ordered the city of Chang'An (long peace) to be built on the site of the former Han capital. The name of the city referred to the long peace of the Han Dynasty.

The Tang Dynasty (beginning in A.D. 618) was the period during which Chang'An became an international commercial and cultural center and grew to be the largest city in the world with a population of around two million. This growth was accompanied by a brilliant period of creativity in all the arts. When the dynasty fell, and the capital was moved elsewhere, the city also declined. The modern city of Xi'an stands on the site of Chang'an and honors the many reminders of its imperial past.

From our twelfth-floor room in a very modern hotel, we had a fabulous view of the famous Bell Tower across the street. Since we had the entire afternoon to explore Xi'an on our own, the Bell Tower was an irresistible first stop. A short but delightful musical performance by players of a two-stringed violin, a sheng, bronze bells, and stones began just as we entered the tower. On the terrace, tourists lined up for a turn at releasing a huge mallet to strike the replica of the equally huge bell. Everyone hoped for a loud gong, a sign of good luck. Originally the bell was used to indicate that the day was beginning. Now the interior of the tower was an art gallery. At the nearby Drum Tower, we saw two drums with diameters of at least six feet. Beating the drum had indicated the end of the working day. Both towers date from the time of the Han emperor, Liu Pang, who was not of noble birth. When earthquakes occurring during his reign destroyed many Xi'an buildings, the emperor was told that the dragon living within the earth was causing the earthquakes because he was upset that the emperor was not a direct dragon descendant. Liu Pang had the two towers built in an attempt to appease the dragon and stop the destruction.

Walking a few more city blocks from the Drum Tower brought us to the Muslim market street and the Great Mosque. The mosque was an interesting mixture of Chinese and Arabic architecture and carving. During the flourishing Tang dynasty, many Muslims had come to cities that were on the Silk Route, such as Chang'an, and their descendants had stayed, maintaining their religious beliefs and customs.

We never learned why the hotel gave us a junior suite with a separate sitting room and a double bed instead of the standard two single beds. We just enjoyed it. For dinner we had spaghetti and ice cream, both ancient Chinese inventions.

Our one-day tour of Xi'an's major sites with Michelle began at the Banpo Neolithic Village, an excavation site of a 6,000- year-old settlement. One of two exhibition buildings showed tools: axes, needles made from bone, fish hooks, and grinding stones, while the other displayed pottery. Large amphoras with carrying ears were shaped with conical bottoms and wider tops. This shape allowed the bottles to be floated in the water, and as they filled, they would stand upright. On some of the later pottery, we saw the beginning of decorations and some runic signs. The face of a person with a fish in his mouth decorated one bowl. We also saw some shell jewelry and evidence that the people had known how to weave.

In the excavation itself, discovered when a textile factory was to be built, the evolution of housing could be seen. Some houses were round, some were half underground, and some were rectangular-shaped. Children were not buried in the general cemetery, but were kept close to their homes in burial pots, a touching practice, perhaps revealing the feelings of these people about their children. Banpo Neolithic Village gave us a fascinating glimpse into the beginnings of civilization in Asia.

About nine miles from Xi'an, at the site of the terra cotta warriors, an introductory film depicted the accidental discovery of the site in 1974 by two peasants digging a well. The movie also related early Chinese history and showed how the statues may have been made. Later,during periods of unrest and war, rebels had burned and broken many of the statues. In addition to the warriors and their horses, in 1980, several bronze pieces were found. One bronze, of a standing chariot driver, carried a removable umbrella. We were intrigued by the smaller turtle-shell covered chariot which supposedly housed the emperor's soul.

Despite the numerous, loud tourist groups, seeing the thousands of life-size warriors standing or kneeling in position, row upon row, was a moving experience. In a newly-excavated section, we could see some of the original paint on the surface of clothing and on the faces of the warriors, buried over two thousand years ago. Although signs were posted prohibiting the taking of photographs, most tourists ignored them.

Lunch in the friendship store was another varied feast including lotus and many hot dishes, such as fried winter melon that tasted like pineapple. Two chefs demonstrated different methods for making noodles. To make broad noodles, the noodle maker vigorously sliced little pieces from a dough slab, hoping that most of them would fall into the boiling water. The other noodle maker lifted, twisted and swirled masses of long thin noodles for a few seconds in boiling water just before serving them to waiting customers.

On our drive back to Xi'an, Michelle regaled us with facts and customs not found in our guidebook. For example, if you want to get a free haircut in Xi'an, look for someone on the street wearing a pink barber's jacket. These are apprentices who cut hair free in order to gain experience. She also told us a joke based on another Chinese custom. Because the locks on toilet stalls in China often do not work, the person inside the stall sings a song to let people waiting know that a stall is occupied. Thus, instead of using our euphemism "I have to powder my nose," Chinese people will say "I have to sing a song." A little boy visiting his American grandmother told her early one morning that he had to "sing a song." She told him to wait a while, as she was still sleepy and she did not want him to disturb other people. He soon returned and insisted that he really had to sing a song and could not wait. Finally the grandmother said, "If you really have to sing a song, go ahead, but only very slowly and softly in my ear."

Back in town, we visited the Forest of Stone Tablets where skill in calligraphy was demonstrated. Important messages were written on stone, a more permanent record than paper. The earliest carving was almost hieroglyphic. Another stone had a cross on it to commemorate the bringing of Christianity to China in 635 by a Nestorian missionary from Syria. One carving that looked like a bamboo tree was really a poem with the calligraphy making up the leaves of the bamboo. Professional inkers laid rice paper on certain stones, then pressed big ink pads on the paper and sold the resulting prints. The Shaanxi Provincial Museum next door had many beautiful carvings, including one of the emperor's four horses and his rhinoceros. Impressed by the gift of a live rhino, he had commemorated it in stone. At a nearby factory that made and sold replicas, the life-size warriors were very attractive, but the cost of shipping was prohibitive. We had to settle for two smaller figures to cram into our already full backpacks.

In the evening, a superb Tang Dynasty dinner and show entertained us with excellent food, talented musicians, graceful dancers, and beautiful costumes. After the seafood and chicken appetizers, we had a black mushroom consomme. Next king prawns with fruit salad whetted our appetite for the succulent beef tenderloin baked in mushroom sauce served with green salad and fried rice. A ginger fruit salad with snow fungus in hawberry syrup, petits fours, and jasmine tea completed the banquet. A lovely costumed hostess filled and re-filled narrow glasses with a hot fermented drink as we ate. Though the menu seemed more western than Chinese, everything was very delicious.

Playing Song of the Orioles, a phenomenal musician imitated actual bird calls on the panpipes. He also performed other lovely melodies. A seemingly modern mandolin sextet was a surprise, but the program insisted that all the music, dance, and clothing were based on either historical documents or designs found on ancient pottery.

Dreary weather the next day did not discourage us from independently taking a local bus to the Big Wild Goose Pagoda. The Buddhist temple and shrine next to it were pleasant to visit prior to hiking up seven flights of stairs to look out at fog and drizzle. Nearby the Shaanxi Provincial History Museum was well organized and complete, beginning with relics from paleolithic times and reaching to about 1860. Many bronze cooking vessels were tripodal, and I was fascinated by an animal-shaped wine-heating container. The lid was also an animal, and the tongue formed the spout. After ordering food in Chinese at a Kentucky Fried Chicken, we walked to South Gate and spent some time strolling on the city wall admiring the decorative red and gold lanterns remaining from a recent festival.

Arriving at the airport for our flight to Chengdu, we were engulfed in a frantic crowd of people mostly pushing and shoving their way forward. Though we were the only Caucasians on the flight, by now I'd learned the proper technique, and we did not end up last in line. When we boarded, however, the seats in the rear of the plane were completely filled by people not assigned to them, and they would not move. After several Chinese people protested, they realized it would do no good, so the boarding passengers just took any seats we could find. No safety instructions were given except to wear seat belts at all times, but even on this short flight to Chengdu, lots of food was served.

In Chengdu we were met by an enthusiastic guide, Little Lee, and Zhan Xiansheng, the driver. Little Lee's English was very hard to understand, so I tried to use what little Chinese I knew to tell him that we needed to buy a map of Emeishan (the mountain we intended to climb). He actually understood me and before dropping us off at our hotel, he said that we would buy the map the next day.

We had the afternoon to explore Chengdu on our own. When we couldn't find a "folkway" exhibit mentioned in our guidebook, I asked a policeman where it was. He explained that Chengdu no longer had one. This conversation, also in Chinese, increased my confidence.

In honor of a conference on the development of China's Western provinces, the park in front of the Mao statue was decorated with many balloons and flowers. Near the river, we noticed some elegant penthouses, but in other streets we saw squalor. Many people were fashionably dressed; we saw very short miniskirts with very high platform shoes and more women with their hair highlighted or dyed a reddish or golden color. The streets were crammed full of multitudes of bicyclists–all in a frantic hurry.

In the morning, Mr. Zhan, our driver, wanted to drop us off at the Baguo

Monastery, where two days later we were to meet him and Little Lee again, after we had climbed Emeishan. But we had expected to be dropped off at the Wannian cable car station, part way up the 10,000- foot mountain. After we insisted that was where we needed to be, Little Lee found a waiting taxi driver who agreed to drive all four of us to the cable car station for 120 yuan (about fifteen dollars). It was worth the price, although I wasn't sure why Mr. Zhan needed to ride with us.

Once there we bought a map, admission tickets, and cable car tickets to the Wannian Temple, even higher on the mountain. Although we had no reservations, we planned to spend the night at Xixiang Chi (Elephant Pond) monastery, a location that would allow us to reach the summit of Emeishan the next day. The monastery was so named because, according to legend, as a blue-haired Buddha flew his elephant over the mountains, they paused at the monastery's site for the elephant to have a bath. No evidence of any kind of pond remained.

Even from Wannian temple, I estimated it would take us at least six hours, depending on the trail condition to reach the monastery. We had no idea how many beds were available at the monastery, so planned to arrive in the early afternoon to increase our chances of getting one. For that reason, we had hoped to be on the trail by ten a.m. If there was "no room at the inn," we would have to hike several more hours to reach the next monastery, not knowing if it had any space, either.

Because the drive from Chengdu to the monastery had been longer than we'd expected, we got a late start up the mountain. It was noon when we reached the Wannian shrine or stupa and briefly looked inside to see a huge blue-haired Puxian Buddha sitting on an enormous white elephant, surrounded by about one thousand small, gilt Buddhas in niches on the high wall and embedded in the ceiling. Then, finding the main trail, we began the ascent, as I worried about what time we would reach the monastery and whether we would have to hike even farther.

Mt. Emei (Emeishan) is one of four mountains held sacred by Buddhists. As early as the second century A.D. monasteries began to appear on the mountain. During the fifteenth century, when Buddhism was at its height in China, the mountain held more than one hundred monasteries. About twenty were still functioning, even after the Communist regime.

Shrouded in misty fog, the steep twisting staircase of uneven, slippery stones climbed endlessly. Through a cloudy veil, we glimpsed picturesque drooping pine branches, lush bamboo forests, beautiful stands of fir and cedar trees, and breathtaking steep precipices and pinnacles. A windy, overcast day on Taishan the week before had convinced us it would be quite cool at higher elevations, so we'd put on our long underwear. Now, as we trudged up towards Emeishan's 10,000-foot summit, we sweated profusely and constantly. The path was not difficult, but we couldn't take any time to rest. At best, we would reach

Elephant Pond Monastery by 6:00 p.m. And this would give us only thirty minutes of daylight for hiking farther, in case no beds were available. I did not want to hike this trail in the dark.

We stopped briefly for a lunch of noodles and a cold drink at a trail-side stand, then kept walking upwards. Everyone we met was descending, moving slowly and carefully. Some people were carried in sedan chairs by two porters; others rode on a single porter's back, "piggy-back" style. *"Ni hao"* (How are you?) was a frequent greeting which we returned or answered with *"Hen hao, shei, shei."* (Very well, thank you). Not many people stopped to chat, however, as even the route down commanded each hiker's full attention.

When we met two hikers from Australia heading down, they told us about the two-dollar bus back to Baguo Monastery, if we tired of walking. The previous day they had walked for four hours in heavy rain to reach the summit, only to find it engulfed in clouds with no view at all. Not much fun or reward for strenuous effort!

Just before 5:00 p.m., when I stopped for a cold drink to energize me for another hour, the vendor told me the monastery was just five minutes ahead. I didn't really believe him, but he was right. By then the high humidity, lack of wind, and our exertion had left us drenched, in danger of a chill. And we knew the monastery was not heated.

"Women yao fangjian?" I hoped I'd used the correct tones and not inadvertently said something insulting or obscene. The young monk beckoned us to follow him through winding, darkening hallways at the side of a central open court where incense burned. As daylight faded, we reached a large room with, surprisingly, a television set and two double beds, one with an electric blanket. The overhead light bulb flickered off and on. We didn't even try the television, but we plugged in the electric blanket, put on all the clothes we had, and crawled under heavy comforters to dry out. My pocketknife set us free when the door lock stuck. Later that night heavy rains started, but we were warm and dry, except when scurrying through hallways to the very primitive *cesuo*. We worried that a continuing rain would send us back down the long, treacherous, slippery stone steps.

We woke early, surprised to find ourselves in sunlight above a "sea of clouds." Munching a few cookies, we headed for the summit, stopping after an hour at an inviting stall where *miantiao* (instant noodles) and *cha* (tea) provided energy for reaching the Golden Summit Cable Car. In just ten minutes, we and other visitors (all Chinese) were strolling in and around Golden Summit Temple, on a glorious sunshine-filled day, enjoying clear views to Gangga Shan, the last snow-capped mountain range before Tibet. Vendors offered dried mushrooms, various herb preparations, and other specialties. A family of baboons teased picture-taking tourists. We enjoyed the spectacular views of the clouds below us, a white sea on which many islands floated. In reality, the "islands" were created by the peaks of nearby mountains piercing the cloud cover. Though we skipped going into the temple, we followed several trails to various special viewpoints, enjoying the scenery and the beginning of fall colors in the few deciduous trees among the feathery pines.

Large bowls of instant noodles could be purchased at the snack bar, which also provided thermoses of boiling water, chopsticks, and a place to sit. As the clerk handed us our bowls of dry noodles, a construction worker who happened to be standing next to us, spoke in Chinese to the clerk and turned to us shaking his head to indicate "no." Then he opened his mouth and waved his hand in front of it. We got his message and noticed the flames decorating the lid of the bowl. The clerk, returning from the storeroom, handed us a milder version of the same noodles. We were grateful for the friendly help from this man who somehow recognized that we probably didn't know what we were doing.

Because Kurt's knee was bothering him a bit, and he was concerned that the slick, uneven stone steps might be even harder to negotiate going downhill, we decided to ride down the mountain. At the bus stop, we found a minivan waiting for just two more passengers. As we traveled through an area world famous for its gigantic bamboo, the kind preferred by pandas, we saw large stacks of the bamboo, piled like logs, where it was being harvested.

Back in town, I used my Chinese to get a clean, comfortable hotel room with a private bath for about twelve dollars. We ate at the hotel, but the food was much too spicy, even with the accompanying beer and the bananas and mandarin oranges we had purchased on the street.

For breakfast we found the Teddy Bear Café where I asked for *shoofing*, and the waitress responded, "pancake?" This was one English word she knew. The pancakes, covered with chocolate syrup and bananas, tasted fabulous after our skimpy dinner. While waiting to be picked up, we enjoyed the well-tended, lush gardens of Baguo Monastery, despite the many disrupted areas where reconstruction was underway.

Driving back to Chengdu with Little Lee and Mr. Zhan, we stopped for most of the afternoon to see the Giant Buddha at LeShan. After the glorious weather on top of Emeishan, it was discouraging to be back in the mist and occasional rain showers. Overlooking the swirling confluence of the Dadu and Min rivers, the location of the Buddha was spectacular. The largest Buddha in the world, the carving was started in 713 by the monk Haitong. At the confluence, many boats had been lost, and Haitong felt the presence of a large Buddha might calm the water. Actually the project did have that effect because the surplus rock that fell into the river while the Buddha was being carved filled up some of the river's treacherous holes. It took ninety years to complete the statue, which is about 200 feet tall, sitting down. His ears are twenty-one feet long.

Little Lee said that a 1962 earthquake had opened the Buddha's eyes, which had been closed when he was originally carved. We thought maybe something had been lost in translation. Even the water-drainage system inside the

Buddha's body hasn't prevented weathering, and a restoration project was being discussed for this national treasure.

On one side of the Buddha, an impressive staircase with a railing descended the cliff steeply, allowing tourists to view the Buddha from below. The path continued past the carving, entering an ascending staircase carved into the rock wall itself. Long lines of people on the staircases, with everyone stopping in scenic spots to take photos of themselves with the Buddha, indicated that the Buddha was an extremely popular destination, even in rainy weather. Gardens, pavilions, and monasteries could be visited in the large park-like area. An impressive statue of DongPa, a poet who loved to drink, was admired by many visitors. DongPa had claimed that the more wine he consumed, the better his poetry became. In the anteroom of one temple, we saw a collection of eighteen Arhat statues (Arhat is a Buddhist term referring to people who have released themselves from the psychological bondage of greed, hate, and delusion.) as well as the four kings of the North, South, East, and West.

While we were waiting for Mr. Zhan at the location he specified, an old man wearing the standard light-blue worker's clothing from the Mao era came by and spoke rapidly while using many imploring hand gestures. Kurt and I both thought he was begging, but Little Lee said the man was urging us to come to his restaurant for dinner. Getting tired of waiting, Kurt walked to the parking lot where we'd been dropped off and found Mr. Zhan waiting there. Our drive back to the Chengdu took us through the middle of the flower, bird, and pet fish market, and then down a very narrow street past an enormous meat market offering all kinds of fly-decorated carcasses.

As we waited for our early morning flight to Kunming, a fellow passenger told us he lived in Kunming and if we needed a place to stay, we should call him. But we didn't need to call. As soon as we arrived in Kunming, Stacey and her driver took us to our very modern hotel which overlooked a central traffic circle decorated with sculptures that made it resemble a pond filled with lily pads. From our room on the twentieth floor, we could see a recently restored mosque.

We had the entire day to explore Kunming on our own. Walking to a recommended restaurant, we stopped at the Western Pagoda, an attractive sculpture in a park. Unlike most pagodas, it was not large enough for anyone to enter. In a nearby terrace, many people drank tea and read newspapers. We also passed stalls where meat, chickens, and geese were hanging outside for sale. The chickens were so small they looked like Cornish game hens. Now we knew why there had been so little meat in chicken dishes we'd ordered.

At the restaurant, we ordered Across the Bridge Noodles, a Yunnan province specialty. First thinly-sliced raw meat and vegetables were brought to the table, then a very hot soup with a thin oil layer on top arrived, and the raw items were dropped into the hot liquid. According to legend, the dish was discovered by a woman bringing food to her husband, who was studying on an

318

island. Usually by the time she crossed the long wooden bridge to reach him, the food she had prepared at home was cold. One morning she was late and just brought the uncooked ingredients and the hot liquid separately. She found that a thin layer of oil kept the soup hot enough to cook the ingredients after she arrived. We couldn't believe how much food there was for the inexpensive price.

When we couldn't find the bus to the Bamboo Temple, we visited the Yunnan Provincial Museum to see bronze drums and Buddhist art from Yunnan province, which borders Vietnam, Laos, Myanmar, and Tibet.

The next day, we traveled seventy miles with Stacey and her driver to visit *Shilin* (Stone Forest). On the way there, we saw many fields of rice, wheat, lotus, and tobacco. We also learned that Yunnan province has some gold mines. Despite early morning rain in Kunming, by the time we reached the Stone Forest, the weather was excellent. Stacey said that the weather in Kunming was as changeable as a boy's heart. An amazing area of weathered and eroded limestone towers, the Stone Forest had many walkways so visitors could stroll amidst the various dramatic formations and see many different parts of the extensive park. Costumed women could be hired as guides, but many of them also graciously posed with tourists for souvenir photos. The women were from the Sani tribe and were dressed to represent the legendary Ashima who still looks for her lost husband. In their elaborate headgear, the women wear two triangles if they are single, one if engaged, and none if married.

Fanciful names had been given to some of the stone shapes, such as "The Lovers," "The Field of Swords," "Woman Sitting Alone," "Ashima,"and "Elephant Rock." Built on the top of a broad formation, a pagoda/pavilion gave those who climbed up a gorgeous view over the entire Stone Forest area. Lunch was very delicious with tofu, pork and mushrooms, and duck. On our way to the Stone Forest, we had noticed many duck-roasting stands where uncooked ducks hung like laundry on a line. Diners select a duck, and it is barbecued on the spot. Stacey said these stands were very popular, and sure enough, when we passed the same stands on our return trip, most of the ducks were gone.

We also stopped at the fairly primitive and dirty Sani village to observe the way of life of these agricultural people. One old man actually said *"Ni hao,"* but most villagers speak only the Sani language. Two little boys tried to hit Kurt with a stick, while another tried to jump on my pack. The fields where crops were growing were quite beautiful, but the living conditions appeared terrible, even though the village was only a few miles from modern high-rise buildings in Kunming.

That night as we walked in Kunming, we saw many people having their necks, legs, and arms massaged by people wearing white coats. One massager was blind. Massages were given on the street next to many vendors selling candy, baked goods, roasted ears of corn, sweet potatoes, and souvenirs from stalls. Other vendors walked back and forth carrying their wares in dual baskets hanging from a yoke.

We thought our early morning flight would give us a full day to explore Guilin on our own. But when we were dropped off at the hotel, our room was not ready so we had to delay climbing the steps of Fubo Hill, just across the street, until we were allowed to check in. From the top of Fubo Hill, we were enchanted by the views of the unusual shapes of the numerous limestone or karst hills, sometimes covered with lush vegetation, through which the town winds itself.

We next took a taxi to the railway station in order to ride the bus to Guilin's Reed Flute Cave. Although I had pointed to the station on the map I showed the driver, he took us to a nearby hotel. But after I said "main train station" in Chinese, he immediately took us there. When an official at the station told us to take a taxi and not the bus, we realized we should have taken a taxi directly to the cave in the first place. Reed Flute Cave was well worth the entry fee of five dollars, despite the large number of tourist groups and the megaphone-using guides leading them. The many interesting formations started right at the entrance to the cave and continued into a very large room. As in many commercial caves in the United States, colored lighting was used for special effects. Nearby we hiked to the top of a knoll for more views over the unusual limestone mounds, some emerging above flat rice paddies.

After a taxi ride back to our hotel, we ate dinner at a family restaurant where we ordered in Chinese. Our after-dinner stroll by the river led us to a bridge that many people were crossing in both directions. On the other side, several rather elegant-looking homes were under construction adjacent to a grubby section of town.

The following day's cruise on the Li River to Yangshuo revealed beautiful scenery wherever we looked. Fantastically-shaped spires covered with lush vegetation invited imaginative names such as "Snail Hill", "Goat Horn Hill", "Five Fingers Hill", and "Dragon Head Hill." Some of the hillsides lacking vegetation, displayed mineral-stain patterns resembling galloping horses, rolling clouds, or two dragons playing with a pearl. Small boys swam amidst the many ducks in the water. Some traders wearing peaked straw hats poled their basket-loaded barges to a market.

Each passenger was given an embroidered red silk ball with five tassels attached to it. In this part of China, if a girl throws such a ball to a boy and he catches it, they are engaged. When we asked the young hostess on the boat if she had "thrown the ball to anyone," she told us she had and would be married in three months. After we enjoyed a delicious lunch on our motor-powered boat, a staff person offered drinks from a bottle containing pickled snakes. We passed on that, not realizing until too late that such a drink conferred excellent health or long life, or something like that. Other sights along the river were water buffalo cows and calves, a beautiful stand of bamboo, and cormorant fishing near the dock in Yangshuo. Actually, it is the cormorants that catch the fish, while the men control the large black birds. A string is tied around the cormorant's neck to prevent it from swallowing the fish it catches. Only after the cormorant's owner has all the fish he wants is the string removed so that the bird can eat.

Arriving in Yangshuo, we found our way from the dock into town, but we had no address for the Paradise Hotel, so we finally asked for directions, not realizing we were only a few steps from our destination. Nestled below one of the towering spires covered with dark green vegetation, the Paradise Hotel had a swimming pool as well as very attractive rooms. When I noticed that my bedside lamp didn't work, I was able to get help using my Chinese and some hand signals. But the problem was more than a burned-out light bulb. The repairman decided to take the fixture apart and replace the controller.

Now we had time to bargain for gifts and for the chop I wanted as a souvenir. Chops are carved stone blocks which are inked and then stamped on documents or letters to indicate signatures. For western tourists, both the Chinese character for your name and your English name are carved on the stone, after you have selected the particular kind of stone you prefer. Everything could be negotiated, and I was glad I knew my Chinese numbers. When Kurt needed a plain underwear tee-shirt, we walked through the Chinese market section of town, but were successful only at an old-fashioned department store.

We didn't realize until later that the crowds of people and the various costumed units of a parade we saw gathering on Yangshuo's main street were both waiting for the opening ceremony in a three-day festival honoring cormorant fishing. We realized something was going on, but it was getting late for us.

In the morning, while we waited for a park to open its gates, we climbed to the top of a nearby pagoda from which we could watch another festival event. Dragon dancers who manipulated the long cloth body of a dragon with sticks as they ran through the streets left the watching crowd amazed at their skill. Four men wearing lion costumes shook their heads and sporadically jumped up and down. An important official wearing an enormous ceremonial red sash and bow made a speech and then rode in a truck followed by musicians in another. While I waited for Kurt to descend from the pagoda, two Chinese women asked Kurt's age and mine, so I asked their ages. They gave us thumbs-up for doing the pagoda climb. As we walked in the park, we saw orchards of pomelos, a citrus fruit as large as a grapefruit. Perhaps we didn't make a good selection when we bought two from a vendor, for the skin was very thick, and the inside was too fibrous and tasteless to justify even the very cheap price.

We planned to walk along the highway to see Moon Hill, but a persistent woman on a motorcycle with a sidecar kept lowering her price until we agreed to ride with her. On the way we passed through a spectacular grouping of the limestone mounds or hills. We also saw people harvesting rice by hand and then threshing it in a small foot-operated threshing machine. Moon Hill was essentially a limestone arch at the top of a hill. The space beneath the arch resembled the shape of a half moon from one spot on the road and a crescent moon from another perspective.

Being a popular tourist spot, Yangshuo had many restaurants. One of our favorites was Lisa's where we enjoyed chicken with pineapple, sweet-and-sour beef, and rice. There we overheard a loud conversation between three men. One of them, a Vietnam vet who was a teacher of English at a school in Guilin, had just had a "stir-up" with his supervisor and had taken a week off. He felt that the Chinese students who were training to be teachers of English learned only by ticking off answers, not by really speaking English. The girls waitressing in Yangshuo had better English skills, in his opinion.

Streets near the dock were full of vendors who called out "Hallo, table cloth," "Hallo, tee shirt." "This one for you." "Lady, lookee, lookee. I make you good price: good for you, bad for me." We often replied *Shei, shei, bu yao* ("Thank you, we don't need.") providing entertainment for the good-natured sellers of an overabundance of goods.

Our transportation to the Guilin airport didn't leave until 5:00 p.m., so we waited in the shade by our hotel's swimming pool, where a Swedish ladies' tour group lounged, taking in the sun. One large woman, facing us, decided to take off her bathing suit top and put on her bra while chatting with her friends. We couldn't stay for her "second act," as our driver arrived.

Amidst massive confusion at the airport, we were given a boarding pass for a flight leaving fifteen minutes later than our scheduled flight. At least both were going to Chongqing (Chunking). Also on this flight was a large Western tour group. One rather obnoxious man pulled other people's luggage out of bins to get his bag in. But when it came time to disembark, the Chinese people trapped him in his seat, not letting him out until everyone else had left. The young man who met us at the airport at 11:00 p.m. and who would take us to the ship the following evening was very glad to see us. He told us that when no westerners arrived on our scheduled flight, he was afraid we had missed it and wouldn't be arriving at all. Then he decided to wait for the next flight arriving from Guilin, just in case.

On our way to the hotel, he told us some interesting facts about Chongqing, the capital of the Ba Kingdom. Originally called Gongzhou, the city received a new name during the Song dynasty. Shortly after he became prince of the city of Gongzhou in 1190, Zhao Dun also became the Emperor of China. To celebrate these two happy events, the emperor renamed his city Chongqing which means double celebration or double happiness. Chongqing also became very important when Japan invaded China in 1937-38, and the Nanking government with Chiang Kaishek relocated to the city, then called Chunking. During the war, Chunking was bombed two hundred times, so very little of historic interest can be found. In the past ten years, hundreds of high rises have been constructed to meet housing needs.

On a hazy Sunday morning as we walked to the wharf area, we paused at a central square to join hundreds of onlookers watching a children's dance performance. Some children were dressed as flowers, some as bumblebees, and some as combat soldiers.

At the Arhat Monastery, where many ancient stone carvings were preserved, the Arhats were very realistic, being squat in shape. Many we had seen elsewhere were tall and slim. A large public park-like area near the wharf attracted families who picnicked while watching the large passenger and freight ships loading and unloading.

Because he was concerned about being bored on our Yangtze River cruise, Kurt wanted to find a foreign-language bookstore. I thought I could find it, but the street we entered was narrow and crowded, with hordes of people everywhere. It did lead us, however, to the Liberation Monument which was surrounded by broad streets, upscale shops, malls, and restaurants. We found an excellent meal for five dollars and noticed that clothing of quite good quality was phenomenally cheap. A padded jacket, for example, was only two dollars. No wonder most people we saw were very well dressed. Eventually we found the book store.

After being dropped off at the ship, we learned that we had a first-class cabin with a private bath and a television--and that there were no other Westerners on board. We had asked to travel on a Chinese ship, and that's what we got. Only one staff person knew any English, and he left after rapidly telling us about optional side trips and a meal plan which must be pre-paid. We declined the pre-paid meals, fearing the food would be too spicy for Kurt, but we did pay for the excursions, since they included a trip into the Lesser Gorges and a visit to Fengdu, known to the Chinese as Ghost City. Sitting on the ship waiting for the excursionists to return had no appeal for us.

Somewhat later two young Chinese women came to the door and explained the procedure for excursions using sign language and more Chinese than English. One of them would let us know whenever it was time to leave the ship by tapping on our door. We had no idea what we would be seeing when, but believed it would all be interesting in some way. They handed us two caps with Chinese letters on the visors. We thought they were souvenirs and put them in our packs. After the first outing, we realized that the visors identified the wearer as part of a particular day-tour group. The ship carried many separate groups, each with its own Chinese guide. We had been added to an already existing group.

As we watched men loading huge bags of cargo onto the lower levels of our ship, the sun set. From a distance, the city lights of Chongqing were quite beautiful, and it was very restful cruising along the river at night. Around midnight we reached Faling where quite a bit of loading and unloading of cargo took place.

Our first excursion turned out to be the visit to Fengdu or Ghost City. It is believed that after death the Chinese souls meet here to be judged and to begin their journey to the underworld. Supposedly this idea originated from a linguistic mistake. During the Han dynasty (206-220) two men, Yin Changsheng and Wang

Fangping, chose to live isolated lives on Ming mountain, near Fengdu. When their families were joined through marriage in the Tang dynasty, their combined family names sounded like *Yinwang* (king of hell). People began to believe that not only the king of hell but also other devils lived on the mountain, and that it was the entry to the underworld. Temples were built where sacrifices could be made in an effort to avoid the worst tortures for leading a sinful life. The first temple was built in 618. There are now about twenty-eight of them that can be visited and other attractions have been added in recent times.

After a 5:00 a.m. tap on the door, around 6:00 a.m., still in the dark, we followed our group's designated Chinese guide, walking across the gangplank and then briskly through town to Ghost City. First we took a chairlift in the fog to go up a hill where we visited a few of the many temples. In one temple we saw a larger-than-life statue of an emperor. Outside another, statues of various demons posed menacingly. One of the more terrifying statues was that of a green-faced monster gleefully devouring children. The temple dedicated to the king of Hell showed Bosch-like scenes of people being tortured for their sins, reminding me of Dante's inferno. Nevertheless, in the midst of these disgusting and horrible scenes, we saw some beauty. On one pagoda, each curving eave ended in the shape of a crane's head, creating a lovely, delicate silhouette. With more than twenty-eight temples and numerous tour groups visiting them, it was hard to stay with our assigned group, but we did see some people we thought we had seen before.

Next we took the cable car down to a trail leading to another area of Ghost City. After passing through the archway of Ghost Street, we encountered more temples and many vendors selling skeletons, skulls, hearts, and "I survived Ghost City" tee-shirts. Beyond this area, ninety-nine steps led up to another entry gate, shaped like an open mouth with dagger-like teeth. Many people climbed all the stairs to visit the walled-in area behind the fearsome gate. Inside the walls was a large house of horrors with many tableaus and very graphic dioramas depicting the underworld and the soul's journey through it. The area was somewhat like a theme park, but most of the scenes were much more violent than any I had seen anywhere. Signs in English and Chinese explained each horrific display, but we didn't have time to read them all, as we were worried about when the ship would leave and how we would find it. After we entered this section of Ghost City, we no longer saw anyone we recognized.

Our plan, when we left Ghost City, was to walk downhill to the river and then turn left, hoping we would recognize our ship among the many at the wharf. As we walked along Main Street, I suddenly recognized a woman and her daughter who had been in our original group. Unfortunately, they didn't know any more than we did. Kurt tried to buy some fruit, since we had only had half a doughnut for breakfast, but the vendor would sell only a large bag, for which we had no room.

Fortunately, I remembered the name of our ship, but when we reached the river, we did not see it. We kept walking to the left, asking people about it. Many other passengers were equally lost, so we were quite relieved to finally see both our ship and the woman we had followed in the morning. Just after we entered our cabin, an attendant knocked on the door to see if we were back This reassured us that the ship's management took some responsibility for their passengers' whereabouts.

Whenever the ship stopped to let some passengers off or on, vendors selling food appeared on the wharf. I pointed and said "*miantiao*" (noodles), then handed money to the sellers, struggling to reach their outstretched hands from the side of the ship and hoping I wouldn't lose my grasp of the purchases they passed to me through the ship's railings. On the four-day trip, we bought most of our food that way.

Traveling through the pleasant countryside in sunny weather, we enjoyed watching other ships and busy laborers. About 5:00 p.m., the ship stopped at Fengjie for another excursion. We followed the crowd, not knowing what to expect, up a hill to a series of steep steps, finally reaching a temple. While waiting in line to enter the rooms inside, where life-sized statues portrayed historic scenes, we met a couple from Ottawa, who were traveling with their Chinese friend from the Wushan University. Having visited China previously, they were much better informed than we were and told us that the temple had been built in the Song, Ming, and Qing dynasties to commemorate the deeds of Zhang Fei, a famous general of the Kingdom of Shu. This temple, famed for its ancient architecture and sculptures, was to be taken apart and carefully moved to avoid its destruction from flooding when the Three Gorges Dam is completed.

On the way back to the ship, we bought potatoes, bananas, persimmons, and two oranges from local people. These items, along with cookies from the ship's snack bar plus our two bowls of noodles, gave us a well-filled pantry. Just before our ship left, a barge came alongside it and attached itself with a hook on the end of a long pole, while someone from the barge offered cooked food for sale. That evening as a Western-style cruise ship passed us, we could see fancy chandeliers in their elegant dining room.

Early on a misty morning, we entered Qutang Gorge, the first of the famous Three Gorges. Only about five miles long, Qutang Gorge is the smallest and shortest of the three, but the water flows most rapidly through it. Unfortunately, the heavy mist and fog prevented us from seeing much of this gorge.

Just before entering Wu Gorge, as the sun burned off the fog, we docked at Wushan, and were taken by bus to board a smaller boat for a fabulous trip through the Three Lesser Gorges located on the Daning River. Beautiful, steep crags lined both sides of the river through very narrow gorges. The river was at most only sixty feet wide, and the current was quite swift. Twice I saw monkeys and once some ducks. When we stopped for lunch, local people sold wonderful food from stands: fresh fried fish, turkey legs, succulent noodles, soft drinks, and beer. Wandering around enjoying the scene, we were startled when someone yelled at us to go to the boat. We had misunderstood the instructions about our departure time. Although we weren't the last ones to return, we had lost our good seats. On the return trip we saw travertine hanging stalactites, caves, and waterfalls. In one desolate spot along the shoreline, a mountain goat perched on an isolated crag, seemingly with no visible access. At first, I thought the goat was a statue carved from the rock. High suspension bridges dazzled us, and finally on a tan-colored cliff face, a dark image of a Buddha, god, or devil appeared. There were similar mineral-stained areas on the cliffs, but I had to believe this one had been enhanced by a skilled sculptor.

After we returned to the larger ship, we continued through the twenty-five mile long Wu Gorge. This second gorge was quite dramatic with cliffs rising to almost 3,000 feet. Beautiful vistas and gorgeous mountain scenery attracted most passengers to the top deck. Many people were taking photographs and pointing to a crag that resembled the profile of a robed emperor. Suddenly quite a few people started to talk to us in Chinese. This had also happened to Alan on his trip. I had difficulty understanding their questions, except for those about our ages. When the Chinese friend of the Ottawa couple started chatting with us, we learned that he, like Kurt, was a physical chemist. He told us that the ship we were on, a luxury Chinese tourist ship, cost about one-third the price of the Western cruise ships.

Xiling Gorge, about fifty miles long, was the last gorge before the locks of the Gezhouba Dam. Along the way through this third and longest gorge, we saw white markers indicating what the water level would be after the Three Gorges Dam was completed. This made it clear which towns and farms would be inundated. We could see construction of new towns higher on the hills to which the displaced residents would be moved. Although the new housing will certainly have more amenities than the old, the rich riverside land, where crops had been easily cultivated, can never be replaced. Supposedly the dam will serve as flood control of the Yangtse as well as providing more hydroelectric power, but the effectiveness of both has been questioned.

Just at twilight, we reached the amazing site of the Three Gorges Dam–a huge construction area. It looked like a small city, and work continued into the night as the area was very well lighted.

Later as we were getting ready for bed, someone knocked at the door and told us that the ship's motor was broken and we would be moved to another ship. We were ready immediately, but first the ship had to go through the locks of the already existing Gezhouba Dam. Because the locks were enormous, we had a very long wait for the gates to close. Then the ship was lowered a distance equal to the height of the tall Western cruise ships.

Many people disembarked at Yichang where we transferred to the replacement ship. The new ship was bigger but not as nice as the old one, although the snack bar was better stocked. In our room, water from a shower resisted going down the drain, and in the morning we discovered that a broken handle on the toilet prevented it from being flushed.

Now the countryside became very flat on all sides, and the river spread out. Although the boat kept moving all night, progress was very slow. We ate our noodles and bought some stale cake as a change from stale cookies. The river became so wide it resembled one of our Great Lakes, and many of the barges we saw carried coal.

Our scheduled tour of Yueyuang Pagoda was two hours late. Originally built in 716 during the Tang Dynasty, the pagoda was rebuilt in 1045 by Fang Zhongyan when he was exiled to the city of Yueyuang, then a backwater. A poet and minister in the court of the Song emperor Renzong, Fang Zhongyan fell into disfavor for advising Renzong not to depose his empress. Irritated by this advice, Renzong deposed the empress and exiled Fang Zhongyan. Yearning for the beauty he had experienced at court, Fang Zhongyan attempted to recreate that environment at Yueyang. His poem describing the pagoda's beauty and his concern about China and the condition of its people is highly revered. The pagoda, redone in 1867, was indeed very beautiful and filled with ornate furniture, wood carving, and statuary.

Many passengers lingered at the pagoda and its surrounding park so long that they had to run to board the already moving ship. The Canadians were almost left behind because they were trying to buy milk for their coffee. Earlier in the day, they had warned us not to drink the boiling water because it came directly from the filthy river. They had put some in a plastic bag in order to have a hot shower and saw little bits of things floating in the water. Because we had already used the boiling water for our noodles, we hoped there would be no ill effects. When we checked our water supply in the thermos, it was perfectly clear. Although this third day was somewhat tedious, lacking the previous spectacular scenery, it did provide a picture-worthy sunset on the river.

When we finally arrived in Wuhan about 1:00 a.m., we were surprised and relieved to see Wendy, the young woman assigned to take us to our hotel and to the airport the following afternoon. She had seen that our original ship had been cancelled and decided to meet the next ship scheduled to arrive. We slept late till 9:00 a.m., then took a taxi to the Hubei Provincial Museum, repository of all that had been excavated from Marquis Yi's tomb. We had seen some of the bronze bells when they traveled to the Sackler Museum in Washington D.C. Urns, jades, wine coolers, flutes, qins, and the coffin itself were all on exhibit. In addition, a performance by musicians using the stones, bells, kotos, and stringed instruments included a woman who embellished a beautiful traditional dance with the graceful movements of her elongated sleeves. The concert concluded with a rousing version of Beethoven's *Ode to Joy.*

Trying to find East Lake Park, we ended up instead at Mao's villa, where we took the one-dollar tour led by a girl originally from Chongqing. She also showed us a coffee shop where we had cups and cups of tea while admiring the lake. Finally we found an entrance to the enormous park which contained many lakes, an alligator/crocodile farm, zodiac topiary, various amusement rides, and an area called Houses of the World. Most of these miniature buildings looked fairly similar except for the signs identifying the country each represented. Threatening weather discouraged us from taking a boat ride on the lake.

The next day we had until noon to explore Jiefang Park, near our hotel in the middle of town. This delightful area, surrounded by trees, was a haven for many people relaxing there. Some were line dancing, some performed a version of tai chi that used swords, and some played stringed instruments. Groups of school or pre-school children lined up for rides of various kinds such as the dragon swing and a huge Ferris wheel. We visited a tall pagoda standing in the midst of many models of pagodas in different styles. Only the view from the top level of the pagoda revealed the many commercial skyscrapers and the rest of this large city surrounding the peaceful tree-enclosed city park.

After Wendy dropped us off at the Wuhan airport, we gulped when we saw that we would be traveling in a small plane with propellers. But we arrived safely at Tunxi, where we were met by David. After introducing us to Mr. Xie, the driver, David left to take care of other business, and we never saw him again. Mr. Xie's English was no better than my Chinese, but we managed to communicate as he drove us to the Yungfu Hotel near the cable car entrance and the eastern steps of Huangshan (Yellow Mountain). We planned to climb up the eastern stairs to the top of the mountain, to stay overnight at the Beihai Hotel on the summit, and then to descend the western steps to Taoyuan (Peach Blossom) Hotel near the hot springs on the other side of the mountain. Not wanting to carry our full backpacks all that way, we asked Mr. Xie to drop the big packs off at the Taoyuan Hotel where we'd be staying two days later. He assured us that it was no problem, or at least that's what we thought he said.

The Yungfu Hotel was very attractive, but there was no heat. It was now November, we were in a mountainous area, and the temperatures were quite cool. But we were comfortable wearing our long underwear under the thick quilts provided by the hotel. An excellent breakfast gave us a good start for the day's hike to the summit.

Despite the large numbers of porters carrying all sorts of goods up the eastern stairs, we made good time and were on the summit of Huangshan by 10:30 a.m. More and more tourists arrived as the day went on. With many trails and destinations on the summit, it wasn't very clear where the Beihai Hotel was located. Finally we found a sign for it, and fortunately, a room was available. Not only did the room have heat, but the hotel provided down jackets for anyone who planned to get up to see the sunrise over the Dawn Pavilion. We spent the rest of the day hiking the spectacular trails in this fascinating area, making sure that we walked to various formations such as Monkey Looking Out to the Sea and the Dawn Pavilion. The trail to Xi Hai Hotel and another hotel, even more isolated, led through stone tunnels and over cantilevered steps. Wild and wonderful scenery made us feel we were part of a Chinese painting. Relishing the superb weather, we wished we had scheduled a second day for the mountain top. Instead of buying noodles for dinner, we splurged for the Hot Pot, but many of the items were of dubious origin and the wine provided was atrocious.

Hoping to have time to pause now and then, we got an early start the next morning. The trail heading toward the western steps was often carved out of stone and involved some rock scrambling. It was everything we'd hoped for, providing fabulous scenery and exciting hiking. Views from Bright Top Peak, Lotus Peak, and the Jade Screen Hotel were thrilling. Without the trail, it would have been impossible to reach some of these spots. The Jade Screen Hotel, for example, was perched on a rock surrounded by high smooth rock walls. A spectacularly steep staircase carved into the cliffside provided the only safe access. What a job it must have been to create any trail on and through this formidable terrain! Sometimes there were railings, sometimes not. Alternate routes for bad weather were available. At times, tunnels had been cut through the cliff itself. In other places, a short ladder to another level took us to an unexpected turn in order to avoid a steep drop-off, and then the trail continued.

In some places stone formations resembled animals, and one formation looked like a profile of a Chinese scholar. On many tall boulders, poems and sayings had been carved in beautiful calligraphy. With such fabulous weather, many couples, families, and larger groups were enjoying day excursions and picnics. We saw very few who were not Chinese. The trail took us near a cable car going down the mountain, but we weren't sure if it ended up anywhere near our hotel, so we kept walking, even though we saw many people taking it. Our map in Chinese showed several cable cars ending on different sides of the huge mountain.

Because Kurt's knees began to bother him, we took more rest stops, not really knowing how much farther we had to go. As we reached the terminus of a cable car, we saw a minivan that offered to take us to Peach Blossom Hotel for $2.50–well worth it. Our big packs were waiting for us and the room was quite attractive.

The next day, Mr. Xie arrived promptly at 8:00 a.m. to drive us to Hangzhou. The five-hour ride over terrible roads was somewhat tiring even with a stop for lunch. Mr. Xie chose a small roadside cafe he knew, where we were taken into the kitchen to pick out the food we wanted to eat. For thirty yuan (about $3.50), we had smoked chicken, peas and corn, cabbage soup, rice, and tea for three people served family-style–*pianyi* (very cheap). Because there was more food than we could eat, Mr. Xie finished it all.

The China Merchants' Hotel was so new that Mr. Xie's map didn't show its location. Before we found it, we saw quite a bit of Huangzhou. At every red traffic light, Mr. Xie asked other drivers for directions, but these weren't always accurate. Although the hotel catered to many tour groups, we were the only Westerners staying there. The hotel was not yet licensed to cash travelers' checks, but an English-speaking staff member offered to take us to a bank. One bank was closed, and the other would not accept travelers' checks, but it did give me a cash advance on my Visa card.

Misty weather in the morning convinced us to visit the Zhejiang Provincial Museum instead of taking a boat ride on West Lake. This museum on Solitary Hill Island had once been an emperor's summer palace. Some of the artifacts were from 7000-5000 B.C., and the entire history of China could be studied. Marble decorative pillows were exquisite, though I don't think I'd like to sleep on them. Another room, dedicated to a history of ceramics from simple pottery to celadon, included pottery bells. An exhibit of furniture displayed a huge table with fabulous mother-of-pearl inlay work. An exquisite bed and an elaborately carved bridal sedan chair were decorated with animal-bone inlay. Visiting the coin collection, we learned that small seashells were China's first medium of exchange. When shells became scarce, the Chinese began making "shells" of bronze. Even today, the written Chinese character for money includes the character for the word "shell." We also explored the grotesque rockery's many niches and crevices and admired the lovely gifts presented to Hangzhou from its sister cities throughout the world

In the adjoining park where many bridal couples were having their pictures taken in especially scenic spots, two delicate bronze cranes stood in a pond in front of the lovely Crane Releasing Pavilion. Although the pavilion's name may refer to releasing of birds, it more likely refers to the releasing of someone's virtues, a Buddhist tradition associated with death. It could also refer to the releasing of the spirit from the bondage of the material world. This pavilion or pagoda was built as a memorial to a reclusive poet, Lin Hejing, who had once lived on Solitary Hill Island, eschewing fame and political office. He devoted himself to meditation, raising plum trees, and caring for a pet crane, claiming that the flowers of the plum tree were his wife and that the crane was his son. Near this pavilion was an extensive exhibit of chops. Many of them were shaped like small animals and were exquisitely carved. The earliest chops were from the Zhou period about 1100 B.C.

To save time, we took a taxi to Lingyin Si, the temple of inspired seclusion, located in a park at the edge of town. As we entered the temple, we passed through the hall with the usual four heavenly guardians to see a Buddha protected by two dragons. A magnificent sixty-foot Buddha carved from camphor wood sat in the next hall. Behind him was a fantastic and amazing montage of more than 150 small figures of mortals and mythical creatures in various poses on carved hills and mounds. Even more fascinating was a room full of life-sized carvings of 500 Arhats and an ornately decorated altar with coiling dragons. Resembling Roman Catholic saints who often carry symbols representing their sufferings, the Arhats also carried symbolic items or were surrounded by elements relating to personal history. One had a head growing out of his chest. Another had a monkey sitting on his arm. Others had dragons chewing on them or chains weighing them down. I wanted to learn each Arhat's story, but no book in English was available.

Across the street from this complex was Feilai Feng, the "peak that flew from afar." The mountain received its name when an Indian monk visiting Hangzhou in the third century said that the mountain looked exactly like one in India and asked when it had flown to China. The entire mountainside was full of niches housing Buddhas and other creatures. Of the 330 sculptures, the earliest was from 951 A.D. and consisted of a group of three Buddhist deities. Paths led up, through, and among the grottoes and niches. Many tourists were scrambling all over this area to have their pictures taken in front of their favorite carvings. It was a fascinating place, but when the rain started making the rocks very slippery, we hurried on to the sculpture garden to see some gigantic, larger-than-life stone carvings of historic groups. This area resembled stone sculptures we'd seen in Southern India.

When the rain became a downpour, we tried to leave. The first taxi driver we found said he couldn't go to our destination. But there were no taxis at the stop where we'd been dropped off earlier. By then we were fairly drenched, but had no choice. We walked back to the bus stop and took the number seven. We knew it would take us back to West Lake, and from there we could get a taxi to the hotel. Because the bus was crammed with passengers, we missed our stop and had to walk back in the dark to the Kentucky Fried Chicken cafe, where we dried out a bit while consuming a strawberry sundae. It felt like a miracle to find an available taxi when we came out.

Because Kurt had no dry shirts, he wore a pajama top under his sweater when we went to have dinner in the hotel. For a total of six dollars, we had beef and vegetables, fried rice, soup, fruit, and beer. We had hoped to hear the election results from the United States, but the race was so close that the winner would not be known until polls closed in the far Western states.

Experienced travelers in China, we were now able to find our seats on the afternoon train to Nanjing without any help. I sat next to two women from Canberra, Australia, who were on a recruiting visit, hoping to convince rich Chinese families to send their children to high school or college in Canberra. Narelle, the Director of Education, was responsible for fifty schools. Her reaction to many comments ("dee, dee, dee"), seemed strange until I remembered having heard it in Australia. Her assistant, Lily, originally from Beijing, had married an Australian when he was living and teaching in Beijing for several years. Narelle and Lily had bought scooters, then costing one hundred dollars in the United States, for twenty dollars. Apparently Lily was skilled at bargaining.

When I said that we'd seen men pulling a plow, Lily told us that when she was six years old, she and her three siblings had been separated from their parents and sent with their grandmother to a labor camp for six years. There they raised and ate corn to survive, and the four children had pulled a plow steered by the grandmother. Reunited later with their mother and father, who had been sent to a different labor camp, the children did not feel close to their parents. Although they later realized that it was not their parents' wish to leave them, Lily said, an odd cold feeling still remained within. Her mother and father will not speak of what happened to them, saying that it is in the past and they wish to forget about it.

Our other companion was a professor of ecology from Nanjing University who had been to the United States with a group and had visited the United Kingdom four times. We became a bit concerned when we realized that there were two train stations in Nanjing, so Lily used her cell phone to determine the location of our hotel. Professor Zhong wrote the name of the hotel in Chinese on a card and said that if no one was waiting for us at the station, he would call a taxi for us. We bought a box dinner from a vendor on the train, and the Australians offered everyone chocolate. From the window, I saw many mulberry bushes being cultivated for feeding silkworms. The bushes were laid out much like vineyards, so that workers could walk between the rows harvesting the silkworm cocoons when they were ready.

It was almost dusk when we were met by Yvonne at the main train station. She delivered us to the Mandarin Garden Hotel, saw that we were checked in, and left. In the foyer of the hotel we saw lots of black marble, elegant statuary, fountains, plush furniture, and large exotic floral arrangements. Our room, in the cheaper wing of the hotel, was still quite good. After dinner, Kurt and I wandered for about an hour in a pedestrian plaza behind the hotel--a lively section of Nanjing called Fuzimiao. Back in our room, we learned from television that the United States's presidential election had been the strangest in many years and that the outcome now depended on a recount in Florida. Gore had conceded, but then retracted his concession–absolutely amazing!

Because we had only one day for Nanjing, we took a taxi for $2.50 to Zijinshan or Purple Mountain to visit the Sun Yatsen mausoleum, museum, and study. We climbed every one of the hundreds of steps in the enormous and imposing stone stairway leading to the Ming-style tomb with its beautiful marble gateway and roof of blue-glazed tile. Sun Yatsen had wished to be buried in Nanjing, but probably not in such a grandiose tomb, as he always preferred simplicity. Regarded by many as the founder of modern China, Sun Yatsen had been given an imperial memorial, though rumor has it that his body may have been taken to Taiwan in 1949 by the Nationalists.

For the rest of this sunny, very pleasant day, we explored Purple Mountain's other features. Formerly part of a tomb, the beamless house, a vaulted building made entirely of brick with a very high ceiling, was now a memorial to famous Chinese individuals from the 1920s. Dioramas related some of the history of that time. We admired the Linggu pagoda, a nine-story octagonal building 180 feet high. Earlier in our trip, we would have eagerly paid the fee to climb to the top, but now we were content to take photographs from the ground level.

After a glimpse at an amusement park also located in the area, we walked to the tomb of Hong Wu, one of the three Ming emperors not buried at Beijing's Ming tomb area. The tomb, still not excavated, was completed in 1383. After a very long walk, we saw several memorial buildings, but we could not find the Sacred Way with its carved animals and other guardians. Then, as we exited the park where the tomb was located, we saw the entrance to the Sacred Way across the street in Plum Blossom Hill Park. Somewhat similar to the sculptures of Beijing's Sacred Way, the carved figures here were some of the earliest still standing and included one mythical animal that had a scaly body, a cow's tail, deer's hooves, and one horn.

After I told a cab driver, "*Fuzimiao*," and we arrived there, Kurt finally conceded that I could actually communicate in Chinese. On our way to dinner, we accidentally strolled through a crowded, vibrant, and vivid market that sold pigeons for food and finches for pets. Live fish and frogs, kept in small water-filled plastic bathtubs, waited for buyers.

No one in the *jaozi* (boiled dumpling) store spoke English, and we didn't know how many *jaozi* were enough for a meal. We ordered twenty-four beef dumplings with soy sauce, and for one dollar had a very tasty dinner.

Later we wandered around the very lively streets in Fuzimiao. Pagodas, a Confucius temple, and shops along the river bank were all outlined with lights. On the Qinhuai, paddle boats and floating restaurants, also decorated with small lights, created an attractive scene as many people strolled in the area, crossing the arched bridges over the river to a favorite dining spot with a pleasing view.

Right after breakfast the next day, we hiked quickly to the Zhonghua gate and the Nanjing city wall, where we took a few pictures. The six sections of the massive city gates provided a hiding place behind each entry where troops could ambush any enemy who happened to get by one or more of the gates. We were back just in time to board the train for Suzhou, the garden city.

Gardens surrounded our hotel in Suzhou, the Nan Lin, and water cascading over a high wall of rocks just outside the entrance created a lovely, exotic atmosphere. The November weather, however, was not so nice, having turned cold and misty. We wore wooly hats and gloves to visit the nearby Master of Nets Garden.

Suzhou once had over one hundred gardens. Viewed as places of quiet contemplation, each garden contained certain key elements: rocks, water, and picturesque bamboo or pine trees. The gardens had been created by rich officials and scholars as private refuges where they could relax from the stress of their daily duties. Master of the Nets, the smallest garden, was laid out in the twelfth century, abandoned, and then restored in the eighteenth century. The residential area had several rooms, and a courtyard in the inner garden was furnished with Ming-style furniture and lanterns. Many visitors marveled at the small model of the entire garden created from rocks, paper, and silk. We were fascinated by the rockeries, the mosaic patterns made with stones on the ground, the surprising

333

views, the weeping willows, little hidden nooks, and the many chrysanthemums blooming in pots. Disturbing the tranquil ambience of the garden were some shouting and running teenagers, but they eventually left.

In this touristy town, many signs were in English, and much English was spoken at our hotel, quite a change for us. As we walked back to our hotel, the hawkers of various services were fairly aggressive, probably because the number of tourists was dwindling. When I said *"Bu yao"* (not interested) to an English-speaking pedicab hustler, he switched entirely to Chinese and continued his sales pitch at high speed

Although the rain stopped in the morning, the day remained very cloudy, windy, and cold. Nonetheless, we took a taxi to the Humble Administrator's Garden across town. The administrator may have been humble, but his garden was not. Quite large with huge ponds, rockeries, bridges, buildings, pavilions, and many arrangements of chrysanthemums, it was full of tourist groups (mostly Chinese) feverishly taking photos. Many picturesque views of trees could be seen through latticed windows, and at one pavilion, classical Chinese dances were performed gracefully and beautifully.

At the Lion Grove Garden, in contrast, the rockeries had trails at various levels. Many were dead ends, but others continued, after a twist through tunnels and hidden steps, to a trail on a lower level. Even a small waterfall had been constructed in this limited space.

Our next stop was the North Pagoda, an adjoining temple, and the plum blossom garden where we saw the largest gold fish or carp we had ever seen. Near the pagoda was a beautiful mural depicting various parts of Suzhou. The drizzle began again as we went into a noodle soup shop and successfully got what we ordered. On the way back to the hotel, we stopped at the Tao Mystery Temple, the oldest in Suzhou, which had a stele with a carving of Lao-Tzu (author of *The Way*) on it. Instead of candles, this temple had electric lights on top of the pillars. Nearby many shops were selling silk, a Suzhou specialty.

We traveled by train to Shanghai, our final stop, and from the station took a taxi to our hotel, not knowing that we could have easily walked there. For sightseeing downtown, we rode a convenient metro to the People's Park. In the center of Shanghai, we admired the modern architecture of the newly-built Grand Theatre, the exotic-looking fountains, the Shanghai Museum, and the urban planning exhibition hall. These low, attractive buildings provided a dramatic contrast to the city's skyscrapers. For example, the museum, constructed of brown stone, was only two stories high, and resembled an ancient, gigantic earthen, lidded bowl. On display were materials recently found in Inner Mongolia. Another huge area contained bronzes of various kinds from 2200-1600 B.C.

On the second floor we found wonderful, evocative abstract paintings with light and dark contrasts suggesting calligraphic swipes made with brushes and paints. The collection of beautifully carved jade pieces was extensive. A golden emperor's chair and a screen inlaid with ivory were stunning examples of exuberant Qing furniture, while the furniture from the Ming period was simpler, having more elegant lines. Indigenous costumes and crafts were displayed in the national minorities section. Several times we were approached by young Chinese girls with cameras who wanted their pictures taken with Kurt. He thought perhaps they found his beard unusual, but he didn't discourage their attention.

To reach the famous Bund, we walked through a pedestrian shopping street which offered all the latest items. Quite photogenic were the many European buildings built in the 1930s when the Bund area was Shanghai's Wall Street. The Bund itself, an embankment constructed to protect the city from floods, serves as a huge waterfront park, attracting many tourists and locals. With the haze, fog, mist, and cold weather continuing, there wasn't much point in taking the elevator to the top of the newly-built Pearl tower, eating in its revolving restaurant, or taking a boat ride on the Pudong River.

On our last day, we visited the temple of the white jade Buddha. The sculpture was surrounded by little gold Buddhas, and additional small Buddhas were being unwrapped and installed in ceiling niches. A second large jade Buddha was reclining in the gift shop, where we couldn't resist buying a wood carving of a fisherman.

Next we took the subway to the French Concession, or Frenchtown, an area inhabited mainly by White Russian emigres in the 1920s and 1930s. At that time, the area licensed prostitution and opium smoking, attracting a number of China's underworld figures. Outstanding among many Art Deco buildings was the Jin Jiang Hotel, the ultimate at the time it was built. It reminded us somewhat of the Kennedy-Warren building in Washington, D.C. Even now, the area was fairly upscale, with many trendy shops and a variety of foreign restaurants.

At the Pudong airport, on the other side of the Huang Po river, a large, boisterous tour group from Dayton, Ohio, were celebrating their return to the United States. We quietly thought about all the experiences we'd had and the incredible variety of sights we had seen. We enthusiastically told each other, "*Hen hao Luxing*" (It was a very good trip). Although we were in China for thirty-eight days and had seen much more on our own than many tour groups see, we still felt we had barely scratched the surface of this intriguing, vast, and fantastic country.